Recht und Digitalisierung | Digitization and the Law

Herausgegeben von | Edited by

Prof. Dr. Roland Broemel
Jun.-Prof. Dr. Lea Katharina Kumkar
Prof. Dr. Jörn Lüdemann
Prof. Dr. Rupprecht Podszun
Prof. Dr. Heike Schweitzer †

Band | Volume 23

Yannic Duller

Data Access and Portability

A Taxonomy of European Data Rights

Nomos

The publication of this work was made possible by funding from Ars Iuris Vienna – Doctoral School of the University of Vienna. We would like to express our sincere thanks for this support.

The Deutsche Nationalbibliothek lists this publication in the Deutsche Nationalbibliografie; detailed bibliographic data are available on the Internet at http://dnb.d-nb.de

ISBN 978-3-7560-3319-5 (Print)
978-3-7489-6253-3 (ePDF)

Online Version
Nomos eLibrary

1st Edition 2025

Foreword

This book was originally submitted as a doctoral dissertation to the Faculty of Law at the University of Vienna in August 2024. While the text has been slightly revised and updated for publication, the central arguments and structure remain the same as in the original version.

I am deeply grateful to Professor Christiane Wendehorst for supervising my dissertation and for the generous support and guidance she offered throughout the process. I also thank her for inviting me to join the research project "Principles of a Data Economy" as a project assistant. Working on that project profoundly shaped my thinking on many of the themes explored in this book and offered valuable insight into the broader context of data law in Europe and beyond.

I would also like to express my sincere thanks to Professor Matthias Lehmann and Professor Thomas Jaeger for serving as reviewers of the dissertation and taking the time to engage with the thesis in great detail—even though it turned out to be considerably longer than initially anticipated, and much longer than reviewers typically hope for. Their close reading and detailed feedback are deeply appreciated.

I am also grateful to the *ars iuris* doctoral school for their generous support throughout the dissertation process. The Socratic sessions they organised offered an invaluable opportunity to present and critically discuss key aspects of the work with peers, whose thoughtful feedback significantly contributed to the development of the arguments. I am also particularly thankful for *ars iuris*' financial contribution, without which the publication of this book in its present form would not have been possible.

Warm thanks are also due to my colleagues at the Department of Civil Law at the University of Vienna. Their willingness to listen, share ideas, and take time to discuss legal puzzles—large and small—made all the difference during the writing process. The many hallway conversations and lunch time exchanges were often as valuable as structured research.

I am especially grateful to my parents, whose support has always been unconditional. They encouraged me to pursue my interests in my own time and never put pressure on me to deliver, even when the process was long and uncertain. Their quiet confidence in me was an anchor throughout.

Finally, I want to thank my friends from university, who made the hours spent in the library something to look forward to. Their company brought lightness and laughter to the routine of study and turned the long journey through legal education into something I will remember with real fondness.

Vienna, June 2025
Yannic Duller

Table of Contents

Abstract

In recent years, the European legislature has introduced a growing number of data access and portability rights to address a fundamental structural imbalance in the digital economy: the de facto control over data by dominant actors, largely determined by technical and economic conditions rather than by legal entitlement. This control often leads to an uneven distribution of data resources, disproportionately benefitting large platforms while putting smaller market participants, consumers, and start-ups at a disadvantage.

Earlier policy discussions focused on the idea of introducing a general property right in data. However, this approach has largely been abandoned, particularly because data are non-rivalrous: exclusive control would risk hampering innovation and reinforcing monopolistic tendencies. Instead, EU data law has moved toward the establishment of contextual, purpose-driven access and portability rights aimed at enabling participation rather than exclusivity.

This book offers a systematic legal analysis of some of the most significant access and portability rights in the EU legal order. It examines their scope, conditions, and objectives, while also evaluating their effectiveness, coherence, and potential shortcomings. Recent legislative developments—such as the GDPR's portability right (Article 20), the Digital Markets Act, and the Data Act—signal a shift in EU policy: data are now treated as a regulatable resource, and access and portability are seen as tools to foster innovation, competition, and fairness.

The book develops a functional taxonomy of these rights, distinguishing between three categories:

(1) **Access rights for co-generated data**, granted to individuals who contributed to the generation of the data and who may access and reuse it for personal purposes, typically free of charge;
(2) **Access rights in the public interest**, granted to third parties not involved in data generation, justified by broader economic or societal objectives, and typically subject to fair, reasonable, and non-discriminatory (FRAND) remuneration;

(3) **Portability rights in the narrower sense**, where the data subject can request direct transfer of data to a third party, creating a tripartite relationship with asymmetrical entitlements.

By introducing this classification, the book contributes to the conceptual foundations of EU data law. It aims to enhance the coherence, accessibility, and future development of a fragmented but increasingly central area of digital regulation.

1 Introduction

Since the advent of digitalisation, an unprecedented amount of data has been created, and with the emergence of new technologies, like IoT-products, and the increased connectivity of economy and society, this trend will even be accelerated. The European Commission estimates that the amount of data produced worldwide by 2025 will be five times as much as in 2018, namely 175 Zettabytes, with one Zettabyte being a billion Terabytes.[1] However, as markets are becoming more and more data-driven, the demand for data is also increasing at the same time. This increase in demand is primarily owed to new technological developments. Large and reliable datasets are necessary in order to train artificial intelligence and ensure its proper functioning, and with the possibilities of modern data analytics, traditionally less data-intensive sectors, like agriculture, are developing a need for accurate and reliable data.[2] Data has become a crucial resource to develop innovative services and products, reduce costs and improve efficiency, which in turn leads to economic growth, the creation of jobs and societal progress.[3] Hence, in the digital economy, access to data determines success not only for individual companies but also for society as a whole, or as the European Commission has put it: data is "the lifeblood of the digital economy".[4]

Unlike traditional resources, like oil, wood or steel, data has an intangible and non-rivalrous nature and can therefore be shared and reused across different sectors for different purposes with limited costs and without exhausting the initial resource. Sharing and reusing data in a different context and merging it with other datasets can not only be done without exhausting the data, but may, in many instances, lead to an increased value extraction because data has no intrinsic value. The value of data rather depends on its point of use and the initial data holder is not necessarily best equipped to

1 COM(2020) 66 final of 19 February 2020, 2.

2 OECD, 'Enhancing Access to and Sharing of Data: Reconciling Risks and Benefits for Data Re-Use across Societies' (2019) 28; SWD(2017) 2 final of 10 January 2017.

3 COM(2017) 9 final of 10 January 2017.

4 COM(2020) 66 final of 19 February 2020 1.

extract value of the data they hold.[5] Different types of market players may be in a position to extract value from the same set of data for their specific need, leading to an increase in overall welfare.

Facilitating data access and data sharing is not a policy objective that only emerged in the past couple of years. For more than two decades, the EU has made efforts to increase the availability of publicly held data for the private sector. The arguments that have been used back then are fairly similar to those brought forward today: improved access to public data strengthens the competitiveness of the European information industry, especially of SMEs, which in turn leads to economic growth and the creation of new jobs.[6] That the efforts to increase the availability of public sector data started at the end of the 20th century is not a mere coincidence. At the same time, the mass roll-out of the internet began, which allowed an easy and low-cost transfer of digital information, and thus enabled the market to fully benefit from the intangible and non-rivalrous nature of data. Especially the lack of clear rules for accessing and exploiting data was seen as an issue for the European single market. Hence, it was already in 2003 that the European legislators adopted the Public Sector Information (PSI) Directive,[7] which established a minimum set of rules for the re-use of information held by the public sector. Since then, the notion that public data should be open by default has gained global recognition[8] and the EU has introduced further legislative measures to increase the availability of publicly held data.[9]

While public data was at the centre of the EU's efforts to increase the re-use of data and strengthen the digital economy, over the past few years, the focus has shifted towards privately held data. This shift of priorities may be explained by the achievements that have already been made regarding the availability of public data and/or the amount of data that is held by the private sector. At the end of the 20th century, when initiatives on the re-use of publicly held data were first pursued, the public sector was the

5 Martina Barbero and others, 'Study on Emerging Issues of Data Ownership, Interoperability, (Re-)Usability and Access to Data, and Liability: Final Report' (Deloitte 2018).

6 COM(1998) 585 final of 20 January 1999, 5.

7 Directive 2003/98/EC of the European Parliament and of the Council of 17 November 2003 on the re-use of public sector information OJ 2013 L 345/90.

8 OECD, 'Recommendation of the Council for Enhanced Access and More Effective Use of Public Sector Information' (2008); G8, 'Open Data Charter' (2013).

9 See Directive (EU) 2019/1024 of the European Parliament and of the Council of 20 June 2019 on open data and the re-use of public sector information, OJ 2019 L 172/56; COM(2020) 767 final of 25 November 2020.

biggest single information content resource for the creation of value-added information services.[10] With the success of internet companies and the digitalisation of many—traditionally analogue—activities, the amount of data held by private entities has increased significantly.

However, legislative interventions in the private sector would not be necessary if market players could simply access the necessary data from data holders under fair and reasonable conditions. While the need for reliable and high-quality data increases, companies are reluctant to share their data with each other.[11] The majority of data holders are keeping their data in-house and do not subcontract it to other entities for further reuse.[12] Of course companies may have good reasons not to grant access to their data. For example, personal data can only be shared within the limits of data protection law. Even if data is shared in accordance with data protection law, potential customers might mistrust companies that sell personal data to third parties. In order to evade possible violations of data protection law and loss of customer trust, companies might choose not to share data at all. However, there are also less 'noble' reasons not to share data, like the fear of losing the competitive edge vis-à-vis innovative SMEs or eliminating competition on the downstream market.[13]

This reluctance of companies to share their data—for whatever reasons—leads to the creation of what has been called data silos. The term is used to describe the fact that the generators of data are keeping their data to themselves.[14] Consequently, the data is analysed in isolated silos, which leads to economic inefficiencies, as the combined data will often be more valuable than the sum of the isolated parts.[15] The aggregation of data in silos may also render it necessary for companies to generate and store datasets similar to already existing ones, which is not only inefficient from an economic but also from an ecological point of view. Furthermore, the unavailability of data may constitute a market entry barrier for SMEs and

10 COM(1998) 585 final of 20 January 1999, 6.

11 OECD, 'Enhancing Access to and Sharing of Data' (n 2) 17.

12 COM(2017) 9 final of 10 January 2017, 9; OECD, 'Enhancing Access to and Sharing of Data: Reconciling Risks and Benefits for Data Re-Use across Societies' (n 2).

13 Barbero and others (n 5) 79.

14 OECD, 'Data-Driven Innovation: Big Data for Growth and Well-Being' (2015) 55; COM(2017) 9 final of 10 January 2017 8; Gabriella Cattaneo and others, 'The European Data Market Monitoring Tool' (IDC & Lisbon Council 2020) 55.

15 OECD, 'Data-Driven Innovation' (n 14).

is likely to impede innovation, as data is a prerequisite for many digital services and products.[16]

The aggregation and control over large datasets by a single company may also result in market power, which can extend far beyond the company's primary and even secondary markets. This extended competitive advantage may best be demonstrated by the success of large internet companies in the industrial sector. Large and reliable datasets that are collected in the internet sector are not only a key resource for the development of smart products and services, but they also provide insights into consumer behaviour, which allows efficient targeting of potential customers. Hence, it is no surprise that Google's affiliate company, Waymo, seems to have the competitive edge in the market of driverless cars over traditional automotive companies. Expanding to the industrial sector also allows internet intermediaries to utilise the data produced by smart products, increasing the datasets in their control, which in turn leads to even more market power and enhances market tipping tendencies.[17]

The outlined examples demonstrate that market-based solutions alone do not necessarily lead to fair and innovation-friendly outcomes.[18] Based on these considerations, discussions both on an academic and policy level arose, as to whether and how legal interventions could facilitate the sharing of privately held data and thus break up data silos.

Initially, the European legislator wanted to introduce an ownership-like right to address the problems caused by limited access to and unfair allocation of privately held data.[19] However, concerns were raised that while ownership might create incentives for data production, the issue is not that not enough data is produced but that the existing data is unfairly distributed and/or underutilised. Moreover, the issues that would justify a legal intervention do not arise in the same form or to the same extent across all sectors of the digital economy. They depend, inter alia, on the different interests parties may have in the data, a company's market power or its position in the value chain.[20] Due to the mounting criticism, the Commission eventually abandoned the idea of a data ownership right.

16 COM(2020) 66 final of 19 February 2020.
17 Josef Drexl, 'Designing Competitive Markets for Industrial Data – Between Propertisation and Access' (2017) 8 JIPITEC 257, [35-36].
18 COM(2017) 9 final of 10 January 2017, 10.
19 SWD(2017) 2 final of 10 January 2017.
20 Lothar Determann, 'No One Owns Data' (2018) 70 Hastings Law Journal 1, 39; Josef Drexl, 'On the Future EU Legal Framework for the Digital Economy: A Competition-

In response to the recommendations by academics, the Commission considered data access and portability rights as the most appropriate tool to address the challenges caused by data silos.[21] Before 2020, the GDPR's right to data-portability was the only horizontally applicable portability right. Additionally, several sector-specific regimes existed. In the ensuing years, however, the European legislator significantly expanded this framework and introduced a diverse array of access and portability rights aimed at addressing a variety of issues within the data economy. As these rights are targeted at a variety of different market failures, they vary in terms of scope, modalities, underlying concepts, and rationales. The proliferation of these rights emphasises their central role in the EU's efforts to regulate the digital economy. Access and portability right have evolved from singular regulatory tools scatter across mostly sectoral Regulations and Directives to pillars of the EU data law. Especially the data rights set forth in the Digital Markets Act and the Data Act are expected to have a great impact on the digital economy and data markets.[22]

1.1 Trajectory and research questions

The analysis begins by clarifying the notion of 'data' and its distinction from other economic resources (Chapter 2). Building on this foundation, Chapter 3 examines the challenges that arise from the de facto control of data and the limited accessibility for other actors, which have led to the introduction of rights to data access and data portability. Chapter 4 explores the possibility of invoking Article 102 TFEU as a legal basis for ex-post

Based Response to the "Ownership and Access" Debate' in Sebastian Lohsse, Reiner Schulze and Dirk Staudenmayer (eds), *Trading Data in the Digital Economy: Legal Concepts and Tools: Münster Colloquia on EU Law and the Digital Economy III* (Nomos; Hart Publishing 2017) 235; Wolfgang Kerber, 'A New (Intellectual) Property Right for Non-Personal Data? An Economic Analysis' [2016] GRUR International 989, 997; Wolfgang Kerber, 'Governance of Data: Exclusive Property vs. Access' (2016) 47 International Review of Intellectual Property and Competition Law 759, 761; see also Simon Geiregat, 'The Data Act: Start of a New Era for Data Ownership?' [2022] SSRN Electronic Journal 9 <https://www.ssrn.com/abstract=4214704> accessed 8 April 2024.

21 See COM(2020) 66 final of 19 February 2020, 13.

22 See e.g. Pinar Akman, 'Regulating Competition in Digital Platform Markets: A Critical Assessment of the Framework and Approach of the EU Digital Markets Act' (2021) 47 European Law Review 85; Friso Bostoen, 'Understanding the Digital Markets Act' (2023) 68 The Antitrust Bulletin 263.

access to data and sets out why competition law alone cannot effectively address the structural concerns identified in the preceding chapter.

Chapters 5 to 9 provide a detailed examination of selected statutory data access and portability rights under EU law. These chapters analyse the scope of each right, the conditions under which they can be exercised, and the objectives they pursue. Rather than aiming for an exhaustive compilation, the selection seeks to reflect the diversity of access and portability rights across regulatory domains. The analysis also considers legal uncertainties and practical shortcomings—actual, potential, or asserted—that affect the application of these rights.

Despite their heterogeneity, recurring themes and normative patterns begin to emerge across the different instruments. Chapter 10 identifies these underlying concepts and common principles, with the aim of developing a taxonomy of data access and portability rights. This taxonomy provides a structured overview of the current landscape of data rights in the European Union and seeks to contribute to a more coherent understanding of their regulatory logic.

The following five questions guide the analysis throughout:

- What are the specific data access and portability rights currently established in European Union law?
- How do these rights function in practice—what is their scope, and what are their modalities?
- Are there overlaps between different access and portability rights, and if so, how do these overlaps affect their practical application?
- To what extent is the legal design of these rights adequate for achieving their intended regulatory objectives?
- Do these rights—despite their diversity—rely on shared principles or structural commonalities?

As the players in the data economy are usually spread across different countries and data flows are seldom limited to national borders, data regulation is an issue that is mainly dealt with at EU level. The study therefore, adopts an EU perspective when it comes to answering the above-mentioned research questions. The rationale behind this delimitation is to provide a comprehensive and coherent assessment of EU data rights in their current form, unaffected by the specificities of national legal systems. In view of the recent tendency of the European legislator to adopt Regulations, which are directly applicable across all Member States, this seems particularly appropriate. Adopting an EU law perspective also means that even when the access or portability rights are laid down in a Directive, the provisions of the Directive and not the transposing national law are assessed. This focus ensures a uniform analysis, providing insights into the intentions and frameworks established at the EU level without distractions from the variations that may occur during national implementation. While national laws also play an important role in the overall structure of data regulation and would also merit analysis, they fall outside the scope of this work.

1.2 Methodology

In order to answer the research questions set out above, different perspectives on the law[23] are required. For the first three research questions, an internal perspective is adopted, where the law is perceived as a normative framework. The internal perspective is focused on finding or selecting the one correct interpretation array from the multiplicity of all possible interpretations by way of interpretative means.[24] The starting point is to identify the relevant sources of law, which lay down access and portability rights (RQ 1).[25] Once the source of the law is identified, the normative content has to be established.[26] This means analysing how the access and portability rights are applied, what their effects are (RQ 2) and how the interactions with other rights might affect their application (RQ 3). While the true meaning of the law may sometimes be evident, there are other

23 The perspectival compass for legal reasoning used in this section was developed by Christiane Wendehorst, 'Von Arbeit im Recht, am Recht und über Recht. Konsequenzen für das Lückenproblem in der Rechtsvergleichung' in Andreas Heldrich and others (eds), *Festschrift für Claus-Wilhelm Canaris zum 70. Geburtstag* (Beck 2007) and furhter refined in Christiane Wendehorst, 'The State as a Foundation of Private Law Reasoning' (2008) 56 The American Journal of Comparative Law 567 and Christiane Wendehorst, 'Dogmatik im Privatrecht – Versuch einer thematischen Grundlegung' in Christoph Bezemek (ed), *Rechtsdogmatik – Stand und Perspektiven* (Manz 2023).

24 Wendehorst, 'Dogmatik im Privatrecht – Versuch einer thematischen Grundlegung' (n 23) 138; Thomas Lobinger, 'Perspektiven der Privatrechtsdogmatik am Beispiel des allgemeinen Gleichbehandlungsrechts' (2016) 216 Archiv für die civilistische Praxis 28, 37; Franz Bydlinski, *Juristische Methodenlehre Und Rechtsbegriff* (2nd edn, Verlag Österreich 2011) 16; Wendehorst, 'The State as a Foundation of Private Law Reasoning' (n 23) 570.

25 Wendehorst, 'The State as a Foundation of Private Law Reasoning' (n 23) 575.

26 Wendehorst, 'The State as a Foundation of Private Law Reasoning' (n 23) 580; Lobinger (n 24) 37; Bydlinski (n 24) 9; Wendehorst, 'Dogmatik im Privatrecht – Versuch einer thematischen Grundlegung' (n 23) 141.

instances where the legal rules remain unclear or incomplete. In such situations, a thorough interpretation of the law becomes necessary to determine its intended meaning.[27] For example, by means of interpretation, it needs to be established what kind of data Article 20 GDPR[28] covers, when it refers to 'data [...], which [the data subject] has provided to a controller'. The analysis resorts to the methods of legal interpretation for secondary EU legislation that are being used by the ECJ and have been restated by legal scholars. Particularly, German scholars refer to the four traditional elements of legal interpretation—grammatical, systematic, historical, and teleological interpretation—that typically used in national laws of the German legal tradition,[29] also in the context of EU secondary law, albeit with some adaptations.[30] However, the ECJ does not use this terminology but refers to wording, context, and purpose when interpreting provisions of EU secondary law.[31] This difference, however, is one of terminology and not of substance, as the scholars referring to the four 'classic' elements of interpretation acknowledge that the ECJ has attached a specific normative meaning to each method that reflects the peculiarities of EU secondary legislation,[32] such as its multilingual character[33] and their policy-driven rationales.[34] For example, the *effet utile* doctrine, which is unique to the interpretation of

27 Bydlinski (n 24) 402 ff; Wendehorst, 'The State as a Foundation of Private Law Reasoning' (n 23) 580.

28 Regulation (EU) 2016/679 of the European Parliament and of the Council of 27 April 2016 on the protection of natural persons with regard to the processing of personal data and on the free movement of such data, and repealing Directive 95/46/EC (General Data Protection Regulation), OJ L 2016 /119, 1.

29 Karl Riesenhuber, in Karl Riesenhuber (ed), *European Legal Methodology* (2nd edn, Intersentia 2021) 256 ff.; Karl Larenz, *Methodenlehre der Rechtswissenschaft* (6th edn, Springer 2013) 312 ff.

30 See Riesenhuber (n 29) 256 ff.

31 ECJ, C-306/16, *Maio Marques da Rosa, EU:C:2017:844*, para 38 ff

32 See for exmaple Riesenhuber (n 29) 260, 263 and 265.

33 Riesenhuber (n 29) 258.

34 Christiane Wendehorst, 'Regulierungsprivatrecht Verhaltenssteuerung durch Privatrecht am Beispiel des europäischen Verbrauchervertragsrechts' in Eva Schumann (ed), *Das erziehende Gesetz* (De Gruyter 2014) 133 ff.; Christiane Wendehorst, 'Methodenlehre und Privatrecht in Europa' in Clemens Jabloner and others (eds), *Vom praktischen Wert der Methode, Festschrift für Heinz Mayer zum 65. Geburtstag* (Manz 2011) 829; Hans-W Micklitz, 'Europäisches Regulierungsprivatrecht: Plädoyer für ein neues Denken' (2009) 6 Zeitschrift für Gemeinschaftsprivatrecht 254; Christoph U Schmid, 'The Instrumentalist Conception of the Acquis Communautaire in Consumer Law and Its Implications on A European Contract Law Code' (2005) 1 211, 215 ff.

EU law, is considered to be part of teleological interpretation.[35] Instead of explaining the different methods of interpretation in abstract terms here in more detail, the methods are outlined when they are used to interpret a specific legal provision.

The internal perspective mirrors the approach taken by judges when adjudicating cases.[36] Since the judge needs to decide the case, under the internal perspective in its purest form, the right answer cannot be left open, and the 'correct' interpretation needs to be found. This is the case even when multiple interpretations seem equally valid.[37] Generally, the analysis adheres to this pure form of the internal perspective and thus takes a clear stance where multiple interpretations are possible. However, this does not imply that the conclusions drawn are the only correct ones or that alternative interpretations lack validity. To account for this, the approach occasionally departs from the strict internal perspective and acknowledges the existence of multiple plausible readings, presenting them alongside one another while ultimately endorsing a preferred interpretation.

To address the fourth research question—assessing the appropriateness of the analysed data access and portability rights in achieving their respective objectives—the analysis shifts from the internal to the sovereign perspective. This perspective goes beyond interpreting the law and critically evaluates whether the legal provisions function as effective instruments for realising their intended policy aims. The question moves from 'What is the right interpretation of the law?' to 'Is the law is good or bad in achieving its objective?'[38] The sovereign perspective is not neutral toward the law, as it requires a normative assessment that is inherently more subjective than the objective analysis of legal content.[39] Albeit more subjective, the sovereign perspective may not simply be ignored because laws are not an end in themselves but are instruments aimed at achieving normative goals.[40] Hence, assessing whether a law fulfils these goals provides input for legal debate and policy discussions. To counter the subjectiveness of this perspective, the reasoning behind each evaluation is explicitly stated, allow-

35 Riesenhuber (n 29) 269; Reiner Schulze, in Reiner Schulze (ed), *Auslegung europäischen Privatrechts und angeglichenen Rechts* (Nomos 1999) 13.

36 Robert Alexy, *Begriff und Geltung des Rechts* (3rd edn, Karl Alber 2016) 47.

37 Wendehorst, 'The State as a Foundation of Private Law Reasoning' (n 23) 581.

38 Wendehorst, 'The State as a Foundation of Private Law Reasoning' (n 23) 571.

39 Wendehorst, 'Dogmatik im Privatrecht – Versuch einer thematischen Grundlegung' (n 23) 139; Wendehorst, 'The State as a Foundation of Private Law Reasoning' (n 23) 571.

40 Riesenhuber (n 29) 269.

ing others to understand the basis of the conclusions drawn. To enrich the analysis and ensure a balanced view, alternative arguments and dissenting opinions are also presented and analysed. This approach helps to ensure that the conclusions, if not objective, are at least comprehensible and can therefore contribute to further debates.

For the fifth and final research question, the analysis takes an external perspective, where the law is viewed as a factual framework that is observed from outside. The external perspective focuses on describing and categorising the law as it exists, with the goal of providing an accurate and objective restatement of existing laws. A key task is to delineate the similarities and differences across various legal provisions.[41] Although the reasoning from the external perspective does not follow the methods of interpretation of the internal perspective, it is an objective view of the law. Hence, any restatement of the law from an external perspective must aim to be as correct, complete and as objective as possible.[42] Taking the external perspective is necessary, as answering the fifth research question entails a comprehensive restatement of the current framework of data access and portability rights in EU law. This enables the identification of common principles and characteristics of the different provisions.

41 Bydlinski (n 24) 13 f.; Wendehorst, 'The State as a Foundation of Private Law Reasoning' (n 23) 571.

42 Wendehorst, 'The State as a Foundation of Private Law Reasoning' (n 23) 585.

2 Data and Its Characteristics

As the subject of this book is data access and portability rights, it needs to be established what the term 'data' entails in this context. The following Chapter establishes how data and information should be understood for the purposes of the analysis and aims to provide a terminological framework for the subsequent examination of the research questions. Furthermore, this Chapter looks at the special characteristics of data as an economic resource.

2.1 What is data?

Writing about the data economy inevitably raises questions of terminology, since no uniform or generally recognised definition of 'data' exists.[43] The understanding of the term 'data' varies depending on the scientific discipline and field of research. Hence, a whole array of diverging conceptual understandings exists. The resulting terminological ambiguities have complicated the legal and interdisciplinary discussions about the data economy.

2.1.1 Definitions of data

Legal research seems particularly plagued with terminological inconsistencies. In fact, lawyers frequently talk past each other when using the term 'data' because they are referring to different facets or concepts of data. With the GDPR,[44] the Digital Content Directive[45] and the Digital Markets Act,[46] the European legislator has introduced three diverging definitions of data

---

43 Regulation (EU) 2016/679 of the European Parliament and of the Council of 27 April 2016 on the protection of natural persons with regard to the processing of personal data and on the free movement of such data, and repealing Directive 95/46/EC (General Data Protection Regulation), OJ L 2016/119, 1.

44 Article 4(1)Regulation (EU) 2016/679 (GDPR).

45 Article 2(1) Directive (EU) 2019/770 of the European Parliament and of the Council of 20 May 2019 on certain aspects concerning contracts for the supply of digital content and digital services, OJ L 2019/136, 1 (DCSD).

46 Article 2(24) Regulation (EU) 2022/1925 of the European Parliament and of the Council of 14 September 2022 on contestable and fair markets in the digital sector

within a matter of a couple of years. This has contributed to the existing confusion, in particular about the difference between the term 'information' on the one hand and 'data' on the other.

2.1.1.1 Data as information

Arguably, EU law's most established definition of data can be found in the GDPR, which defines 'personal data' as information relating to an identified or identifiable natural person.[47] The synonymous use of information and data reflects common parlance. According to the Oxford English Dictionary, data means 'an item of information'[48] and the Black's Law Dictionary defines 'datum' (the singular of 'data') as 'a piece of information'.[49] However, the GDPR's definition needs to be seen in the light of its objective: the protection of information about individuals. To define data as information in the context of data protection law is, therefore, not wrong and even mandated by the subject matter.[50] It is, however, an unfortunate choice of words, as the interchangeable use of data and information conflicts with definitions in other scientific areas. From a pure terminological standpoint, the US approach of calling data protection law privacy law and using the term 'personal information' instead of 'personal data' therefore seems beneficial.

2.1.1.2 Data as patterns without meaning

That the GDPR's understanding of data is far from universal becomes particularly apparent when compared to the well-established terminology in information theory, which clearly distinguishes between data and information. The data–information–knowledge–wisdom hierarchy (DIKW) or information hierarchy is a central model that has been used to contextualise

---

and amending Directives (EU) 2019/1937 and (EU) 2020/1828 (Digital Markets Act), OJ L 2022/265, 1.

47 Article 4(1) Regulation (EU) 2016/679 (GDPR).

48 'Data, n' (OED *Online*, March 2021), <https://www-oed-com.uaccess.univie.ac.at/view/Entry/296948?rskey=uyawRt&result=1&isAdvanced=false> accessed 16 March 2021.

49 'Datum, n' (Black's Law Dictionary 11th ed, 2019).

50 Contra Louisa Specht, 'Ausschließlichkeitsrechte an Daten – Notwendigkeit, Schutzumfang, Alternativen' (2016) 32 Computer und Recht 288, 290.

the respective terms in information science since the late 1980s.[51] The DIKW hierarchy itself has been the subject of definitional debates, and several different versions have been developed. Some have suggested adding extra levels,[52] while others have proposed removing certain levels of the hierarchy[53]. However, the different models share the common understanding that data is at the bottom of the hierarchy and should be understood as uncategorised and unprocessed facts or observations, which lack context and are therefore patterns without meaning or value. Information (the next level in the hierarchy) is deduced from data by interpreting the data and giving it meaning and value in a certain context.[54]

2.1.1.3 Data as representation of information

In computer science, data is understood as the representation of information available in a formalised way, usable for communication, interpretation or processing.[55] One of the most frequently referenced definitions in this context is the one by the International Organisation for Standardization (ISO), which defines data as 'a reinterpretable representation of information in a formalized manner, suitable for communication, interpretation or processing, which however does not have to be in an electronic or machine-readable format.'[56]

In the understanding of computer science, information and data are two distinct terms that are, however, closely linked to each other. Data is the physical or digital manifestation of an abstract idea. Without such representation, information only exists on an intellectual level and cannot

51 See Milan Zeleny, 'Management Support Systems: Towards Integrated Knowledge Management' (1987) 7 Human Systems Management 59; Russell Ackoff, 'From Data to Wisdom' (1989) 16 Journal of Applied Systems Analysis 3.

52 Zeleny (n 51).

53 Dave Chaffey and Steve Wood, *Business Information Management: Improving Performance Using Information Systems* (Prentice Hall 2005).

54 Jennifer Rowley, 'The Wisdom Hierarchy: Representations of the DIKW Hierarchy' (2007) 33 Journal of Information Science 163, 170; Sasa Baskarada and Andy Koronios, 'Data, Information, Knowledge, Wisdom (DIKW): A Semiotic Theoretical and Empirical Exploration of the Hierarchy and Its Quality Dimension' (2013) 18 Australasian Journal of Information Systems 5, 7.

55 Michael Sonntag, in Dietmar Jahnel, Peter Mader, and Elisabeth Staudegger (eds), *Handbuch IT-Recht* (Verlag Österreich 2020).

56 ISO 'Information Technology – Vocabulary' (2015) ISO/IEC Standard No. 2382 <https://www.iso.org/standard/63598.html> accessed 16 March 2021.

be processed or stored outside of the human mind.[57] The same information can, of course, be represented in different forms and needs to be adapted depending on the addressee. For example, next week's weather forecast can, for further processing or interpretation by humans, be written down on a piece of paper in complete sentences or be represented by a graph with symbols and numbers (see 2.2.4.1).

However, for information to be processed by a computer, it needs to be represented in the form of binary code, i.e. strings of zeros and ones. These **bi**nary digi**ts** (commonly referred to as **bits)** are, simply put, instructions given to the computer, whereby '0' signals no flow of electricity and '1' means electricity is allowed to flow. A bit, i.e. a one or a zero, is the smallest unit in computer science, and everything that is processed by a computer can ultimately be broken down into bits. The more complex a file is, the more bits it contains. The computer itself, however, does not process individual bits but always groups of at least eight bits, which are then called bytes.[58] For humans, binary code is at least difficult to comprehend and even impossible to understand once it reaches a certain length. However, that information is represented by only two different states—electric impulse or no electric impulse—allows computers the rapid processing of any input.[59]

2.1.2 Data in the digital economy

The computer science understanding of data seems to have gained general acceptance in the context of legal issues related to the digital economy. The United Nations Commission on International Trade Law refers to the ISO standard for the definition of data in a paper outlining the legal challenges posed by the digital economy.[60] Furthermore, the Principles for a Data Economy, a joint project by the American Law Institute and the European Law Institute, define data as 'information recorded in any form or medium

---

57 Peter Pepper, *Grundlagen Der Informatik* (2nd edn, R Oldenbourg 2018) 20.

58 Heinz Gumm and Manfred Sommer, *Einführung in die Informatik* (9th edn, De Gruyter Oldenbourg 2011) 28.

59 George Heath, 'Origins of the Binary Code' (1972) 227 Scientific American 76; Igor Aleksander, 'Understanding Information Bit by Bit' in Graham Farmelo (ed), *It Must be Beautiful: Great Equations of Modern Science* (Granta 2002).

60 United Nations Commission on International Trade Law, Legal issues related to the digital economy – data transactions (2020).

or as it is being transmitted' and digital data as 'information recorded in digital form'. The reason for deviating from the wording of the ISO standard is that the terms 'reinterpretable' and 'formalized' raise questions of interpretation themselves. Furthermore, 'processing' might be understood overly broad in the EU and other countries, which have adopted a similar data protection terminology. Also the European legislator has picked up the understanding of data as representation of information in the context of the data economy. The Digital Markets Act, which regulates platforms in order to ensure fair markets in the digital sector, defines data as 'any digital representation of acts, facts or information and any compilation of such acts, facts or information, including in the form of sound, visual or audiovisual recording' (Article 2(24) DMA). The same definition can be found in the Data Governance Act[61] and in the Data Act.[62]

The origins of adopting the understanding of data as representation of information from computer science in a legal context can be traced back to the debate on data ownership. *Zech*, first in his detailed work on the protection of information but also consistently throughout later papers, defines data as 'machine-readable coded information' and refers to the ISO definition.[63] This understanding has been picked up by various scholars, who have contributed to the data ownership discussion.[64] From there, the computer science definition of data seems to have spread to broader debates on how to adopt a legal framework for the data economy.[65]

61 Article 2(1) Regulation (EU) 2022/868 of the European Parliament and of the Council of 30 May 2022 on European data governance and amending Regulation (EU) 2018/1724 (Data Governance Act) OJ L 2022/152, 1.

62 Article 2(1) Regulation (EU) 2023/2854 of the European Parliament and of the Council of 13 December 2023 on harmonised rules on fair access to and use of data and amending Regulation (EU) 2017/2394 and Directive (EU) 2020/1828 (Data Act), OJ L, 2023/2854.

63 Herbert Zech, *Information als Schutzgegenstand* (Mohr Siebeck 2012) 32; Herbert Zech, '„Industrie 4.0" – Rechtsrahmen für eine Datenwirtschaft im digitalen Binnenmarkt' [2015] GRUR 1151, 1153; Herbert Zech, 'Daten als Wirtschaftsgut – Überlegungen zu einem „Recht des Datenerzeugers"' (2015) 31 CR 137, 138.

64 Marc Amstutz, 'Dateneigentum' (2018) 218 AcP 438, 448; Maximilian Becker, 'Lauterkeitsrechtlicher Leistungsschutz für Daten' [2017] GRUR 346, 347.

65 See e.g. Paul Craig and Gráinne de Búrca (eds), 'The Evolution of European Data Law', *The Evolution of EU Law* (3rd edn, OUP).

2.1.3 The concept of data used in the context of this analysis

No universally valid answer can be given to the question: What is data? As with many terms, it is not necessarily helpful to use the exact same definition irrespective of the context. However, the research conducted so far has shown that there is a global trend in legal matters related to the digital economy to follow the computer science approach and define data as the machine-readable (or digital) representation of information. This understanding is compelling in that the representation of information through binary code is what made the digital economy possible in the first place. Only with the aid of digital technologies, in particular computers and the internet, data can be shared and reused without hardly any costs and the special characteristics of data, such as non-rivalry and simultaneous use (see 2.6),[66] can be exploited to their full extent.

2.2 What is Information?

The established definition of data as the (digital) representation of information can only be a starting point and is, as such, not useful, because it immediately triggers another question: what is information? It is a question that already occupied Plato and Aristotle[67] and has since then been the research subject of a plethora of scholars from different scientific disciplines. The various angles from which the term 'information' has been examined have produced even more definitions than for the term data.[68] None of the definitions are universally valid but rather claim correctness only for the respective factual context. Hence, the difficulty of this chapter is not to find a definition of information, but to establish one that—at the very least—is reconcilable with the definition of data and, at best, further helps to conceptualise the understanding of data in the context of this analysis.

66 OECD, 'Data-Driven Innovation' (n 14) 20.

67 For extensive elaborations on the origins of the term 'information' see Rafael Capurro, *Information* (Saur 1978) 16.

68 Shannon Martin, *Bits, Bytes, and Big Brother: Federal Information Control in the Technological Age* (Praeger 1995) 19.

2.2.1 Information as transfer of knowledge

As generally recognised, the starting point for legal interpretation should be the general understanding of the term.[69] In everyday language, the term information refers to the transfer of knowledge. According to the English Oxford Dictionary, information is 'the imparting of knowledge in general' or 'knowledge communicated concerning some particular fact, subject, or event'[70]. This concept of information requires the involvement of a sender and recipient of the transferred knowledge and thus implicitly relates to the human consciousness.[71] Another property that is commonly assigned to information is that information expands the recipient's level of knowledge.[72] Hence, the message of the sender must contain some degree of novelty for the recipient. Or, to put it differently: what is already known to the recipient cannot be information.[73]

Information is not synonymous with knowledge as such but refers to the human act of transferring knowledge, i.e. informing someone. This act presupposes some kind of physical or digital manifestation of information,[74] which otherwise exists only in the human mind. For example, sound waves transfer orally given information,[75] while ink and paper can be manifestations of written information.[76] The manifestation allows information to exist independently of human consciousness, which is also the criterion

69 Riesenhuber (n 29) 256; Christian Baldus and Friederike Vogel, 'Gedanken zu einer europäischen Auslegungslehre grammatikalisches und historisches Element' in Maximilian Wallerath and Peter Krause (eds), *Fiat iustitia, Recht als Aufgabe der Vernunft* (2006) 247 ff, However, it is also pointed out that given the diversity of languages in the Community, it is difficult to find a reliable interpretation, which necessitates recourse to other methods such as teleological and historical interpretation.

70 'Information, n' (OED *Online*, March 2021), <https://www-oed-com.uaccess.univie.ac.at/view/Entry/95568?redirectedFrom=information#eid> accessed 16 March 2021.

71 Capurro (n 67) 199.

72 Capurro (n 67) 202.

73 Winfried Nöth, *Handbook of Semiotics* (Indiana University Press 1990) 134.

74 Andreas Wiebe, 'Information als Schutzgegenstand im System des geistigen Eigentums' in Herbert Fiedler and Hanns Ullrich (eds), *Information als Wirtschaftsgut* (Otto Schmidt 1997) 100.

75 David Ritchie, *Information* (Sage Publications 1991) 10.

76 The argument that the knowledge is physically manifested by the electrical impulses in the human brain seems far-fetched because, despite the impressive achievements of neuroscience to detect and track neural activity, it is not possible to tie individual electrical impulses to certain pieces of knowledge. For the technique used to capture brain activity, see Joel M Kralj and others, 'Optical Recording of Action Potentials in Mammalian Neurons Using a Microbial Rhodopsin' (2012) 9 Nature Methods 90.

that distinguishes knowledge from information. Knowledge can be stored as information, for example, as bits in a digital file or as text in a book. *Zech,* therefore, understands 'knowledge as a special form of information that is bound to the human mind.'[77]

More relevant from a legal point of view than the rather philosophical delineation between knowledge and information is to clearly distinguish the tangible (or digital) embodiment from the information itself. The same information can be stored on various different media. Therefore, information does not necessarily share the fate of the medium. If a digital file embodying a piece of information is deleted from the hard drive of a computer, the same information may still exist in another file stored on a cloud server. Due to technical progress, there are, of course, a growing number of information carriers and thus ways to transfer information. From the carrier or medium, the recipient deduces the information in a process of comprehension.[78] What kind of information the recipient ultimately derives depends on the recipient's individual abilities and knowledge.[79]

This understanding of information allows a rather seamless reconciliation with the established definition of data: a binary code is the digital carrier for information that transfers knowledge from a sender to a recipient. However, the common understanding that information needs to be comprehensible by the human mind and—at least to some extent—expand the recipient's knowledge is too narrow for the context of the digital economy. Technological advancements have made it possible to process information that is not intended to reach a human recipient and may not be comprehensible to humans, but nonetheless has value for actors in the digital economy. For example, the binary code of software represents information, which is not intended for a human recipient and only gains meaning when processed by a computer. Furthermore, AI systems may be able to extract information from raw data that is rather meaningless to humans.[80] Nevertheless, the common understanding is a sound point of departure for the further examination of the concept of information in the context of the digital economy.

77 Zech, *Information als Schutzgegenstand* (n 63) 28.
78 Raymond T Nimmer and Patricia Ann Krauthaus, 'Information as a Commodity: New Imperatives of Commercial Law' (1992) 55 Law and Contemporary Problems 103, 105.
79 Specht (n 50) 290.
80 Zech, *Information als Schutzgegenstand* (n 63) 176.

2.2.2 Information as reduced uncertainty

Information science has developed its own understanding of information, which is very distinct from the common use of the term. To determine the capacity of system to transfer information, information theory uses a quantitative understanding of information[81] and defines information as 'knowledge which reduces or removes uncertainty about the occurrence of a specific event from a given set of possible events'.[82] From a mathematical perspective, information is thus understood solely as the statistical property of a message, independent of its meaning. For example, the letter 'a' in the unfinished sentence 'Give me the a-' does not have any meaning but still has information, as it excludes all English nouns that do not begin with the letter 'a'. The more alternatives are excluded, the higher the amount of information. Hence, a less common first letter would have a higher amount of information than the letter 'a' because even more alternatives are eliminated.[83]

This mathematical-statistical approach thus understands information as a measurement of the improbability of a random event.[84] Or, to put it differently, information is the opposite of uncertainty.[85] This understanding leaves the recipient out of the equation because the concept of information is independent of the amount of knowledge conveyed by a statement or the meaning of message.[86] By excluding any human elements from the definition, the notion of information becomes very precise and has for this

---

81 Claude Shannon and Warren Weaver, *The Mathematical Theory of Communication* (14. [print.]., Univ of Illinois Press 1949) 538: 'In estimating the capacity of a physical system to transmit information we should ignore the question of interpretation, make each selection perfectly arbitrary, and base our result on the possibility of the receiver's distinguishing the result from of selecting any one symbol from that of selecting any other. By these means the psychological factors and their variations are eliminated and it becomes to set up a definite quantitative measure of information based on physical considerations alone.'

82 ISO 'Information Technology – Vocabulary' (2015) ISO/IEC Standard No. 2382 <https://www.iso.org/standard/63598.html> accessed 16 March 2021

83 Nöth (n 73) 135; Shannon and Weaver (n 81) 20.

84 Shannon and Weaver (n 81) 22.

85 Zech, *Information als Schutzgegenstand* (n 63) 14.

86 Yehoshua Bar-Hillel, 'An Examination of Information Theory' (1955) 22 Philosophy of Science 86, 94.

reason been picked up by physics,[87] biology and various other scientific disciplines.[88]

The precise and narrow definition of mathematics and statistics, however, does not convince for legal purposes. First, due to its detachment from the common understanding of information, it would be a constant source of misunderstandings[89]. Secondly, law, which regulates human affairs, cannot be based on a purely abstract concept of information that ignores the meaning of information for the human recipient.[90] For humans, the information value of a signal is not the probability of its occurrence but the content it transports. Actors in the data economy do not assign value to data because they represent a statistical probability. Only if some kind of knowledge can be extracted from data is it considered a valuable asset. Hence, regulation that deals with the increased demand for data and aims to ensure a fair attribution cannot be based on a purely quantitative concept of information but needs to recognise the various interests, actors may have in the information represented by a dataset. The increased need for data is created by the potential insights that can be gained from information. This is true even if the information may not be comprehensible for humans, but only for an AI. The person operating the AI system only has an interest in acquiring or generating data from which the AI can derive 'conclusions'. Data, which can be processed by an AI, but can neither be used for training the AI system nor as basis for output, is of no value for the operator. Information in the context of this analysis, thus presupposes that it has a meaning for recipients, be they human or machine.

2.2.3 Semiotics

The theory of signs (semiotics) has developed a concept of information that uses the common understanding as a starting point but further delineates between the sign and meaning levels of information. By distinguishing between the syntactic, semantic and pragmatic layers of information,[91] the

---

87 Leon Brillouin, *Scientific Uncertainty, and Information* (Elsevier 1964) 12.

88 See Capurro (n 67) 216 with further references for the different diciplines.

89 See Bar-Hillel (n 86) 94 on the terminilogical confusion even in the scientific community.

90 Jean Nicolas Druey, *Information als Gegenstand des Rechts : Entwurf einer Grundlegung* (Schulthess, Nomos 1995) 9.

91 Charles Morris, *Signs, Language, and Behavior*, vol 56 (Prentice-Hall 1946).

semiotics have subdivided the broad and diffuse notion of information into logical and delimited concepts and, at the same time, introduced a precise and practical terminology. Due to these properties, legal scholars regularly resort to the semiotic concept of information to address legal challenges related to data and information.[92]

The syntactic layer only concerns the signs, such as letters or bits, and their relationship to each other, while the semantic layer is the intellectual content, which is transported by the signs. The pragmatic layer concerns the effects the content has on the recipient and thus takes into account the recipient's background knowledge and abilities.[93] The layers are in a hierarchical relationship, i.e. each layer includes the preceding ones. It also needs to be emphasised that all three layers focus on different aspects of the same piece of information.[94] Some authors also use the term 'physical layer of information' to distinguish the signs from their physical carrier.[95]

2.2.4 Layers of information

The terminology and the basic distinction between the sign level and meaning level should also be used to address legal issues in the digital economy. The semiotics provides a particularly well-suited basis for discussions, because the above-established definition of data can be integrated into the three-layered concept of information. However, it should be noted that the semiotic concept of information was developed for the purposes of its own discipline. Legal science has adopted the general considerations of semiotics but adapted them to better suit its own purposes.[96] The following description of the three different layers of information should not be

92 Ulrich Sieber, 'Informationsrecht und Recht der Informationstechnik – Die Konstituierung eines Rechtsgebietes in Gegenstand, Grundfragen und Zielen' [1989] NJW 2569, 2572; Egbert J Dommering and P Bernt Hugenholtz, *Protecting Works of Fact* (Springer 1991) 13; Wiebe, 'Information als Schutzgegenstand im System des geistigen Eigentums' (n 74) 100; Michael Kloepfer, *Informationsrecht* (Beck 2002) 24; Zech, *Information als Schutzgegenstand* (n 63); Specht (n 50) 290; Nico Schur, *Die Lizenzierung von Daten* (Mohr Siebeck 2020) 26.

93 Dommering and Hugenholtz (n 92) 13; Wiebe, 'Information als Schutzgegenstand im System des geistigen Eigentums' (n 74) 100; Schur (n 92) 29.

94 Wiebe, 'Information als Schutzgegenstand im System des geistigen Eigentums' (n 74) 101; Schur (n 92) 28.

95 Herbert Zech, 'Data as a Tradeable Commodity' in Alberto De Franceschi (ed), *European Contract Law and the Digital Single Market* (Intersentia 2016) 54.

96 *Cf.* Zech, *Information als Schutzgegenstand* (n 38) 37 and Rafael Capurro (n 42) 218.

mistaken for an outline of the semiotic understanding. The aim is rather to introduce a terminology inspired by the conceptual framework of semiotics that can be used to describe and understand legal concepts in the digital economy.

2.2.4.1 Syntactic layer

The syntactic level focuses on the signs that represent information for a potential observer. Such signs can be letters, digits, electronic or magnetic impulses, and even patterns of soundwaves.[97] However, the signs have to follow certain operational rules in order to be processed by a potential recipient.[98] For example, a written text can only be understood if the words correspond to the vocabulary of a language and follow the grammatical rules. If information, on the other hand, is intended to be processed by a computer, it needs to be represented as binary digits that follow an encoding standard.

By determining information on a syntactic level, information becomes independent of its meaning. In most instances, the syntactic layer will also carry semantic information, but this need not necessarily be the case. The sentence 'Colorless green ideas sleep furiously.'[99] is information on a syntactic level because it is composed of English words and follows the rules of grammar. It can be processed by anyone who reads this text but does not contain any semantic information, as the sentence is without any meaning.

It also needs to be pointed out that different signs may represent the same semantic information. On a syntactic level, Shakespeare's Hamlet may have the form of a text (a linguistic code independent of the concrete document or book) or a digital audio file (a binary code independent of the concrete storage medium).[100] The conveyed content stays the same

Where legislation, such as Article 20 GDPR or Article 6(9) DMA, sets out the requirement that data should be provided in a machine-readable format, this refers to the syntactic layer of information. The actors in the digital economy will usually only have an interest in the semantic layer

97 David Ritchie (n 75) 11.

98 Dommering and Hugenholtz (n 92) 13.

99 Norman Chomsky, 'Three Models for the Description of Language' (1956) 2 IRE Transactions on Information Theory 113, 116.

100 Zech, *Information als Schutzgegenstand* (n 63) 38.

if the information can be processed with the help of machines. Without the correct syntax, data cannot be used as an asset, resource or tradeable commodity.

2.2.4.2 Semantic layer

The semantic layer refers to the intellectual content of information. We speak of semantic information if a recipient can extract meaning from the syntactic layer. The yardstick for semantic informativity, however, is not a specific recipient, but a hypothetical recipient with universal knowledge.[101] Hence, syntactic information will carry semantic information independently of whether it actually reaches a specific recipient.[102] For example, the content of Shakespeare's Hamlet can be extracted from letters or signs, irrespective of whether they follow the rules of English, German or Japanese language. On the semantic level, it is irrelevant that the individual recipient may not be able to process the content without knowing Japanese, German or English.

The GDPR's definition of personal data understands information only on its semantic level.[103] 'Any information relating to an identified or identifiable natural person' is considered personal data.[104] Which signs are used to transport the information is just as irrelevant as whether the information is comprehensible for a specific recipient. As long as an ideal recipient is able to extract (semantic) information from the signs that relate to an identifiable natural person, the information will qualify as personal data. However, the syntactic level becomes relevant if a controller wants to use technical means (such as data mining or data matching) to derive new semantic information from several separate pieces of semantic information.[105]

101 Nöth (n 73) 141.

102 Bar-Hillel (n 86) 96.

103 See Zech, *Information als Schutzgegenstand* (n 63) 215; Zech, 'Data as a Tradeable Commodity' (n 95) 54.

104 Article 4(1) Regulation (EU) 2016/679 (GDPR).

105 See Zech, *Information als Schutzgegenstand* (n 63) 38.

2.2.4.3 Pragmatic layer

The effect information has on a concrete recipient is referred to as the pragmatic layer.[106] The focus is on the meaning or content of information, but not from the perspective of an ideal recipient, but that of a concrete one. It depends on the personal capabilities and background knowledge of the individual recipient whether pragmatic information can be inferred from semantic information.[107] It has already been pointed out that Shakespeare's Hamlet in Japanese is information on a syntactic and semantic level but does not contain pragmatic information for anyone without sufficient knowledge of Japanese. In this example, it may, however, be possible to change the syntactic layer in a way that the semantic information becomes comprehensible for the recipient (see 2.2.4.1).

Information rights, such as Article 15(1) GDPR, which gives the data subject the right to request information about the processing of their personal data concerns, refer to the pragmatic level (see 3.4). The information has to be given in a manner that it can be understood by the data subject who made the request. In contrast, the pragmatic level is irrelevant for the GDPR's data portability right.[108] Article 20(1) GDPR allows data subjects to retrieve their personal data from the controller in a structured, commonly used and machine-readable format and to transmit it to another controller. The retrieved information, however, does not have to be comprehensible to the data subject. It is sufficient if the information is machine-readable (syntactic level) and relates to the data subject (semantic level).

2.2.5 Physical manifestation of information

The importance of distinguishing between information and the physical carrier has already been pointed out (see 2.2.1). Based on the three-layered understanding of information, the ambivalent relation of information and its physical manifestation can be described more precisely. On the one hand, syntactic information does not share the fate of the physical carrier, as the same sequence of signs can have different physical manifestations. Every English copy of Hamlet carries the same syntactic information. If one

106 Sieber (n 92) 2573.
107 Druey (n 90) 8; Schur (n 92) 27.
108 Article 20 Regulation (EU) 2016/679 (GDPR).

copy is destroyed, the syntactic information is not lost. This independence gives syntactic information a non-exclusive and non-rival nature. Syntactic information can also be described as an abstraction of the various physical embodiments.[109]

While syntactic information is independent of the concrete embodiment, the physical manifestation is at the same time a prerequisite for the existence of syntactic information.[110] In order to be processed by humans or machines, the sequence of signs needs to be stored on at least one physical carrier.[111] To put it differently, the physical manifestation brings the syntactic information into existence, but the signs are independent as long as one carrier exists. By writing down the words that make up Hamlet, Shakespeare has created the syntactic information, which was then reproduced and stored on different physical carriers. If all copies of Hamlet are destroyed, the syntactic information ceases to exist.

Data is also syntactic information (binary code) that only exists if it has a machine-readable physical manifestation (data carrier). Binary code can physically be stored either by magnetic lines (e.g. floppy disks and traditional hard drives), as tiny bumps (pits) on an optical disk (e.g. CDs and DVDs) or by low-voltage switches called transistors (e.g. SD cards and SSD hard drives in modern laptops and computers).[112]

The dependency of information on the physical manifestation becomes particularly apparent if the carrier has a volatile nature. The patterns of human speech disappear if the sound waves fade out. A digital audio recording can preserve the semantic information by transforming the sound waves into pulses that correspond to patterns of binary digits (data), which are then stored on a magnetic surface or an optical disc (data carrier).

2.2.6 The concept of information used in the context of this analysis

It can be concluded that information is not a homogeneous concept that can be expressed with a universally valid definition. The understanding of the term is rather dependent on the scientific discipline and pursued purpose. Legal science has drawn inspiration from semiotics, which divides information into three different layers, as the differentiation between

109 Zech, *Information als Schutzgegenstand* (n 63) 41.
110 Zech, *Information als Schutzgegenstand* (n 63) 54.
111 See David Ritchie (n 75) 10.
112 Gumm and Sommer (n 58) 49.

syntactic, semantic and pragmatic levels of information reduces the terminological ambiguities. The need for nuanced terminology becomes particularly important when comparing legal concepts that concern different layers of information. For example, without establishing that data may represent syntactic, semantic or pragmatic information, it becomes difficult to delineate data access and portability rights from information duties (3.4).

2.3 Reconciling the notion of data and information

It has been established that in the context of the digital economy, data is to be understood as machine-readable information. The three-layered concept of information cannot only be reconciled with the definition but also allows for further concretisation of the term. By definition, digital data is syntactic information, as it is the string of binary digits that allows machine processing. The binary code needs to be stored on at least one data carrier, but is otherwise independent of the concrete embodiment and can therefore be used simultaneously by multiple actors and be shared without exhausting the resource. The 'format' of data usually refers to the syntactic level of data.

While the syntactic layer gives data its specific characteristic, it is only when it carries semantic information that data becomes a valuable resource. Depending on the semantic content, data can be used to automate processes, develop new products and business models or target customers.[113] Hence, data is often specified by referring to its semantic layer, e.g. personal data, customer data, vehicle data, engine data (see 2.5). The 'quality' of data usually describes how well the data is suited for a specific purpose (e.g. is the data correct, representative and unbiased) and therefore also refers to the content, i.e. the semantic information, of data.

From the perspective of an individual market participant, however, the value of data depends on the ability to extract pragmatic information. Thus, it is not only the semantic content of data that determines its value, but also background knowledge, context and personal capabilities.[114] For an individual, the value of a dataset may, thus, depend on whether the holder also has access to the metadata that gives context to the actual dataset. Furthermore,

113 See OECD, 'Data-Driven Innovation' (n 14) 23.

114 Datenethikkommission, 'Gutachten der Datenethikkommission' (Bundesministerium des Innern, für Bau und Heimat; Bundesministerium der Justiz und für Verbraucherschutz 2019) 52.

large datasets are useful only if the holder has the technological means to process and draw conclusions from the data. Only with the increased capabilities of processing and analysing big streams of data and the reduced storage costs companies are able to exploit pragmatic information from data on large scale.[115] Before these technological advancements, the semantic information of large unstructured datasets had to remain mostly untapped and was therefore without pragmatic value for companies.

2.4 The informational purpose of data

Since computers can only process electric impulses, the instructions that make up a computer program also consist of binary code. If the string of zeros and ones that make up software is translated into programming language, it contains information that can be understood by humans. Hence, software would also fall under the above-established definition of data. Moreover, cryptocurrencies, such as bitcoin, and utility tokens only exist in a digital form and thus also comprise a string of ones and zeros.[116] However, the problem of data silos does not describe the aggregation of large amounts of cryptocurrency or assets in the hands of a few market players and the data access debate is not about access to software, which in most cases will be protected by intellectual property rights.

While 'mere' data, software and cryptocurrencies are all machine-readable and carry some kind of information, they serve very different purposes. The data that is labelled 'the lifeblood the digital economy' is data, which is primarily obtained or generated to extract information from it. By comparison, software derives its value from the fact that it exerts some kind of computational control in a processing device.[117] Cryptocurrencies, on the other hand, are considered valuable because they represent a specific

115 Gintare Surblyte, 'Data as a Digital Resource' [2016] SSRN Electronic Journal 3 <http://www.ssrn.com/abstract=2849303> accessed 17 April 2020; See OECD, 'Data-Driven Innovation' (n 14) 143.

116 Zech, '„Industrie 4.0“ – Rechtsrahmen für eine Datenwirtschaft im digitalen Binnenmarkt' (n 63) 1153.

117 IEEE Standard Glossary of Software Engineering Terminology, IEEE Std 610.12 – 1990; see also Recital 10 Directive 2009/24/EC of the European Parliament and of the Council of 23 April 2009 on the legal protection of computer programs, OJ L 2009/111, 16.

asset.[118] The informational aspect is not the focus of software and crypto assets. It can therefore be differentiated between informational, functional and representative data.[119]

While computer science clearly delineates software (or computer programs) from 'mere data', EU law has diluted this distinction by introducing the term digital content. The Digital Content Directive (DCD) defines digital content as 'data which are produced and supplied in digital form' and lists as examples 'computer programmes, applications, video files, audiofiles, music files, digital games, e-books or other e-publications'. While Recital 23 clarifies that the digital representations of value, such as electronic vouchers, e-coupons or cryptocurrencies, i.e. representative data, are not covered by the DCD, its broad definition would cover functional data as well as data with a prevailing informational purpose. However, the objective of the DCD is to introduce contractual rights for consumers similar to those applicable to contracts for traditional goods. Therefore, it can be assumed that the DCD primarily targets the functional dimension of data rather than the dimension of data as information recorded.[120]

2.5 Categories of data

Data can be classified into various categories based on its nature, origin, and the legal frameworks governing its use. This section outlines some of the categories of data, such as personal and non-personal data, user-generated and machine-generated data, and co-generated data, which are relevant when assessing data access and portability rights.

118 Article 1(2)(d) Directive (EU) 2018/843 of the European Parliament and of the Council of 30 May 2018 amending Directive (EU) 2015/849 on the prevention of the use of the financial system for the purposes of money laundering or terrorist financing, and amending Directives 2009/138/EC and 2013/36/EU OJ L 2018/156, 43, which defines virtual currencies as 'a digital representation of value that is not issued or guaranteed by a central bank or a public authority'.

119 Christiane Wendehorst, in MüKoEGBGB (Beck 2021) Art 43, paras 270 ff; Neil Cohen and Christiane Wendehorst, 'Principles for a Data Economy' (ALI/ELI 2023) <https://europeanlawinstitute.eu/fileadmin/user_upload/p_eli/Publications/ALI-ELI_Principles_for_a_Data_Economy.pdf> Principle 2(1); Data Governance Working Group, 'A Framework Paper for GPAI's Work on Data Governance' (GPAI 2020) 6.

120 Wendehorst, MüKoEGBGB Art 43 (n 99), para 299.

2.5.1 Personal vs non-personal data

Whether the GDPR applies to data has a significant influence on the activities that can lawfully be performed on the data. Therefore, policymakers and actors in the data economy pay much attention to the distinction between personal and non-personal data. The GDPR's regime applies if the processed data is personal. Since there is no gradual applicability of the GDPR,[121] the question whether data is personal is not a matter of degree, but one that can be answered with yes or no.

2.5.1.1 Personal data

The GDPR's objective is not to introduce a protective regime for data as such but to protect the fundamental right to privacy, i.e. the information about natural persons.[122] Hence, the GDPR only applies to personal data, which is defined in Article 4(1) GDPR as 'any information relating to an identified or identifiable natural person ('data subject'); an identifiable natural person is one who can be identified, directly or indirectly, in particular by reference to an identifier such as a name, an identification number, location data, an online identifier or to one or more factors specific to the physical, physiological, genetic, mental, economic, cultural or social identity of that natural person'. Since the GDPR's predecessor, the Data Protection Directive (DPD),[123] contained an almost identical definition, the guidance issued by Article 29 working party on the concept of personal data under DPD, as well as CJEU case law on Article 2(a) DPD can still be used.[124] The definition of personal data is based on four elements: 'any information', 'relating to', 'identified or identifiable' and 'natural person'.[125]

---

121 See Moritz Karg, in Spiros Simitis, Gerrit Hornung and Indra Spiecker (eds), *Datenschutzrecht: DSGVO mit BDSG* (Nomos 2019) Art 4(1) DSGVO, para 14.

122 Achim Klabunde, in Eugen Ehmann and Martin Selmayr (eds), *DS-GVO: Datenschutz-Grundverordnung: Kommentar* (2nd edn, Beck 2018) Art 4(1), para 7.

123 Directive 95/46/EC of the European Parliament and of the Council of 24 October 1995 on the protection of individuals with regard to the processing of personal data and on the free movement of such data, OJ L 1995/281, 31.

124 Daniel Rücker, in Daniel Rücker and Tobias Kugler (eds), *New European General Data Protection Regulation: A Practitioner's Guide* (Nomos 2017) para 67 see also Opinion of AG Kokott, Case C 434/16, Nowak, EU:C:2017:582, para 3.

125 Article 29 Working Party, 'Opinion 4/2007 on the Concept of Personal Data' WP 136 6.

2.5.1.1.1 'Any information' may be personal data

It has already been pointed out under 2.2.4.2 that the GDPR's understanding of 'information' relates to the semantic layer. Hence, the type of data, format and storage medium are irrelevant for the categorisation as personal data. Information may be factual and verifiable statements concerning a person (e.g. student S has the matriculation number X) as well as subjective assessments or opinions (e.g. student S is an active participant in lectures). The information does not need to be correct or true.[126] In fact, the GDPR gives data subjects a specific remedy to rectify inaccurate or incomplete personal data.[127] The word 'any' underlines that data may be personal irrespective of whether the information is particularly private or of a rather general nature.[128] However, the GDPR also recognises the specific category of sensitive data (see 2.5.1.3).

2.5.1.1.2 The relationship between the information and a natural person

In order to qualify as personal data, information needs to relate to a natural person, referred to as 'data subject' in the GDPR.[129] The link to an individual is obvious if the information is 'about' a person, i.e. if it refers to an individual's identity, characteristics or behaviour (content element). However, according to the Article 29 Working Party, information also 'relates' to an individual if the information is used for the purpose of evaluating, treating in a certain way or influencing the status or behaviour of an individual (purpose element). The link is also sufficiently close if the information is likely to have an impact on a specific person's rights and interests, such as being treated differently than other persons (result element).[130]

In the decision *Nowak*,[131] the ECJ held that the written answers in a professional examination fulfil all three of these different elements that determine whether information relates to an individual. On a content level, the answers reflect the candidate's knowledge and competence in a given

126 Article 29 Working Party, 'Opinion 4/2007' (n 103) 6; Klabunde (n 100) DSGVO Art 4(1), para 9.
127 See Article 16 GDPR.
128 ECJ, C-434/16, *Nowak*, EU:C:2017:994, para 34; Rücker (n 124) para 74.
129 Article 4(1) GDPR.
130 Article 29 Working Party, 'Opinion 4/2007' (n 103) 10.
131 ECJ, C-434/16, *Nowak*, EU:C:2017:994.

field. The purpose for collecting these answers is to evaluate the candidate's abilities and suitability for a certain profession. Finally, the answers determine whether the candidate passes or fails the exam, which influences the candidate's chances of exercising the pursued profession or obtaining an aspired post.[132] The three elements, however, are alternative conditions. Thus, for information to qualify as personal data, it is sufficient that one of the elements is present. This also means the same piece of information may relate to different persons simultaneously, as the elements may be present with regard to different individuals.[133]

Due to this broad understanding, data that primarily relates to an object and not an individual may also be considered personal data. For example, the value of a property is not information about an individual and thus is not considered personal data if used for statistical evaluations of property value during the COVID pandemic in a particular area. However, if the information is used for the purpose of determining the tax obligation of the individual owning the property, the property value would fall under the definition of personal data.[134]

In the IoT context, the question whether data relates to an object or a natural person is particularly relevant. While some of the data generated by connected devices undoubtedly qualifies as personal data, one of the three elements can also be present in data relating primarily to technical aspects of the device. Delineating personal and non-personal IoT can therefore not be done on a general basis but requires a case-by-case analysis.[135] For example, while data on tyre pressure or brake wear collected by a connected vehicle is technical on its outset, it may also be used for assessing the owner's driving behaviour and handling of the car for insurance purposes.[136] In this case the data is used for the purpose of evaluation, and the car owner is treated differently than other persons based on this data. Regarding technical data, which is not stored for a longer period of time but is continuously deleted or overwritten, it will hardly be possible to create a

---

132 ECJ, C-434/16, *Nowak*, EU:C:2017:994, para 35 ff.

133 ECJ, C-434/16, *Nowak*, EU:C:2017:994, para 45; Article 29 Working Party, 'Opinion 4/2007' (n 125) 11.

134 Article 29 Working Party, 'Opinion 4/2007' (n 103) 9.

135 Rolf Schwartmann and Robin Lucien Mühlenbeck, in Rolf Schwartmann and others (eds), *DS-GVO/BDSG: Datenschutz-Grundverordnung, Bundesdatenschutzgesetz (Heidelberger Kommentar)* (2nd edn, CF Müller 2020) Art 4(1), para 30.

136 Benedikt Buchner, 'Datenschutz im vernetzten Automobil' (2015) 39 Datenschutz und Datensicherheit 372, 373.

sufficiently close link to a natural person. Therefore, such volatile data that is only stored for a few seconds will usually not qualify as personal data.

2.5.1.1.3 'Natural persons' as data subjects

The requirement of 'natural person' limits the concept of personal data to information relating to human beings that have the capacity to be the subject of legal relationships. Recital 27 clarifies that the GPDR does not apply to data on deceased persons but leaves Member States leeway to introduce a protective regime also for such data. Information on legal persons also falls outside the definition of personal data.[137] However, a piece of information primarily relating to a dead or legal person may also contain elements that connect it to a (living) natural person.[138] Information about a small legal entity may, for instance, provide insight into the behaviour of its legal representative,[139] or the health data of dead a person could reveal a genetical disease in relatives.[140] In such cases the data is personal.

Not specifically addressed by the GDPR is the question whether data relating to unborn children is personal data. Since the legal capacity afforded to conceived but still unborn children differs among Member States, the decision whether information on unborn children is protected should, according to the Article 29 WP, be left to national law.[141]

2.5.1.1.4 An 'identified or identifiable' data subject

In order to qualify as personal data, the information needs to relate to a natural person who is either identified or identifiable. Since 'identifiability' is a lower threshold than 'identified' and the GDPR's legal effects do not depend on which of the elements is present, identifiability' is the practically significant one.' An identifiable natural person is one who can be identified,

137 Recital 14 GDPR.

138 Article 29 Working Party, 'Opinion 4/2007' (n 125) 23; Moritz Karg, in Spiros Simitis, Gerrit Hornung and Indra Spiecker (eds), *Datenschutzrecht: DSGVO mit BDSG* (Nomos 2019) Art 4(1) DSGVO, para 44.

139 Manuel Klar and Jürgen Kühling, in Jürgen Kühling and Benedikt Buchner (eds), *Datenschutz-Grundverordnung/BDSG: Kommentar* (2nd edn, Beck 2018) Art 4(1) DSGVO, para 4.

140 Article 29 Working Party, 'Opinion 4/2007' (n 125) 22.

141 Article 29 Working Party, 'Opinion 4/2007' (n 103) 23.

directly or indirectly, in particular by reference to an identifier such as a name, an identification number, location data, an online identifier or to one or more factors specific to the physical, physiological, genetic, mental, economic, cultural or social identity of that natural person.'[142] In essence, the requirement of 'identifiability' describes the possibility to single someone out from a group of people.[143] This requirement highlights the objective of data protection law, which is to protect natural persons from impairments of their privacy. Even the most sensitive information does not need protection if it is impossible to link it to a natural person.

It can be distinguished between information that allows to directly identify a person and information that only allows for identification if combined with other information.[144] Traditional direct identifiers are name, fingerprints but also characteristics so unique that someone can be identified without much effort (e.g. first female president of the European Commission). However, the GDPR not only applies if a piece of information uniquely identifies a natural person but also if the identification is only possible indirectly.[145] Hence, even seemingly non-personal information may qualify as personal data, either because the information can be tied to information directly identifying an individual, or because the aggregation of several pieces of information results in a unique combination that can be ascribed to a specific person.[146] For example, address, age and gender may be sufficient in order to uniquely identify a natural person.

The element 'identifiable', of course, raises the question whether the information and means of the concrete controller are the benchmark to determine if an identifying link to a natural person can be established,[147] or whether the hypothetical possibility is sufficient.[148] The GDPR combines

---

142 Article 4(1) GDPR

143 Article 29 Working Party, 'Opinion 4/2007' (n 103) 12.

144 ECJ, C-582/14, *Breyer*, EU:C:2016:779, paras 40 f; Article 29 Working Party, 'Opinion 4/2007' (n 125) 13.

145 ECJ, C-582/14, *Breyer*, EU:C:2016:779, para 41.

146 Moritz Karg (n 138) Art 4(1) DSGVO, para 53.

147 See AG München, SU vom 30.09.2008 – 133 C 5677/08; OVG Münster, Beschluss vom 17.2.2009 – 13 B 33/09 (VG Köln); for further references see Stefan Brink and Jens Eckhardt, 'Wann ist ein Datum ein personenbezogenes Datum?' [2015] ZD 205, 210; Ulrich Sachs, 'Datenschutzrechtliche Bestimmbarkeit von IP-Adressen' (2010) 26 CR 547, 548; Nikolaus Forgó and Tina Krügel, 'Der Personenbezug von Geodaten' [2010] MMR 17, 18.

148 See Ingrid Pahlen-Brandt, 'Datenschutz braucht scharfe Instrumente Beitrag zur Diskussion um „personenbezogene Daten"' (2008) 32 Datenschutz und Datensi-

elements from both of these approaches.[149] According to Recital 26, in order to 'determine whether a natural person is identifiable, account should be taken of all the means reasonably likely to be used, such as singling out, either by the controller or by another person to identify the natural person directly or indirectly.' Hence, it is not necessary that all the information enabling the identification of the data subject is in the hands of a single person, but the means need to be reasonably likely to be used by the controller or third person to identify the data subject.[150] To determine whether the means are reasonably likely to be used, Recital 26 stipulates that all objective factors should be considered and lists the costs and the amount of time required for identification, the available technology at the time of the processing and technological developments as examples for such factors. To put it differently, identification is not possible if the necessary means would require disproportionate efforts and identification therefore seems unlikely. According to CJEU, the means are also not reasonably likely to be used if they are prohibited by law.[151] On the other hand, where the processing of information only makes sense if it can be linked to natural person, it needs to be assumed that the controller will have the means to identify the data subject. For example, the purpose of deploying a video surveillance system is to identify individuals recorded by the system. Therefore, the whole application is considered to process information about identifiable individuals, even if identification only takes place in very limited cases.[152]

2.5.1.2 Pseudonymised data

The GDPR defines 'pseudonymisation' as the 'processing of personal data in such a manner that the personal data can no longer be attributed to a specific data subject without the use of additional information, provided that such additional information is kept separately and is subject to technical and organisational measures to ensure that the personal data

---

cherheit – DuD 34, 39; Thilo Weichert, 'Der Personenbezug von Geodaten' (2007) 31 Datenschutz und Datensicherheit – DuD 113, 115.

149 Moritz Karg (n 138) Art 4(1) DSGVO, para 60.

150 ECJ, C-582/14, *Breyer*, EU:C:2016:779, para 42, 45

151 ECJ, C-582/14, *Breyer*, EU:C:2016:779, para 46; Opinion of AG Sánchez-Bordona, C-582/14, *Breyer*, EU:C:2016:339, para 68.

152 Article 29 Working Party, 'Opinion 4/2007' (n 103) 16.

are not attributed to an identified or identifiable natural person'.[153] While pseudonymisation of data reduces the link between information and the data subject, the information can still be retraced to a natural person. A typical example is that the controller of personal data replaces the names of individuals with a random code but keeps a separately stored list (the so-called key) that links the codes to the names. Since this list is reasonably likely to be used to identify the individual, the data still qualifies as personal data under the GDPR even though the personal identifier has been replaced with a random number.[154] If the link between the information and the data subject has been reduced to the point that it can no longer be established with means reasonably likely to be used, the data has been 'anonymised' and is no longer considered personal data (see 2.5.1.4).[155] Hence, pseudonymised data can be described as a subcategory of personal data where the linkability has been reduced.

In order to answer the question whether data has merely been pseudonymised or anonymised, it needs to be assessed whether a controller has the necessary means to backtrack the information to the individual and establish its identity. Since no general answer can be given as to what means are reasonably likely to be used (see 2.5.1.4), an assessment for each individual case is necessary. The delineation between pseudonymisation and anonymisation is particularly difficult if the original controller encrypts the data and transfers it to a third party without passing on the key to decrypt the code. Does the new controller (recipient) have means that are reasonably likely to be used to establish a link between the random number and the name of the individual? The lack of access to the key is certainly a strong indicator that the measure has an anonymising effect for the data recipient.[156] However, there may be cases where the random number is linked to a combination of indirect identifiers, which are so unique that a recipient would still be able to link the information to a natural person. In this case, the information would qualify as personal data despite the fact that recipients do not have access to the key that could decrypt the data.[157]

Even though pseudonymised data qualifies as personal data, pseudonymisation may significantly reduce the privacy risks for the data

153 Article 4(5) GDPR.
154 Recital 26 GDPR; Article 29 Working Party, 'Opinion 4/2007' (n 103) 18.
155 Article 29 Working Party, 'Opinion 05/2014 on Anonymisation Techniques' WP 216, 10.
156 Article 29 Working Party, 'Opinion 4/2007' (n 103) 18 ff.
157 Article 29 Working Party, 'Opinion 05/2014' (n 133) 22.

subject. The GDPR explicitly mentions pseudonymisation as an example of a technical/organisational measure that may be used in order to comply with the principle of privacy by design.[158] Pseudonymisation may also be used by a controller to comply with the principle of data minimisation.[159] Moreover, according to Article 6(4) GDPR, a controller, when ascertaining whether processing for another purpose is compatible with the purpose for which the personal data was initially collected, shall, *inter alia*, take into account the existence of appropriate safeguards, such as pseudonymisation of the data.[160] This means pseudonymisation may legitimise a change of purpose that would otherwise not be allowed.[161]

2.5.1.3 Sensitive data

The GDPR provides additional protection to personal data that is, by its nature, particularly sensitive and poses an enhanced risk to fundamental rights and freedoms.[162] Such sensitive data includes information revealing racial or ethnic origin, political opinions, religious or philosophical beliefs, or trade union membership, and the processing of genetic data, biometric data for the purpose of uniquely identifying a natural person, data concerning health or data concerning a natural person's sex life or sexual orientation.[163]

2.5.1.4 Non-Personal Data

Any information that does not relate to an identifiable natural person falls outside the scope of the GDPR and is labelled non-personal or anonymised data. While the GDPR does not define anonymised or non-personal data, Recital 26 GDPR provides that 'the principles of data protection should [...] not apply to anonymous information, namely information which does

158 Article 25(1) GDPR; Recital 78 GDPR.
159 According to Article 5(1)(c) 'personal data shall be adequate, relevant and limited to what is necessary in relation to the purposes for which they are processed'.
160 See Rolf Schwartmann and Steffen Weiß (eds), 'Whitepaper zur Pseudonymisierung' (Fokusgruppe Datenschutz des Digital-Gipfels 2017) 14 ff.
161 Article 29 Working Party, 'Opinion 03/2013 on Purpose Limitation' WP 203 26.
162 Recital 51 GDPR.
163 Article 9(1) GDPR.

not relate to an identified or identifiable natural person or to personal data rendered anonymous in such a manner that the data subject is not or no longer identifiable.' That non-personal data is the counterpart to personal data also follows from the Free Flow of Non-Personal Data Regulation,[164] which defines data as any data that is not personal data as defined by Article 4(1) GDPR.[165] It can be distinguished between data that is non-personal in nature, i.e. that has never related to a natural person, and data that had been personal but the link to the natural person was removed.[166]

Like personal data, the nature of non-personal data is dynamic and context-dependent and may therefore change over time.[167] For example, due to the increasing interconnectedness of information resulting from technical developments, situations may arise in which previously non-personal data can be linked to a natural person and thus qualifies as personal data.[168] Therefore, controllers are under a duty to continuously review whether information processed as anonymous can still be considered as such.[169]

New means of de-anonymisation also pose a problem to parties engaging in data transactions, as it becomes increasingly difficult to ensure that the transferred data does not fall under the data protection regime. One strategy to mitigate the risk of anonymised data becoming personal data is by not actually transferring a copy of the dataset but providing the data recipient with access to data within a system that remains in control of the original data holder (so-called in situ access). By maintaining control over the environment where the data is accessed and analysed, the original data

---

164 Regulation (EU) 2018/1807 of the European Parliament and of the Council of 14 November 2018 on a framework for the free flow of non-personal data in the European Union, OJ L 2019/303, 59.

165 Article 3(1) Free Flow of Non-Personal Data Regulation.

166 Marit Hansen, in Spiros Simitis, Gerrit Hornung and Indra Spiecker (eds), *Datenschutzrecht: DSGVO mit BDSG* (Nomos 2019) Art 4(5) DSGVO, para 13; EDPS, 'Comments of the EDPS on a Proposal for a Regulation of the European Parliament and of the Council on a Framework for the Free-Flow of Non-Personal Data in the European Union' (2018) 7.

167 EDPS, 'EDPS 2018' (n 166) 7.

168 Inge Graef, Raphael Gellert and Martin Husovec, 'Towards a Holistic Regulatory Approach for the European Data Economy' [2018] SSRN Electronic Journal 5 <https://www.ssrn.com/abstract=3256189> accessed 9 November 2021.

169 Manuel Klar and Jürgen Kühling (n 139) Art 4(1) DSGVO, para 22; Moritz Karg (n 138) Art 4(1) DSGVO, para 63.

holder can ensure that appropriate security measures are in place to prevent any re-identification of the data.[170]

2.5.1.5 Mixed datasets

Very often, a dataset will consist of both personal and non-personal data. In such constellations, the question arises whether the whole dataset qualifies as personal data. Due to the broad understanding of personal data, seemingly non-personal data of a 'mixed dataset', such as machine-generated or commercial data, will already qualify as personal data when the data can be linked to personal identifiers.[171]

For cases where truly non-personal data is combined with personal data, Article 2(2) of the Free Flow of Non-Personal Data Regulation stipulates that the GDPR shall apply to the whole dataset if the personal data is inextricably linked to the non-personal data. The European Commission has further specified that the GDPR shall apply regardless of the extent to which personal data is included in a mixed dataset. Hence, a mixed dataset is treated as personal data even if the inextricably linked personal data only represents a marginal share of the dataset.[172]

The Free Flow of Non-Personal Data Regulation does not define the notion of 'inextricably linked'. According to the Commission's guidance, it refers both to situations where separating the personal and non-personal data would be impossible as well as where the controller considers the separation to be economically inefficient or technically unfeasible.[173]

2.5.2 Categorisation according to the data's origin

Data, regardless of its semantic content, can originate from different sources and can be categorised accordingly. The categories 'user-generated' and 'machine-generated' not only describe who but also how the syntactic information was first generated. Since this categorisation refers to the data's origin, it is irrelevant which actions are later performed on the data.

170 Jacques Crémer, Yves-Alexandre de Montjoye and Heike Schweitzer, 'Competition Policy for the Digital Era' (2019) 86.

171 EDPS, 'EDPS 2018' (n 166) 4.

172 COM(2019) 250 final of 29 May 2019, 9.

173 COM(2019) 250 final of 29 May 2019, 10.

2.5.2.1 User-generated data

If the data is generated by an activity performed by a person, such data is referred to as user-generated data. The category is very broad and includes data actively entered in online forms, data generated by the use of credit or debit cards and even data generated by a public surveillance camera. Within the category of user-generated data, it can be distinguished between actively 'provided data' and data generated by observing a person's activities ('observed data').

Originally, these categories were used only for personal data.[174] However, a natural person's activities may also generate non-personal data. For example, by (digitally) typing down lottery tips, an individual generates data that is not personal. Furthermore, the user whose activities lead to the generation of data may also be a legal person. Where retailers provide data about their business activities to an online marketplace, the data should be considered user-generated, irrespective of whether the retailer is a legal or natural person. Since the adjectives 'provided' and 'observed' are helpful to describe a party's contribution to the generation of data, the terms should be used without regard to the semantic content of the data.[175] The classification of data as personal or non-personal therefore needs to be seen separately from the question of whether data is user-generated or machine-generated (see 2.5.2.2).

2.5.2.1.1 Provided data

Data falls in the category of 'provided data' if a person takes an action which purposefully leads to the generation of data. The person does not need to consider the full implications of their actions, but it is sufficient that the person is aware that they are fully involved in the generation of the data. Such actions include registering on a social media platform, entering credit card information for online purchases, or posting on social media.[176] A person can also be actively involved in the generation of non-personal

174 OECD, 'Enhancing Access to and Sharing of Data' (n 2) 30; Martin Abrams, 'The Origins of Personal Data and Its Implications for Governance' [2014] SSRN Electronic Journal 4 ff <http://www.ssrn.com/abstract=2510927> accessed 11 November 2021.

175 See also Stefan Schmidt, *Zugang zu Daten nach europäischem Kartellrecht* (Mohr Siebeck 2020) 41.

176 Abrams (n 174) 6.

data, e.g. by participating in an anonymised survey, or if a legal person provides data about its financial situation to a credit institute.

The term 'volunteered data' is occasionally used synonymously[177] but is somewhat misleading, as there may be situations where data is generated actively and purposefully but not voluntarily. For example, if people were required to complete a COVID contact tracing form after contracting the virus, the data cannot be assumed to have been provided voluntarily, as some people may have chosen not to provide the data if it had not been required by law.

2.5.2.1.2 Observed Data

Observed data is generated when a person undertakes an action or activity that is observed and recorded. The observed person is not actively involved in the generation but plays only a passive role. The extent to which persons are aware that they are being observed may vary within this category. The observed person may be notified that their actions are recorded, but observations may also be conducted clandestinely. Examples are location tracking by apps, observation of online shopping behaviour, or the analysis of driving behaviour by the sensors of a connected vehicle. If the observed person is a natural person, the data will qualify as personal data unless appropriate anonymisation measures are applied.[178]

Observed data necessarily involves at least two actors that contribute to the generation of data (regarding the term 'co-generated data' see 2.5.3): the person whose activities are being observed and the person observing and recording the data.[179]

2.5.2.2 Machine-generated data

In its Communication on the Data Economy, the European Commission describes 'machine-generated data' as 'data created without the direct inter-

177 E.g. Christian Reimsbach-Kounatze, 'Enhancing Access to and Sharing of Data: Striking the Balance between Openness and Control over Data' in Bundesministerium der Justiz und für Verbraucherschutz and Max-Planck-Institut für Innovation und Wettbewerb (eds), *Data Access, Consumer Interests and Public Welfare* (Nomos 2021) 57; OECD, 'Enhancing Access to and Sharing of Data' (n 2).

178 Abrams (n 174) 6.

179 Schmidt (n 175) 42.

vention of a human by computer processes, applications or services, or by sensors processing information received from equipment, software or machinery, whether virtual or real.' Such data may include the recording of internal technical processes (e.g. the maintenance status of a machine) or of physical input that is recorded by some sort of sensor or camera (e.g. the soil quality of farm land).

Since observed data will often also be generated by some kind of sensor, the question arises as to how the category of user-generated data can be delineated from machine-generated data. It has rightly been pointed out that this line is difficult to draw because even sensor data documenting natural phenomena, such as room temperature, may give insights into human actions (e.g. the temperature may vary depending on how many people are in the room or when windows are opened).[180] What distinguishes machine generated data from observed data, however, is that the latter is a direct record of a person's activities. Inferring conclusions about human behaviour from machine-generated data, on the other hand, requires some sort of additional processing and can only be done indirectly. In the latter case, the party's contribution to data generation is marginal.

Where references to a natural person can be deduced, machine-generated data may qualify as personal data. Therefore, the term machine-generated data is not synonymous with non-personal data.

2.5.2.3 Aggregated, derived and inferred data

Both user- and machine-generated data may often be the basis for the generation of new data. There are multiple ways to generate data on the basis of other data, such as analysing, combining or linking raw data. The term 'aggregated data' usually refers to combining initially separated datasets, while 'derived' and 'inferred' data are often used as synonyms to describe data that was generated by applying statistical or computational procedures to draw conclusions from raw datasets.[181]

180 See Nestor Duch-Brown, Bertin Martens and Frank Mueller-Langer, 'The Economics of Ownership, Access and Trade in Digital Data' (2017) Digital Economy Working Paper 2017-01, 7 who have critised the unclear use of the term 'machine generated data'.

181 See Data Governance Working Group, 'The Role of Data in AI' (GPAI 2020) 19; OECD, 'Enhancing Access to and Sharing of Data' (n 2) 31; Japanese Ministry of Economy, Trade and Industry (METI), 'Contract Guidelines on Utilization of

With the help of data analytics and artificial intelligence (AI), controllers may be able to link separate pieces of information or identify patterns in datasets and generate more sophisticated data. The aggregation of data will often precede such data analysis, as more enhanced inferences can be drawn from large and diverse datasets. Due to the fact that more insights and consequently more economic value can be extracted from combined datasets, the value of an aggregated set can exceed the sum of the values of the separate sets.[182]

The labels 'derived', 'inferred' or 'aggregated', as such, do not imply whether the data is personal or not. However, the possibility to infer information about individuals by aggregating, extracting or analysing data that is non-personal on its outset,[183] needs to be considered when determining the means reasonably likely to be used to identify an individual (see 2.5.1.4).

2.5.3 Co-generated data

While the categories 'user-generated', 'machine-generated' or 'inferred data' indicate how data was generated, they are indifferent to the fact that data will often be generated by multiple persons that may play very different roles in the generation process. Observed data, for example, will necessarily involve the person who is the subject of the data (i.e. the person being observed) and the person recording the activity or behaviour (i.e. the person observing). In its Principles for a Data Economy,[184] the American (ALI) and European Law Institute (ELI) have therefore developed and coined the term 'co-generated data', which has been picked up by the European

AI and Data: Data Section' (2018) 1'the term "derived data" refers to data that is newly generated through processing, analysis, editing, integration, etc. of any data'; Duch-Brown, Martens and Mueller-Langer (n 180) 37.

182 Bertin Martens and others, 'Business-to-Business Data Sharing: An Economic and Legal Analysis' (Joint Research Centre 2020) 5.

183 See Arvind Narayanan and Vitaly Shmatikov, 'How to Break Anonymity of the Netflix Prize Dataset' (2006) abs/cs/0610105 CoRR <http://arxiv.org/abs/cs/0610105> who demonstrated how supposedly anonymous movie ratings of Netflix subscribers can be linked to identifiable individuals by combining, analysing and cross-referencing data publicly available on the internet.

184 Neil Cohen and Christiane Wendehorst (n 120); a final draft was published online already in 2021, see Neil Cohen and Christiane Wendehorst, 'Principles for a Data Economy (ELI Final Council Draft)' (ALI/ELI 2021) <https://www.principlesforadataeconomy.org/fileadmin/user_upload/p_principlesforadataeconomy/Files/Principles_for_a_Data_Economy_ELI_Final_Council_Draft.pdf>.

Commission[185], UNCITRAL[186] as well as other institutional actors.[187] The Principles define 'co-generated data as data to the generation of which a person other than the controller has contributed'[188] and specify four different factors that determine what counts as co-generation of data.

The strongest form of contribution is by either being the person who is the subject of the information (e.g. data about the shopping preferences of a natural person), or the owner or operator of an asset that is the subject of that information (e.g. data on the maintenance status of machinery, which is held by the producer of the machinery and not the owner or operator). A person may also contribute to the generation by pursuing an activity that produces the data (driving a connected vehicle), or by owning or operating a product or service that produced the data (owning a connected vehicle). A less significant contribution is compiling or structuring already existing data in such a way that something of new quality is created, e.g. a database. The weakest form of contribution is to develop a product or service (e.g. a sensor or software) that is used to generate the data.[189]

A party's share in the generation of the data depends on which and how many of these four factors are met, on the remoteness of the contribution, and the specificity of the contribution (i.e. a contribution carries less weight if the same contribution could have been made by any other party). A party's share also needs to be seen in relation to the contributions of other parties involved. However, contributions of a party that are insignificant in the circumstances should be considered irrelevant.[190]

2.6 The economic characteristics of data

Due to technological advancements that have made the means to efficiently collect, store and process large amounts of (digital) data more readily available and more affordable, data has become a valuable resource beyond the internet sector. It provides companies a new basis for more efficient deci-

185 COM(2020) 66 final of 19 February 2020 10.

186 UNCITRAL, Legal issues related to digital economy – proposal for future work on data transactions (2022, A/CN.9/1117), available at <https://documents.un.org/doc/undoc/gen/v22/024/80/pdf/v2202480.pdf?token=pQdRcYRTSsaaLgNAcd&fe=true> accessed 10 June 2024.

187 Datenethikkommission (n 114) 89 ff; Data Governance Working Group (n 119).

188 Neil Cohen and Christiane Wendehorst (n 119) Principle 3(1)(h).

189 Neil Cohen and Christiane Wendehorst (n 119) Principle 18(1).

190 Neil Cohen and Christiane Wendehorst (n 119) Principle 18(2), (3).

sion-making across the entire value chain, as relevant and high-quality data may reduce costs in manufacturing and production, improve logistics, and provide valuable insights for sales and marketing. Access to data also plays an important role in developing innovative services and products. In the IoT sector, which has gained an increasingly important role for commercial actors (e.g. integrated production and distribution chains, and smart manufacturing) as well as private actors (e.g. smart home applications, and connected cars), access to data is a prerequisite for interconnecting devices and providing complementary services to IoT ecosystems. Moreover, huge datasets are necessary to train AI systems and develop new and reliable applications. The potential of data and its endless possibilities of use have created a demand across almost all sectors of the economy, from health and education to finance and mobility.[191]

2.6.1 The non-rivalrous nature of data

A characteristic feature of data is that it can be used simultaneously by multiple parties without diminishing its availability or value. For example, a consumer behaviour dataset can be used by a marketing team to target advertising campaigns, by a product development team to design new products and by customer service to improve customer interaction—all at the same time, without exhausting the dataset. Moreover, the cost associated with data primarily arises at the point of collection and initial processing. Once data is collected, the marginal cost of another party using it is close to zero. This is because data can be duplicated and distributed at minimal cost. This non-rivalrous nature is what makes data fundamentally different from traditional resources, where use by one person physically prevents simultaneous use by another and often leads to depletion of the resource. Moreover, reproducing physical goods can typically only be done with significant costs.[192]

191 See Crémer, de Montjoye and Schweitzer (n 170) 72.

192 Martens and others (n 182) 12; OECD, 'Enhancing Access to and Sharing of Data' (n 2) 17; Vera Demary and Christian Rusche, 'Data Sharing im E-Commerce: Rechtliche und ökonomische Grundlagen' (Institut der deutschen Wirtschaft 2019) 33; Duch-Brown, Martens and Mueller-Langer (n 180) 12.

2.6.2 (Non-)exclusivity of data

Since data is a non-rivalrous resource, data is, in principle, also non-excludable. The use of data by one person does not automatically prevent others from accessing the data and using it for their purposes. In contrast, the physical control of tangible objects by one party directly prevents another from using the same object at the same time. Despite its natural non-excludability, technical protection measures that restrict access to data can be put in place to ensure that only authorised users can access or use the data. The person controlling who can access the data through technical means becomes the de facto holder and can potentially charge for access and derive economic benefits from controlling a non-rivalrous resource.[193]

A certain degree of excludability may also be achieved by legal means. For example, the person holding the data may enter into a contract with a data recipient that lays down restrictions on how the recipient may process, share, or redistribute the data, and/or stipulations on the purposes for which the data can be used. However, contractual excludability is limited to the parties of the agreement. If third parties acquire the data, either through leakage, unauthorised dissemination, or other means, they are not bound by the terms of the contract.[194] For instance, if a company A shares data with company B under a data sharing agreement that includes non-disclosure and usage restrictions, company B is legally bound to adhere to these terms. However, if an employee of company B leaks this data to a third party, C, who was not a party to the original agreement, C is not legally bound by the agreement's terms and may use the data freely, provided that the C did not know or did not ought to have known that the data transfer would breach the contractual obligations towards A.[195]

The law also grants *erga omnes* rights with regard to data that can be enforced against anyone. For example, the GDPR gives individuals the right to access, correct, delete, or restrict the processing of their personal data. Whilst this right gives data subjects a form of excludable control, this legal position is not transferable and does not give data subjects full control

193 Martens and others (n 182) 13; Herbert Zech, 'Besitz an Daten?' in Tereza Pertot, Martin Schmidt-Kessel and Fabio Padovini (eds), *Rechte an Daten* (Mohr Siebeck 2020) 93.

194 Determann (n 20) 9; Zech, 'Daten als Wirtschaftsgut – Überlegungen zu einem „Recht des Datenerzeugers"' (n 63) 140.

195 For the effects of a breach of contract on the downstream recipient, see Neil Cohen and Christiane Wendehorst (n 119) Principle 34.

over their data.[196] Another example is the EU Database Directive, which grants the creators of a database *sui-generis* right to prevent others from using their database.[197] However, it is not the data as such that is protected because the *sui-generis* right only prevents others from extracting qualitative and quantitative substantial parts of the database.[198] Excludability with regard to data can also be established by the Trade Secrets Directive if the data contains information that has commercial value because it is secret.[199] However, trade secret law does not confer exclusive property-like rights over data. The protection depends on the actual existence of the secret, which means that the legal protection is lost once the secrecy of the data is lost. Hence, if data were to be leaked to the public, the data holder could not stop third parties from using that data based on trade secrets law.[200]

The excludability conferred by various laws regarding data does not equate to full ownership in the traditional sense, which gives the right to possess, exclude and transfer the owned object.[201] Instead, these rights focus on preventing harm or misuse by placing limitations on how data can be used. Since the law does not assign data to a specific person, the control of data is primarily based on factual circumstances, that is, who stores the data on the server and prevents it from being accessed by others through technical measures. Legal excludability may either reinforce or weaken the de facto control of the data holder. For instance, in the case of trade secrets, where the de facto holder is typically also the trade secret holder, the de facto control is enhanced, as the trade secrets law prevents others from legally using, disclosing, or disseminating the information without consent

196 Zech, 'Daten als Wirtschaftsgut – Überlegungen zu einem „Recht des Datenerzeugers“' (n 63) 141.

197 Article 7 Directive 96/9/EC of the European Parliament and of the Council of 11 March 1996 on the legal protection of databases, OJ L 1996/77, 20.

198 Kerber, 'A New (Intellectual) Property Right for Non-Personal Data? An Economic Analysis' (n 20) 991; Zech, '„Industrie 4.0“ – Rechtsrahmen für eine Datenwirtschaft im digitalen Binnenmarkt' (n 63) 1158.

199 Article 2 Directive (EU) 2016/943 of the European Parliament and of the Council of 8 June 2016 on the protection of undisclosed know-how and business information (trade secrets) against their unlawful acquisition, use and disclosure, OJ L 2016/157, 1.

200 Kerber, 'A New (Intellectual) Property Right for Non-Personal Data? An Economic Analysis' (n 20) 991; Andreas Wiebe, 'Protection of Industrial Data – a New Property Right for the Digital Economy?' [2016] GRUR International 877, 880; Zech, '„Industrie 4.0“ – Rechtsrahmen für eine Datenwirtschaft im digitalen Binnenmarkt' (n 63) 1156.

201 Determann (n 20) 9.

(Article 4(2) Trade Secrets Directive). On the other hand, by imposing stringent requirements on the processing of personal data, the GDPR limits the data controller's ability to freely use the data despite de facto control. Access and portability rights add another layer. These rights allow persons who do not have factual control over their data to access and potentially transfer their data to another person, without restricting the original data holder's ability to use the data simultaneously.

3 The Rationale for Affording Access and Portability Rights

The flipside of data-driven innovation is that companies lacking access to the relevant data are at a significant disadvantage. Recent years have shown that the business models in many areas of the digital economy have led to the accumulation of large amounts of data in the hands of only a few market players. However, the allocation of the data is not determined by the legal system—since the introduction of data ownership has, for good reasons, been abandoned—but by factual circumstances. If the de facto holders are not willing to share the data they control, it may have negative effects on competition, innovation and societal welfare.[202] The following Chapter first outlines the different issues that may arise from the de facto control of data and limited accessibility of other parties. It then describes why the concept of data ownership would not have been capable of solving these issues.

3.1 Ever-growing market power of digital conglomerates

The largest data holders, Google (Alphabet), Amazon, Facebook (Meta), Apple, and Microsoft (GAFAM), have significantly expanded their field of operations to a variety of sectors over the past two decades. Google, which started as a search engine provider, has since then developed an internet browser, an operating system for smartphones, smartphone hardware and is a pioneer in the development of self-driving cars. The online book retailing platform Amazon has become one of the market leaders in cloud computing services, entered into competition with grocery stores, and offers products ranging from electronics to sports equipment.[203] What

---

202 Wolfgang Kerber, 'Updating Competition Policy for the Digital Economy? An Analysis of Recent Reports in Germany, UK, EU, and Australia' [2019] SSRN Electronic Journal 30 f <https://www.ssrn.com/abstract=3469624>.

203 Nicolas Petit, 'Technology Giants, the Moligopoly Hypothezis and Holistic Competition: A Primer' [2016] SSRN Electronic Journal 15 ff <https://www.ssrn.com/abstract=2856502> accessed 14 January 2022; Reinhardt Krause, 'Meet The New Digital Conglomerates: Google, Facebook, Amazon ... And Apple? | Stock News & Stock Market Analysis – IBD' (*Investor's Business Daily*, 11 June 2016) <https://www.inves-

drives the conglomerate expansion of digital companies is they are operating on markets that constantly evolving and developing and are therefore at a constant risk of being driven out of business. Kodak, Nokia and Myspace are just a few of the names that come to mind. Against this backdrop, it makes sense for digital companies to focus their innovation efforts not only on existing products and markets, but to try to discover the next transformative technology and to expand their market power to adjacent and peripheral markets and disrupt incumbent players.[204]

Access to large amounts of data is an enabling factor for the rapid expansion of digital companies and their conglomerate structures. Detailed user and customer data collected on the core market not only allows the data holding companies to improve their existing services and products but also to develop new products and services that meet their users' preferences. By venturing into new market sectors, even more diverse datasets can be collected, which allows the creation of more detailed and meaningful consumer profiles. Due to their access to data on user preferences, new products and services can be advertised, targeting the customers' needs and weaknesses. Moreover, control over large amounts of data usually goes hand in hand with special expertise in data analytics, the development of algorithms and AI. These key technologies enable innovation in many different sectors and can therefore give a significant competitive advantage on both adjacent and peripheral markets.[205] Ultimately, the conglomerate structures lead to a cycle in which the existing data is used to create new products and services to increase the contact points with customers, which in turn results in the aggregation of even more diversified and valuable datasets.[206] Such data aggregation and multiple use of data may well have advantages for users, as the quality of the services offered to them increases with ever greater access to increasingly differentiated user profiles. However, the creation of datasets that cannot be replicated in their detail and richness by competitors and to which they also do not have access can lead to the issues described under 3.2.

---

tors.com/news/technology/google-facebook-amazon-apple-digital-conglomerates/> accessed 15 January 2022.

204 Petit (n 203) 3.

205 Heike Schweitzer and others, 'Modernisierung der Missbrauchsaufsicht für marktmächtige Unternehmen' (Bundesministeriums für Wirtschaft und Energie 2018) 85.

206 Yong Lim, 'Tech Wars: Return of the Conglomerate – Throwback or Dawn of a New Series for Competition in the Digital Era?' (2017) 19 Journal of Korean Law 47, 56.

3.1.1 The data power of platforms

Platforms have played an essential role in the mass roll-out of the internet and consequently also in the economic success of internet platform providers. The vast amount of information available on the internet can hardly be utilised without platforms that act as information intermediaries and systematically collect, order and rank the information. Information intermediaries have many different forms and include search engines, trading platforms, social media platforms, price comparison platforms and booking portals.

In economic literature, platforms are also called multi-sided markets, as there are two or multiple different user groups (e.g. buyer and seller, or user and advertiser) that interact via the platform. A characteristic feature of multi-sided markets is indirect network effects, which means that the actions of one group positively or negatively influence the benefit of the other group. The typical example of positive network effects is that an online marketplace gets more attractive for buyers if there are many different sellers offering a variety of different products on the platform. At the same time, more buyers increase the attractiveness of the platform for sellers. It is crucial for the functioning of platforms that all relevant market sides participate in sufficient numbers to make the platform attractive to the opposite side of the market.[207] In order to attract a large number of users to one side of the platform, which in turn draws more users to the other side, platform providers often pursue asymmetric pricing strategies. Users on one side are charged very low prices for the platform services, while the other, less price-sensitive side is overcharged.[208]

In terms of data collection, platform providers are in a particularly privileged position because they benefit significantly from economies of scale. Due to indirect network effects and the fact that the fixed costs for developing, establishing and maintaining a platform are very high, but the variable costs of adding additional users to the platform are close to zero, successful platforms can collect data from a large number of users.[209]

207 See Bertin Martens, 'An Economic Policy Perspective on Online Platforms' (Joint Research Centre 2016) 11 with further references from economic literature.

208 For an extensive economic analysis of overcoming this 'chicken and egg' problem, see Bernard Caillaud and Bruno Jullien, 'Chicken & Egg: Competition among Intermediation Service Providers' (2003) 34 RAND Journal of Economics 309.

209 See Vera Demary and Christian Rusche, 'The Economics of Platforms' (Institut der deutschen Wirtschaft 2018) IW-Analysen, No. 123, 14 'For instance, once an

Furthermore, while traditional companies can only analyse the data of their customers, platform providers collect data from both sides of a market and from a variety of different actors on each side. The diversity of the datasets collected and aggregated by platform providers makes them more valuable than the sum of individual datasets traditional companies hold.[210]

Access to these large amounts of data allows platform providers to boost innovation. For example, the data on supply and demand characteristics allows platform providers to improve search rankings and lower the search costs, adapt and tailor their services to the specific needs of users, and develop new platform features. However, platform providers may also use their data power to actively forestall competition and lock users in their ecosystem.

3.1.1.1 Data leverage on vertically integrated platforms

In economic theory, vertical integration describes the phenomenon that one actor controls two or more successive stages of production and/or distribution. Classic examples are a shoe manufacturer that also runs a shoe retail business,[211] or a furniture retailer that acquires a forestland.[212] Long before the emergence of the digital economy, vertical integration has raised concerns of anticompetitive behaviour, as it allows companies to leverage their market power and extend it to other stages of the production or distribution chain. Vertically integrated companies can also foreclose competition by using one line of business to disadvantage competitors on the other line and boost its own business.[213]

Vertically integrated platforms, where platform providers act not only as intermediaries but also as suppliers on their own platform, have raised additional concerns about possible anti-competitive behaviour. Platform providers may use their data power, which is an inherent side effect of operating a platform, to skew competition in their favour and boost their other

online search engine has established its website and programmed an appropriate algorithm, the total costs for 100 or 1,000 search queries do not differ much'.

210 Martens (n 207) 36.

211 *Brown Shoe Co., Inc. v. United States*, 370 U.S. 294 (1962).

212 'IKEA Group Acquires 25,000 Acre Forest' <https://www.ikea.com/us/en/newsroom/corporate-news/ikea-group-acquires-25-000-acre-forest-in-alabama-latest-investment-furthers-the-ikea-group-pu-b986453f7> accessed 21 January 2022.

213 Lina Khan, 'Amazon's Antitrust Paradox' (2017) 126 Yale Law Journal 710, 731.

lines of business. Instead of using the data collected on both sides of the market only for the purposes of the marketplace itself, e.g. for optimising the intermediation service, providers of vertically integrated platforms can use the insights from their datasets to gain a competitive advantage over other suppliers.

Amazon's business practices brought broader attention to the effects of data leverage on vertically integrated platforms. Amazon's e-commerce platform offers individual traders a reach that goes far beyond that of their own website. As a provider of intermediation services, Amazon collects sales and transaction data of all third-party traders as well as detailed data on consumer behaviour, such as the time customers looked at a product, or which items ended up in the shopping cart but were never purchased. However, Amazon does not only operate a platform but also acts as retailer and competes directly with third-party merchants.[214] Under a number of different labels Amazon offers products ranging from clothing and furniture to household goods and health and beauty products.[215] In the competition with third-party retailers, Amazon can use the data collected on the marketplace to identify successful products and gain information on the price strategies of its competitors in the retail sector. These insights allow Amazon to replicate profitable products and undercut third-party merchants on the price. Moreover, as Amazon is also the platform provider, it can influence the search results and rank its own products higher than those of competitors.[216]

While both of these practices are now prohibited for gatekeeper platforms under the DMA,[217] these examples show the dependence of users on the platform provider. Even though third-party merchants provide their direct competitor with data on their business strategies and the behaviour and preferences of their customers, traders rely on intermediation services like those offered by Amazon due to a lack of alternatives. Amazon's marketplace has reached a critical mass of users on both sides of the market, to the extent that many retailers simply can no longer afford to rely solely on direct (online) sales. Creating their own platforms is not an option for most

214 See Demary and Rusche, 'Data Sharing im E-Commerce: Rechtliche und ökonomische Grundlagen' (n 192) 8.

215 For a list of Amazon's exclusive brands, see https://www.amazon.com/b?ie=UTF8&node=17728530011.

216 Lina M Khan, 'The Seperation of Platforms and Commerce' (2019) 119 Columbia Law Review 973, 984.

217 See Articles 5(2), 6(2) and 6(5) DMA.

of them either, as the capital costs of creating a platform are very high and a larger number of users on the supplier side would be needed to make it attractive to consumers.[218]

The example of Amazon also illustrates that, in addition to vertical integration, data leverage presupposes a significant degree of market dominance by the platform. If suppliers are not dependent on the platforms' intermediation services, they would not provide their competitor with data that can be used against them. Of course, market dominance and vertical integration are competition law problems not specific to the data economy. However, as *Khan* rightly pointed out, it is the ability of platforms to collect large amounts of data and use it in a different context that aggravates the anti-competitive potential of market dominance and vertical integration.[219] It is the strong information asymmetry between the platform provider and its users that allows providers of vertically integrated e-commerce platforms to leverage their power. While it is not uncommon that big conventional retailers introduce their own private labels to compete with third-party suppliers, their leverage is weaker, because a conventional retailer has, if at all, only access to the sales data of third-party suppliers. Platform providers, on the other hand, have sophisticated data of all users on both sides of the market and can therefore more effectively and efficiently manipulate competition.[220]

3.1.1.2 Impediment of multi-homing

In digital platform markets, users can often engage with multiple platforms without significant additional costs. For instance, users may search different travel platforms simultaneously to find the best offer. Contrastingly, in traditional markets like telecommunications or software, multi-homing is less common due to significant barriers, particularly related to monetary costs. For instance, individuals typically maintain only one mobile phone contract or use office software from a single provider because subscribing to multiple services would be costly and impractical. In theory, the ability

218 Demary and Rusche, 'Data Sharing im E-Commerce: Rechtliche und ökonomische Grundlagen' (n 192) 9.

219 Khan (n 213) 783; see also Crémer, de Montjoye and Schweitzer (n 170) 107.

220 Khan (n 213) 782.

for users to multi-home makes digital platform markets less likely to be monopolised by one large player.[221]

However, although multi-homing will typically be possible in platform markets, providers may still try to tie users to their platform by not enabling users to automatically move their data to another provider. In these cases, users are not trapped because they have already invested money in the service, but because they have invested significant amounts of time and effort into setting up and maintaining their profiles on digital platforms.[222] These investments become sunk costs if they decide to switch platforms. For example, users spend considerable time curating their social media presence, connecting with friends, and generating content. This personal investment binds them to the platform, making switching costly not just in terms of data loss but also in terms of social connectivity.[223] Other examples are platforms like Airbnb or Amazon, where business users build reputations through ratings and reviews that are crucial for their success on these platforms. If these data cannot be transferred to other platforms, it would directly affect their business opportunities, creating a significant disincentive to switch. When a large number of users are locked into a platform, new platform providers will face a significant barrier to entry as they will struggle to convince users to abandon their investment in established platforms. This dynamic can lead to monopolistic or oligopolistic conditions where a few large platforms dominate the market, stifling competition and innovation by giving an unfair advantage to incumbent platforms.[224]

3.2 Lack of data access and its consequences

The concentration of data in the hands of a few entities, combined with a reluctance of many companies to share their data, despite the growing

221 Schweitzer and others (n 205) 12.

222 Schmidt (n 175) 478; Nela Grothe, *Datenmacht in der kartellrechtlichen Missbrauchskontrolle* (Nomos 2019) 57 <https://www.nomos-elibrary.de/index.php?doi=10.5771/9783748903437> accessed 13 May 2021; Inge Graef, Sih Yuliana Wahyuningtyas and Peggy Valcke, 'Assessing Data Access Issues in Online Platforms' (2015) 39 Telecommunications Policy 375, 377.

223 Schmidt (n 175) 478; Inge Graef, Jeroen Verschakelen and Peggy Valcke, 'Putting the Right to Data Portability into a Competition Law Perspective' [2013] Law: The Journal of the Higher School of Economics, Annual Review 53, 58.

224 Schmidt (n 175) 478; Duch-Brown, Martens and Mueller-Langer (n 180) 44.

demand for high-quality, reliable data, is creating significant challenges in the digital economy. Data can be reused within a different context or merged with other datasets without exhausting the resource. Different actors may be able to derive different value from the same dataset and aggregated datasets typically become more valuable than when they are kept segmented.[225] Moreover, since economic success in the digital economy will often depend on sufficient access to the relevant data, data holders may be incentivised to deny data access in order to solidify their market power. Finally, the de facto control and denial of data access deprives those who have contributed to the creation of the data of their legitimate interest in using this data for their own purposes.

3.2.1 Inefficient use of data

The non-rivalrous nature of data is the reason why a lack of data sharing and re-use can be a source of significant economic inefficiency. If data is not shared, others needing access to similar data have to collect or generate the same data independently, leading to duplicated collection efforts and increased costs across the economy. Multiplying the resource expenditure on similar datasets could be avoided if only one person invests in gathering a particular set of data, but many can benefit from its use. This would lead to economic welfare gains, as the collection costs could be spread over numerous applications and users. Moreover, since data does not diminish with use, restricting its access means that potential insights and value derivable from the data are lost. Other persons may be able to create value-added services and products based on the data input that the original data collector may not have thought of.[226] For example, traffic data collected by navigation apps could also be used for urban planning and congestion management, areas that are not the primary business focus of the data collector.

Moreover, by restricting data access, potential synergies from combining datasets may be lost. This is because merging complementary datasets may allow for a more comprehensive analysis, revealing patterns and relationships that might remain obscured when datasets are analysed independent-

225 Barbero and others (n 5); Martens and others (n 182) 5.

226 Martens and others (n 182) 12; Demary and Rusche, 'Data Sharing im E-Commerce: Rechtliche und ökonomische Grundlagen' (n 192) 37.

ly. Hence, it may be possible to derive greater insights and value from the combined dataset than from each dataset in isolation.[227] For example, integrating data on customer transactions with online browsing data can provide a more comprehensive picture of consumer behaviour, leading to more effective marketing strategies.

3.2.2 Data as an essential resource

Large data holders can impede competition on aftermarkets and the roll-out of innovative services or products that could threaten their market power by denying (real-time) access to data that is indispensable for the development of a product or service and cannot otherwise be replicated or acquired on the market. For example, innovative fintech companies that want to offer services, which could simplify (online) payment transactions for the general public, are dependent on the willingness of established banks to grant access to the data that is necessary to perform such services. Since these third-party providers are likely to compete with established banks for a lucrative line of business in the financial sector, the banks have an incentive to forestall any competition by denying access to the data required to offer the competing services.

Furthermore, the development of AI and self-learning algorithms, which are becoming a decisive competitive factor in many fields of economic activity, requires access to large amounts of training data. Data access denial by large data holders may block market entries or drive competitors out of the market.[228]

3.2.3 Unfair distribution of co-generated data

Where multiple actors have contributed to the generation of data but only one actor has factual control over the co-generated data, the distribution of the data may give rise to unfair commercial practices by the data holder. Particularly in IoT ecosystems, several stakeholders will contribute to the

227 Richard Feasey and Alexandre de Streel, 'Data Sharing for Digital Markets Contestability' (CERRE 2020) 21; Martens and others (n 182) 12; Duch-Brown, Martens and Mueller-Langer (n 180) 9; Daniel Rubinfeld and Michal Gal, 'Access Barriers to Big Data' (2017) 59 Arizona Law Review 339, 352.

228 Schweitzer and others (n 205) 136.

production of data and also have an interest in accessing the produced datasets for their purposes. The party having de facto control over the generated data is in a stronger bargaining position and may either charge high fees for the access or deny access at all. For example, the manufacturer of a smart tractor buys certain parts, such as motor and sensors, from third parties. The motor and sensor data that is generated during the operation of the tractor is, however, stored exclusively on the servers of the tractor manufacturer. In order to improve their products, the producers of the motor and sensors have an interest in accessing the data but are dependent on the goodwill of the tractor manufacturer.[229]

3.2.4 Lock-in effects

From an end user perspective, denied access will regularly lead to lock-in effects. End users may be discouraged from switching to a different provider if the initial provider/data holder denies porting of user-generated data to the new provider. For example, a farm corporation would only want to switch to another smart tractor manufacturer if data on soil quality and past yields held by the manufacturer of the old tractor fleet can be ported. Without access to this data, the farm corporation could not make full use of the analytical tools of the new smart tractors.[230]

Exclusive control over data may not only allow data holders to solidify their market power in the core market, but also to transfer market power to aftermarkets and adjacent markets. By denying data access, data holders can block companies from entering the aftermarkets or offering complementary services, locking the end user in the data holder's ecosystem.[231] For example, a third-party service provider that offers an analysis of the combined datasets from all the machinery used on a farm would require

229 See Neil Cohen and Christiane Wendehorst (n 119) Principle 18.

230 Christiane Wendehorst, 'Konsument:innen in der Datenökonomie' in Maria Raiffenstein and Beate Blaschek (eds), *Konsumentenpolitisches Jahrbuch* (Verlag Österreich 2023) 218; Boris Paal and Moritz Hennemann, 'Big Data as an Asset' (ABIDA – ASSESSING BIG DATA 2018) 25; Graef, Verschakelen and Valcke (n 223) 57 f.; Monopolkommission, 'Wettbewerbspolitik: Herausforderung digitale Märkte' (2015) Sondergutachten 68 109.

231 Crémer, de Montjoye and Schweitzer (n 170) 88; EDPS, 'Privacy and Competitiveness in the Age of Big Data: The Interplay between Data Protection, Competition Law and Consumer Protection in the Digital Economy' (2014) 29 <https://edps.europa.eu/sites/edp/files/publication/14-03-26_competitition_law_big_data_en.pdf.>.

access to the data of all the smart agriculture equipment. Manufacturers that have de facto control over the collected data could use their position to offer analytic services themselves and, by denying access, squeeze out third-party service providers. This would force farmers to buy all products from one manufacturer because otherwise, an analysis that combines the data of all the machines deployed on the farm would not be possible.[232]

3.3 *From data ownership to data access*

Before the European legislator started introducing data access and portability rights on a broader scale to ensure more equitable data use, there was a quite vivid debate on whether an exclusive right with regard to data ('data ownership') should be recognised.[233] One of the most widely adopted justification for granting property rights, is rooted in the utilitarian and economic theory that property rights provide an incentive to create and improve products or technologies by ensuring that creators can reap the benefits of their investments.[234] Regarding data, it was argued that recog-

232 Wolfgang Kerber, 'Rights on Data: The EU Communication "Building a European Data Economy" from an Economic Perspective' in Sebastian Lohsse, Reiner Schulze and Dirk Staudenmayer (eds), *Trading Data in the Digital Economy: Legal Concepts and Tools: Münster Colloquia on EU Law and the Digital Economy III* (Nomos; Hart Publishing 2017) 127; Josef Drexl, 'Neue Regeln für die Europäische Datenwirtschaft? (Part 1)' [2017] NZKart 339, 342.

233 Pro data ownership Zech, 'Daten als Wirtschaftsgut – Überlegungen zu einem „Recht des Datenerzeugers"' (n 63); Gerrit Hornung and Thilo Goeble, '„Data Ownership" im vernetzten Automobil' (2015) 31 Die rechtliche Analyse des wirtschaftlichenWerts von Automobildaten und ihr Beitrag zum besseren Verständnis der Informationsordnung 265; Thomas Hoeren, 'Dateneigentum. Versuch einer Anwendung von § 303a StGB im Zivilrecht' [2013] MMR 491. Contra; Determann (n 20); Josef Drexl and others, 'Position Statement of the Max Planck Institute for Innovation and Competition of 26 April 2017 on the European Commission's "Public Consultation on Building the European Data Economy"' (Max Planck Institute 2017); Bernt Hugenholtz, 'Data Property in the System of Intellectual Property Law: Welcome Guest or Misfit?' in Sebastian Lohsse, Reiner Schulze and Dirk Staudenmayer (eds), *Trading Data in the Digital Economy: Legal Concepts and Tools: Münster Colloquia on EU Law and the Digital Economy III* (Nomos; Hart Publishing 2017).

234 Determann (n 20) 9; Eric Posner and Glen Weyl, 'Property Is Only Another Name for Monopoly' (2017) 9 Journal of Legal Analysis 51, 51; Estelle Derclaye, 'Eudemonic Intellectual Property: Patents and Related Rights as Engines of Happiness, Peace, and Sustainability' (2012) 14 Vanderbilt Journal of Entertainment & Technology Law 495, 499 ff; Peter Horsley, 'Property Rights Viewed from Emerging Relational

nising exclusive rights to data could help facilitate the creation of more efficient data markets. These markets would allow for the efficient exchange and trading of data, thereby maximising its economic value. The idea is that the prospect of owning data and controlling its subsequent use could lead to enhanced data harvesting, as companies would be motivated to collect and refine data to maximise its value. Without property rights, companies might be less willing to license or share their data with others, as the lack of legal entitlement could lead to concerns about losing control over the data they possess resulting in competitive disadvantages.[235] In Germany in particular, the automotive industry lobbied for the introduction of such a right—with the manufacturers as owners, of course. Such an exclusive allocation that protects the data against use by third parties was believed to strengthen the position of manufacturers, especially vis-à-vis the tech corporations from the US that are entering the automotive sector.[236] Based on these considerations, the European Commission discussed the creation of a new data producer right with the aim of improving the tradability of non-personal data as an economic good as a possible legislative approach.[237]

However, the proposition of establishing a property-like right in data raised substantial concerns. It was argued that there is no apparent incentive problem regarding the production or analysis of data, as the digital economy has been experiencing an exponential increase in both the generation and utilisation of data—a trend that can be expected to continue. The problems of the data economy are rather rooted in power imbalances and lack of access that lead to competitive distortions and unfair distribution of benefits from data within value networks (see 3.2 and 3.1.). Introducing a new exclusive right for data is not an appropriate tool to address these issues and could even enhance imbalances.[238] Since the 'owner' would be

---

Perspectives' in David Grinlinton and Prue Taylor (eds), *Property Rights and Sustainability* (Brill, Nijhoff 2011) 89.

235 Zech, *Information als Schutzgegenstand* (n 63) 279 ff., 423; Zech, 'Daten als Wirtschaftsgut – Überlegungen zu einem „Recht des Datenerzeugers"' (n 63) 144 f.; Zech, '„Industrie 4.0" – Rechtsrahmen für eine Datenwirtschaft im digitalen Binnenmarkt' (n 63) 1160; see also Philipp Denker and others, '„Eigentumsordnung" für Mobilitätsdaten?' (Bundesministerium für Verkehr und digitale Infrastruktur 2017) 86, 109 <https://www.uni-kassel.de/fb07/index.php?eID=dumpFile&t=f&f=4043&token=5408d0e9eac3fa0fda9271f06e5d67cc84b646e8>.

236 See Hornung and Goeble (n 233) 272.

237 SWD(2017) 2 final of 10 January 2017.

238 Determann (n 20) 39; Drexl, 'On the Future EU Legal Framework for the Digital Economy: A Competition-Based Response to the "Ownership and Access" Debate'

able to transfer the ownership right or grant an exclusive licence, a party with superior bargaining power would be able to get access to the data for free or at a very low price. Conversely, if the data ownership right is conferred to the party with a powerful market position, they may use the legal exclusivity to expand their data silos and exclude others from its use or charge high prices.[239] Moreover, the difficulty of specifying what exactly would be protected under a data ownership right and who would be the rightful holders, especially when data is contributed by multiple sources, could lead to considerable legal uncertainty that might result in significant economic burdens and stifle innovation.[240]

The proposed alternative is to introduce access and portability rights that are targeted to address a specific market failure. The economic justification for prioritising access over exclusivity with data hinges on its non-rivalrous character. In contrast to ownership rights, which are negative rights to exclude others from usage, data access rights are positive rights that allow multiple parties to use the same data for different purposes. For non-rivalrous goods like data, social welfare is maximised when as many parties as possible who find value in the data are able to use it. This is in contrast to rivalrous goods, where the optimal allocation is that goods are consumed by the party who values them the most.[241] In a functioning market, companies should be able to acquire the data they need as input for developing new and innovative products and services through market transactions. However, when market barriers, such as monopolistic control, high costs, or strategic withholding of data, exist, legislative intervention

(n 20) 235; Kerber, 'A New (Intellectual) Property Right for Non-Personal Data? An Economic Analysis' (n 20) 997; Kerber, 'Governance of Data: Exclusive Property vs. Access' (n 20) 761; see also Geiregat (n 20) 9.

239 Drexl, 'On the Future EU Legal Framework for the Digital Economy: A Competition-Based Response to the "Ownership and Access" Debate' (n 20) 235.

240 Determann (n 20) 35; Drexl, 'Designing Competitive Markets for Industrial Data – Between Propertisation and Access' (n 17) 260; Kerber, 'A New (Intellectual) Property Right for Non-Personal Data? An Economic Analysis' (n 20) 997; Kerber, 'Governance of Data: Exclusive Property vs. Access' (n 20) 761.

241 OECD, 'Data-Driven Innovation' (n 14) 196; Daria Kim, 'No One's Ownership as the Status Quo and a Possible Way Forward: A Note on the Public Consultation on Building a European Data Economy' (2018) 13 Journal of Intellectual Property Law & Practice 154, 164; Heike Schweitzer and Martin Peitz, 'Datenmärkte in der digitalisierten Wirtschaft: Funktionsdefizite und Regelungsbedarf?' (Zentrum für Europäische Wirtschaftsforschung 2017) Discussion Paper 17-043 77.

might be necessary to ensure that persons who have a legitimate interest in obtaining the data can do so.[242]

Eventually, the European Commission abandoned the idea of data ownership and considered ex-ante access rights as the proper way to promote a fair distribution of data and address the issues present in the data economy.[243] Even before the Commission took this strategic decision, access and portability rights existed in the acquis, most notably in the GDPR, but also in sector specific instruments, such as the Payment Services Directive II or the Type Approval Regulation. However, since the deliberate decision to address the problems arising from the lack of access to data with access and portability rights, the European legislator has, within a relatively short period of time, introduced a number of far-reaching data rights in the Data Act and the Digital Markets Act. Access and portability rights specify ex ante who must disclose what kind of data to whom under what circumstances. In contrast to ex-post access based on competition law (see 4), they increase legal certainty for the actors of the data economy. The downside of ex ante regulation that introduces data access and portability rights, however, is that it may either under- or overregulate a certain issue. This is because the legislator has to anticipate the possible access scenarios and formulate abstract rules that are neither too broad nor too narrow to achieve the intended purpose. These challenges are also the reason why some of the existing rights to data access and portability have met criticism.

3.4 Information duties

The data portability and access rights that are the subject of this analysis need to be delineated from information duties and disclosure obligations, which can be found in abundance across the entire acquis. While the objective of information duties is to enable the rightsholder to gain knowledge of certain facts, data access and portability rights aim to facilitate the reuse of data in a different context. A typical example of an information duty is

242 Rolf Weber and Florent Thouvenin, 'Dateneigentum und Datenzugangsrechte – Bausteine der Informationsgesellschaft?' [2018] ZSR 43, 65; Drexl, 'On the Future EU Legal Framework for the Digital Economy: A Competition-Based Response to the "Ownership and Access" Debate' (n 20) 236; Drexl and others (n 233) 9; Kerber, 'A New (Intellectual) Property Right for Non-Personal Data? An Economic Analysis' (n 20) 998.

243 COM(2020) 66 final of 19 February 2020, 13.

the obligation of a trader to disclose information about the characteristics of the sold goods to the consumer.[244] Another example is Article 26 Digital Services Act (DSA),[245] which obliges the providers of online platforms that present advertisements to provide certain information regarding their ads.

3.4.1 Mere information duties

Due to the vast number and diverse range of information duties, it is challenging to establish abstract criteria for distinguishing between data portability/access rights and information duties. Generally, it can be said that information duties pertain to the semantic layer (2.2.4.2) of information, as their primary objective is to enable rightsholders to extract knowledge from the provided information. The form in which the semantic information is transmitted, i.e. the syntactic level (2.2.4.1), is irrelevant for achieving this goal. In contrast, the objective of data access and portability rights, on the other hand, is to leverage the unique features of digital data, such as non-rivalry and simultaneous use, to facilitate the reuse of data for other purposes. To achieve this goal, it is essential that the information is represented in binary code, as this enables it to be machine-readable. Only if the information is machine-readable, it can be easily processed, analysed, and shared by computers, making it efficient and cost-effective to reuse the information. Conversely, if the information were not machine-readable, it would create a significant barrier to reuse, as it would typically require significant time and resources to manually process, analyse or transfer the information

However, merely analysing whether a provision requires the transfer of information in digital format or not is not sufficient to distinguish between data access/portability rights and information duties. This is because some information duties, such as Article 7(6) Consumer Rights Directive, provide that the information must be provided on a durable medium, which includes emails, i.e. information in a digital format. The primary purpose of the said provision is to inform the consumer about the characteristics of the sold goods, yet the provision also regulates the syntactic layer, in other words, how the data is to be transferred. It is therefore necessary to identify

244 Article 6(1) Consumer Rights Directive.

245 Regulation (EU) 2022/2065 of the European Parliament and of the Council of 19 October 2022 on a Single Market for Digital Services and amending Directive 2000/31/EC (Digital Services Act).

other points of difference that can be used to determine whether a right should be classified as an access/portability right or an information duty.

Another distinguishing feature of access and portability rights is that they cover data that has a certain (economic) value for the data holder, the rightsholder and/or the recipient. Due to its value, the data holder, the rightsholder or both have an inherent interest in the generation of the relevant data. Hence, the data would exist even if access or portability rights were not in place. In contrast, the information that must be provided under information duties has no value for the addressee beyond the fulfilment of the legal requirements. Such information is not intended to be further processed for deriving economic value; its only purpose is to inform. For example, the Type Approval Regulation and the PSD II grant access to data that is an essential resource for independent repair service providers and payment service providers. Under the REACH Regulation, data which has an economic value for the manufacturers of chemical substances is accessed. On the other hand, Article 6 Consumer Rights Directive does not require traders to share the information with consumers because it is economically valuable, but to increase transparency in b2c relations.

3.4.2 Information duties facilitating data rights

In a special category of mere information are those duties that are intended to inform the data controller about the nature and scope of the data under his control. Examples of such information duties are Article 3(2) and (3) DA, Article 9(1) P2B Regulation and Article 15(1) GDPR. In principle, these rights are mere information duties, just as the ones described in the previous section. They do not directly grant a right to access data, but provide information about data. However, they are closely related to access and portability because these information duties provide a basis for more informed decisions regarding the exercise of access or portability rights. The underlying rationale is that in order to make a decision about whether and how to exercise one's right to access or transfer data, it is imperative to first understand the scope and nature of the data in question.[246] More-

246 With regard to Article 3(2) and (3) DA, see Heike Schweitzer and Axel Metzger, 'Data Access under the Draft Data Act, Competition Law and the DMA: Opening the Data Treasures for Cowmpetition and Innovation?' (2023) 72 GRUR International 337, 53; Martin Schmidt-Kessel, 'Heraus- und Weitergabe von IoT-Gerätedaten' [2024] MMR 75, 79; reagrding Article 9(1) P2B Regulation, see Rupprecht Podszun,

over, these information duties may also reveal instances of unauthorised processing. By receiving information about the data controlled by the data holder, the rights holder may discover that the data holder possesses data that should not have been collected or retained. This may prompt further actions, such as requests for data erasure or complaints to supervisory authorities.[247]

in Christoph Busch (ed), *Verordnung (EU) 2019/1150 zur Förderung von Fairness und Transparenz für gewerbliche Nutzer von Online-Vermittlungsdiensten (P2B-VO): Kommentar* (Beck 2022) Article 9 P2B Regulation, para [128]; with regard to Article 15(1) GDPR, see Alexander Dix, in Indra Spiecker gen. Döhmann, Euangelos Papakōnstantinu and Gerrit Hornung (eds), *General data protection regulation: article-by-article commentary* (Beck, Hart, Nomos 2023) Article 15 GDPR, para [1]; Eugen Ehmann, in Eugen Ehmann and Martin Selmayr (eds), *DS-GVO: Datenschutz-Grundverordnung: Kommentar* (2nd edn, Beck 2018) Article 15 GDPR, para [1].

247 See Alexander Dix, in Spiros Simitis, Gerrit Hornung and Indra Spiecker (eds), *Datenschutzrecht: DSGVO mit BDSG* (Nomos 2019) Article 15 GDPR, para [1]; Ehmann (n 246) Article 15 GDPR, para [1].

4 The Essential Facility Doctrine (Article 102 TFEU)

As has been pointed out above, the aggregation of large datasets in the hands of a single market player can lead to competitive imbalances (see 3). Hence, Article 102 TFEU, which prohibits the abuse of a dominant position, seems like an obvious legal instrument to invoke in situations where large data holders deny access to their data. Indeed, the essential facility doctrine (EFD), which has been developed on the basis of Article 102 TFEU, is discussed as a possible solution for cases of denied access to data. According to the EFD, the refusal of a dominant player to grant access to a resource that is essential to a downstream market without objective justification constitutes abusive conduct within the meaning of Article 102 TFEU. However, the unique features of data give rise to legal questions on how to apply the EFD to cases of denied access.

This Chapter first describes some general concepts of competition law, such as the relevant market, market dominance and abuse, that are also relevant in EFD constellations. Then, the requirements of the 'exceptional circumstances' that need to be present in order to successfully rely on the EFD are outlined. The main focus of the Chapter is to analyse and discuss the challenges of applying the exceptional circumstances test, which has been developed for traditional non-rivalrous resources, to data. In the last section, the main findings are briefly summarised.

4.1 Abuse of a dominant position

At EU level, Article 102 TFEU prohibits 'any abuse by one or more undertakings of a dominant position within the internal market or in a substantial part of it [...] as incompatible with the internal market in so far as it may affect trade between Member States.' The core rationale is that an undertaking's dominant position lessens the positive effects of competition on the relevant market and therefore certain behaviour that would further impair genuine undistorted competition on the internal market needs to be restricted.[248]

248 *Cf.* ECJ, C-322/81, Michelin, ECLI:EU:C:1983:313, para 53.

The application of EU competition law requires that the agreements or practices on the part of undertakings may affect trade between Member States. This 'effect on interstate trade criterion' has been interpreted rather broadly. According to the ECJ and EGC, it is met if it is possible to foresee with a sufficient degree of probability that the concerted practice may have an influence, direct or indirect, actual or potential, on the pattern of trade between Member States, capable of hindering the attainment of the objectives of a single market between States.[249] This broad understanding means that any abuse rendering access to the national market more difficult is to be considered an appreciable effect on interstate trade.[250] For example, even if abusive practices by an undertaking holding a dominant position in one Member State are limited to that country, they may be capable of affecting trade on the internal market: by repeatedly engaging in exclusionary practices towards direct competitors, competitors from other EU countries may be discouraged to enter the market.[251]

4.1.1 Relation between Article 102 TFEU and national competition law

In the national laws of the Member States, prohibitions comparable to Article 102 TFEU can be found.[252] If abusive behaviour affects both domestic trade and trade between member states, the applicability requirements of EU and national competition law may be fulfilled. The CJEU repeatedly held that one case can be subject to proceedings under EU and national competition law.[253] On the basis of the authorisation provided for in Article 103(2)(e) TFEU, the European legislator enacted Regulation 1/2003[254] which clarifies the relationship between national competition law and Article 101 *et seq* TFEU. Article 3 of this Regulation lays down a priority rule obliging the national authorities and courts to apply EU law in paral-

249 See EGC, Case T-62/98, *Volkswagen v. Commission*, EU:T:2000:180 and the cases cited there.

250 European Commission, Guidelines on the effect on trade concept contained in Articles 81 and 82 of the Treaty, OJ C 2004/101, 81, para 96.

251 European Commission, Guidelines on the effect on trade concept contained in Articles 81 and 82 of the Treaty, OJ C 2004/101, 81, para 94.

252 See, e.g. § 5 (Austrian) KartG and § 19 (German) GWB.

253 ECJ, C-617/17, *PZU Zycie*, EU:C:2019:283, para 25.

254 Council Regulation (EC) No 1/2003 of 16 December 2002 on the implementation of the rules on competition laid down in Articles 81 and 82 of the Treaty, OJ L 2003/1, 1.

lel alongside their own national law if the abusive behaviour may affect interstate trade.[255] According to Article 3(2) Regulation 1/2003, agreements or concerted practices that are not prohibited under EU law may not be prohibited by national competition law. This convergence rule, however, does not apply to unilateral practices. Hence, Member States may prohibit unilateral behaviour capable of affecting trade between Member States even if it occurs below the level of dominance or is not considered abusive under Article 102 TFEU.[256]

Due to the priority rule and the fact that competitive distortions by large holders that operate in several MS will regularly have the potential to affect interstate trade, research in this Chapter will primarily focus on Article 102 TFEU.

4.1.2 Market dominance

The application of Article 102 requires an assessment of the undertaking's market power. According to the case law of the ECJ, an undertaking has a dominant position in the relevant market if it is able to prevent effective competition from being maintained because it can behave to an appreciable extent independently of its competitors, its customers and ultimately of consumers.[257] The concept of dominance has a structural element (the undertaking has to be in a position of strength), a behavioural element (the undertaking's ability to take decision independently of competition) and an element linking these two elements, namely the possibility to prevent

255 Manfred Rehbinder, in Torsten Körber, Heike Schweitzer and Daniel Zimmer (eds), *Immenga/Mestmäcker Wettbewerbsrecht* (6th edn, Beck 2019) VO 1/2003 Artikel 3, para 12; see also Laurence Idot, 'The Future of Regulation No. 1/2003: New Relations Between EU and National Laws' (2020) 11 Journal of European Competition Law & Practice 409 criticising the parallel application of EU law and national law.

256 Communication from the Commission to the European Parliament and Council – Report on the
functioning of Regulation 1/2003, COM(2009) 206, 6; Commission Staff Working Paper
accompanying the Report on the functioning of Regulation 1/2003, SEC(2009) 574, 49 ff.

257 ECJ, C-27/76, United Brands, ECLI:EU:C:1978:22, para 65; ECJ, C-457/10, *AstraZeneca*, EU:C: 2012:770, para 175.

effective competition.[258] Market dominance as such is not prohibited under competition law. However, once an undertaking reaches this threshold, it bears a special responsibility,[259] and certain conduct that would normally be part of competition on the merits is considered abusive because of the undertaking's capability to impair genuine, undistorted competition.[260]

It has been repeatedly held that a combination of various factors which, taken separately are not necessarily decisive, constitute a dominant market position and therefore a case-by-case analysis is required.[261] However, possessing a very high market share over an extended period of time on the relevant market is always a strong indication for a dominant position. In general, a market share of 50 % is the threshold above which the CJEU presumes a dominant position, unless the company can show that competition is not affected due to exceptional circumstances.[262]

Other factors that are of overriding importance for assessing the competitive structure of the market are: (i) the position of the undertaking's competitors and their market power (ii) the barriers for new companies to enter the market or for existing competitors to expand and (iii) constraints imposed by the bargaining strength of the undertaking's customers (countervailing buyer power). This list is not exhaustive; depending on the type of market and its conditions, new factors may be added, and the relative weight between the factors may change.[263]

---

258 Martin Herz and Hans Vedder, in Hermann-Josef Blanke and Stelio Mangiameli (eds), *Treaty on the Functioning of the European Union – A Commentary* (Springer 2021) Article 102 TFEU, para 10.

259 ECJ, C-322/81, *Michelin*, ECLI:EU:C:1983:313, para 57.

260 Heike Schweitzer and Ernst-Joachim Mestmäcker, *Europäisches Wettbewerbsrecht* (3rd edn, Beck 2014) § 16 para 44.

261 ECJ, C-457/10, *AstraZeneca*, EU:C: 2012:770, para 176

262 ECJ, C-85/76, *Hoffmann-La Roche*, ECLI:EU:C:1979:36, para 41; ECJ, C-62/86, *AKZO v Commission*, ECLI:EU:C:1991:286, para 60; ECJ, C-457/10, *AstraZeneca*, EU:C: 2012:770, Rn. 176.

263 Communication from the Commission, Guidance on the Commission's enforcement priorities in
applying Article 82 of the EC Treaty to abusive exclusionary conduct by dominant undertakings, OJ C 2009/45, 8.

4.1.2.1 Collective dominance

According to Article 102, a dominant position may also be held jointly by two or more undertakings together.[264] The phrase 'one or *more* undertakings' does not refer to different legal entities that belong to the same corporate group and enjoy no economic independence, as those are treated as a single entity,[265] but is understood more broadly. A collective dominant position can be held by legally and economically independent firms if they are able together, 'in particular because of factors giving rise to a connection between them, to adopt a common policy on the market and to act to a considerable extent independently of their competitors, customers and, ultimately, consumers.'[266] Factors that may constitute a connection that amounts to a collective entity may be agreements but also other economic ties that bind the concerned undertakings, such as vertical and horizontal integration.[267] Once it has been established that the undertakings act as a collective entity it is assessed whether they together hold a dominant position in the relevant market (see 4.1.2).[268]

While collective dominance presupposes that, from an economic point of view, the undertakings present themselves or act together on a particular market as a collective entity,[269] they do not need to behave in the same way in every respect in the market. In other words, the existence of collective dominance is inferred from the position held jointly by the undertakings in question, but the abuse does not necessarily have to be committed by all the undertakings involved.[270] Of course, holding a collective dominant position is in itself not a violation of Article 102.[271] Hence, the undertakings that

264 European Commission, Guidance on the Commission's enforcement priorities in applying Article 82 of the EC Treaty to abusive exclusionary conduct by dominant undertakings, OJ C 2009/45, 4.

265 See ECJ, C-22/71, *Béguelin Import*, EU:C:1971:113 para 8.

266 ECJ, Joined Cases C-68/94 and C-30/95 *France and Others v Commission*, EU:C:1998:148, para 221; EGC, Case T-228/97, *Irish Sugar v Commission*, EU:T:1999:246, para 46.

267 Peter Lewisch, in Thomas Jaeger and Karl Stöger (eds), *EUV/AEUV* Art 102 TFEU, para 84.

268 ECJ, Joined cases C-395/96 P and C-396/9, *Compagnie Maritime Belge Transports*, EU:C:2000:132, para 37 and 38.

269 ECJ, Joined cases C-395/96 P and C-396/9, *Compagnie Maritime Belge Transports*, EU:C:2000:132, para 36.

270 EGC, T-228/97, *Irish Sugar v Commission*, EU:T:1999:246, para 66.

271 ECJ, Joined cases C-395/96 P and C-396/9, *Compagnie Maritime Belge Transports*, EU:C:2000:132, para 37

are part of the collective entity but did not engage in the abusive conduct would not face any legal consequences based on Article 102 TFEU.[272]

4.1.3 The relevant market

The definition of the relevant market establishes the framework within which competition law, including Article 102 TFEU, is applied. Hence, before any of the factors outlined above can be assessed, it is necessary to define the relevant market.[273] A more narrowly defined market increases the probability of finding that an undertaking has a dominant position, while a broader definition has the opposite effect.[274]

The basic idea is that all companies, which are capable of exerting effective competitive pressure on an undertaking, are part of the same relevant market. The concept of 'relevant market' has both a product and a geographical dimension. Competitive restraints exist if a group of products or a geographic area are substitutable. Hence, the relevant market comprises all products or geographic areas that are to some extent substitutable. It can be distinguished between substitutability on the demand and on the supply side.[275]

4.1.3.1 Demand substitution

Demand substitutability means that consumers are able to respond to a worsening of a company's sales conditions. If the prices increase, can consumers switch to available substitute products or to suppliers in other countries? The assessment of demand substitutability is ultimately a question of which range of products consumers consider to be substitutes. The methodology used by the Commission for this analysis is the so-called SSNIP[276] (small but significant and non-transitory increase in price) test.[277]

---

272 Lewisch (n 267) Art 102 TFEU, para 90.

273 ECJ, C- 6/72, *Continental Can v. Commission*, ECLI:EU:C:1973:22, para 32.

274 Martin Herz and Hans Vedder (n 258) Article 102 TFEU, para 11.

275 Commission Notice on the definition of relevant market for the purposes of Community competition law, OJ C 1997/372, 5, paras 2 ff.

276 Also referred to as 'hypothetical monopolist test' or '5 % test'.

277 Commission Notice on the definition of relevant market for the purposes of Community competition law, OJ C 1997/372, 5, paras 15 ff.

The test examines how consumers would react if a hypothetical monopolist would permanently increase its prices by 5 % to 10 % for the product under investigation, assuming that the price of all other goods remains constant. If the undertaking's customers would switch to readily available substitutes or to suppliers located elsewhere to an extent that the price increase is unprofitable because of the resulting loss of sales, the substitute products and areas are considered to be part of the relevant market. If a hypothetical monopolist would not be able to profitably raise the price, the product or geographical dimension is expanded, and the test is applied again, until a range of products is identified for which a price increase would not induce a sufficient substitution in demand. The crux of the matter is whether the higher profit per unit is sufficient to compensate for the lost sales volume.[278]

For example, if a (hypothetical) monopolist in the energy drink sector in Austria were not able to profitably raise the prices, because consumers would switch to other caffeinated sodas, such as cola, mate or green tea drinks, these sodas would be part of the relevant market. In a second step, the test is extended to other potential substitutes on the same geographical market. Would consumers switch to coffee if the price of all caffeinated sodas is increased by 5 %? If not, coffee would not be part of the relevant market because the hypothetical monopolist is able to raise prices without losing profits.

4.1.3.2 Supply substitution

When defining the relevant market, supply substitutability needs to be taken into account only if it has a similar disciplinary effect on the competitive behaviour in terms of effectiveness and immediacy as demand substitutability. This is the case when an undertaking from a different market can react to increases in price by switching its production to the relevant products and market these products within a short time without incurring significant costs or risks.[279] For example, even if consumers of brown bread would not switch to other bread in case a hypothetical monopolist would increase

278 On how to calculate whether a price increase is profitable see Simon Bishop and Markus Baldauf, 'Theoretische Grundlagen und praktische Anwendung wettbewerbsökonomischer Methoden in Bezug auf die Abgrenzung des relevanten Marktes' (RBB Economics 2006) 36 ff.

279 Commission Notice on the definition of relevant market for the purposes of Community competition law, OJ C 1997/372, 5, paras 20 ff.

the price, other bakeries would be prepared to adjust their production to brown bread with negligible costs and in a short timeframe. Thus, different kinds of bread would not constitute separate markets for competition law purposes.

4.1.4 Abuse

Having a dominant position in a market is not in itself an abusive conduct. However, once the dominance threshold is passed, undertakings have a special responsibility not to further reduce the already weakened competition and therefore certain business practices are no longer allowed.[280]

Article 102 demonstratively lists four types of behaviour that are considered abusive if conducted by a dominant undertaking:

> '(a) directly or indirectly imposing unfair purchase or selling prices or other unfair trading conditions;
> (b) limiting production, markets or technical development to the prejudice of consumers;
> (c) applying dissimilar conditions to equivalent transactions with other trading parties, thereby placing them at a competitive disadvantage;
> (d) making the conclusion of contracts subject to acceptance by the other parties of supplementary obligations which, by their nature or according to commercial usage, have no connection with the subject of such contracts.'

The forms of abuse listed in Article 102 are not exhaustive. The CJEU defined abuse as behaviour of a dominant undertaking that 'is such as to influence the structure of a market where, as a result of the very presence of the undertaking in question, the degree of competition is weakened and which, through recourse to methods different from those which condition normal competition in products and services on the basis of the transactions of commercial operators, has the effect of hindering the maintenance of the degree of competition still existing in the market or growth of that competition'[281]

Typically, it is distinguished between exclusionary abuses, which intend to exclude competitors from the market or prevent them from entering

280 ECJ, C-322/81, *Michelin*, ECLI:EU:C:1983:313, para 57.
281 ECJ, C-85/76, Hoffmann-La Roche, EU:C:1979:36, para 91.

it, and exploitative abuses, where the dominant company exploits its economic power (e.g. by charging excessive or discriminatory prices). Both kinds of abuse may not only be carried out through unilateral conduct but also through agreements, in which case they are also subject to Article 101 TFEU.[282]

4.2 The history of the Essential Facility Doctrine

In a string of cases, the CJEU has held that a dominant market player's refusal to grant access to a resource that is essential for a downstream market without objective justification may constitute an exclusionary abuse that is prohibited under Article 102 TFEU. The denial of access has a market leveraging effect and allows the dominant undertaking to expand its position into related but economically self-contained markets (secondary or downstream markets) to gain an unjustified competitive advantage in that market.[283]

While the CJEU deals with these cases under the labels 'refusal to deal' or 'refusal to supply', the more figurative term 'essential facility doctrine' is often used in scholarly discussions. As the name suggests, the essential facility doctrine (EFD) was originally developed for cases of denied access to physical facilities and can be traced back to the 1912 US Supreme Court decision *Terminal Railroad*. In this case, the US Supreme Court ordered an association of railroad companies, which had acquired all existing railroad bridges that led over the Mississippi River and into Saint Louis, to provide competitors access to the bridges under reasonable conditions.[284]

More than half a century later, the CJEU handed down its first 'refusal to deal' decision. The case concerned the conduct of the chemical group *Commercial Solvents,*[285] which supplied the pharma company Zoja with the raw material aminobutanol that is used for the production of anti-tuberculosis drugs. After a subsidiary of Commercial Solvents started to produce its own aminobutanol-based drugs, Commercial Solvents stopped supplying the

282 European Commission, Guidelines on the effect on trade concept contained in Articles 81 and 82 of the Treaty, OJ C 2004/101, 81, para 73.

283 See Matthias Lamping, 'Refusal to License as an Abuse of Market Dominance - From Commercial Solvents to Microsoft' in Reto Hilty and Kung-Chung Liu (eds), *Compulsory Licensing* (2015) 132.

284 *United States v. Terminal Railroad Association of St. Louis, 224 U.S.* 383 (1912), 409–411.

285 ECJ, Joined Cases C-6/73 and 7/73, *Commercial Solvents Corporation*, EU:C:1974:18.

raw material to its long-term customer Zoja. Due to Commercial Solvents' dominant position on the market for aminobutanol, Zoja was not able to obtain a different source of supply. The CJEU upheld the Commission's decision that Commercial Solvents is abusing its dominant position on the market for aminobutanol to eliminate competition on the downstream market.

Although the essential facilities doctrine has its origins in US competition law, it is still a controversial legal concept in the US, to say the least. Lower US courts[286] and scholars[287] have inferred the existence of the EFD from a series of Supreme Court decisions,[288] but the highest US court has never explicitly relied on the EFD, and thus it is still unclear whether the doctrine can be considered established law.[289]

The CJEU, on the other hand, has taken a more progressive approach and continuously expanded the scope of the EFD.[290] It has been clarified that the 'resource' to which access is denied needs to be understood broadly and does not only cover physical facilities, such as ports[291] and raw

286 See e.g., Alaska Airlines, Inc. v. United Airlines, Inc., 948 F.2d 536, 544 & n.11 (9th Cir. 1991); Twin
Labs., Inc. v. Weider Health & Fitness, 900 F.2d 566, 570 (2d Cir. 1990); MCI Communications Corp. v. AT&T Co., 708 F.2d 1081 (7th Cir. 1983).

287 See e.g., Emma Hagemann, 'Essential Facilities, Essential Patents, and the Essential Oversight of Qualcomm' [2021] SSRN Electronic Journal <https://papers.ssrn.com/sol3/papers.cfm?abstract_id=3893771>; Thomas Cotter, 'The Essential Facilities Doctrine' [2008] SSRN Electronic Journal <https://ssrn.com/abstract=1125368> accessed 9 March 2022; Robert Pitofsky, Donna Patterson and Jonathan Hooks, 'The Essential Facilities Doctrine under United States Antitrust Law' (2002) 70 Antitrust LJ 443; Abbott Lipsky and Gregory Sidak, 'Essential Facilities' (1998) 51 Stan L Rev 1187.

288 *United States v. Terminal Railroad Association of St. Louis*, 224 U.S. 383 (1912); *Associated Press v. United States*, 326 U.S. 1 (1945); *Otter Tail Power Co. v. United States*, 410 U.S. 366 (1973); *Aspen Skiing Co. v. Aspen Highlands Skiing Corp.*, 472 U.S. 585 (1985).

289 In *Verizon Communications Inc. v. Law Offices of Curtis V. Trinko, LLP*, 540 U.S. 398 (2004) the US Supreme Court did not impose access based on competition law because the applicable Telecommunications Act extensive contained specific provision for access. The Supreme Court, however, states that this 'conclusion would be unchanged **even if** we considered to be established law the "essential facilities" doctrine **crafted by some lower courts** [emphasis added]' and that there is 'no need either to recognize [the essential facilities doctrine] or to repudiate it here'.

290 For a detailed description of the development of the EFD in the US and the EU see Inge Graef, *EU Competition Law, Data Protection and Online Platforms: Data as Essential Facility* (Kluwer 2016) 155 ff.

291 Commission Decision 94/119/EG, *Port of Rødby*, OJ L 1994/55, 52.

materials,[292] but also the supply of services,[293] and even IP-rights.[294] In *Magill*, TV stations refused to grant a copyright license of their TV listings to a publisher that sought to offer comprehensive programme guides to consumers.[295] The *Microsoft* case concerned interoperability information, which was indispensable for producing programs that are compatible with Windows.[296] The CJEU's apparent openness to applying the EFD to intangible resources is the reason why the EFD is extensively discussed as a possible solution to address cases of denied access to data.

4.2.1 The exceptional circumstances test

Since the objective of Article 102 TFEU—and competition law in general—is not to protect the interests of a specific competitor but to prevent distortion of competition and safeguard the interests of consumers in general, the mere fact that a dominant undertaking uses an essential facility for its own competitive advantage does not justify legal intervention. Imposing a duty to deal will certainly lead to short-term benefits for the consumers, as competition for substitute products or services and price will increase in the downstream market. However, in the long run, such an obligation can also harm the interests of consumers, as it may decrease the willingness of dominant companies to invest in innovation. Moreover, competitors do not have an incentive to develop a competing facility if they can free ride on the investments made by the dominant market player.[297] The application of the EFD presupposes the refusal to deal by a dominant market player controlling an essential asset puts competition as an institution—either on a downstream or adjacent market—at risk. Applying the EFD not only requires balancing the prospective social and procompetitive benefits against the negative effects of reducing the incentives to innovate, but also a careful balancing of the public interest in free competition against the dominant

292 ECJ, Joined Cases C-6/73 and 7/73, *Commercial Solvents Corporation*, EU:C:1974:18.

293 ECJ, Case 311/84, *Télémarketing*, EU:C:1985:394.

294 ECJ, C-418/01, *IMS Health*, ECLI:EU:C:2004:25.

295 ECJ, Joined Cases C-241/91 P and C-242/91 P, *RTE and ITP (Magill)*, EU:C:1995:98.

296 EGC, T-201/04, *Microsoft v Commission*, EU:T:2007:289.

297 AG Jacobs, C-7/97, *Bronner*, EU:C:1998:264, paras 56–58; European Commission, Guidance on the Commission's enforcement priorities in applying Article 82 of the EC Treaty to abusive exclusionary conduct by dominant undertakings, OJ C 2009/45, 7, para 75; Graef, *EU Competition Law, Data Protection and Online Platforms: Data as Essential Facility* (n 290) 180.

undertaking's individual interests of private autonomy, right to property and the freedom to conduct business.[298]

The CJEU has repeatedly held that limiting access to an essential resource by interrupting an existing commercial relationship or refusing to enter into a new one constitutes an abuse of a dominant position only under 'exceptional circumstances'. From its case law, it can be inferred that the CJEU considers four criteria to determine when such exceptional circumstances are present: (1) access to the facility needs to be indispensable (2) refusal would eliminate all effective competition (3) refused access hinders the introduction of a new product (4) there is no objective justification for the refusal.[299] Moreover, since the EFD prohibits the leveraging of market power from the primary market, in which the holder of the essential facility is dominant, to a downstream or adjacent market, it is necessary to define two relevant markets.[300]

4.2.1.1 Defining two relevant markets

The first step when applying the EFD is to define the primary (or upstream) market in order to assess whether the holder of the essential facility has a dominant position in that market. In a second step, the market for the product or service that the company would offer if it had access to the essential facility is defined. Without defining the relevant secondary (or downstream) market, it would not be possible to assess whether the refusal would eliminate all effective competition on that market and impede the development of a new product.[301]

On the one hand, the primary market and the secondary market need to be independent from each other because otherwise, the conduct of the essential facility holder would not constitute an illegitimate expansion of market power. On the other hand, the refusal to supply only leads to com-

298 Schmidt (n 175) 256.

299 See ECJ, C-418/01, *IMS Health*, EU:C:2004:25, para 37; ECJ, C-7/97, *Bronner*, EU:C:1998:569, para 40; Joined Cases C-241/91 P and C-242/91 P, *RTE and ITP (Magill)*, EU:C:1995:98, paras 53–56.

300 EGC, T-201/04 Microsoft v Commission EU:T:2007:289, para 335; Graef, *EU Competition Law, Data Protection and Online Platforms: Data as Essential Facility* (n 290) 210 ff; Liyang Hou, 'The Essential Facilities Doctrine: What Was Wrong in Microsoft?' (2012) 43 International Review of Intellectual Property and Competition Law 451, 453.

301 Hou (n 300) 453.

petitive distortions on the secondary market if both markets are related to some extent.[302] In the *Commercial Solvents* case, there was a(n) (upstream) market for the raw material aminobutanol on which Commercial Solvents had a dominant position and a separate yet related market for anti-tuberculosis drugs based on aminobutanol.[303]

To establish the two relevant markets, the general approach of assessing demand and supply substitutability (see 4.1.3) is employed. However, another peculiarity of the EFD is that, according to the CJEU, it is sufficient that there is a hypothetical market for the primary product. This means the EFD can be applied even if the essential facility has never been supplied to a third party and thus no actual market for the product does exist.[304] In these constellations, the traditional methods used to define the relevant market are difficult to apply. Competition authorities and courts can only rely on assumptions of how the hypothetical market would function and not on actual market evidence.[305]

The concept of hypothetical or potential primary markets was established in the CJEU's *Magill* decision. In *Magill*, television broadcasters offered their programme listings free of charge to certain newspapers but did not market them independently. Although technically no market for programme listing existed before Magill, the publisher of a TV guide, requested a copyright license, the CJEU held that the TV stations have a dominant position on the market for TV programme information.[306] This approach was taken one step further in the decision *IMS Health*. IMS

302 Lamping (n 283) 134.

303 ECJ, Joined Cases C-6/73 and 7/73, *Commercial Solvents Corporation*, EU:C:1974:18, paras 21, 22.

304 See Commission Notice on the definition of relevant market for the purposes of Community competition law, OJ C 1997/372, 5, para 79.

305 Graef, *EU Competition Law, Data Protection and Online Platforms: Data as Essential Facility* (n 290) 214; Hou (n 300) 453.

306 Joined Cases C-241/91 P and C-242/91 P, *RTE and ITP (Magill)*, EU:C:1995:98, para 37; see also Opinion of AG Tizzano, C-418/01, *IMS Health*, EU:C:2003:537, paras 55–57 referring to the decisions *Magill* and *Bronner*. The case ECJ, C-7/97, *Bronner*, EU:C:1998:569 concerned two Austrian newspaper publishers: Mediaprint and Oscar Bronner. Mediaprint developed and operated the only nationwide home-delivery scheme for newspapers and refused to include the newspaper published by Oscar Bronner. The fact that the home delivery service was not marketed separately did not a priori exclude the possibility of identifying a separate market and the ECJ ordered the national court to assess whether the homedelivery schemes constituted a separate market that can be distinguished from the market for daily newspapers themselves.

provided data on regional sales of pharmaceutical products in Germany to pharmaceutical laboratories. The information was formatted according to a copyrighted brick structure that represented geographical areas in Germany and had become the industry standard. IMS' refusal to license the brick structure, prevented the competitor NDC to effectively compete in the market for providing data on regional sales of pharmaceutical products (in more detail under 4.2.1.4).[307] IMS has used the brick structure when supplying data to clients but has never independently marketed it. The ECJ held that a hypothetical market can be identified if two different production stages exist, which are interconnected because the input from the primary market is indispensable for the output on the secondary market.[308] The other condition is that 'there is an actual demand for [products or services] on the part of undertakings which seek to carry on the business for which they are indispensable.'[309]

While *Magill* concerned a quite traditional essential facility constellation, the application of the hypothetical market concept in *IMS Health* resulted in a significant expansion of the EFD. In *Magill*, no market for programme listings existed at the time, but the fact that TV stations provided some of the information to daily newspapers made it clear that the tv stations were in principle willing and capable of marketing their listings as a separate product.[310] Another similarity with other EFD cases is that Magill was not a direct competitor of the TV stations and did not intend to compete with the TV stations on the market for programme listings or on the market for broadcasting. In *IMS Health*, the brick structure has only been used for internal purposes to provide regionally structured pharmaceutical data and has never been supplied to a third party. Furthermore, NDC and IMS were direct competitors on the market for providing regional pharmaceutical data. By defining a hypothetical market, NDC would be able to use the building block structure to compete with the dominant undertaking in the only market that actually exists.[311]

The concept of a hypothetical primary market has led to criticism in legal and economic literature. It has been argued that without the need to

307 ECJ, C-418/01, *IMS Health*, EU:C:2004:25, paras 3–7.

308 ECJ, C-418/01, *IMS Health*, EU:C:2004:25, para 45.

309 ECJ, C-418/01, *IMS Health*, EU:C:2004:25, para 44.

310 Graef, *EU Competition Law, Data Protection and Online Platforms: Data as Essential Facility* (n 290) 211.

311 Graef, *EU Competition Law, Data Protection and Online Platforms: Data as Essential Facility* (n 290) 213.

define an existing market, the EFD becomes too broad, and its application would create a significant disincentive to invest in innovation and new production processes.[312] Furthermore, it has been pointed out that if the distinction between primary market and secondary market is as artificial as in *IMS Health*, the conduct of the dominant undertaking can hardly be qualified as leveraging market power to another market. The conduct of the dominant undertaking would therefore no longer be a traditional EFD constellation but rather 'a selective refusal to contract which reserves to the owner of the essential facility the market opportunities created thereby.'[313] However, without the possibility to apply the EFD also to hypothetical primary markets, dominant market players could evade the application of competition law by not marketing products or services separately that are an essential input for downstream competitors.[314]

Clearly, the ECJ was aware of the fact that the concept of a hypothetical primary market significantly expands the EFD and moves it away from its traditional field of application. After all, in *Magill* and *IMS Health*, the ECJ not only defined a hypothetical market but also established the 'new product' criterion. Only if the refusal to supply impedes the development of a new product for which there is clear and unsatisfied consumer demand, the conduct of the dominant undertaking constitutes an abuse (see 4.2.1.4).[315] The 'new product' rule prevents the undertaking seeking access from simply coping the product or service of the dominant undertaking. However, the concept of hypothetical markets may still lead to direct horizontal competition, as it is not necessary that the new product constitutes a self-contained market that is different from the market where the requested undertaking is active.

312 Damien Geradin, 'Limiting the Scope of Article 82 EC: What Can the EU Learn from the U.S. Supreme Court's Judgment in Trinko in the Wake of Microsoft, IMS, and Deutsche Telekom' (2004) 41 Common Market Law Review 1519, 1530.

313 See Lamping (n 283) 137.

314 Graef, *EU Competition Law, Data Protection and Online Platforms: Data as Essential Facility* (n 290) 212.

315 See Joined Cases C-241/91 P and C-242/91 P, *RTE and ITP (Magill)*, EU:C:1995:98, para 54; ECJ, C-418/01, *IMS Health*, EU:C:2004:25, para 37.

4.2.1.2 Indispensability

The indispensability criterion concerns the relationship between the primary market and the secondary market and consists of two elements. First, it needs to be established whether the primary product or service is an objectively necessary input for the secondary product. The objective need for access to a particular input can usually be established based on general knowledge of the sector concerned.[316] For example, the *Ladbroke* case concerned a Belgian bookmaker that requested a license to televise French horse races in its betting outlets. While live broadcasting of horse races would have certainly enhanced the experience for Ladbroke's customers, the EGC held that the broadcasting rights are not indispensable for providing gambling services. The EGC argued that since the transfer takes place only after the bets have been placed, its absence cannot affect the bettors' decision-making and prevent a bookmaker from conducting its business. This conclusion was supported by the fact that the applicant was already present on the Belgian betting market and had a significant share in the market for betting on French horse races.[317]

Once it is established that the primary product is an objectively necessary input, the second step is to assess whether there are no actual or potential substitutes for the input that competitors in the downstream market could resort to in order to compensate for the negative consequences of the refusal.[318] The indispensability requirement is not met if it is legally and technically possible as well as economically viable for a substitute facility to be created in the foreseeable future;[319] whether competitors will in fact make the investment is, however, not decisive.[320] In *Bronner*, the ECJ clarified that the question of whether it is possible to create a substitute facility is not assessed on the basis of the applicant's capabilities but with regard to a hypothetical undertaking comparable in size to the requested

316 Graef, *EU Competition Law, Data Protection and Online Platforms: Data as Essential Facility* (n 290) 216; Hou (n 300) 458; Christian Evans Ahlborn, 'The Logic & Limits of the Exceptional Circumstances Test in Magill and IMS Health European Union' (2004) 28 Fordham Int Law J 1109, 1122.

317 EGC, T-504/93, *Ladbroke v Commission*, EU:T:1997:84, para 132.

318 Joined Cases C-241/91 P and C-242/91 P, *RTE and ITP (Magill)*, EU:C:1995:98, para 52 and 53; ECJ, C-7/97, *Bronner*, EU:C:1998:569, paras 44 and 45; Commission Notice on the definition of relevant market for the purposes of Community competition law, OJ C 1997/372, 5, para 83.

319 See ECJ, C-7/97, *Bronner*, EU:C:1998:569, paras 44 and 45.

320 Ahlborn (n 316) 1123.

undertaking.[321] Only if no effective substitutes exist, an undertaking's survival on the secondary market—at least in the long run—depends on the access to the primary product and legal intervention is justified.[322]

It has been rightly pointed out that the second element of the indispensability criterion has similarities to the primary market definition, as both concepts revolve around the question of substitutability of the requested product. It has been argued that the difference is the degree of substitutability that is required, which is higher in the context of the indispensability assessment than for the market definition.[323] The decisive difference, however, seems to be a matter of perspective and not of degree. When defining the market, substitutability is assessed from the consumer perspective, whereas the indispensability criterion asks whether a substitute exists from the competitor's perspective. Taking the facts of the *Bronner* case as an example: a national court may come to the conclusion that consumers would not switch from a home delivery scheme to other distribution channels (e.g. sale in shops and at kiosks or delivery by post) if the price of the scheme would be significantly increased over a longer period time. Hence, home delivery systems for newspapers would constitute a separate relevant market. However, at the same time, the court could find that distributing daily newspapers by post and through sale in shops and at kiosks are substitutes that allow competitors to compete with the requested undertaking in the newspaper market efficiently.

4.2.1.3 Excluding competition in the secondary market

The second criterion of the exceptional circumstances test is that the refusal to supply is liable to eliminate competition in the secondary market. There is a close connection to the indispensability criterion, as the elimination of competition on the secondary market follows from the indispensability of the essential facility for the economic activity of the requesting undertaking. In *Magill*, the ECJ held that the TV broadcaster's reserved to themselves the secondary market of weekly television guides by excluding all competition in that market since they denied access to the basic information, which is the raw material indispensable for the compilation of

321 ECJ, C-7/97, *Bronner*, EU:C:1998:569, para 46.

322 See Hou (n 300) 460.

323 Graef, *EU Competition Law, Data Protection and Online Platforms: Data as Essential Facility* (n 290) 219.

such a guide.[324] Although the ECJ listed indispensability and eliminating all competition as two distinct conditions in the decisions *Bronner* and *IMS Health*,[325] some scholars have argued that the elimination of competition is an inevitable consequence of the indispensability requirement and thus not a separate criterion.[326]

While it is true that both criteria are dependent on each other and need to be assessed jointly,[327] they should be treated as separate requirements.[328] The exclusion of the competition criterion determines the degree to which the indispensability of the essential resource needs to affect competition in order to meet the exceptional circumstances test. This becomes apparent when comparing the different thresholds applied by the ECJ and the EGC. In *Magill*, *Bronner* and *IMS Health*, the ECJ held that the refusal needs to be capable of eliminating *all* competition on the secondary market.[329] In *Microsoft*, the EGC followed the Commission's approach[330] and only required that the requested undertaking's conduct is liable, *or likely* to eliminate all *effective* competition. Accordingly, the requirement can be met even if competitors of the dominant undertaking with marginal market positions still exist on the downstream market.[331] The EGC also argued that due to the preventive purpose of Article 102 TFEU, intervention is justified even before competition is completely eliminated. Otherwise, the Commission would have to wait until competitors have been eliminated from the market or their elimination is imminent before acting based on

324 Joined Cases C-241/91 P and C-242/91 P, *RTE and ITP (Magill)*, EU:C:1995:98, para 56.

325 ECJ, C-7/97, *Bronner*, EU:C:1998:569, para 41; ECJ, C-418/01, *IMS Health*, EU:C:2004:25, para 52.

326 Hou (n 300) 460; Net Le, 'What Does "Capable of Eliminating All Competition" Mean?' (2005) 26 European Competition Law Review 6, 7.

327 Katharina Apel, *Die kartellrechtliche Zwangslizenz im Lichte des europäischen Wettbewerbsrechts* (Nomos 2015) 373; Rüdiger Wilhelmi, 'Lizenzverweigerung als Missbrauch einer marktbeherrschenden Stellung in der Gemeinschaftsrechtsprechung' [2009] WPR 1431, 1438.

328 See Commission Notice on the definition of relevant market for the purposes of Community competition law, OJ C 1997/372, 5, para 85; Graef, *EU Competition Law, Data Protection and Online Platforms: Data as Essential Facility* (n 290) 222.

329 Joined Cases C-241/91 P and C-242/91 P, *RTE and ITP (Magill)*, EU:C:1995:98, para 56; ECJ, C-7/97, *Bronner*, EU:C:1998:569, para 41; ECJ, C-418/01, *IMS Health*, EU:C:2004:25, para 52.

330 Commission Notice on the definition of relevant market for the purposes of Community competition law, OJ C 1997/372, 5, para 85.

331 EGC, T-201/04 *Microsoft v Commission* EU:T:2007:289, para 563.

Article 102 TFEU.[332] Irrespective of whether ECJ will follow the EGC and Commission in future cases, the arguments of the EGC demonstrate that the elimination of competition criterion provides additional nuances to the exceptional circumstances test and should therefore be considered a separate requirement.

Another element of the 'eliminating effective competition' criterion is that it is interpreted by Commentators as requiring that the essential facility holder is already active on the downstream market and aims to reserve that market to itself. Hence, the requirement would not be met if the requesting undertaking intends to enter a downstream market on which the essential facilities holder is not (yet) active.[333] It is argued that the essential facilities holder would not have any incentives to refuse access if it is not active on the downstream market, because it does not have to protect its position on that market and could create an additional source of revenue by charging third parties for the access.[334] However, as argued under 4.3.4, a different interpretation is at least conceivable.

4.2.1.4 New product rule

The new product rule is not part of the general exceptional circumstances test, but is only applied if the essential facility is an IP right.[335] It was originally developed in *Magill* and was further refined in *IMS Health.* According to the ECJ, the refusal to license can be regarded as abusive only if it prevents the emergence of a new product for which there is potential consumer demand. The requesting undertaking may not simply duplicate the goods or services already offered on the secondary market by the owner of the intellectual property right.[336]

The new product rule not only has a narrower scope of application than the indispensability and the exclusion of competition criteria but also serves a different purpose. While the latter two requirements are intended

332 EGC, T-201/04 *Microsoft v Commission* EU:T:2007:289, para 561.

333 Giuseppe Colangelo and Mariateresa Maggiolino, 'Big Data as Misleading Facilities' (2017) 13 European Competition Journal 249, 269; Josef Drexl, 'Neue Regeln für die Europäische Datenwirtschaft? (Part 2)' [2017] NZKart 415, 419; Graef, *EU Competition Law, Data Protection and Online Platforms: Data as Essential Facility* (n 290) 220.

334 See Schmidt (n 175) 385.

335 See EGC, T-201/04 *Microsoft v Commission* EU:T:2007:289, para 334

336 C-418/01, *IMS Health*, EU:C:2004:25, para 49.

to determine the leverage effects of the requested undertaking's conduct, the new product rule's purpose is to resolve the tension between competition and intellectual property law. By granting a temporary, exclusive right to the creator of an intangible asset, IP law, like competition law, is intended to promote innovation and competition. The fact that nobody else can use the intellectual property and the prospect of a considerable financial return are incentives to invest in innovation that is valued by consumers. IP law prevents competitors from simply duplicating the protected products and competing on price, thereby creating an incentive to invest in innovation to create a potentially even more competitive product, which benefits consumers in a more long-lasting way than competition on price. Therefore, it is said that IP law forestalls static competition by duplication (price competition) but facilitates dynamic competition by substitution, i.e. competition in innovation.[337] The objective of strengthening competition is also what distinguishes intellectual property from property in tangible assets, which of course is characterised by a right to exclude others as well.[338] Since both competition and IP law facilitate innovation, there is an inherent tension when curtailing IP rights based on the EFD. The underlying notion of the new product rule is that an IP right is not (no longer) contributing to competition in innovation if it prevents the emergence of a new product for which there is potential consumer demand.[339]

Among legal and economic scholars, the new product rule has led to much disagreement. Some agree with the CJEU and consider it to be the central element that delimitates competition and intellectual property law and ensures that competition by substitution is not forsaken for competi-

337 Graef, *EU Competition Law, Data Protection and Online Platforms: Data as Essential Facility* (n 290) 194; Apel (n 327) 379; Josef Drexl, 'Abuse of Dominance in Licensing and Refusal to License: A "More Economic Approach" to Competition by Imitation and the Competition by Substitution' in Claus-Dieter Ehlermann and Isabela Atanasiu (eds), *European Competition Law Annual 2005: The Interaction Between Competition Law and Intellectual Property Law* (Hart Publishing 2007) 648; Josef Drexl, 'Intellectual Property and Antitrust Law IMS Health and Trinko – Antitrust Placebo for Consumers Instead of Sound Economics in Refusal-to-Deal Cases' (2004) 35 International Review of Intellectual Property and Competition Law 788, 792.

338 Wilhelmi (n 327) 1440.

339 Graef, *EU Competition Law, Data Protection and Online Platforms: Data as Essential Facility* (n 290) 197.

tion by imitation.[340] Others have criticised the new product on various different grounds.[341]

It has been argued that the CJEU's reasoning is flawed for two reasons. The first issue is that in some instances, the scope of protection afforded by IP rights is too broad and consequently not only limits competition by imitation but also by substitution. This was the case in *Magill*, where it was argued that the listings of TV programs are not worthy of copyright protection in the first place because it amounts to a control of ideas that automatically impeded competition on the market for TV guides. As this issue is rooted in a failure of the IP systems, solutions should be sought at that level rather than in competition law.[342]

The second argument is that the new product rule is not suitable to delineate situations in which IP protection promotes dynamic competition from those in which it does not. While the reasoning of the CJEU seems convincing at first glance, the new product requirement will restore competition only in situations where the IP system itself fails because the scope of protection is so broad as to also exclude competition by substitution (i.e. *Magill*-Constellation). However, the new product rule is not the adequate criterion in situations where IP protection is appropriate in scope and would, in principle, be suited to facilitate competition by substitution, but due to certain external market failures, this objective is not reached. An example of this constellation is *IMS Health*. IMS used the 1860-brick structure to provide pharmaceutical companies with data on the sales of drugs based on regions in Germany, which became the de facto industry standard. The pharmaceutical companies had contributed to the development of the brick structure, and due to switching costs and network effects, they were not willing to use a different structure. The applicant in the *IMS Health* case had tried to provide pharmaceutical data based on a new 2201-brick

340 Ahlborn (n 316) 1139; Wilhelmi (n 327) 1445; Apel (n 327) 397.

341 E.g. François Lévêque, 'Innovation, Leveraging and Essential Facilities: Interoperability Licensing in the Microsoft Case' (2005) 28 World Competition 71, 75 ff; Damien Geradin (n 312) 1531; Kung-Chung Liu, 'Rationalising the Regime of Compulsory Patent Licensing by the Essential Facilities Doctrine' (2008) 39 International Review of Intellectual Property and Competition Law 757, 773.

342 Drexl, 'Abuse of Dominance in Licensing and Refusal to License: A "More Economic Approach" to Competition by Imitation and the Competition by Substitution' (n 337) 651 ff; Drexl, 'Intellectual Property and Antitrust Law IMS Health and Trinko – Antitrust Placebo for Consumers Instead of Sound Economics in Refusal-to-Deal Cases' (n 337) 805 ff; see also Graef, *EU Competition Law, Data Protection and Online Platforms: Data as Essential Facility* (n 290) 194 ff.

structure (competition by substitution), but due to the lock-in effects, there was no demand. Therefore, competitors on the market for providing pharmaceutical data would need to use IMS Health's brick structure, but could not do so because of copyright protection. Due to the market conditions, IMS Health would be overcompensated for its investment in developing the brick structure. In these constellations, IP law fails to promote competition by substitution due to external market conditions. Therefore, it would be justified to restore competition by affording a compulsory license against a reasonable royalty and allowing imitation.[343]

This line of reasoning goes one step further by arguing that the distinction between competition by substitution and competition by imitation should be used in order to determine whether the new product requirement is met. Refusals to license should not be treated differently than refusals to deal involving tangible assets. Instead, it should be assessed whether external market failures exist. In case no external market failures are present, the requesting undertaking is required to indicate a specific product it would like to introduce that is not merely a duplication in order to hold a refusal to deal abusive under Article 102 TFEU. However, should the characteristics of the market at issue be of such nature that competition by substitution is not possible, the requesting undertaking should be allowed to compete by imitation and introduce a product similar to that of the essential facility holder.[344]

Apart from the fundamental question of whether the new product rule is an appropriate criterion for IP rights cases, there has been a debate on how much novelty is required for a product to be 'new'. Much of the discussion revolved around the question whether a product is new only if it is not in competition with the goods or services of the right holder. Or, in other words, whether the new product must constitute a different relevant market than the one in which the rightsholder operates.[345] This was suggested by AG Gulman in his *Magill* Opinion, where he stated

343 Drexl, 'Abuse of Dominance in Licensing and Refusal to License: A "More Economic Approach" to Competition by Imitation and the Competition by Substitution' (n 337) 651 ff; Drexl, 'Intellectual Property and Antitrust Law IMS Health and Trinko – Antitrust Placebo for Consumers Instead of Sound Economics in Refusal-to-Deal Cases' (n 337) 805 ff; see also Graef, *EU Competition Law, Data Protection and Online Platforms: Data as Essential Facility* (n 290) 224 ff.

344 Graef, *EU Competition Law, Data Protection and Online Platforms: Data as Essential Facility* (n 290) 225 ff.

345 The view that the new product may not compete with the products of the essential facility holder is of course irreconcilable with the view that the 'eliminating all

that 'there is an abuse of a dominant position if a copyright owner by means of his copyright prevents the emergence of a product *which does not compete* with his product [emphasis not added].'[346] Contrary to the ECJ,[347] AG Gulman concluded that the new product requirement was not met because the comprehensive weekly television guide would compete with the weekly guides of the individual broadcasters and meet the same consumer needs.[348]

In *IMS Health*, AG Tizzano expressed the opinion that the new product requirement is met if the applicant 'does not wish to limit itself essentially to duplicating the goods or services already offered on the secondary market by the owner of the intellectual property right but intends to produce goods or services of a different nature which, *although in competition with those of the owner of the right*, answer specific consumer requirements not satisfied by existing goods or service [emphasis added].'[349] The ECJ followed the AG's Opinion but did not explicitly address whether the new product may be in competition with those of the owner of the IP right.[350] However, regarding consumer demand, the ECJ has been more lenient than AG Tizanno. According to the Court, there does not need to be specific consumer demand, as required by the AG, but potential consumer demand for the new product is sufficient.[351]

Commentators have argued that requiring the new product not to compete with products or services of the rightsholder may even run counter to the criterion's objective to promote innovation in the secondary market. If the new product is different to an extent that it constitutes a separate relevant market, competition on the secondary market would not benefit from the compulsory license.[352] The new product rule only wants to restrict

competition' criterion requires that the essential facility holder is already active on the downstream market (4.2.1.3). This is discussed in more detail under 4.3.4.

346 Opnion of AG Gulman, Joined Cases C-241/91 P and C-242/91 P, RTE and ITP (Magill), EU:C:1994:210, para 96.

347 ECJ, Joined Cases C-241/91 P and C-242/91 P, RTE and ITP (Magill), EU:C:1995:98 para 56.

348 Opnion of AG Gulman, Joined Cases C-241/91 P and C-242/91 P, RTE and ITP (Magill), EU:C:1994:210, para 98.

349 Opinion of AG Tizzano, C-418/01, IMS Health, EU:C:2003:537, para 61.

350 ECJ, C-418/01, *IMS Health*, EU:C:2004:25, para 49.

351 ECJ, C-418/01, *IMS Health*, EU:C:2004:25, para 49.

352 Graef, *EU Competition Law, Data Protection and Online Platforms: Data as Essential Facility* (n 290) 201; Ekaterina Rousseva, *Rethinking Exclusionary Abuses in EU Competition Law* (Hart 2010) 124.

competition by imitation but promote the development of similar products, which provide additional benefits for consumers.[353] Hence, it can be argued that the benchmark for the degree of novelty is rather low.

In its *Microsoft* decision, the EGC deviated from the ECJ's new product requirement and held that it is sufficient if the refusal limits technical developments.[354] The EGC argued that 'the appearance of a new product cannot be the only parameter which determines whether a refusal to license an intellectual property right is capable of causing prejudice to consumers'[355] within the meaning of Article 102(b) TFEU. The essential difference between the *Microsoft* and the *IMS Health* requirement is the standard of proof. The ECJ's new product rule requires that the applicant proves that the product is not a mere duplication, and consequently, the applicant needs to specify the novelty of the product they will offer once access is obtained. Under the *Microsoft* requirement, the standard of proof is significantly lower, as the applicant only needs to show that they are capable of bringing technical developments to the market without specifying the novelty of the product or proving that there is potential consumer demand for it.[356]

4.2.1.5 No objective justification

The final requirement of the exceptional circumstances test is that the refusal cannot be justified by objective considerations.[357] Once the competition authority has demonstrated that the (two) three requirements are met, it is for the dominant undertaking to prove that the justification prevails over the exceptional circumstances.[358] A possible justification is the objection that the duty to supply would eliminate the dominant undertaking's incentives to continue to invest in innovation in the future or lead to structural changes in the market that would negatively affect the develop-

353 Wilhelmi (n 327) 1444; Apel (n 327) 384.
354 EGC, T-201/04 Microsoft v Commission EU:T:2007:289, para 647.
355 EGC, T-201/04 Microsoft v Commission EU:T:2007:289, para 647.
356 Rousseva (n 352) 123.
357 ECJ, C-418/01, *IMS Health*, EU:C:2004:25, para 37; ECJ, C-7/97, *Bronner*, EU:C:1998:569, para 40; Joined Cases C-241/91 P and C-242/91 P, *RTE and ITP (Magill)*, EU:C:1995:98, paras 53–56.
358 EGC, T-201/04, *Microsoft v Commission*, EU:T:2007:289, para 688.

ment of follow-on innovation by competitors.[359] However, vague, general and theoretical arguments that a duty to supply would have a significant negative impact on the dominant undertaking's incentives to innovate are not sufficient.[360] Another objective justification may be capacity constraints in supply, for example when dominant undertaking would no longer be able to satisfy its own need on the secondary market to an extent that it endangers its own business operation.[361] In a similar vein, the ECJ clarified that the dominant undertaking may refuse to supply if the access request is out of the ordinary in terms of quantity to an extent that it needs to be considered improper commercial behaviour.[362]

4.2.2 Flexibility of the exceptional circumstances test

The exceptional circumstances test can certainly be seen as an attempt to objectify the balance of interests at stake, as the ECJ, the EGC and the Commission have repeatedly resorted to the four requirements when evaluating an undertaking's refusal to deal. However, it should be kept in mind that the primary objective of the ECJ and the EGC is it to react to the particularities of an individual case and not to lay down abstract rules. This explains the divergences in applying the requirements of the exceptional circumstances test. Moreover, it means that the four criteria are not exhaustive. This has also been made clear by the Commission in its *Microsoft* decision. The Commission stated that 'there is no persuasiveness to an approach that would advocate the existence of an exhaustive checklist of exceptional circumstances and would have the Commission disregard *a limine* other circumstances of exceptional character that may deserve to be taken into account when assessing a refusal to supply.'[363] In the follow-up decision, the EGC applied the established exceptional circumstances test

359 See Commission Notice on the definition of relevant market for the purposes of Community competition law, OJ C 1997/372, 5, para 89.

360 EGC, T-201/04, *Microsoft v Commission*, EU:T:2007:289, para 696–698.

361 ECJ, Joined Cases C-6/73 and 7/73, *Commercial Solvents Corporation*, EU:C:1974:18, para 26 and 27.

362 ECJ, C-27/76, *United Brands*, EU:C:1978:22, para 187; ECJ, Joined Cases C-468/06 to C-478/06, *GlaxoSmithKline*, EU:C:2008:504, para 70, 76; Graef, *EU Competition Law, Data Protection and Online Platforms: Data as Essential Facility* (n 290) 230.

363 Commission Decision C-3/37.792, *Microsoft*, OJ L 2007/32, 23, para 555.

but argued that it would assess additional circumstances invoked by the Commission if one or more requirements were absent.[364]

4.3 The denial of data access

At least at first glance, the EFD seems to be a very fitting instrument for cases of denied access to data (see 3). On the one hand, the exclusive control over large and diverse datasets may allow undertakings to distort competition in adjacent or downstream markets. On the other hand, the generation and storage of data also require investments from the data holder. Like in traditional EFD constellations, these interests need to be balanced against each other. Since the CJEU, in its previous case law, has adopted a very broad understanding of essential facilities, which also includes information protected by IP rights, it can be argued that the EFD could be applied to both single-source data and big data.

So far, however, there have been no cases where a dominant company was ordered to share their data on the basis of Article 102 TFEU. A closer look reveals that applying the requirements of the 'exceptional circumstances' test for compulsory licensing, which were developed in the abovementioned cases, to situations of denied access to data raises various issues. Not only are there several legal uncertainties, but in each case, difficult factual and economic questions need to be addressed. For an undertaking seeking access, this means that data access is only a potential remedy at the end of a lengthy procedure, the outcome of which is difficult to predict.

4.3.1 Defining the relevant data market

The first step in examining whether the refusal to provide access to data constitutes an abuse under the EFD is to delineate the two relevant markets (4.2.1.1). The application of the EFD requires that the data holder has a dominant position in the primary market and that the refusal to provide access eliminates competition in the secondary market.[365] Similar to the IP rights cases, the crux of the matter is the definition of the primary market.

---

364 EGC, T-201/04 *Microsoft v Commission* EU:T:2007:289, para 336.

365 Regarding the data dependent secondary market, see 4.3.3.1.

Based on the insights gained from the CJEU's IP rights decisions, it can be argued that because data has an economic value and has become a tradable commodity, a separate data market needs to be defined.[366] In *Magill*, the relevant primary market for the application of the EFD was not the broadcasting market in which the essential facility holders conducted their main business, but a separate market for (copyright protected) TV listing information, even though this information was not independently marketed.[367] The same approach can be used for data markets. Since the data market is different from the market where the requested data was generated, the core business of the data holder is not relevant for defining the relevant data market. For example, insurance companies, automobile associations and manufacturers of connected vehicles may all generate data on the risk profiles of drivers. Such data can constitute a market within its own right, irrespective of its origin, given that the datasets from the different actors are substitutable. Since the economic value of data is a result of its semantic content and the size of the dataset, it is irrelevant which product, service or activity led to the creation of the data. Therefore, in cases where the accumulation of large datasets is a consequence of operating a platform, the difficult questions regarding the definition of two-sided markets[368] do not need to be addressed in this context.[369] EFD constellations concern competition *for* data, i.e. for input necessary for data-based business models, and not competition *with* data.[370]

366 See Pamela Jones Harbour and Tara Isa Koslov, 'Section 2 In A Web 2.0 World: An Expanded Vision of Relevant Product Markets' (2010) 76 Antitrust Law Journal 769, 773 who have first proposed defining a separate data market and argued that 'this approach to market definition would be consistent with marketplace reality: Internet-based firms often derive great value from user data, far beyond the initial purposes for which the data initially might have been shared or collected, and this value often has important competitive consequence'; see also Schmidt (n 175) 400.

367 Joined Cases C-241/91 P and C-242/91 P, *RTE and ITP (Magill)*, EU:C:1995:98, para 47.

368 On this issue see, inter alia, Lapo Filistrucchi and others, 'Market Definition in Two-Sided Markets: Theory and Practice' (2014) 10 Journal of Competition Law & Economics 293; Ralf Dewenter, Jürgen Rösch and Anna Terschüren, 'Abgrenzung zweiseitiger Märkte am Beispiel von Internetsuchmaschinen' [2014] NZKart 367.

369 See also Schmidt (n 175) 400.

370 Paal and Hennemann (n 230) 44; see also Grothe (n 222) 102.

4.3.1.1 Data as tradable commodity on the market

Defining the relevant data market is rather straightforward if the requested data is traded as a commodity either directly by the data holders or by data brokers.[371] When datasets are sold to customers, competition authorities and courts could assess to what degree customers would substitute certain data in response to a hypothetical small but permanent price increase (demand substitutability, see 4.1.3.1).[372] However, the existence of an actual data market also renders it unlikely that the requested data is exclusively held by one undertaking and the requesting undertaking is unable to actually or potentially create or access any substitutes.[373]

4.3.1.2 Hypothetical data markets

The EFD is more likely to be invoked in scenarios where the requested data is used exclusively for internal purposes, and the data holder does not engage in any data exchanges or transactions. This constellation is similar to the *IMS Health* case, where the copyright-protected brick structure was used only when supplying data to clients but had never been marketed independently. Even though the requested data is only used internally by the data holder, a hypothetical or potential data market can be identified if the conditions set out by the ECJ in *IMS Health* are met: (i) an actual demand for the data exists, (ii) the input from the primary market is indispensable for the output on the secondary market and (iii) two different production stages can be identified, (see 4.2.1.1).[374] Since the indispensability of the input is already considered when defining the hypothetical market, the distinction between market definition and the exceptional circumstances test, which also assess the indispensability, gets blurred.[375] The fact that the existence of a hypothetical data market depends on whether the data is indispensable for the services or products that the requesting undertaking

371 See Grothe (n 222) 103; Darren Tucker and Hill B Wellford, 'Big Mistakes Regarding Big Data' [2014] The Antitrust Source 1, 8.

372 Charlotte Breuvart, Étienne Chassaing and Anne-Sophie Perraut, 'Big Data and Competition Law in the Digital Sector: Lessons from the European Commission's Merger Control Practice and Recent National Initiatives' [2016] Concurrences 41, 43.

373 Schmidt (n 175) 397.

374 ECJ, C-418/01, *IMS Health*, EU:C:2004:25, para 44 and 45.

375 See the critical remarks of Hou (n 300) 453.

wants to offer also means that it cannot be defined in the abstract, but only based on the circumstances of each individual case.[376]

The SSNIP test cannot be used to assess the substitutability of data on the demand side if the requested data is not traded on an existing market, as there is no initial price that can be increased. In case no quantitative test, which estimates the elasticities and cross-price elasticities for the demand of a product, can be applied, demand substitutability must be established according to qualitative criteria. Whether the requested data has only a limited degree of interchangeability with other data and therefore constitutes a separate market depends on the extent to which the requested data has particular characteristics that render it an essential input for the requesting undertaking to operate on the secondary market.[377]

When determining the qualitative properties of the requested data, the primary aspect is the semantic level, i.e. the informational content of the data.[378] For example, data on the online behaviour of consumers is qualitatively different to data on the performance of an IoT product. However, establishing the substitutability of the requested data requires a different approach depending on whether the access is requested to specific pieces of data (single source data) or to large compilations of data ('big data').

4.3.1.2.1 Hypothetical single source data market

If an undertaking seeks access to semantic information that, by its nature, can only be generated and is exclusively held by the requested undertaking (single source data), it will usually be the semantic content that renders it an objectively necessary input (see also 4.3.3.2). This constellation is comparable to the *Magill* case: due to the specificity of the semantic information and the fact that the data is held by one undertaking, there are no substitutes available. Hence, such data would constitute a separate market even if it is not copyright protected.[379] The semantic information, however, is not the only factor. From the perspective of the requesting undertaking,

376 Schmidt (n 175) 403.

377 See ECJ, C-7/97, *Bronner*, EU:C:1998:569 para 33 with further reference to case law; see also Opinion AG Jacobs, C-7/97, *Bronner*, EU:C:1998:264 para 30 and Opinion of AG Tizzano, C-418/01, *IMS Health*, EU:C:2003:537, para 59.

378 Ralf Dewenter and Hendrik Lüth, 'Datenhandel und Platformen' (ABIDA – ASSESSING BIG DATA 2018) 12.

379 Schmidt (n 175) 406.

the timeliness and form of supply may also play a role in determining whether the data can be substituted. For example, an independent payment service provider needs real-time access to the relevant transaction data once the account holder initiates a transaction. The same semantic information is of no use to the payment service provider if it is supplied only with a significant delay, as the payers would be unable to complete the transfer.[380]

4.3.1.2.2 Hypothetical big data market

In case the subject of the access request is 'big data', the size, diversity, and representativeness of the dataset need to be taken into consideration. These factors generally increase the quality and reliability of larger data collections.[381] While the semantic level is also relevant for big data, the focus is not on the semantic information of the individual pieces of data per se, but on the conclusions that can be drawn from the dataset as a whole. It is important to keep in mind that, under certain circumstances, different semantic information may allow for the same conclusions to be drawn. For example, movement patterns of the population can be established based on telecommunication data held by a telecom operator, but also based on the data collected by the provider of navigational apps.[382]

On the other hand, the mere fact that two datasets contain similar semantic information does not necessarily make them interchangeable if one of the datasets is significantly larger and contains more granular and diverse information. An example is the difference between online and offline data. While traditional companies, such as retailers, telecom operators, banks and insurance companies, collect data about consumer behaviour in the respective sector, such datasets may not be comparable in terms of their scope and specificity to datasets collected by large internet platforms. An offline retailer and an e-commerce platform both collect data on their customers' purchasing behaviour. The dataset of the e-commerce platform, however, will also include data on the search history of its customers, the time customers looked at a product, or items that ended up in the shopping

380 This scenario is covered by the PSD II Directive, see 9.1

381 Drexl, 'Designing Competitive Markets for Industrial Data – Between Propertisation and Access' (n 17) 281.

382 Dewenter and Lüth (n 378) 12.

cart but were never purchased.[383] In big data scenarios, the characteristics of the dataset as a whole need to be taken into consideration.

4.3.2 Dominance in the data market

The EFD only applies if the data holder has a dominant position in the previously defined data market. In traditional competition law cases, a high market share is usually a strong indicator of an undertaking's dominant position (see 4.1.2). Since data is a non-rivalrous good that has no intrinsic value, the question arises how to establish the existence of a dominant position in a data market. The analysis depends on whether a 'real' market or only a hypothetical market for data can be identified.

In case a 'real' data market exists because the data holder engages in data transactions and grants third parties access to its data against remuneration, it is possible to calculate market shares. However, since it is difficult to abstractly quantify the value of different data, it has been argued that neither the quantity nor quality of data controlled are suitable indicators of market power. It has therefore been suggested to assess an undertaking's ability to monetise the controlled data and compare the data-related turnover to that of other data-trading companies on the market. The revenue serves as an indicator of how successful an undertaking is in the respective data market. By calculating the market shares based on the share of the total profit of the companies active in the relevant data market not only the value of the dataset itself is taken into account, but also the success of the company in monetising the data.[384]

In hypothetical markets, the market share cannot be the decisive factor. Since the actual demand for the data and the indispensability of the input for the secondary market are taken into consideration already at the level of market definition, the hypothetical data market is defined with regard to the specific access request (see 4.3.1.2). Hence, data holders will always exclusively control the requested data on a hypothetical market and conse-

383 Inge Graef, 'Market Definition and Market Power in Data: The Case of Online Platforms' (2015) 38 World Competition 473, 497 argues that a comparison can be drawn to the distinction between offline and online advertising made by the Commission in its *US Google/DoubleClick* merger decision (Case No COMP/M.4731).

384 Graef, *EU Competition Law, Data Protection and Online Platforms: Data as Essential Facility* (n 290) 266; but see Schmidt (n 175) who points out that it may be difficult in pratice to include only data of the relevant market in such an analysis.

quently have a market share of 100 %. Despite the absence of any real competition in hypothetical data markets, competitive constraints may still exist due to potential competition.[385] An undertaking is put under competitive pressure, if it is likely that other undertakings either hold similar data or are able to generate the requested data.[386] Additional constraints may be imposed by the bargaining strength of the requesting undertaking. If the requesting data undertaking has a high market share either on the market in which the requested data was generated or on the secondary market, the undertaking dominant on the hypothetical data market would not be able to act to an appreciable extent independently of competitive pressure. Such strength may not only result from the requesting undertaking's size but also from its commercial significance for the data holder.[387] By taking the bargaining power of the requesting undertaking into account, it can be ensured that the EFD does not enable data flows from innovative newcomers to already big data companies and their data silos.

It is important to note that the concept of 'data-power' (*Datenmacht*), which has received much attention from commentators, is irrelevant for determining an undertaking's dominance in the data market. The concept of 'data-power' is used to describe the fact that control over large datasets can generate market power that allows the data holder to act independently from other market participants.[388] For example, Austrian and German competition law explicitly recognise the concept of data-power and provide that an undertaking's access to data is to be taken into account when assessing market dominance, in addition to other criteria such as financial strength and relationship to other companies in the market.[389] This means

385 Communication from the Commission, Guidance on the Commission's enforcement priorities in
applying Article 82 of the EC Treaty to abusive exclusionary conduct by dominant undertakings, OJ C 2009/45, 8.

386 Graef, *EU Competition Law, Data Protection and Online Platforms: Data as Essential Facility* (n 290) 266.

387 *Cf* the concept of 'countervailing buyer power' used by the Commission, see Communication from the Commission, Guidance on the Commission's enforcement priorities in applying Article 82 of the EC Treaty to abusive exclusionary conduct by dominant undertakings, OJ C 2009/45, 8.

388 See e.g. Simon Deuring, *Datenmacht: Zugang als Herausforderung* (Nomos 2021); Grothe (n 222); Andreas Heinemann, 'Big Data im Kartellrecht' in Markus Notter and others (eds), *Europäische Idee und Integration – mittendrin und nicht dabei? liber amicorum für Andreas Kellerhals* (Schulthess 2018) 311.

389 See § 4(1) KartG (Austrian Federal Cartel Act) and § 18(2) GWB (German Competition Act).

that when determining whether a platform provider holds a dominant position in a certain market, the platform provider's control over data is one criterion that needs to be taken into account. However, it has rightly been pointed out that the concept of data power is relevant only if the data is used to compete in a market that is different from the (hypothetical) data market (i.e. competition *with* data) and not if the competition is *for* the data. Control over the relevant data is a prerequisite for being a competitor in the data market in the first place.[390]

4.3.3 Indispensability of the data input

The denial of access to data is abusive only if it is established that the requested data is indispensable for competition on the secondary market. As outlined above (4.2.1.2), the indispensability is assessed in two steps. First, it needs to be established whether the data is an objectively necessary input. If the objective necessity is affirmed, the second step is to examine whether there are no actual or potential substitutes for the data input. Substitutes exist if the data can be acquired from other sources or if there are no technical, legal or economic barriers that prevent the requesting undertaking from generating the data itself.

Typically, it is rather straightforward to delineate the facility to which access was sought and assess whether this facility is in fact indispensable in traditional EFD-cases. However, due to data's non-rivalrous nature and context-dependency, this exercise is more difficult in data-related access cases. The requesting undertaking will usually be interested in receiving semantic information in some kind of machine-readable format. The same semantic information may be represented in different syntactic code and can therefore be held by multiple actors at the same time. Furthermore, if the inferences that can be derived from the semantic information are the essential input for competition in the downstream market, it needs to be taken into account that different semantic information may allow for the same conclusions to be drawn.

In order to be able to determine the indispensability of the data input, a distinction must be made as to whether single source data or big data is requested. On the second stage of the indispensability test, additional considerations need to be taken into account if the requested data is personal data (see 4.3.3.4).

390 Schmidt (n 175) 216.

4.3.3.1 Data-dependent secondary market

Already from the outset, the indispensability requirement cannot be met if no data-dependent secondary market exists. This may be the case if the secondary product or service can also be provided without the additional functions that require data as input. If a market analysis indicates that products or services that depend on data are part of the same secondary market as those that do not offer additional data-dependent services, then access to that data cannot be considered essential for competition in that market.[391] For example, the SSNIP test may show that users of smart fridges, which require access to inventory data from online grocery stores to automatically reorder their preferred items, would be willing to switch to traditional fridges if the prices of smart fridges were to rise. In such a scenario, the grocery shops' inventory data would not be essential to compete in the refrigerator market.

The EFD can only be applied if a separate, data-dependent secondary market exists. The Commission has confirmed the existence of such a data-dependent data market with regard to the advertising market in its *Google/DoubleClick* merger decision. Instead of defining a market that encompasses the provision of advertising space in all types of media, the Commission held that offline and online advertising are two separate markets. The decisive difference is that in the online advertising market, advertisers can precisely target their audience by combining data regarding geographical location, time of day, areas of interest, previous purchasing record of the user and search preferences.[392] Market investigations may even reveal that it needs to be distinguished further between various forms of online advertising (e.g. between search ads, which target the user based precisely on their revealed interests, and non-search ads, which target consumers based on more general criteria such as the context of the website and the geolocation). The findings of the Commission in this regard were inconclusive, however.[393]

The advertising market is an example of how the scope of the relevant market influences the assessment of whether and which data is a necessary input to compete efficiently. The narrower the data-dependent secondary

391 Schmidt (n 175) 432 ff.

392 Commission Decision M.4731, *Google/ DoubleClick,* C(2008) 927 final, para 45.

393 See Commission Decision M.4731, *Google/ DoubleClick,* C(2008) 927 final, para 48 ff.

market is defined, the more likely it is that certain data constitutes an indispensable input.

4.3.3.2 Indispensability of single source data

Assessing whether data is an objectively necessary input for providing a certain product or service is the least challenging if the requested data is non-personal, single-source data. Such data is created, for example, when the requested undertaking offers a specific service or product that generates data unique to that product or service. As already pointed out above (see 4.3.1.2.1), data that is generated and exclusively held by the requested undertaking may constitute a separate hypothetical market. Usually, the characteristics and quality of single source data can be clearly described and delineated. It can be the semantic content that renders it an objectively necessary input. This constellation is again comparable to the *Magill* case, except that the requested data is not copyright protected. However, if the requested input is real-time data generated by a product, service or activity, it is the timeliness that renders the data exclusive. Thus, where access to the historical data is not sufficient, real-time data qualifies as single source data at the relevant time. Examples can be found in the IoT market, where compatible products or services depend on access to such real-time data. In case the subject of the access request is single source data, it should not be very difficult for competition authorities or courts to assess whether the requested data is an objectively necessary input for providing a particular service or product on the data-dependent secondary market.[394]

Once it is established that single source data is an objectively necessary input for the product in question, the requesting undertaking has to demonstrate that it is unable to duplicate the input data or create substitute data. The ECJ clarified that the benchmark is not the capabilities of the requesting undertaking but that of a hypothetical competitor that has similar means as the essential facilities holder.[395]

Since non-personal single source data is per definition data, which is generated and held exclusively by the requested undertaking, the only option for the requesting undertaking would be to enter the market where

394 See Schmidt (n 175) 440; Sebastian Louven, 'Braucht es mehr materielles Kartellrecht für digitale Plattformen?' (2019) 17 ZWeR 154, 171.

395 ECJ, C-7/97, *Bronner*, EU:C:1998:569, para 46.

the data was generated, i.e. the upstream market of the data market. By creating its own data-collecting product or service, the requesting undertaking would be able to generate data similar to the requested data and allow competition in the secondary market. Such a parallel market entry of the requesting market would facilitate competition both in the market upstream of the data market and in the secondary market. However, competitors of the requested undertaking cannot be expected to enter the market if it would be economically ruinous either due to market conditions or the necessary investment costs.[396] Arguably, this would be the case if the investment costs to enter the upstream market are disproportionate to potential revenues that could be generated by the product or service. Where the data is the mere by-product of an economic activity, this would also indicate that a market entry cannot be reasonably expected from the requesting undertaking. In other constellations, entering the upstream market is already from the outset an unviable option. In *Magill*, for example, entering the TV broadcasting market would not have enabled Magill to produce a comprehensive weekly TV Guide that lists the programmes of *all* TV stations.

4.3.3.3 Indispensability of big data

The application of the indispensability test proves to be more difficult when access to big data is requested. If the requested data is not single-source, the semantic information of the data can also be obtained by other means. For example, traffic data collected by a navigation app provider is based on publicly available information and can be reproduced by anyone putting in the effort.[397] The same applies to actively provided personal data. Giving a company access to personal data like address, email or phone number does not prevent natural persons from providing the same data to others. Undertakings that require access to such data could either become active on the data market as well and collect the data themselves or buy it from data holders.

Moreover, the asserted indispensability may not necessarily be rooted in the concrete semantic content of the big data, but rather in the inferences that can be drawn from it. In these cases, the requested data is substitutable

396 See Rubinfeld and Gal (n 227) 357.
397 See Schmidt (n 175) 455.

by other big data that allows for the same conclusions to be drawn. Due to the context dependency of data, the substitutability can only be assessed in light of the service or product the requesting undertaking intends to offer and therefore requires a case-by-case analysis.[398] For example, a search engine platform provides targeted and individualised ads that match the consumers' preferences based on the search data of its users. However, such individual ads may also be provided by analysing the transaction and search data of e-commerce platforms.[399] Hence, search engine data and data collected by an e-commerce platform are—from the perspective of an undertaking seeking to enter the market of individualised advertising—substitutable, even though their semantic content is different.

Although the semantic information of the single data points is not unique, an undertaking may still argue that the whole dataset is an indispensable input that cannot be duplicated or substituted due to its size and diversity.[400] The requesting undertaking would have to demonstrate that technical, legal or economic barriers prevent the requesting undertaking from replicating a dataset that matches the size and quality of requested big data. This has to be done taking into account the high threshold established in the *Bronner* decision. According to the ECJ, it is not sufficient to argue that it would not be possible for the requesting undertaking to gather a similar dataset due to its limited financial resources. Only if an 'enterprising'[401] competitor would be unable to replicate the dataset with a similar investment as the requested undertaking, duplication is not a realistic alternative and access to the existing data is therefore indispensable.[402] For example, it is difficult and costly to generate navigation data, which is an essential input for navigation devices, as it requires employees that travel along different routes. While the human, temporal and financial costs for

398 See Graef, *EU Competition Law, Data Protection and Online Platforms: Data as Essential Facility* (n 292) 271 'For example, if the specific data needed to operate a search engine of good quality can only be obtained through serving customers, other data that is available from third parties will not form an adequate substitute for the search data of the incumbent search engine provider'.

399 Schmidt (n 175) 449; Rubinfeld and Gal (n 227) 362.

400 Drexl, 'Neue Regeln für die Europäische Datenwirtschaft? (Part 2)' (n 333) 419.

401 Opinion AG Jacobs, C-7/97, *Bronner*, EU:C:1998:264, para 68.

402 ECJ, C-7/97, *Bronner*, EU:C:1998:569, para 45; Opinion AG Jacobs, C-7/97, *Bronner*, EU:C:1998:264, para 68; see also Anna Blume Huttenlauch, in Ulrich Loewenheim and others (eds), *Kartellrecht: Kommentar zum deutschen und europäischen Recht* (4th edn, Beck 2020) Article 102 AUEV, para 280.

the requesting undertaking would be high, they would not be higher than those of the data holder.[403]

However, due to economies of scale and network effects, there may be scenarios where collecting a dataset that is similar in size and quality to the requested big data may only be possible with significantly higher financial costs. An example of such a scenario can be found in the Commission's merger decision *Thompson/Reuters*.[404] The costs for replicating the financial data held by the merging parties were considered too high for new market entrants and therefore constituted a barrier to entry. For new entrants, the cost of creating a competitive dataset that is as rich in historical data would be higher than the investment costs of the merging firms because historical financial data is not as readily available as current financial data and thus can only be collected manually with considerable effort.[405] Contrary to new market entrants, Thomson and Reuters were able to continuously expand their dataset over time by gathering the current data of each year and did not have to acquire all historical data at once.[406] If the costs for replicating big data exceed the investment costs of the data holder, the *Bronner*-threshold is passed, and competition authorities or courts could find that the duplication is not a viable alternative.

The costs for generating a dataset that is similar in size to the requested data can also be higher than the investment costs of the data holder, if the dataset was acquired under non-competitive conditions, such as through public funding. In the French *GDF Suez*[407] case and the Belgian *Nationale Loterij*[408] case, the competition authorities held that the data generated by former public monopolists during the time when they still enjoyed a legal monopoly cannot easily be replicated by new entrants.[409] In this scenario the requirement of the *Bronner* decision would also be met.

Like in single-source data constellations, the question of whether the requesting undertaking can be expected to become active on a market upstream of the relevant data market in order to substitute or duplicate the

403 Schmidt (n 175) 455.

404 Commission Decision M.4726, *Thomson/Reuters*, C(2008) 654 final.

405 Commission Decision M.4726, *Thomson/Reuters*, C(2008) 654 final, para 360 ff.

406 See Schmidt (n 175) 454.

407 Autorité de la concurrence, Decision n°14-MC-02 (GDF Suez), 9 September 2014.

408 Belgian Competition Authority, Decision n°BMA-2015-P/K-27-AUD, 22 September 2015.

409 Thomas Tombal, *Imposing Data Sharing among Private Actors: A Tale of Evolving Balances* (Wolters Kluwer 2022) 238.

requested data also needs to be addressed with regard to big data. Since it is primarily the size and quality of the dataset rather than the semantic content of the individual pieces of data points that renders it (potentially) indispensable, several upstream markets, which allow the collection of similar data, may exist. The requesting undertaking would not necessarily have to offer the same service or product that the data holder used to generate the requested data. It would also be possible to offer a product or service that generates data with different semantic content but nonetheless enables similar inferences. For example, data on consumer preferences for targeted advertising can be collected by various different platform providers[410] as well as by producers of smart goods.

However, it needs to be taken into account that the requested data may be a mere by-product of an economic activity. For example, large datasets on the geological conditions of certain regions may be the by-product of deep drilling activities conducted to gather valuable underground resources. In such a scenario, it can hardly be expected that requesting undertaking would need to enter the upstream market in order to duplicate the data.[411] Ultimately, the barriers to entry need to be assessed on a case-by-case basis, as they depend on the specific features of the industry and the upstream markets at stake.[412]

Should the duplication of the requested big data only be possible by creating a platform, the much-debated topic of entry barriers to platform markets would need to be addressed.[413] Economic literature is divided on this issue. Some argue that platforms heavily profit from a positive feedback loop: Access to large amounts of data allows platform providers to offer better services. Better services attract more users, which in turn allows the collection of even more data. This leads to significant economies of scale and strengthens the position of established platforms to an extent that it becomes an insurmountable obstacle for potential market entrants.[414] Others oppose the argument that platform markets will eventually tip due to network effects and feedback loops. They argue that even for the same

410 Commission Decision M.7217, Facebook/WhatsApp, C(2014) 7239 final, 188.

411 Rubinfeld and Gal (n 227) 357; see also Tombal (n 409) 239.

412 Colangelo and Maggiolino (n 333) 259.

413 Colangelo and Maggiolino (n 333) 261.

414 David Evans and Richard Schmalensee, *Matchmakers: The New Economics of Multisided Platforms* (Harvard Business Review Press 2016); E.g. Nathan Newman, 'Search, Antitrust, and the Economics of the Control of User Data' (2014) 30 Yale Journal on Regulation 401, 406.

type of online activity, users will often utilise various online platforms (multi-homing). Moreover, the quality of platform services does not solely depend on access to data but also—and perhaps primarily—on engineering resources as well as technological investments and innovation. To strengthen this line of argumentation, it is often referred to historical examples, where incumbent platforms (such as Myspace or Yahoo!) were quickly replaced by firms that offered better products or services.[415] However, in EFD cases, this question does not have to be addressed in the abstract, rather an economic analysis of the concrete platform market(s) under investigation would be required.

Due to all these variables, it is time-consuming and costly to demonstrate that it is indeed impossible or unreasonably difficult for the requesting undertaking to substitute the big data by entering an upstream market.

4.3.3.4 Effects of the right to data portability on the indispensability test

If the data requested is personal data, another complex facet is added to the indispensability test. While big data will regularly be comprised of information about individuals, personal single-source data is rather the exception. On the one hand, it has to be information about a natural person that is not known to the natural person itself. On the other hand, the requested undertaking must be the only one capable of collecting such data, e.g. due to technical means and/or a special relationship to the natural person. An example is the transactional and behavioural data collected and exclusively controlled by a platform about the customers of independent third-party retailers (see 3.1.1.1). Such data is unique because the customers do not actively provide that data and can therefore not replicate it. Moreover, the platform is the only one capable of collecting such data, due to its role as a gatekeeper.

The application of the EFD could be opposed on the grounds that GDPR's right to data portability (Article 20 GDPR) enables sufficient access to the requested personal data. Article 20 GDPR gives data subjects the right to request that the controller of provided personal data transfers the

415 E.g. Anja Lambrecht and Catherine Tucker, 'Can Big Data Protect a Firm from Competition?' [2015] SSRN Electronic Journal <https://ssrn.com/abstract=2705530> accessed 20 April 2022; Andres V Lerner, 'The Role of "Big Data" in Online Platform Competition' [2014] SSRN Electronic Journal <http://www.ssrn.com/abstract=2482780> accessed 15 January 2022.

data to a selected third party (see Chapter 5). It could be argued that Article 20 GDPR allows the requesting undertaking to duplicate the requested personal data by contacting the data subjects and urging them to exercise their data portability right.[416] If the data subjects value the data-dependent services or products the requesting undertaking intends to offer, they will agree to transfer their personal data to the requesting undertaking.

However, it has also been argued that the mere existence of the data portability right does not necessarily mean that effective competition is possible. Article 20 GDPR affords the right to have personal data transferred exclusively to data subjects and does not give competitors a right to access the data. Hence, the requesting undertaking can only benefit indirectly from the portability and is entirely dependent on the discretion of the data subjects.[417] The requesting undertaking may be able to convince data subjects to exercise their portability right, but this would presuppose that it is in a position to contact the data subjects. Often third parties do not know whose data they want to access and/or do not have the means to contact them efficiently.[418] Especially when the requested dataset is very large, it is unlikely that a sufficient number of data subjects can be reached and convinced to exercise their portability right. It also needs to be taken into account that the right to data portability does not apply to inferred personal data (see 5.1.4). Moreover, Article 20 GDPR only allows the one-off supply of personal data and not a continuous transfer of personal data (see 5.6.1). Therefore, Article 20 GDPR is an unsuitable legal instrument to duplicate the requested input if access to large datasets, inferred personal data or real-time personal data is necessary.

Ultimately, it must be irrelevant for assessing the competitiveness whether legal or factual obstacles impede the requesting undertaking from duplicating the requested input.[419] The mere existence of a portability right is not sufficient to ensure facilitated market access. Competition authorities have to evaluate the specific market circumstances and assess whether the requesting undertaking could actually benefit from the data portability right. If this question is answered in the affirmative, the indispensability requirement is not met. However, competition authorities may also come to the conclusion that either factual circumstances or the limited scope of

416 The question whether personal data can be accessed based on the EFD without consent is addressed under 4.3.6.

417 Louven (n 394) 171.

418 See Datenethikkommission (n 114) 136.

419 *cf Louven (n 394) 171.*

the portability right render it impossible or unreasonably difficult[420] for the requesting undertaking to obtain a copy of the requested data. In this case, facilitated market access requires measures that go beyond the effects the data portability right has to offer.

4.3.3.5 Constructive refusals to provide access

As shown above, the indispensability requirement criterion raises many difficult economic and legal questions that need to be evaluated on a case-by-case basis. However, addressing these issues can be omitted if the requested undertaking is required to provide access by law, but does so only under unfair conditions.[421]

In its *Slovak Telekom* decision, the ECJ confirmed the Commission's and the EGC's view that the indispensability condition does not apply to so-called constructive refusals to deal (i.e. access under unfair conditions). The Court argued that in case of an outright refusal, the indispensability requirement determines whether the requested 'undertaking has a genuinely tight grip on the market by virtue of that infrastructure'.[422] Slovak Telekom was, however, subject to a sector-specific regulatory obligation requiring it to grant access to the requested infrastructure, which Slovak Telekom did, but only under unfair conditions. The ECJ pointed out that the objective of the statutory access obligation is to strike a balance between encouraging the requesting undertaking and its competitors to invest and innovate and ensuring effective competition in the market. Since the legislator already took these interests into account, it is not necessary to repeat the same balancing exercise by assessing the indispensability of the input.[423] Abolishing the indispensability requirement is also justified by the argument that competition law does not force the undertaking to give access to its infrastructure but only to adapt the conditions of access. Hence, the measures taken by the competition authority or court are less invasive to the requested undertaking's freedom of contract and right to property.[424]

420 See ECJ, C-7/97, *Bronner*, EU:C:1998:569, para 44.

421 Tombal (n 409) 240.

422 ECJ, C-165/19 P, *Slovak Telekom*, EU:C:2021:239, para 49.

423 ECJ, C-165/19 P, *Slovak Telekom*, EU:C:2021:239, paras 54–60; see also Tombal (n 409) 231.

424 ECJ, C-165/19 P, *Slovak Telekom*, EU:C:2021:239, para 51.

In light of the Court's reasoning, it seems questionable whether the indispensability requirement applies if the requested undertaking voluntarily, but under unfair conditions, grants access to the requested data. The fact that competition authorities or courts do not need to compel access, since it has already been granted on a voluntary basis, suggests that the indispensability test could be dispensed with. However, the decisive argument of the ECJ seems to be that assessing the indispensability can be omitted only if competition authorities or courts can rely on the balancing exercise of the legislator. Hence, only if access is granted because a statutory provision requires it, albeit under unfair conditions, the indispensability requirement does not apply.[425]

4.3.4 Excluding competition on the data-dependent secondary market

The requirement of 'excluding competition on a secondary market' may also pose a challenge to applying the EFD to cases of denied data access. As described above (see 4.2.1.3), the criterion is interpreted as requiring the dominant undertaking to be active on the secondary market. This understanding is based on the rationale that it would be unreasonable for a company to deny access to input that is necessary to provide a product or service if it is not competing in the downstream market because it does not have to fear losing the competitive edge. Moreover, the undertaking could generate additional revenue by charging for the access.

However, scenarios, where the undertaking holding the essential input is not (yet) operating in the secondary market but still refuses to grant access, are likely to occur more frequently in the digital economy.[426] It is a distinctive feature of data that the same data may be used for multiple purposes. Hence, data an undertaking controls may turn out to be a very valuable input in various different sectors and undertakings may be unwilling to give up their potential first mover advantage.[427] By denying data access, data holders may try to forestall competition in data-dependent markets, in case they decide to enter that secondary market at a later stage (future offensive leverage). Even if data holders do not have any intentions to expand their current operations, they may still fear that access seekers will disrupt their

425 But see Tombal (n 409) 240 who seems to arrive at a different conclusion.
426 Colangelo and Maggiolino (n 333) 273.
427 Drexl, 'Designing Competitive Markets for Industrial Data – Between Propertisation and Access' (n 17) 282.

business with innovative products or services (defensive leverage).[428] Given the rapid evolution of digital markets, disruptive innovation can emerge quickly and shake-up not only certain markets but whole industries and cause previously successful incumbents to stumble.[429]

This view that the 'excluding competition' criterion is not fulfilled if the refusal to supply prevents access seekers 'only' from entering or opening up new markets in which the data holder itself is not active is based on the wording of the ECJ.[430] In *Magill*, the Court stated that the dominant undertakings '*reserved to themselves* the secondary market [...]by excluding all competition on that market'.[431] Proponents of this understanding have rightly been arguing that the EFD should apply even if the dominant data holder is not active in the secondary market because it might engage in future offensive or defensive leveraging tactics, but that this would require ECJ to depart from its settled case law.[432]

However, the ECJ's rulings would also permit a broader reading of the 'excluding competition' requirement. The Court never explicitly stated that the dominant undertaking being active on the downstream market is a condition for holding the refusal to deal abusive. In fact, it can also be argued that a dominant undertaking is 'reserving the secondary market to itself', when it refuses to give access because the undertaking is planning to become active on the downstream market itself in the near future or because it wants to prevent the emergence of new (disruptive) markets.

4.3.5 A new product required?

The new product requirement has been applied only to cases involving the refusal to license an intellectual property right. As outlined above

428 Feasey and de Streel (n 227) 36; see also Tombal (n 409) 241.

429 Feasey and de Streel (n 227) 36.

430 E.g. Tombal (n 409) 241; Inge Graef, 'Rethinking the Essential Facilities Doctrine for the EU Digital Economy' [2019] SSRN Electronic Journal 20 <https://papers.ssrn.com/sol3/papers.cfm?abstract_id=3371457> accessed 24 June 2022; Drexl, 'Neue Regeln für die Europäische Datenwirtschaft? (Part 2)' (n 333) 419; Graef, *EU Competition Law, Data Protection and Online Platforms: Data as Essential Facility* (n 290) 220.

431 ECJ, Joined Cases C-241/91 P and C-242/91 P, *RTE and ITP (Magill)*, EU:C:1995:98, 56, see also ECJ, C-418/01, *IMS Health*, EU:C:2004:25, para 52.

432 Tombal (n 409) 242; Feasey and de Streel (n 227) 36; Graef, *EU Competition Law, Data Protection and Online Platforms: Data as Essential Facility* (n 290) 274.

4.2.1.4, the requesting undertaking needs to demonstrate that based on the requested input, it intends to introduce a service/product that is new, or at least improved (if the EGC's *Microsoft* threshold is applied), compared to those of the dominant undertaking's products on the secondary market. The application of this rule makes sense only if both the dominant undertaking and the requesting undertaking are competitors in the same secondary market. The new product test intends to ensure that competition by imitation is restricted in favour of promoting the development of similar products, which provide additional benefits for consumers.[433] If, as suggested above, the EFD is applied also to cases where the dominant undertaking is not (yet) active on the secondary market, assessing the novelty of the product or service the requesting undertaking intends to offer would be a futile exercise.

It can be questioned whether the new product rule is an appropriate criterion also for refusals to share data. According to the ECJ, the additional requirement is necessary to strike a balance between competition and IP law, which both intend to facilitate innovation. Only if an IP right prevents the emergence of a new product for which there is potential consumer demand, IP law does not contribute to competition in innovation and judicial intervention is justified (see 4.2.1.4). Hence, it would not be necessary to apply the new product test if the requested data is not subject to IP protection.

However, as outlined under 4.2.1.4, it has also been argued that the applicability of the new product test should depend on whether external market failures are present in the market, irrespective of whether the data is protected by IP rights. If market failures, such as network effects and/or switching costs, render it commercially unviable for competitors to introduce a new product, the new product condition should be dropped in order to restore competition by allowing duplication. In case no external market failures exist, legal intervention should be limited to facilitating competition in innovation, and the new product condition should be applied strictly.[434]

---

433 Drexl, 'Designing Competitive Markets for Industrial Data – Between Propertisation and Access' (n 17) 283.

434 Graef, 'Rethinking the Essential Facilities Doctrine for the EU Digital Economy' (n 430) 21; see also Tombal (n 409) 245.

4.3.6 Data protection as objective justification for refused access?

The absence of an objective justification for the refusal is the last condition of the exceptional circumstances test. If the requested datasets contain personal data, the dominant undertaking may invoke its duties under data protection law, in particular the GDPR, to justify the refusal to allow access.[435] And indeed, at first glance, there seems to be an inherent tension between competition law, which—if the other conditions of the exceptional circumstances test are met—requires access to personal data in order to ensure effective competition and forester innovation, and the GDPR, which is based on the principles of data minimisation and purpose limitation.[436] However, the GDPR does not prohibit the sharing of personal data but rather ensures that there is a legal basis for the processing and that no more data is made available than necessary for the purpose of the processing. The GDPR's Recitals even explicitly clarify that its objective is not only to protect the right to the protection of personal data but also to ensure the free flow of personal data within the internal market.[437] Competition law, on the other hand, only enables access to personal data if it enhances consumer welfare. While data protection concerns cannot be simply brushed aside but rather need to be reconciled with competition law, obligations under the GDPR are certainly not a knockout argument against data sharing based on the EFD.[438]

Although the protection of the requested personal data may generally be considered as an objective justification, data access based on EFD can also be aligned with the GDPR.[439] In fact, competition authorities and courts need to ensure that the remedy of imposing data sharing is in compliance with the GDPR. This presupposes that there is a lawful basis for both the transfer of the requested data by the dominant undertaking and the subsequent processing by the requesting undertaking, once the

---

435 See Graef, *EU Competition Law, Data Protection and Online Platforms: Data as Essential Facility* (n 290) 276.

436 see Tombal (n 409) 348.

437 Recitals 3 and 9 GDPR.

438 Contra Grothe (n 222) 178; Torsten Körber, 'Konzeptionelle Erfassung digitaler Plattformen und adäquate Regulierungsstrategien' [2017] ZUM 93 who ignore that consent is not the only legal basis for processing personal data.

439 Contra e.g. Sebastian Telle, 'Kartellrechtlicher Zugangsanspruch zu Daten nach der essential facility doctrine' in Moritz Hennemann and Andreas Sattler (eds), *Immaterialgüter und Digitalisierung: Junge Wissenschaft zum Gewerblichen Rechtsschutz, Urheber- und Medienrecht*, vol 2 (Nomos 2017) 83.

data has been received.[440] Otherwise, the processing would infringe the data subjects' fundamental right to data protection. Of course, a legal basis is necessary only if the requested personal data cannot be anonymised before the transfer, either because anonymisation would render the data unfit for the purposes pursued by the requesting undertaking[441] or because it is technically not feasible to achieve true anonymisation.[442]

4.3.6.1 Legal basis for transferring the data to the requested undertaking

The dominant undertaking, as the initial data holder, is already processing the requested data based on one of the legal grounds of Article 6(1) GDPR. Transferring the data to the requesting undertaking is a form of processing that will, in most cases, not be compatible with the initial purpose of processing, as has been rightly pointed out.[443] According to Article 6(4) GDPR, processing personal data for a purpose that is incompatible with the purpose for which the data was initially collected is lawful only if it can be based the legal grounds of 'consent' (lit a), 'legal obligation' (lit c) or 'performance of a task carried out in the public interest' (lit e). The other lawful bases listed in Article 6(1) GDPR cannot legitimise further processing incompatible with the original purpose.[444] Theoretically, relying on consent is an option, but it would be too complicated and uncertain in practice to contact every affected data subject and ask for their consent

440 Christiane Wendehorst, 'Of Elephants in the Room and Paper Tigers: How to Reconcile Data Protection and the Data Economy' in Sebastian Lohsse, Reiner Schulze and Dirk Staudenmayer (eds), *Trading Data in the Digital Economy: Legal Concepts and Tools: Münster Colloquia on EU Law and the Digital Economy III* (Nomos; Hart Publishing 2017) 334 ff; see Tombal (n 409) 350 ff who has applied Wendehorst's view that data transfers require a lawful basis at two levels to mandatory data access based on the EFD.

441 Stefan Schmidt, 'Daten als Zugangsobjekt: Braucht es ein "Daten für alle"-Gesetz?' [2018] Wirtschaft und Wettbewerb 549, 549.

442 Tombal (n 409) 349; Schmidt (n 175) 501; Josef Drexl, 'Legal Challenges of the Changing Role of Personal and Non-Personal Data in the Data Economy' in Alberto De Franceschi and Reiner Schulze (eds), *Digital Revolution – New Challenges for Law: Data Protection, Artificial Intelligence, Smart Products, Blockchain Technology and Virtual Currencies* (Beck; Nomos 2019) 20; Wendehorst, 'Of Elephants in the Room and Paper Tigers: How to Reconcile Data Protection and the Data Economy' (n 440) 330.

443 Tombal (n 409) 351.

444 Horst Heberlein, in Eugen Ehmann and Martin Selmayr (eds), *DS-GVO: Datenschutz-Grundverordnung: Kommentar* (2nd edn, Beck 2018) Article 6 para 51.

(see also under 4.3.6.2). Hence, it is to be assessed whether a decision by a competition authority or court ordering a dominant undertaking to share the requested data with a competitor qualifies as legal obligation that justifies the data transfer.

Recital 45 clarifies that processing carried out in accordance with a legal obligation to which the controller is subject needs to have a basis in Union or Member State law. The decision to share data with third parties is imposed on the basis of Article 102 TFEU,[445] i.e. directly applicable primary law.[446] A specific law for each individual processing is not required.[447] Strengthening free and effective competition in the internal market for the benefit of consumers is also an objective in the public interest,[448] and the dominant undertaking holder does not have a choice whether or not to fulfil the obligation.[449] Hence, according to some commentators, an obligation to share personal data with the requesting undertaking imposed on the basis of competition law amounts to a legal obligation within the meaning of the GDPR.[450]

However, others argue that Article 102 TFEU is too general and can therefore not justify the transfer of personal data. This view is based on Recital 41 GDPR which clarifies that the 'legal basis or legislative measure should be clear and precise and its application should be foreseeable to persons subject to it, in accordance with the case-law of the Court of Justice of the European Union and the European Court of Human Rights.' It is asserted that Article 102 TFEU does not meet this standard.[451] To strengthen this argument, it is put forward that three different groups of legal grounds for processing can be distinguished (i) consent of the data subject, (ii) cases where legitimate interests are presumed to some extent (Article 6(1)(b) to (e) GDPR), and (iii) cases where legitimate interests

445 Schmidt (n 175) 497.

446 Boris Paal, in Boris Paal and Daniel Pauly (eds), *Datenschutz-Grundverordnung* (3rd edn, Beck 2021) Article 6 GDPR, para [35].

447 Recital 45 GDPR.

448 Tombal (n 409).

449 Article 29 Working Party, 'Opinion 06/2014 on the Notion of Legitimate Interests of the Data Controller under Article 7 of Directive 95/46/EC' WP 217, 19.

450 Graef, *EU Competition Law, Data Protection and Online Platforms: Data as Essential Facility* (n 290) 319; more cautious Tombal (n 409) 356.

451 Vikas Kathuria and Jure Globocnik, 'Exclusionary Conduct in Data-Driven Markets: Limitations of Data Sharing Remedy' (2020) 8 Journal of Antitrust Enforcement 511, 22.

outweigh the rights and freedoms of the data subject in a balancing test.[452] Article 6(1)(c) GDPR falls in the second category because the balancing exercise had already been carried out in a democratic procedure when adopting the law in question and hence does not need to be done again. However, it is said that this does not apply to Article 102 TFEU, because when adopted, the fundamental right to data protection was not balanced against the objective of ensuring a competitive environment.[453]

The argument that Article 102 TFEU is not specific enough is fairly bold because it would suggest that a central provision of EU primary law is not sufficiently clear and foreseeable to meet the standards set by the CJEU and the ECtHR and therefore 'cannot be considered as "law".'[454] The ECtHR's case law rather supports the opposing argument, as it explicitly recognises that laws may—depending on the content of the instrument, the field it is designed to cover and the number and status of those to whom it is addressed—be vague to a certain degree, and that interpretation and application are questions of practice.[455] In EFD cases, it is the decision of the competition authority or court that specifies the legal obligation laid down in Article 102 TFEU.[456] It determines the purpose of processing, describes the types of personal data affected and may include additional measures to ensure lawful and fair processing. As elaborated below in more detail (4.3.6.2), the competition authority has to ensure that its decision does not disproportionately affect the data subjects' interests and rights, e.g. by informing the consumers, so they can exercise their right to object. Since a duty to share data is imposed only after the competition authority or court balanced the affected interests, a decision based on Article 102 TFEU falls neatly into the second group of legal grounds for processing.

---

452 This categorisation was proposed by Opinion of AG Bobek, Case C-13/16, *Valsts policijas*, EU:C:2017:43, para 56.

453 Kathuria and Globocnik (n 451) 23.

454 ECJ, Joined Cases C-465/00, C-138/01 and C-139/01, *Österreichischer Rundfunk*, EU:C:2003:294, para 77 ff; *Rekvényi v Hungary*, App no 25390/94 (ECtHR 20 May 1999), para 34.

455 *Rekvényi v Hungary*, App no 25390/94 (ECtHR 20 May 1999), para 34.

456 See Article 29 Working Party, 'Opinion 06/2014 on the Notion of Legitimate Interests of the Data Controller under Article 7 of Directive 95/46/EC' (n 449) 20 according to which it is sufficient if the legislation sets only a general objective, while more specific obligations are imposed at a different level, such as a binding decision of a public authority in a concrete case.

4.3.6.2 Legal basis for the processing by the requesting undertaking (data recipient)

Once the dominant data holder has transferred the data, the requesting undertaking requires a legal basis for processing the received personal data. However, the decision based on Article 102 TFEU does not impose any obligations on the requesting undertaking. Hence, processing the essential data is not necessary for complying with a legal obligation to which the requesting undertaking is subject. The recipient's processing activities rather need to be based on one of the other six legal grounds of Article 6(1) GDPR. The changed purpose of the processing has already been legitimised by the legal basis used for transferring the data from the controller to the requesting undertaking and thus, the available legal grounds are not limited.[457]

The most obvious legal basis for the recipient is Article 6(1)(f) GDPR. The processing of the essential data by the applicant pursues the legitimate interest of offering products or services that would restore competition and increase consumer welfare. Since all other requirements of the exceptional circumstances are met, there are also no other remedies available that would achieve this objective. However, Article 6(1)(f) GDPR requires that the legitimate interest of restoring competition is balanced against the data subject's fundamental right to the protection of personal data.[458] Only if the former prevails, the requesting undertaking's processing of the requested data is compatible with the GDPR.

Whether the data subjects' interests outweigh the recipient's legitimate interests will depend on the concrete purpose for which the data is processed by the requested undertaking and whether sufficient safeguards can be put in place. In particular, the competition authority or court needs to ensure that the data subjects are still able to exercise their rights under GDPR, such as the right to object to the processing and the right to data portability. This can be achieved by ordering the dominant undertaking to notify the affected data subjects that their personal data is shared with the requesting undertaking in order to comply with competition law. At the very least, the data subjects must be informed about the type of personal data (email address, telephone number, etc.) that will be shared, the pur-

457 Tombal (n 409) 357.
458 Tombal (n 409) 359.

pose for which the requesting undertaking will process the data[459] and that they have a right to object to the data processing.

Such an approach was adopted by the French Competition Authority (French Autorité de la concurrence) in the *GDF Suez* case.[460] The competition authority held that GDF Suez had abused its dominant position in the market for natural gas and ordered it to give other market players access to certain customer data (e.g. names, addresses, telephone numbers and consumption profiles) in order to allow competitors to contact potential new customers. In order to ensure compliance with data protection law, the competition authority required GDF Suez to inform the affected customers that their data is to be transmitted for marketing purposes to other gas suppliers unless they object.[461] The French competition authority's efforts to reconcile competition law and data protection law are underlined by the fact that it had consulted the French data protection authority (CNIL) before imposing the measure.it has been argued that competition authorities cooperating with data protection authorities should be the norm in data access cases. The latter should be responsible for supervising the correct implementation of the remedy from a personal data protection perspective.[462]

In case the requested data contains sensitive data, the specific requirements listed in Article 9(2) GDPR apply in addition to the general conditions for lawful processing.[463]. Article 9(2)(g) GDPR is similar to the legal ground provided for in Article 6(1)(f) GDPR, but requires that the sensitive data may only be processed if 'necessary for reasons of *substantial* [emphasis added] public interest, on the basis of Union or Member State law which shall be proportionate to the aim pursued, respect the essence of the right to data protection and provide for suitable and specific measures to safeguard the fundamental rights and the interests of the data subject'.

459 The dominant undertaking knows the purpose for which the data are going to be processed because the requesting company has to specify its intention in order to prove the indispensability of the data input (see 4.3.3).

460 Autorité de la concurrence, Decision n°14-MC-02 (GDF Suez).

461 Interpreting the decision in the same way Tombal (n 409) 354; Graef, *EU Competition Law, Data Protection and Online Platforms: Data as Essential Facility* (n 290) 318 ff; but see Kathuria and Globocnik (n 451) 28 who argue that informing the data subjects was a form of 'opt-out consent', which back then may have been admissible because the Data Protection Directive did not require explicit consent.

462 Tombal (n 409) 363.

463 Recital 51 GDPR.

Hence, competition authorities have to give even more weight to the interests of the data subjects if the requested data is sensitive.

Should the competent competition authority conclude that the objective of restoring effective competition does not outweigh the legitimate interests of the data subject (e.g. because the personal data is processed for purposes that would significantly harm the interest of the data subjects), the denial of data access is objectively justified. Seeking access from the affected data subjects will usually not be an option. Especially if the requested dataset is large, it is unlikely that a sufficient number of approvals can be obtained within a reasonable time. Should there be a constellation where contacting the data subjects is not a mere theoretical but also a practical option (e.g. the dataset is mostly non-personal but contains personal data of only a few data subjects), it is at first glance conceivable that the competition authority may instruct the dominant undertaking to reach out to the affected data subjects and seek their consent. However, it must be borne in mind that if the requesting undertaking is able to contact the data subjects and urge them to exercise their data portability right, the indispensability requirement is not met, and data access based on the EFD is not possible (see 4.3.3.4).

4.3.7 Compulsory access to essential data as an ex-post remedy

Once it is established that all conditions of the exceptional circumstances test are met, the Commission may, according to Article 7(1) of Regulation 1/2003, impose any behavioural or structural remedies, as long as they are proportionate to the infringement committed and necessary to bring the infringement effectively to an end. Remedies need to be delineated from fines, which are intended to deter firms from engaging in anticompetitive behaviour, and from damages that need to be paid to compensate private parties for their losses.[464]

In line with the IP rights cases, the appropriate remedy to end the abusive denial of data access is to impose an obligation to conclude a contract for the transfer of the requested data on reasonable and non-discriminatory

464 Ariel Ezrachi and Mariateresa Maggiolino, 'European Competition Law, Compulsory Licensing, and Innovation' (2012) 8 Journal of Competition Law and Economics 595, 611.

terms.[465] For example, in *Magill*, the Commission decision, which was upheld by the ECJ, imposed a duty on the broadcasters to license the copyright protected TV listings on a non-discriminatory basis in order to enable the entry on to the market of comprehensive TV guides. Beneficiaries of this duty-to-license were not only the requesting undertaking but any third party considering producing a comparative television guide as well as existing competitors in the broadcasting space. The Commission decision clarified that the broadcasters did not have to license the information for free, but could request 'reasonable' royalties.[466] Similarly, in the *Microsoft* case, the Commission ordered Microsoft to make available the requested interoperability information to any undertaking having an interest in developing and distributing work group server operating system products on reasonable and non-discriminatory terms. The Commission explicitly clarified that imposing unreasonable conditions regarding the access to, or the use of, the information would render the duty to supply ineffective.[467] The remedy may also not discriminate between different requesting undertakings, as this would lead to new distortions of competition.[468]

It should be noted that the Commission decision merely requires the dominant undertaking to enter into a contractual relationship that would end the abusive behaviour but does not stipulate the content of such an agreement. As the Commission is not a 'price commissioner', it is left to the parties to negotiate the terms of the agreement, agree on reasonable royalty and conclude the contract.[469] The Commission only ensures that the agreement is capable of eliminating the anti-competitive effects and that no additional abuse takes place (e.g. by imposing unfair conditions or linking unrelated products or licences).[470] For example, in follow-up proceedings to the initial *Microsoft* decision, it was assessed whether Microsoft had complied with its obligation to grant access on reasonable and non-discriminatory terms. After the Commission had assessed the innovative character of the interoperability information and analysed the pricing of similar

465 Schmidt (n 175) 525; Graef, *EU Competition Law, Data Protection and Online Platforms: Data as Essential Facility* (n 290) 277.

466 Commission Decision 89/205/EEC, *Magill*, OJ L 1989/78, 43, para 27.

467 Commission Decision C-3/37.792, *Microsoft*, OJ L 2007/32, 23, para 1005.

468 Commission Decision C-3/37.792, *Microsoft*, OJ L 2007/32, 23, para 1006.

469 See EGC, T-167/08, Microsoft v Commission, ECLI:EU:T:2012:323 para 96 stating that 'it is not for the Commission to impose upon the parties its own choice from among all the various potential courses of action which are in conformity with the Treaty or with a decision imposing behavioural remedies'.

470 Lamping (n 283) 143.

interoperability information, it came to the conclusion that Microsoft's remuneration scheme was unreasonable.[471] Microsoft appealed against the decision based on the argument that the Commission may not impose a penalty payment for infringing the initial decision because it had not determined which remuneration rate it considered reasonable. The EGC rejected the argument and confirmed that it is sufficient if the decision lays down that the dominant undertaking is obliged to share data with competitors on the basis of reasonable and non-discriminatory conditions.[472]

4.4 Summary

The CJEU has continuously expanded the EFD's scope of application over the past decades. According to the Court's case law, an essential facility does not necessarily have to be a physical infrastructure but may also be information protected by IP rights. The EFD may even be applied if the requested input has never been marketed independently and had been used only for internal purposes. This progressive approach allows the conclusion that also the refusal to supply data by a dominant undertaking may constitute an abuse within the meaning of Article 102 TFEU if all conditions of the exceptional circumstances test are met. As an ex-post remedy, the dominant data holder may be obliged to allow access to the requested data under reasonable and non-discriminatory terms. However, the Commission decision does not specify what a reasonable rate is but leaves negotiating fair and adequate terms to the parties. While the exceptional circumstances test is generally flexible enough to be applied to cases of denied data access, several peculiarities need to be taken into account.

If the requested data is used exclusively for internal purposes and the data holder does not engage in any data exchanges or transactions a hypothetical primary market needs to be defined in line with the *IMS Health* decision. Since the requested data is not traded on an existing market, demand-side substitutability has to be assessed based on qualitative criteria of the data, i.e. the data's characteristics. This requires a different approach

471 Commission Decision C-3/37.792, *Microsoft*, OJ C 2009/166, 20, para 280.

472 EGC, T-167/08, Microsoft v Commission, ECLI:EU:T:2012:323, para 100 'That being so, the Commission fulfils its obligation to state reasons when it sets out clearly and unequivocally the reasons why the remuneration rates charged by Microsoft were unreasonable, there being no need for that purpose for reasoning dealing specifically with the possibility of the Commission imposing a periodic penalty payment without first specifying a reasonable rate.'

depending on whether the requested input is single source data or big data. The particular characteristics of single source data that render it an essential input for the requesting undertaking to operate on the secondary market will usually be the semantic content or the timeliness of the data. In case the subject of the access request is 'big data', particularly the size, diversity and representativeness of the dataset need to be taken into consideration to establish the data's qualitative criteria.

Due to data's non-rivalrous nature and context-dependency assessing the indispensability of the data input is more difficult than in traditional EFD-cases, particularly if the requested data is big data. Although challenging, an undertaking may still be able to prove that a big dataset is an indispensable input that cannot be duplicated or substituted due to its size and diversity. However, it is not sufficient to argue that it would not be possible for the requesting undertaking to gather a similar dataset due to its limited financial resources. The requesting undertaking has to demonstrate that the costs for replicating big data exceed the investment costs of the data holder.

When assessing indispensability, the right to data portability (Article 20 GDPR) must be taken into account when personal data are involved. While Article 20 GDPR may enable the requesting undertaking to duplicate the requested personal data by contacting the data subjects and urging them to exercise their data portability right, the fact that the GDPR applies does not in itself mean that the indispensability test cannot be met. It rather needs to be assessed whether specific market circumstances and the limited scope of the portability right allow the requesting undertaking to actually benefit from Article 20 GDPR.

The requirement of 'excluding competition on the secondary market' does not require that the dominant undertaking is active on the downstream secondary market. It is sufficient that the undertaking is planning to become active on the downstream market itself in the near future or wants to prevent the emergence of new disruptive markets that would weaken its position on the primary market.

The new product requirement should not be abolished if the requested data is used exclusively for internal purposes and the data holder does not engage in any data exchange unless external market failures render it impossible to compete on innovation.

Although the EFD is flexible enough to be used also in cases of unfairly denied data access, it has several shortcomings in addressing situations of unfairly denied data access. The complex legal and factual questions that need to be addressed when defining the relevant market and assessing the conditions of the exceptional circumstances test, lead to lengthy procedures. Since compulsory data access may only be granted at the end of such procedures, the EFD is not capable of bringing swift and reliable relief to companies that require data access. Competition law can only intervene after the anti-competitive behaviour took place.

However, even with statutory access and portability rights in place, competition law will not be relegated to irrelevance. Especially in the fast-changing digital economy, competition law can complement more targeted measures, as it applies horizontally and is flexible enough to react to different constellations that have not been anticipated by lawmakers and may pave the way for future legislation.

5 The General Data Protection Regulation

The GDPR is not only aimed at the protection of personal data of individuals, a fundamental right protected by the Charter of Fundamental Rights[473], but also at ensuring the free flow of personal data in the digital single market. While, the GDPR's requirements and principles, such as purpose limitation or data minimisation, certainly set limits to the sharing of data between companies, the right to data portability (RtDP), which is laid down in Article 20 GDPR, is directed at facilitating the re-use of data.[474] The GDPR's RtDP is actually composed of two distinct rights: According to Article 20(1) GDPR, data subjects have the right to retrieve the personal data they have provided in a machine-readable format and to transmit the data to another controller (indirect portability). Where technically feasible, Article 20(2) GDPR gives data subjects the right to have their data transferred directly from the initial controller to the new controller (direct portability).[475] The data subject may request the retrieval or direct transmission of its personal data only from the controller but not from a processor.[476]

The proclaimed primary objective of the GDPR's RtDP is to strengthen the informational self-determination of individuals by giving them more control over their data. This empowerment shall enable data subjects to switch between suppliers and overcome lock-in situations, which in turn also facilitates competition, as it lowers the entry barrier for market entrants.[477] A side-effect of the RtDP is that the receiving company gets access to datasets it might otherwise not have, which can encourage the

473 Art 8 Charter of Fundamental Rights of the European Union, OJ 2012 C 326/391.

474 Recital 4 GDPR.

475 Article 20(2) GDPR.

476 Carlo Piltz, in Peter Gola and Dirk Heckmann (eds), *Datenschutz-Grundverordnung, Bundesdatenschutzgesetz: DS-GVO / BDSG* (3rd edn, Beck 2022) Article 20 GDPR, paras [5] – [8].

477 Ruth Janal, 'Data Portability under the GDPR: A Blueprint for Access Rights?' in Bundesministerium der Justiz und für Verbraucherschutz and Max-Planck-Institut für Innovation und Wettbewerb (eds), *Data Access, Consumer Interests and Public Welfare* (Nomos 2021) 320; Ruth Janal, 'Data Portability – A Tale of Two Concepts' (2017) 8 JIPITEC 59, 59.

development of new products and services.[478] That the RtDP is not a data protection norm in the strict sense, but rather is designed to facilitate the flow of data between companies is underlined by the fact that exercising the right does not require the initial data holder to erase the data.[479]

Like Article 102 TFEU, the RtDP has a rather broad scope of application, as the GDPR applies horizontally and is not limited to certain sectors of the economy. However, while competition law affords a data access right only if it mitigates competitive restraints, data subjects have a general right to request the transmission of personal data to another data holder for any purpose irrespective of whether any market failures are present.[480]

5.1 Requirements of GDPR's RtDP

The scope of the RtDP is limited by a number of conditions—the specifics of which are still being discussed in the legal literature. First, the RtDP can only be invoked for processing that was carried out by automatic means and was based on the individual's consent or necessary for the performance of the contract.[481] In addition, the RtDP only applies to personal data 'concerning' and 'provided by' the data subject. Despite the guidelines issued by the Data Protection Working Party,[482] which are not legally binding, but have authoritative status, it is still discussed in literature what exactly is to be considered 'provided' data (5.1.4).[483] A notable exception, which will also need to be examined, is that the exercise of the RtDP shall not adversely affect the rights of third parties (5.1.5).[484] It is also discussed whether the

478 *Gutachten Der Datenethikkommission* (n 23), 136.
479 Article 29 Working Party, 'Guidelines on the Right to Data Portability' (2016) WP 242 rev.01 7.
480 Inge Graef, Martin Husovec and Nadezhda Purtova, 'Data Portability and Data Control: Lessons for an Emerging Concept in EU Law' (2018) 19 German Law Journal 1359, 1363.
481 Article 20(1) GDPR.
482 Article 29 Working Party, 'Guidelines on the Right to Data Portability' (n 479).
483 See Inge Graef, Thomas Tombal and Alexandre de Streel, 'Limits and Enablers of Data Sharing. An Analytical Framework for EU Competition, Data Protection and Consumer Law' [2019] SSRN Electronic Journal <https://www.ssrn.com/abstract=3494212> accessed 20 April 2020; Janal, 'Data Portability - A Tale of Two Concepts' (n 477) 61.
484 Article 20(4) GDPR.

RtDP facilitates only one-off data sharing[485] or also a continuous supply of data,[486] the latter of which is often required for complementary services (5.6.1).

5.1.1 Data processed by automated means

The GDPR not only applies to the processing of personal data by automated means but also to the 'processing other than by automated means of personal data which form part of a filing system or are intended to form part of a filing system'. The right to data portability (RtDP), on the other hand, has a more limited scope of applicability. According to Article 20(1) (b) GDPR, the RtDP only applies to the processing of personal data that is carried out by automated means. As a result, data in non-digital formats, such as paper files, are excluded from the scope of the RtDP.[487] This limitation is reasonable because only digital data that can be shared and reused without hardly any costs and thus has the potential to be welfare-enhancing without being overly burdensome for the controller.

5.1.2 Data concerning the data subject

Article 20 GDPR allows data subjects only to port personal data concerning them. Hence, anonymous data or personal data that does not concern the person requesting portability is not within the scope of Article 20 GDPR.[488] While personal data is a broad concept that also covers pseudonymised data (see 2.5.1.1), the applicability of the RtDP to pseudonymised data is limited by Article 11(2) GDPR. According to this provision, controllers are not required to meet data portability requests, if they are able to demonstrate that they are not in a position to identify the data subject unless the individual provides additional information that enables their

485 Inge Graef, Martin Husovec and Jasper van den Boom, 'Spill-Overs in Data Governance: The Relationship Between the GDPR's Right to Data Portability and EU Sector-Specific Data Access Regimes' [2020] EuCML 3, 12.

486 Heike Schweitzer, 'Datenzugang in der Datenökonomie: Eckpfeiler einer neuen Informationsordnung' [2019] GRUR 569, 576.

487 Stephanie Elfering, *Unlocking the Right to Data Portability* (Nomos 2019) 24; Article 29 Working Party, 'Guidelines on the Right to Data Portability' (n 479) 9.

488 Article 29 Working Party, 'Guidelines on the Right to Data Portability' (n 479) 9.

identification. Thus, even if it is theoretically possible to identify the data subject, controllers do not have to use all reasonable means to re-identify the data subject of pseudonymised data for the sole purpose of complying with a portability request. Moreover, according to Article 11(1) GDPR, data controllers are not required to maintain data in an identifiable form solely for the purpose of enabling data subjects to exercise their rights under the GDPR.[489]

Often, personal data will not only concern one but multiple individuals (so-called 'multi-data subject constellations'). As long as the data subject making the portability request has 'provided' the data, personal data relating to several individuals is also covered by Article 20 GDPR. However, Article 20(4) GDPR stipulates that the RtDP should not adversely affect the rights and freedoms of others. Hence, in these multi-data subject constellations, the interests of the other individuals concerned by the set of personal data need to be taken into account (see 5.1.5).[490]

5.1.3 Data being processed based on consent or contract

The GDPR's RtDP only applies in cases where personal data is processed by automated means and is either based on the data subject's consent or necessary for the performance of a contract. Personal data processed on any other legal grounds is not subject to the RtDP. Despite this limitation, the Working Party 29 (WP29) recommends that data portability should be adopted by controllers as a best practice, even in cases where it is not required by law.[491]

The wording of the GDPR seems to be too broad because it would also exclude unlawfully processed data from the scope of the RtDP. It can hardly be justified to deny data subjects the right to retrieve their data that is processed in violation of the law from the controller and transfer it to a new controller. The purpose of Article 20(1)(a) GDPR is to exempt data controllers from the data portability requirement if the processing of data is based on the legal grounds specified in Article 6(1)(c) to (f) and Article

489 Graef, Husovec and Purtova (n 480) 1372.

490 Paal (n 446) Article 20 GDPR, para [17a]; Tobias Herbst, in Jürgen Kühling and Benedikt Buchner (eds), *Datenschutz-Grundverordnung/BDSG: Kommentar* (2nd edn, Beck 2018) Article 20 GDPR, para [3]; Article 29 Working Party, 'Guidelines on the Right to Data Portability' (n 479) 11.

491 Article 29 Working Party, 'Guidelines on the Right to Data Portability' (n 479) 8.

9(2)(b) to (j) GDPR. Controllers should not be able to escape their obligations under Article 20 GDPR by not complying with the requirements of lawful processing.[492]

In light of the GDPR's objectives, it is reasonable that the RtDP does not apply to data processed for the performance of a task in the public interest vested in the controller, nor to the processing of data necessary for the compliance with a legal obligation to which the controller is subject. Data that is processed for these two purposes is typically not the cause for consumer lock-ins. Moreover, complying with the RtDP may often be in conflict with the task in the public interest pursued by the controller or the legal obligation. For instance, it would jeopardise the objectives of anti-money laundering law, if financial institutions had an obligation to transmit the personal data that they have to collect in order to comply with their legal obligation to fight money laundering.

However, the fact that Article 20 GDPR only applies if data is processed based on the consent of the data subject or is necessary for the performance of a contract but not for processing necessary for the purposes of the legitimate interests pursued by the controller or a third party opens up a loophole for controllers. By relying on 'legitimate interests', which is a widely used 'fall-back' option for controllers,[493] instead of consent or contract, they can simply escape their obligations under Article 20 GDPR.[494]

5.1.4 Personal data 'provided' by the data subject

The data subject may only port personal data they have 'provided' to the controller. There is general agreement that the term 'providing' implies that an active and conscious action by the data subject is required. This condi-

492 Janal, 'Data Portability under the GDPR: A Blueprint for Access Rights?' (n 477) 327; Elfering (n 487) 24; Josef Drexl, 'Data Access and Control in the Era of Connected Devices' (BEUC 2018) 152; Janal, 'Data Portability – A Tale of Two Concepts' (n 477) 62; contra Kai von Lewinski, in Heinrich Amadeus Wolff and Stefan Brink (eds), *BeckOK Datenschutzrecht* (42nd edn, 2022) Article 20 GDPR, para [36].

493 Tombal (n 409) 141.

494 John Thomas and others, 'Response to the Public Consultation on the Data Act' (European Law Institute 2021) 37 <https://www.europeanlawinstitute.eu/fileadmin/user_upload/p_eli/Projects/Data_Economy/ELI_Response_Public_Consultation_on_a_Data_Act.pdf> accessed 23 January 2023.

tion is certainly met if the data subject wilfully and purposefully—without necessarily understanding the full implications of its actions—makes personal data available to the controller. Such acts may be registering on a social media platform, entering credit card information for online purchases, or posting on social media (see 2.5.2.1.1 on 'provided data'). It is also clear that the term 'provided' excludes any personal data that has been derived or inferred by the controller through means of data aggregation or analysis (see 2.5.2.3).[495] This means that the financial data submitted to a bank by a credit applicant would be covered by the RtDP, but not the credit score that the bank generated on the basis of the financial data.

Much controversy revolves around data that does not fall within the two categories described above. Opposing views have been expressed with regard to data that has been generated by observing actions or activities of an individual ('observed data', see 2.5.2.1.2), which includes data, such as the online shopping history as well as heart rate and sleeping rhythm measured by a smartwatch.

The Article 29 Working Party is the most prominent proponent of a rather broad interpretation of the term 'provided by'. In its guidelines, the WP29 argues that Article 20 GDPR should also cover data resulting from the observation of data subjects' activities in order to give the RtDP its 'full value'.[496] According to this more purposive interpretation, 'provided by the data subject' does not mean that data subjects have to transmit the data to the controller, but only that they are in some way actively involved in the creation of the data (e.g. by wearing a smart device or browsing the website of the controller). Only derived and inferred data resulting from a subsequent analysis of observed or actively provided data should be excluded from the scope of Article 20 GDPR. However, beyond the *effet utile* argument, the WP 29 does not offer any additional reasoning for its views. In legal literature, it has been argued that Recital 60 sentence 4[497]

---

495 Piltz (n 476) Article 20 GDPR, paras [15] – [17]; Janal, 'Data Portability under the GDPR: A Blueprint for Access Rights?' (n 477) 327; Miriam Westphal and Marco Wichtermann, 'Datenportierung nach Art. 20 DS-GVO' [2019] ZD 191, 191; Janal, 'Data Portability – A Tale of Two Concepts' (n 477) 61; Article 29 Working Party, 'Guidelines on the Right to Data Portability' (n 479) 9; Tim Jülicher, Charlotte Röttgen and Max v Schönfeld, 'Das Recht auf Datenübertragbarkeit – Ein datenschutzrechtliches Novum' [2016] ZD 356, 359.

496 Article 29 Working Party, 'Guidelines on the Right to Data Portability' (n 479) 9.

497 Recital 60 GDPR: 'Where the personal data are collected from the data subject, the data subject should also be informed whether he or she is obliged to provide the personal data and of the consequences, where he or she does not provide such data.'

supports a broad interpretation, as the term 'provided' is used to paraphrase the '*collection* of personal data *from* the data subject'. This wording would suggest that under the GDPR, data can be 'provided' even if the data subject's role is a rather passive one.[498]

Other commentators advocate a narrower interpretation based on the wording of Article 20 GDPR and a systematic interpretation of the GDPR. They argue that 'to provide' is synonymous with 'to make available' and thus implies that a person is taking some kind of active action to give or supply something to someone else. The expressions used in other language versions ('bereitstellen', 'fournir' 'facilitar') are also typically used to describe an active and conscious decision to make something available to another person.[499] It would contradict this understanding of the term 'provided' if 'observed data' resulting from an observation by the data controller were also included under providing. It has also been brought forward that Article 13 GDPR uses the phrase 'personal data relating to a data subject [...] *collected from the data subject*', which is broader than data 'provided by' the data subject.[500] Another line of reasoning for a narrow scope of the RtDP is that there would be no clear distinction from the right of access under Article 15 GDPR if Article 20 GDPR were to apply to data not actively provided. The right to access applies to all data relating to the data subject but does not oblige the controller to provide the data in a structured, commonly used and machine-readable format.[501] It has even been asserted that a broad scope could be to the determent of the data subject's data sovereignty. There may be situations where data subjects only want to port data actively disclosed to the old controller because they do not want the new controller to gain insights about their past behaviour. If the RtDP had a broad scope, the data subject would need to explicitly specify which data should be transferred to the new controller in order to avoid

498 Janal, 'Data Portability under the GDPR: A Blueprint for Access Rights?' (n 477) 328; Janal, 'Data Portability – A Tale of Two Concepts' (n 477) 61.

499 Michael Strubel, 'Anwendungsbereich des Rechts auf Datenübertragbarkeit' [2017] ZD 355, 358; Piltz (n 476) Article 20 GDPR para 17.

500 CIPL, 'Comments by the Centre for Information Policy Leadership on the Article 29 Data Protection Working Party's "Guidelines on the Right to Data Portability" Adopted on 13 December 2016' (2017) 8; Orla Lynskey, in Christopher Kuner and others (eds), *The EU General Data Protection Regulation (GDPR): A Commentary* (Oxford University Press 2020) 503.

501 Westphal and Wichtermann (n 495) 192.

the transfer of data observed by the old controller. This additional effort may discourage data subjects from exercising their RtDP altogether.[502]

While decision fatigue certainly is a problem in the data economy that might warrant legal intervention to protect data subjects from their own decisions,[503] limiting the scope of Article 20 GDPR is a paternalistic measure that does not enhance the informational self-determination of the data subjects. Rather the opposite is the case: it would deprive data subjects of their autonomy to decide for themselves what happens to data of which they are the subject. It is in the very essence of informational self-determination that it requires a certain effort and diligence on the part of the data subject.

Moreover, as argued by the WP29, it would contradict the telos of the provision if only actively provided data were covered by Article 20 GDPR.[504] Usually, this kind of data can be easily reproduced by the data subject and hence is not likely to be the cause of a lock-in and does not deprive data subjects of their informational self-determination. For example, when switching from one bicycle ride tracker application to another one, users will not be interested in porting data they have actively provided as part of their user profile, such as name, e-mail address and date of birth. What might discourage them from switching to another provider is if important statistics such as distance, pace, altitude, calories burned and location, which were observed while using the app and allow users to track their performance, cannot be integrated into the new app. Since a too narrow scope of application would defeat the RtDP's intended purpose, the arguments in favour of applying Article 20 GDPR to both provided and observed data are more compelling.[505]

Although the desire to address the issue of user lock-in on social media platforms was the initial motivation for introducing the RtDP,[506] the effectiveness of Article 20 GDPR for this purpose is rather limited because only data that has been provided *by* the data subject itself is covered. Often,

---

502 Westphal and Wichtermann (n 495) 192; Piltz (n 476) Article 20 GDPR, para [18].

503 Regarding the risk that the RtDP predominantly enables data flows to already large and powerful data holders because they are in a better position to approach the data subjects and persuade or nudges them to exercise their RtDP, see 5.6.3.

504 see also Elfering (n 487) 28.

505 See also Drexl, 'Data Access and Control in the Era of Connected Devices' (n 492) 108; Jülicher, Röttgen and v Schönfeld (n 495) 359 who arrive at the same conclusion.

506 COM(2010) 609 final, 7 ff; Alexander Dix in Spiros Simitis, Gerrit Hornung and Indra Spiecker (eds), *Datenschutzrecht: DSGVO mit BDSG* (Nomos 2019) Article 20 GDPR, para [2]; Elfering (n 457) 19.

the person who provides personal data to a controller is not the (only) person to whom the semantic content of that data relates.[507] For example, images or videos on a social media platform showing the data subject are not covered by the GDPR's RtDP if they have been uploaded by other users of the platform.

It can also be disputed whether Article 20 GDPR allows data subjects to port the chat history of communication services since the data subject only 'provides' one side of the conversation. These considerations also apply to comments or likes left by other social media users on the posts of the data subject. The language of Article 20 GDPR would suggest communication addressed to the data subject is not encompassed.[508] However, since social networks are primarily about user interaction, excluding such data would run against the RtDP's rationale of preventing lock-ins.[509] A more comprehensive interpretation of the right to data portability could be reconciled with the wording of Article 20 GDPR by recognising that the semantic information contained in emails, chat logs, and comments on posts is highly context-dependent. For example, the message 'Yes' contains no semantic meaning if it is not read in conjunction with the message to which it is responding. Similarly, a 'like' on social media is meaningless information unless one knows what content the user is reacting to. These examples demonstrate that certain personal data (such as individual messages, comments, or likes) cannot be removed from its broader context without losing at least some of its semantic information. It can thus be argued that the chat history of data subject with other individuals and every post on social media, including likes (or other forms of standardised reactions) and comments should be understood as a 'single piece' of personal data covered by Article 20 GDPR. Of course, it needs to be taken into account that, according to Article 20(4) GDPR, intrinsically intertwined personal data relating to several individuals (so-called "multi-data subject" constellations) cannot be ported if the data is likely to be processed in a way that would adversely affect the rights and freedoms of the other, non-consenting data subjects (see 5.1.5).[510]

507 Hans-Georg Kamann and Martin Braun in Eugen Ehmann and Martin Selmayr (eds), *DS-GVO: Datenschutz-Grundverordnung: Kommentar* (2nd edn, Beck 2018) Article 20 GDPR, para [14].

508 Jülicher, Röttgen and v Schönfeld (n 495) 259.

509 Elfering (n 487) 26; Janal, 'Data Portability under the GDPR: A Blueprint for Access Rights?' (n 477) 327; Dix (n 247) Article 20 GDPR, para [7].

510 Article 29 Working Party, 'Guidelines on the Right to Data Portability' (n 479) 11.

Finally, it has rightly been pointed out that personal data which the data controller receives from a third party with the consent of the data subject should be covered by Article 20 GDPR. It cannot make a difference whether the data subject provides the personal data directly or indirectly.[511]

5.1.5 Not adversely affect the rights and freedoms of others

Article 20(4) GDPR stipulates that exercising the RtPD shall not adversely affect the rights and freedoms of others. This provision is intended to resolve potential conflicts of fundamental rights that may arise when exercising the right to data portability.[512] Such a conflict between the RtDP and the rights and freedoms of others may, primarily, arise where the requested personal data relates not only to the requesting person but also to other data subjects (see 5.1.2).[513] The RtDP may also interfere with the trade secrets protection of others. Whether the term 'others' also covers the rights of the initial controller is disputed in legal literature.[514]

Transferring the requested personal data from the initial controller either to the data subject or to another controller constitutes a processing of data within the meaning of Article 4(2) GDPR and therefore requires a legal basis. By exercising their RtDP, the data subject also gives their implicit consent for the necessary processing.[515] However, in multi-data subject constellations, the transfer would need to be covered by the consent of all the affected data subjects. In case the other data subjects are not willing to give their consent or it is not possible to reach them, Article 6(1)(f) GDPR may provide a legal basis for the transfer of data. Under this provision, the personal data may be processed if it is necessary for the purposes of legitimate interests of the controller or third parties, except where such interests are overridden by the interests or fundamental rights and freedoms of the data subject.[516]

---

511 Dix (n 247) Article 20 GDPR, para [8].
512 Strubel (n 499) 360.
513 Strubel (n 499) 360.
514 Kamann and Braun (n 507) Article 20 GDPR, para [35].
515 See Björn Steinrötter, 'Verhältnis von Data Act und DS-GVO' [2023] GRUR 216, 223, who argues the same with regard to Article 4(1) Data Act.
516 Janal, 'Data Portability under the GDPR: A Blueprint for Access Rights?' (n 477) 333; Janal, 'Data Portability – A Tale of Two Concepts' (n 477) 62; Article 29 Working Party, 'Guidelines on the Right to Data Portability' (n 479) 11.

Hence, the interests of the data subject to exercise its RtDP need to be balanced against the interests of the other affected data subjects. Should the interests of the latter prevail, exercising the RtDP would lead to the unlawful processing of personal data and consequently adversely affect the rights of the affected data subjects.[517] Generally, it can be said that the interests of other data subjects are unlikely to outweigh the interests of the person requesting data portability if the new controller processes the data for the same purposes as the initial controller.[518] For example, a data subject's email account contains personal data not only about the account holder but also about individuals with whom the account holder has been in contact. Should the account holder make use of its RtDP to switch to a new email provider, it is unlikely that the rights and freedoms of those third parties are adversely affected, provided that the new account provider processes the data for similar purposes and offers at least a comparable level of data security.[519] Where, on the other hand, the new controller (recipient) is known to improperly access the account data of its users (and to disclose this data to authorities), the assessment would swing the other way. Hence, there is always a need to conduct a case-by-case analysis.

According to the prevailing view, Article 20(4) GDPR should allow the initial controller to refuse the portability request if it would violate the controller's intellectual property rights or require the disclosure of trade secrets. The root of the controversy is arguably Recital 68 sentence 6 because it only mentions the rights and freedoms of other data subjects in relation to Article 20(4) GDPR. However, the WP 29 and several commentators have pointed out that Recital 63, sentence 5 states that the interests of the data controller may be taken into account in relation to Article 15(4) GDPR. The prevailing view is that the similar wording of the two provisions suggests that the term 'others' also includes the controllers against which the right to data portability is directed.[520]

517 Janal, 'Data Portability under the GDPR: A Blueprint for Access Rights?' (n 477) 333; Kamann and Braun (n 507) Article 20 GDPR, para [34]; Janal, 'Data Portability – A Tale of Two Concepts' (n 477) 62.

518 Dix (n 247) Article 20 GDPR, para [18].

519 Article 29 Working Party, 'Guidelines on the Right to Data Portability' (n 479) 11.

520 Von Lewinski (n 492) Article 20 GDPR, para [97]; Janal, 'Data Portability under the GDPR: A Blueprint for Access Rights?' (n 477) 334; Kamann and Braun (n 507) Article 20 GDPR, para [35]; contra Matthias Rudolph, in Rolf Schwartmann and others (eds), *DS-GVO/BDSG: Datenschutz-Grundverordnung, Bundesdatenschutzgesetz* (2nd edn, CF Müller 2020) Article 20 GDPR, para [109]; Elfering (n 487) 29.

However, mere economic interests of the data controller may not be taken into account when considering a request for data portability. The WP29 has also clarified that a potential business risk is in itself not a valid ground for refusing to respond to a portability request.[521] This follows on the one hand, from Article 12(5) GDPR, which requires that such requests be complied with free of charge, and, on the other hand, from the rationale of Article 20 GDPR, which is to allow individuals to change service providers and to use multiple service providers simultaneously without being prevented from doing so by economic considerations.[522]

One of the rights that may be in conflict with the RtDP is the protection afforded by trade secrets law. However, the Trade Secrets Directive only protects trade secret holders against the unlawful acquisition, use, and disclosure of trade secrets. A request for data portability does not constitute an activity that falls under the scope of the Trade Secrets Directive. It has, however, been pointed out that the controller's interest in protecting an existing trade secret may nonetheless be considered under Article 20(4) GDPR.[523] It should be kept in mind though that the threshold for information to qualify as trade secret according to the Trade Secrets Directive is rather high. Hence, data that has been actively transferred by data subjects does not fall within the scope of trade secrets protection. Only observed data or metadata, from which economically valuable inferences can be drawn (e.g. about the controller's business model or company structure) may qualify as trade secret.[524]

The extent of potential conflict between the RtDP and the IP rights,[525] including the copyright protection of software and the sui generis protection databases seems to be overestimated in legal literature. The RtDP only covers data provided by the data subject (see 5.1.4). Any data that has been generated with significant intellectual input from the controller, such as inferred data or software, does not qualify as provided data within the meaning of Article 20 GDPR and is therefore not covered by the RtDP.[526]

521 Article 29 Working Party, 'Guidelines on the Right to Data Portability' (n 479) 12.

522 Janal, 'Data Portability under the GDPR: A Blueprint for Access Rights?' (n 477) 333.

523 Janal, 'Data Portability under the GDPR: A Blueprint for Access Rights?' (n 477) 335.

524 Von Lewinski (n 492) Article 20 GDPR, para [100].

525 Elfering (n 487) 43 ff; Graef, Husovec and Purtova (n 480) 1375 ff.

526 Von Lewinski (n 492) Article 20 GDPR, para [105] – [108].

The personal data requested by a data subject may be protected by the *sui generis* database protection set forth in Article 7 Database Directive (DbD) but only if the requested data amounts to a substantial part of the database. Typically, databases are created for large amounts of data from different sources and the personal data of a single data subject is arguably only an insubstantial part of such databases and would therefore not be covered by the *sui generis* right of DbD. However, it has been argued that controllers may try to narrow the database's size and limit its content to data relating to one individual.[527] In this case the personal data of the data subject requesting portability would be a substantial part of the whole database. Although this is a theoretical possibility, it seems unlikely that this approach would actually be pursued in practice. Controllers would need to demonstrate that they have made a significant investment in each of the databases containing the data of only one individual. This is either not possible because creating such small databases does not require significant investments or, if it actually does require significant investments, very expansive for the controller. Even if a controller would create small databases for every data subject at considerable costs in order to avoid portability requests, the interests of the controller should not outweigh those of the data subjects. After all, the controller is (mis)using the *sui generis* protection of the DbD to deprive data subjects of their legitimate right to have their personal data retrieved and ported.

According to Article 20(4) GDPR, the controller may only refuse to transfer such data which adversely affect the rights and freedoms of others, but not all the data concerning the data subject. If the data excluded from the RtDP's scope is part of a larger dataset, the controller needs to take appropriate measures to protect the affected interests and comply with the portability request. For example, in order to protect the privacy rights of other data subjects, the controller needs to use reasonable means to remove or redact the personal data of other individuals before fulfilling the request for data portability.[528]

527 Elfering (n 487) 50.

528 Rudolph (n 520) Article 20 GDPR, para [114]; Elfering (n 487) 30; Article 29 Working Party, 'Guidelines on the Right to Data Portability' (n 479) 12.

5.2 Indirect portability: retrieve and transmit

Article 20(1) GDPR gives data subjects the right (i) to receive their personal data, and (ii) to transmit them to another controller without hindrance from the original controller. The controller is required to make the personal data accessible (typically via download) in a structured, commonly used, and machine-readable format so that the data can be easily transferred to another controller (see 5.4).[529]

Portability may be requested only from the data controller and not from a processor. In principle, data controllers can be natural and legal persons as well as public authorities. However, Article 20(3) GDPR excludes the RtDP if it would interfere with the performance of a task carried out in the public interest or in the exercise of official authority vested in the controller and consequently limits the RtDP vis-à-vis public authorities significantly. In the case of joint control by two or more persons, data portability may be requested from each controller.[530]

The data subject does not have to put forward a legitimate interest or justification for exercising the RtDP. A specific form for the portability request is not required.[531] Article 12(5) GDPR also clarifies that the data subject may exercise the RtDP free of charge. Only if a data subject's requests for portability are manifestly unfounded or excessive, in particular, due to their repetitive nature, Article 12(5) GDPR entitles the controller to either charge a reasonable fee or refuse to process the request (see 5.6.1).

Actions by the controller that may hinder the data subject to transfer the data to a new controller may be of a technical, factual, financial or legal nature. An example would be encrypting the personal data in a way that it can only be accessed by authorised users (so-called DRM protection).[532] However, the controller does not violate its obligations under Article 20 GDPR if the impediments to the transmission of the data are objectively justified (e.g. that a certain mode of transfer would constitute a serious cybersecurity risk to the controller's systems).[533]

529 Dix (n 247) Article 20 GDPR, para [11].
530 Rudolph (n 520) Article 20 GDPR, para [31] – [34].
531 Von Lewinski (n 492) 62.
532 DRM Protection is, inter alia, used for e-books to restrict the number of devices and/or limit the use to a specific e-book reader app.
533 Rudolph (n 520) Article 20 GDPR, para [86], [87]; Article 29 Working Party, 'Guidelines on the Right to Data Portability' (n 479) 15.

Once the data subject has filed the request for portability, the controller has to make the data available without delay, but no later than one month after receipt of the request. This one-month time frame may be extended to a maximum of three months in complex cases, on the condition that the data subject has been apprised of the reasons for the delay within one month of the initial request (Article 12(3) GDPR). Data controllers must respect the obligation to respond within the given terms, even if it concerns a refusal. Pursuant to Article 12(4) GDPR, the controller needs to inform the data subject of the reasons for not taking action and about the possibility of lodging a complaint with a supervisory authority and seeking a judicial remedy, no later than one month after receiving the request. Hence, data controllers cannot simply remain silent when confronted with a data portability request.[534]

Article 20(3) GDPR stipulates that the right to erasure is not affected by the RtDP. This means the initial controller does not need to delete the ported data, provided the controller can still base the processing on a legal ground. Hence, after the data subject exercises its RtDP the personal data of the data subject will be held both by the initial controller and the new controller. Data subjects may, of course, exercise their right to erasure (Article 17 GDPR) together with the data portability request.[535] Article 20(3) GDPR highlights the fact that the RtDP is not a traditional data protection norm that is intended to limit the use of personal data, but to make data available to other players in the data economy.

5.3 Direct portability (where technically feasible)

Instead of first retrieving the data from the initial controller and then forwarding the data to the new controller, the data subject may, according to Article 20(2) GDPR also request that the data be directly transferred to the new controller, but only where technically feasible. Article 20(2) GDPR refers to Article 20(1) GDPR, which indicates that direct portability is not a separate right but only a modification regarding the mode of transfer. Hence, the scope and the requirements (except for technical feasibility) are identical to those for indirect portability under Article 20(1) GDPR.

---

534 Von Lewinski (n 492) Article 20 GDPR, para [64]; Article 29 Working Party, 'Guidelines on the Right to Data Portability' (n 479) 14.

535 Paal (n 446) Article 20 GDPR; Article 29 Working Party, 'Guidelines on the Right to Data Portability' (n 479) 7.

The wording of Article 20(2) GDPR would suggest that the controller must actively act and carry out the transfer once requested by the data subject. However, the provision is understood as allowing the controller to automate this process. In practice, this will usually be done by an application programming interface (API), which allows data transfer to other systems using the same API. In order to verify that the call to the API has been authorised by the user whose data is being accessed, the APIs need to be combined with a so-called access delegation protocol.[536] In other words, APIs establish a communication between two systems, which allows transferring and receiving data in a secure manner. The use of APIs allows data subjects to initiate automated transfers to a selected new controller during their use of the service of the original controller.[537] The data subject may even be able to initiate the direct transfer in the user interface of the receiving (new) controller by, inter alia, clicking on a button 'import data from the provider X'.

The initial controller only has to transfer the data directly to the new controller if technically feasible. Recital 68 GDPR specifies that Article 20(2) GDPR 'should not create an obligation for the controllers to adopt or maintain processing systems which are technically compatible.' Hence, the initial controller is not obliged to create an API that is supported by the receiving controller. However, the controller needs to explore other means of enabling the direct transfer to the extent that they are technically feasible.[538] Whether the assessment of what is technically possible should be based on a subjective or an objective standard is not clarified by the GDPR. A subjective approach seems more convincing because it avoids imposing a disproportionate burden on smaller players. What is technically feasible for large data holders, may often require unreasonable economic efforts from smaller controllers. Hence, the relevant standard should be the technical capabilities available to the controller in question.[539]

---

536 Jan Krämer, Pierre Senellart and Alexandre de Streel, 'Making Data Portability More Effective for the Digital Economy' (CERRE 2020) 41.

537 Herbst (n 490) Article 20 GDPR, para [25].

538 Dix (n 247) Article 20 GDPR, para [14].

539 Herbst (n 490) Article 20 GDPR, para [27]; see also von Lewinski (n 492) Article 20 GDPR, para [89]; Rudolph (n 520) Article 20 GDPR, para [93].

5.4 Structured, commonly used and machine-readable format

The effectiveness of the RtDP depends to a great extent on whether the data is provided in a format that can easily be processed by the new controller. The GDPR stipulates that the initial controller needs to transmit the data in a structured, commonly used and machine-readable format.

In the initial proposal for the GDPR, the Commission was given the competence to adopt an implementing act that would specify the electronic format.[540] Due to the wide range of potential data types that could be processed by data controllers, the possibility to specify the data format was abandoned. According to the WP 29, 'structured, commonly used and machine-readable' should be understood as minimum requirements to enable reuse of the data by the individual or another controller, i.e. the interoperability of the data.[541]

What is to be considered a suitable format may vary across different industries. In certain sectors, such as health care, generally accepted formats already exist. Where this is not the case, data controllers should select data formats that are widely accepted and thus allow for a high degree of flexibility.[542] CSV, JSON, and XML, for example, are not only machine-readable and structured data formats but they are also widely supported and can be easily imported into a variety of different systems.[543] Pdf files or formats that are subject to costly licensing constraints, on the other hand, would not ensure sufficient reusability of the data and thus not meet the requirements of the GDPR.[544]

The sectoral approach regarding data formats leads to difficulties for data subjects who want to transmit their data across sectors. For example, the data format commonly used in the healthcare sector may not be supported by controllers from other industries. Does the data subject have the right to request transmission of the data in a generally accepted format instead of a sector-specific data format? The language of Article 20 GDPR would suggest that the data subject does not have the right to choose between different permissible data formats. As long as the format meets the require-

540 COM(2012) 11 final of 25 January 2012, Article 18(3).

541 Article 29 Working Party, 'Guidelines on the Right to Data Portability' (n 479) 17.

542 Article 29 Working Party, 'Guidelines on the Right to Data Portability' (n 479) 17.

543 Krämer, Senellart and de Streel (n 536) 37; Article 29 Working Party, 'Guidelines on the Right to Data Portability' (n 479) 18.

544 Rudolph (n 520) Article 20 GDPR, para [73]; Article 29 Working Party, 'Guidelines on the Right to Data Portability' (n 479) 17.

ments 'machine-readable, structured and commonly used', the controller complies with its obligations under Article 20 GDPR. However, Article 12(2) GDPR lays down a duty of the controller to facilitate the exercise of the data subject's RtDP.[545] Therefore, the data subject is entitled to demand the cooperation of the controller to a proportionate extent. This includes the adaptation of transmission formats as long as it does not amount to an unreasonable burden for the controller.[546]

5.5 Relationship to Article 15(3) GDPR

As described in Section 3.4.2, Article 15(1) GDPR lays down an information duty aimed at enabling data subjects to make more informed decisions regarding the exercise of their rights under the GDPR, including their RtDP. In order for data subjects to efficiently exercise their data rights, they need to know what personal data has been processed and is still controlled by the processor.[547] Article 15(1) is therefore considered the cornerstone of data protection rights.[548]

While it is clear Article 15(1) GDPR itself, is a mere information duty that increases transparency but does not give data subjects actual control over the processed data,[549] the nature of Article 15(3) GDPR and its relation to Article 20 GDPR is much less clear. The provision, which was added relatively late in the legislative process by the European Parliament,[550] provides that the controller shall provide a copy of the personal data undergoing processing. Although Article 15(3) GDPR does not explicitly allow the data

545 See for more detail Sabine Quaas, in Heinrich Amadeus Wolff and Stefan Brink (eds), *BeckOK Datenschutzrecht* (42nd edn, 2022) Article 12 GDPR, para [32].

546 *Cf.* Herbst (n 490) Article 20 GDPR, para [27].

547 Dix (n 246) Article 15 GDPR, para [1]; Paal (n 446) Article 15 GDPR, para [3]; Ehmann (n 246) Article 15 GDPR, para [1].

548 Dix (n 246) Article 15, para [1]; Ehmann (n 246) Article 15, para [1].

549 Indra Spiecker genannt Döhmann, 'The Legal Framework for Access to Data from a Data Protection Viewpoint – Especially under the GDPR' in Bundesministerium der Justiz und für Verbraucherschutz and Max-Planck-Institut für Innovation und Wettbewerb (eds), *Data Access, Consumer Interests and Public Welfare* (Nomos 2021) 191; Paal (n 446) Article 15, para 3.

550 European Parliament legislative resolution of 12 March 2014 on the proposal for a regulation of the European Parliament and of the Council on the protection of individuals with regard to the processing of personal data and on the free movement of such data (General Data Protection Regulation) (COM(2012)0011 — C7-0025/2012 — 2012/0011(COD)), Article 15(2a).

subject to have the data transferred directly to a third party, they could pass on the data, once received they have received the copy. It thus would seem that Article 20 and Article 15(3) GDPR have very similar effects. In fact, Article 15(3) GDPR may even appear to be more attractive for data subject because it is not limited to 'provided data', as Article 20 GDPR is (see 5.1.4), but also covers inferred and derived data.[551]

However, if the data subject or a third party want to (re)use the data for their own purposes, Article 15(3) GDPR is of limited help due to the data format requirements. Article 15(3) GDPR provides that the data shall be provided in a commonly used electronic form. In contrast to Article 20 GDPR, it is not necessary that the format be machine-readable. Hence, a PDF file meets the condition of 'commonly used electronic form', which, although accessible, is not inherently designed for data analysis, manipulation or integration into other systems. Machine-readable formats, like CSV or JSON, on the other hand, allow for easy data extraction and technical reuse.[552] This distinction highlights the different objectives of the two GDPR provisions, with Article 15(3) GDPR prioritising transparency and Article 20 GDPR focusing on making data available to other actors and increasing data usage.

The interplay between Article 15(1) GDPR and the right to receive a copy of personal data under Article 15(3) GDPR has been a topic of considerable debate. Some understand Article 15(3) GDPR as a mere modality of exercising the right granted by Article 15(1) GDPR. According to this view, Article 15(3) GDPR does not introduce a new, independent right.[553] Others have argued that the right to receive a copy under Article 15(3) GDPR should be viewed as an additional and distinct right from the right to access under Article 15(1) GDPR.[554] The ECJ has recently clarified this issue and sided with the former interpretation. The Court explicitly stated that the first sentence of Article 15(3) GDPR cannot be interpreted as establishing a separate right distinct from the right provided for in Article 15(1) GDPR.[555]

551 ECJ, C-487/21, *F.F. v Österreichische Datenschutzbehörde*, EU:C:2023:369, para 28; see also Tombal (n 409) 185.

552 Tombal (n 409) 185.

553 EDPB, 'Guidelines 01/2022 on Data Subject Rights – Right of Access' (2023) 13; Paal (n 446) 33.

554 Dix (n 246) Article 15, para [22]; Matthias Bäcker, in Jürgen Kühling and Benedikt Buchner (eds), *Datenschutz-Grundverordnung/BDSG: Kommentar* (2nd edn, Beck 2018) Article 15, para [39].

555 ECJ, C-307/22, *FT (Copies du dossier médical)*, EU:C:2023:811, para 72.

The fact that the ECJ does not consider Article 15(3) GDPR to be a self-standing right but a modality of Article 15(1) GDPR underscores that its primary objective is ensuring transparency, rather than facilitating data portability or reuse. Hence, Article 15(3) GDPR is more closely related to information duties (3.4.2) that aim to empower individuals to make informed decisions about exercising their access and portability rights, than to the other access and portability rights discussed in this book, which are designed to enable further usage and transfer of data.

5.6 Shortcomings of Article 20 GDPR in light of its objectives

The RtDP laid down in Article 20 GDPR is not a traditional data protection provision, as it is not intended to limit the use of personal data but to give individuals more control over their personal data and strengthen their informational self-determination. Providing individuals with the ability to obtain their personal data in a structured, commonly used, and machine-readable format and to transmit that data to another data controller shall enable them to escape 'lock-in' situations. These may arise if data subjects invest time and resources into the generation of personal data in connection with a specific product or service, and switching to a different one would result in losing access to that data.[556] The RtDP contributes to more data protection, at best, only indirectly by enabling individuals to change to more data protection-friendly services or products and thereby facilitating competition for less privacy-invasive technologies.[557]

A side effect of the GDPR's RtDP is to promote competition between providers in the digital economy. Lock-in effects can limit competition and stifle innovation by making it difficult for new entrants to compete with established companies. Enabling data subjects to switch between different service providers, combine different services, or simultaneously use other innovative services indirectly can therefore foster competition and support

556 Paal (n 446) Article 20 GDPR, para [6]; Herbst (n 490) Article 20 GDPR, para [2]; Jürgen Kühling and Mario Martini, 'Die Datenschutz-Grundverordnung: Revolution oder Evolution im europäischen und deutschen Datenschutzrecht?' [2016] EuZW 448, 450.

557 Paal (n 446) Article 20 GDPR, para [5]; Alexander Roßnagel, Philipp Richter, and Maxi Nebel, 'Besserer Internetdatenschutz für Europa: Vorschläge zur Spezifizierung der DS-GVO' [2013] ZD 103, 108.

innovation.[558] While the direct beneficiaries of the RtDP are the data subjects, the company to which the data is ported gets access to personal data it might otherwise not have. This can put them in a position to challenge incumbents in the personal data business and remedy competitive distortions. Hence, indirect beneficiaries of the RtDP are the receiving controller as well as consumers as a whole, as they benefit from competitive markets.

In the two-year evaluation report of the GDPR, the Commission acknowledged that the RtDP has not contributed to these objectives to the extent that was anticipated (or hoped).[559] This assessment is also backed by empirical evidence.[560] One factor certainly is that data subjects are not sufficiently aware of Article 20 GDPR.[561] However, even if individuals were informed about their RtDP, its effectiveness to achieve the ambitious policy goals outlined above would still be hampered by several shortcomings of the provision as such.

5.6.1 One-time supply only

The ability of the GDPR's RtDP to address lock-in situations of data subjects in the digital economy is significantly limited by the fact that Article 20 GDPR is designed to facilitate the one-time transfer of data but not continuous, real-time transfer.[562] Such a continuous and real-time stream of data, however, is necessary if data subjects want to use complementary services of third parties that build upon the functionality provided by the original service or product.[563] For example, a ski touring app for a smartwatch that is intended to track the skiers progress on backcountry routes

558 Von Lewinski (n 492) Article 20 GDPR, para [11]; Graef, Husovec and Purtova (n 480) 1363; explicitly also COM(2020) 264 final of 24 June 2020, 8; but see Article 29 Working Party, 'Guidelines on the Right to Data Portability' (n 479) 3 stressing that the GDPR is regulating personal data and not competition and pointing to the fact that Article 20 is not limited to data necessary or useful for switching services .

559 COM(2020) 264 final of 24 June 2020, 8.

560 Sophie Kuebler-Wachendorff and others, 'The Right to Data Portability: Conception, Status Quo, and Future Directions' (2021) 44 Informatik Spektrum 264; Sarah Turner and others, 'The Exercisability of the Right to Data Portability in the Emerging Internet of Things (IoT) Environment' (2021) 23 New Media & Society 2861.

561 Kuebler-Wachendorff and others (n 560) 265.

562 Janal, 'Data Portability under the GDPR: A Blueprint for Access Rights?' (n 477) 339; Schweitzer (n 486) 574.

563 Daniel Gill and Jakob Metzger, 'Data Access Through Data Portability' (2022) 8 European Data Protection Law Review 221, 229; Graef, Husovec and van den Boom

needs both real-time and continuous access to the location data collected by the smartwatch. Social media management tools, such as Hootsuite or Buffer, that track metrics such as engagement, reach, and follower growth, and provide users with recommendations for improving their social media strategy are another example of services that rely heavily on real-time data from social media platforms.

The limitation of the GDPR's RtDP to the static one-off supply of data does not follow from Article 20 GDPR but from Article 12 GDPR. According to Article 12(3) GDPR controllers must provide information on actions taken on requests under Articles 15 to 22 GDPR to the data subject without undue delay and in any event within one month of receipt of the request. In complex cases, this period may be extended by an additional two months. It is apparent that this time limit is not conducive to real-time data transfer. Without undue delay is far too expansive a term to ensure instantaneous data transmission. Moreover, Article 12(5) GDPR allows controllers to either refuse a RtDP request or charge a fee for the provision of the data if it is excessive, which may, according to the GDPR, particularly result from the request's repetitive character. Any services that are dependent on real-time availability of personal data would, of course, necessitate repetitive portability requests. While it is true, as WP29 pointed out, that APIs, can lessen the potential burden resulting from repetitive requests,[564] the GDPR does not oblige controllers to adopt or maintain any technical processing systems,[565] such as APIs (see 5.3). Moreover, if automated and continuous portability requests every few seconds do not meet the threshold of 'excessively repetitive', what does? These uncertainties underline that the GDPR's RtDP is a one-off mechanism and not a suitable tool to ensure a constant stream of data between controllers.[566]

Article 20 GDPR may be an appropriate instrument (albeit with limitations, see 5.6.2) to prevent data subjects from being tied to the main product or service, provided there is sufficient competition in the respective market. However, as a result of the one-off supply mechanism, the GDPR's RtDP is not able to tackle lock-ins into the digital ecosystem of one provider, as data-driven ancillary services will regularly require real-time and/or continuous data access. Hence, the decision of whether to allow new

---

(n 485) 13; Jason Furman and others, 'Unlocking Digital Competition: Report of the Digital Competition Expert Panel' (HM Treasury 2019) 68.

564 Article 29 Working Party, 'Guidelines on the Right to Data Portability' (n 479) 15.

565 Recital 68 GDPR.

566 Gill and Metzger (n 563) 229; Graef, Husovec and van den Boom (n 485) 13.

entrants to enter the data-driven aftermarket remains with the provider of the primary product or service.[567]

While the assessment that due to the limitations with regard to one-off data supplies, Article 20 GDPR only partially achieves its goal of strengthening the data subject's position in the digital market and enhancing consumer choice is correct, it can be questioned whether the GDPR would be the right place for such a rule in the first place. This is because the GDPR only applies to personal data; ancillary services and products, however, will often require access to both personal and non-personal data.[568] Furthermore, creating an all-encompassing tool for lock-in effects across all sectors that does not address established and concrete market failures may lead to unwanted effects. Hence, the statement that Article 20 GDPR does not address lock-ins into aftermarkets should be understood less as a criticism than as a mere observation. In sectors, where the limitations of Article 20 GDPR are identified as an actual problem, the European legislator can and already has introduced rights that allow for real-time and continuous data portability (in particular Articles 4 and 5 DA (see 6.7) as well as Articles 6(9) an (10) DMA (see 6.4 and 6.5)).

5.6.2 No duty to import

Article 20 GDPR aims to strengthen the informational self-determination of individuals by giving them the right to take their personal data and move it from one controller to another. However, the RtDP falls short of achieving true empowerment because it enables individuals only to retrieve their data from the initial controller (or even have it directly transferred), but does not give data subjects a remedy to force the new controller to accept that data. The data subject's ability to relocate its data fully depends on the willingness of the new controller.[569] This also means that the GDPR remains a paper tiger with regard to addressing lock-ins in the primary market.

567 Heike Schweitzer and Robert Welker, 'A Legal Framework for Access to Data – A Competition Policy Perspective' in Bundesministerium der Justiz und für Verbraucherschutz and Max-Planck-Institut für Innovation und Wettbewerb (eds), *Data Access, Consumer Interests and Public Welfare* (Nomos 2021) 119.

568 Thomas and others (n 494) 36.

569 Janal, 'Data Portability – A Tale of Two Concepts' (n 477) 60.

The music streaming sector is particularly illustrative of the negative effects this shortcoming of the GDPR can have on users; the press has therefore referred to this issue as the 'Spotify Gap'. In compliance with Article 20 GDPR, music streaming services enable users to download and transfer their carefully curated playlists as well as other personal data, such as the music streamed in the past 90 days, the number and names of other users and artists they follow, and payment details with one click. However, if users want to move this data from one service (e.g., Spotify) to a competitor (e.g. Apple Music), they will not find an option to import their data.[570]

There is, of course, a practical reason for this limitation of Article 20 GDPR. Data formats and database structures can vary significantly depending on the type of data being collected, the purpose of the data, and the technology used to collect and store the data. Thus, a duty to incorporate data from another controller could place an undue burden on the receiving controller, as it can be quite difficult and/or costly to incorporate data that does not match the format or database structure used by the receiving controller.[571] The problem could be addressed by interoperability requirements and harmonised standards, but it would need to be done on a sectoral basis, since different informal standards for data format and structure have already developed in various industries.[572][573]

5.6.3 Benefiting large data holders

The most central shortcoming of Article 20 GDPR is that the RtDP affects competition between players in the digital economy but is afforded to data subjects irrespective of the existence of a concrete market failure and irrespective of whether the initial controller possesses any relevant degree of market power or even bilateral bargaining power. Hence, it is not ensured that the competitive advantage of getting access to data, which a controller

570 Thomas Heuzeroth, 'Spotify: Hier versagt die DSGVO' (*Die Welt*) <https://www.welt.de/wirtschaft/webwelt/article176720143/Spotify-Hier-versagt-die-DSGVO.html> accessed 22 January 2023.

571 Janal, 'Data Portability – A Tale of Two Concepts' (n 477) 60.

572 *Cf.* Susanne Dehmel, 'Stellungnahme zum Recht auf Datenübertragbarkeit nach Art. 20 Datenschutz-Grundverordnung' (Bitkom 2017) 5.

573 *Cf.* Susanne Dehmel, 'Stellungnahme zum Recht auf Datenübertragbarkeit nach Art. 20 Datenschutz-Grundverordnung' (2017) 5.

otherwise might not have, is to the benefit of market entrants or smaller players.[574]

The design of the GDPR's RtDP may even primarily benefit large companies and thereby solidify competitive imbalances in the data economy and harm end users and SMEs. The European legislator's vision certainly was that the data subject's decision to port its data to another controller is both well-informed and independent. However, since the RtDP benefits not only the data subject but also the controller, which gets access to the data, companies have an interest in actively encouraging data subjects to exercise the RtDP in their favour. Thus, the RtDP may not necessarily be exercised on the initiative of the rightsholder but on that of the company benefitting from the right. Large companies that provide services or products that are widely used by many users are particularly well-positioned to do this, as they can reach out to a large number of data subjects and ask them to exercise their RtDP in the company's favour. Furthermore, these big players will typically also have the technical and financial means in place to allow for the seamless integration of different data formats on a large scale. For example, a widely used 'in-vehicle infotainment (IVI) system', which allows the driver to connect their phones and access various features and apps via the car's dashboard, may ask drivers to import the data collected by the vehicle in order to improve the user experience. The provider of an IVI system that is already installed in vehicles from many different manufacturers could collect a large set of vehicle data using this approach. For market entrants and smaller players that have not yet established a broad user base, it is more difficult to reach out to a large number of data subjects and nudge them into exercising their RtDP in favour of the small company.[575]

Data sharing services that act as intermediaries and exercise the right to portability on behalf of the rightsholder as well as privacy management tools may be able to ensure that ensure that the RtDP is exercised in the favour of the data subject and not of dominant market players. For example, the interface of a privacy management tool could list the data subject's data portability decisions and the recipients of the data, as well as specify the reasons for which the transferred data will be used. Additionally, it could provide an option in the user interface that allows for easy revocation

574 Heike Schweitzer and Robert Welker (n 567) 120; Datenethikkommission (n 114) 136.

575 Wendehorst, 'Konsument:innen in der Datenökonomie' (n 230) 225; Datenethikkommission (n 114) 136; see also Thomas and others (n 494) 38.

of data portability requests.[576] However, such data-sharing services are still in their infancy. With the Data Governance Act, the European Commission is trying to promote their uptake. Whether this will be successful and whether the requirements of DGA will ensure the trustworthiness of the data-sharing services remains to be seen.

5.7 Summary

The analysis of GDPR's RtDP leads to a somewhat paradoxical finding. On the one hand, it can be concluded due to the requirements of Article 20 GDPR and the limits regarding mode of supply and interoperability obligations the RtDP does neither achieve true empowerment of data subjects in the data economy nor sufficiently address lock-ins. Situations in which the right to data portability provides data subjects with a useful tool are rather limited. Social media profiles of users will usually comprise data that is provided by several users and thus is only partly covered by the RtDP's scope. As Article 20 GDPR does not support real-time and continuous data transfers, the RtDP is also often not an appropriate mechanism for data subjects who are trying to escape a provider's digital ecosystem or who simply want to add innovative third-party services to their main product/service. The only practical use case is where data subjects intend to switch between products or services that are largely based on provided and observed data. For example, retrieving the data from a period tracker app to change to a different provider that offers a better service or more privacy protection. But even in these scenarios, a smooth transfer is dependent on the willingness of the new provider to accept and import the data.

On the other hand, it needs to be concluded that a more encompassing, cross-sectoral data portability and interoperability right that applies irrespective of the controller's market power can have counterproductive effects. It may, under certain market conditions, inadvertently benefit already larger data holders and place unduly burdens on SMEs, thereby creating additional entry barriers and stifling innovation.[577] The limitations of Article 20 GDPR that have rendered the RtDP not particularly effective in practice, have also ensured that these negative effects have not materialised to a significant extent. Data sharing services may have the potential to unlock the full potential of the Article 20 GDPR for data subjects but

576 Thomas and others (n 494) 38.

577 see also Heike Schweitzer and Robert Welker (n 567) 120.

at this point, it cannot be anticipated whether data subjects will adopt these services and enable their breakthrough in the market. The uptake of data-sharing services, however, will—among other factors—depend on a legal framework that ensures the trustworthiness of these services while allowing providers to establish a profitable business model. Hence, further research on whether the DGA is an appropriate instrument to achieve this objective is warranted. For the time being, sector-specific legislation that affords individuals and legal persons more comprehensive data portability and access rights in response to specific market failures seems to be the right approach forward. Some of the identified gaps have been closed by newer pieces of obligations. Articles 6(9) and (10) DMA offer end-users of platforms that are operated by large undertakings (so-called gatekeepers) a right to access and transfer the data they have generated continuously and in real-time (DMA (see 6.4 and 6.5). The DA affords a similar right to the users of IoT products (see 6.7).

6 Digital Markets Act

The Digital Markets Act (DMA) is a regulatory response to the challenges posed by the rapid growth and dominance of large digital companies. The DMA is based on the idea that certain digital services give their providers a strong competitive position because they have significant control over the pathways through which users access online content, goods and services, making the providers of these services gatekeepers of digital markets. The gatekeepers operating such 'core platform services' (CPS) benefit from strong network effects, economies of scale, and the strategic accumulation and control of data, which leads to reduced competition and allows the gatekeepers to engage in unfair practices that exploit their users or forestall new market entries (Recitals 2 – 4 DMA). The European legislator deemed traditional competition law not fit to address this issue, as it relies heavily on the detailed assessment of individual cases, requiring extensive fact-finding to determine market power and abusive conduct. Since this process is extremely time-consuming, it was considered ill-suited to the fast-paced nature of the digital economy where market dynamics can change rapidly (Recital 5 DMA).[578]

The DMA, thus, pursues a different approach and introduces a number of ex-ante prohibitions and obligations to prevent practices considered unfair or anticompetitive; many address conducts that were the subject of competition law cases.[579] The rules apply to undertakings that have been designated as gatekeepers by the Commission. In stark contrast to traditional competition law, these rules apply regardless of whether the addressed conduct has had, is likely to have, or is presumed to have any specific adverse effects on competition (Recital 11 DMA). Hence, under the DMA, dominance in core platform markets as is such is considered to be an issue that needs to be addressed, whereas traditional competition law has consistently asserted that holding a dominant position is not itself

578 Björn Herbers, 'Der Digital Markets Act (DMA) kommt – neue Dos and Don'ts für Gatekeeper in der Digitalwirtschaft' [2022] RDi 252, 253; Philipp Baschenhof, 'The Digital Markets Act (DMA): A Procompetitive Recalibration of Data Relations?' [2022] Journal of Law, Technology and Policy 101, 105.

579 For a full overview, see Bostoen (n 22) 282.

problematic.[580] The approach of the DMA is designed to increase legal certainty and ensure a higher level of general deterrence by establishing rules that are not subject to a case-specific analysis (the relationship of the DMA to traditional competition law is discussed in more detail under 6.6.2).[581]

Among the many rules for gatekeepers, there are four that oblige the gatekeeper to give access to data they control. These obligations are laid down in Article 6 DMA, which means that although they are self-executing, the Commission may specify the obligation in more detail in regulatory dialogue with the gatekeeper. In this dialogue, the Commission determines whether the measures taken by the gatekeeper are sufficient to comply with their duties under Article 6 DMA and, if necessary, may order specific implementation measures via an implementing act. This regulatory dialogue may take place at the Commission's own imitative or at the request of the gatekeeper (Article 8(2) DMA). In order to ensure that this process is not abused by gatekeepers to overburden the Commission, Article 8(3) DMA clarifies that the Commission has discretion in deciding whether to engage in the regulatory dialogue requested by gatekeepers. Irrespective of whether a regulatory dialogue took place, the obligations of Article 6 DMA are directly applicable and must be implemented by the gatekeepers. The Commission may even specify the measures that need to be implemented and combine them with a fine (Article 8(4) DMA).[582]

6.1 Asymmetric, entity regulation

A unique feature of the data rights under the DMA is that they are a form of asymmetric, entity regulation. The concept of asymmetric regulation pertains to the practice of imposing varying degrees of regulatory measures on different entities operating within the same industry. The specific level of regulatory constraints typically depends on the size of the undertaking.

580 ECJ, C-209/10, *Post Danmark v Konkurrencerådet,* EU:C:2012:172, para 21; ECJ, C-322/81, *Michelin*, ECLI:EU:C:1983:313, para 57.

581 Herbers (n 578) 253; Akman (n 22) 87 ff; Nicolas Petit, 'The Proposed Digital Markets Act (DMA): A Legal and Policy Review' (2021) 12 Journal of European Competition Law & Practice 529, 530.

582 See Herbers (n 578) 255; Romina Polley and Friedrich Andreas Konrad, 'Der Digital Markets Act – Brüssels neues Regulierungskonzept für Digitale Märkte' [2021] Wirtschaft und Wettbewerb 198, 201.

In other words, smaller entities may have less stringent regulatory requirements compared to larger ones within the same industry. In the case of the DMA, only certain providers of digital services that have been identified as gatekeepers (see 6.2) are the addressees of these data rights. Other firms operating in the same industry but not meeting the criteria of being a gatekeeper are not subjected to the DMA's data-sharing obligations.[583]

The DMA in general, including its data rights, is also a form of 'entity regulation'. This refers to a regulatory approach that subjects entities that meet certain criteria to regulatory obligations because of their relative importance for a certain market. Under the DMA, actors with significant market power that might violate competition rules are identified and preemptive remedies on these actors are imposed, irrespective of their actual conduct or the effects of their conduct.[584] In contrast, 'activity regulation' centres around regulating the specific activities carried out within an industry or sector, regardless of the status of the entity involved. Under this approach, the focus is not primarily on the entity itself but rather on the activities it undertakes.[585]

6.2 Gatekeepers and core platform services

The gatekeeper status of an undertaking is assigned by the Commission. The designation presupposes that the undertaking (i) operates at least one of the core platform services listed in Article 2(2) DMA and (ii) meets certain quantitative thresholds defined in Article 3 DMA. This means that providing a core platform service as such is not sufficient to be designated as a gatekeeper; the undertaking must also hold a significant position within the respective market. Conversely, an undertaking holding a dominant position in a digital market is not subject to the provisions of the DMA, if it does not provide a core platform service.[586]

The DMA recognises ten different core platform services: Online intermediation services, online search engines, online social networking ser-

583 Baschenhof (n 578) 109.

584 Björn Lundqvist, 'Study on the Digital Services Act and Digital Markets Act and Their Possible Impact on Research.' (European Commission 2022) 18 <https://data.europa.eu/doi/10.2777/751853> accessed 31 May 2023.

585 Akman (n 22) 104.

586 Ina Kapusta, 'Pflichten von Gatekeepern im Digital Markets Act' (2023) 20 83, 84; Baschenhof (n 578) 109; Petit (n 581) 532.

vices, video-sharing platform services, messenger services (number-independent interpersonal communication services), operating systems, web browsers, virtual assistants, cloud computing services, and advertising services.[587] The range of services identified reflects the broad scope of digital activities that the DMA aims to regulate, covering practically all the important services offered by the major digital corporations.[588]

Regarding the quantitative requirements, Article 3(1) DMA sets out that the provider must have a significant impact on the internal market. Moreover, the provider must operate a core platform service that serves as a crucial gateway for business users to connect with end users. And thirdly, the provider must either possess an entrenched and durable position in its operations, or it must be foreseeable that it will attain such a position in the near future. Article 3(2) DMA outlines circumstances that, if present, create rebuttable presumptions that an undertaking meets these criteria. The impact criterion is presumed to be met if the undertaking has achieved an EU-wide turnover of € 7.5 billion in each of the last three business years or the average market capitalisation in the last business year amounted to € 75 billion and the undertaking offers the same CPS in at least three EU member states. Regarding the gateway criterion, the undertaking needs to provide a CPS of at least 45 million monthly active end users and at least 10,000 annual active business users in the EU in the last financial year. The durable position is presumed if the undertaking has fulfilled these two requirements in each of the last three financial years.

It is important to point out that an undertaking has a gatekeeper status only with regard to the core platform services listed in the relevant designation decision.[589] This means DMA's obligations apply only to the business activities associated with those services. For instance, if an undertaking is designated a gatekeeper for its online marketplace platform, the DMA's obligations will apply to that marketplace. However, if the same company also provides cloud services that were not listed in the gatekeeper designation, the provider is not bound by DMA's specific gatekeeper obligations with regard to the cloud services. So far, the European Commission has

587 For a detailed description of these services, see Christian Heinze and Tom Kettler, in Björn Steinrötter (ed), *Europäische Plattformregulierung: DSA, DMA, P2B-VO, DGA, DA, AI Act, DSM-RL: Rechtshandbuch* (Nomos 2023) 315 ff.

588 Herbers (n 578) 254.

589 See Akman (n 22) 94.

designated six gatekeepers (Alphabet, Amazon, Apple, ByteDance, Meta, Microsoft), which in total provide 22 core platform services.[590]

6.3 Data access for advertisers and publishers (Article 6(8) DMA)

Article 6(8) DMA lays down two measures to address the lack of transparency in online advertising services provided by gatekeepers to business users. First, gatekeepers are required to give advertisers, publishers, and any third parties authorised by them, such as advertising agencies, access to their performance-measuring tools. This includes tools that track various metrics such as impressions, clicks, conversions, and other relevant data that reflects the performance of advertisements. While some publicly available tools exist, gatekeepers also use internal performance measurement tools tailored for specialised or proprietary needs. These tools may offer deeper insights into user behaviour and detailed performance analytics than those typically accessible to the general public.[591] Additionally, gatekeepers must provide access to essential data needed for the independent verification of advertising inventory. This includes both aggregated data (e.g. data combined from numerous campaigns to provide statistical insights and non-aggregated data (e.g. detailed, granular data on specific advertisements or campaigns).[592]

It is important to point out that, according to the definition of online advertising services in Article 2(2) DMA, Article 6(8) DMA does not apply to undertakings that only offer advertising services but only to advertising services of companies that qualify as gatekeepers because of other core platform services they offer, such as search engines, social networks, or online marketplaces.[593] Recital 58 DMA clarifies that the obligations do not only apply if the advertising services are explicitly listed in the gatekeeper designation decision but also if the advertising services are fully integrated with other CPS of the same undertaking. For example, if a gatekeeper offering an online marketplace also offers advertising services, these would be covered by Article 6(8) DMA.

---

590 The designation decisions can be found here 'DMA Designated Gatekeepers' <https://digital-markets-act.ec.europa.eu/gatekeepers_en> accessed 21 April 2024.

591 Anna Wolf-Posch, in Rupprecht Podszun (ed), *Digital Markets Act: Gesetz über digitale Märkte* (Nomos 2023) Article 6(8) DMA, para [170].

592 Wolf-Posch (n 591) Article 6(8) DMA, para [172].

593 Carsten König, in Björn Steinrötter (ed), *Europäische Plattformregulierung: DSA, DMA, P2B-VO, DGA, DA, AI Act, DSM-RL* (Nomos 2023) 383.

6.3.1 Objectives

The online advertising market is dominated by a few market players.[594] Due to this lack of competition, the online advertising services provided by these gatekeepers suffer from non-transparency and opacity. This means that the processes, algorithms, and data handling practices behind online advertising are not fully disclosed to those placing the advertisements (Recital 58 DMA). However, without insight into metrics like impression counts, click-through rates, and the context in which ads are placed, it is difficult for advertisers that use the services of the gatekeeper to understand how their advertisements are being delivered and how they perform. This creates a power imbalance, where gatekeepers control much of the data that advertisers and publishers need to assess the return on investment for their advertising spend, make informed decisions or negotiate better terms.[595]

By affording advertisers and publishers the right to access the data necessary for independent verification, they can cross-check the claims made by advertising platforms regarding the effectiveness and reach of their advertising services. Having access to reliable and independently verifiable data enables advertisers and publishers to effectively compare the performance of different advertising platforms. Equipped with better information, advertisers and publishers can negotiate more effectively and choose platforms that best meet their advertising goals and budgets. The ability to compare may also drive competition among platforms, as they are incentivised to improve their services and offer better terms to attract and retain clients. This can also be an opportunity for market entrants to demonstrate value and compete on a more level playing field with larger, more established platforms. The increased competition through transparency is intended to drive down prices for online advertising services in the long run.[596] Moreover, the independent assessment may also serve as an indirect check against exclusionary practices by gatekeepers, where certain advertisers or

594 Competition and Markets Authority, 'Online Platforms and Digital Advertising: Market Study' (2020) 212.

595 Competition and Markets Authority (n 594) 297; Furman and others (n 563) 46.

596 Natalia Moreno Belloso and Nicolas Petit, 'The EU Digital Markets Act (DMA): A Competition Hand in a Regulatory Glove' [2023] SSRN Electronic Journal 21 <https://www.ssrn.com/abstract=4358589> accessed 4 September 2023; Wolf-Posch (n 591) Article 6(8) DMA, para [160]; Competition and Markets Authority (n 594) 411.

publishers prioritised or favoured over others, potentially distorting competition.[597]

6.3.2 Rightsholders

The access right is afforded to advertisers and publishers, both terms are not defined by the DMA itself. In the absence of a specific definition by the DMA, the term must be interpreted in accordance with the general meaning of the word, which is a rather broad understanding including any entity that engages in advertising activities.[598] This includes not only commercial companies that advertise to make a profit but also non-profit organisations that promote their interests.

'Publishers' is considered to refer to all providers of online advertising space through core platform services. This includes a variety of actors, such as the operators of a website in the form of a blog or an online newspaper, an app or video content (e.g. via YouTube). In principle, everything that offers a space for the placement of online advertising is covered.[599] It has been argued that such a broad understanding would cover everything that offers a space for the placement of online advertising and thus also include social media, or marketplaces, owned by the same provider as the core platform service. It has therefore been suggested to draw on the understanding of 'publisher' in the Copyright in Digital Single Market Directive[600] and interpret the term as referring to undertakings that invest in the production or acquisition of content and associated rights and have editorial responsibility.[601] It is asserted that this narrower definition of 'publisher' would lead to less complications when implementing the DMA.[602] However, the objective of Article 6(8) DMA to increase transparency and fairness across online advertising market is better served by a broader definition of publisher, as it creates the risk that entities, which play a meaningful role in the online advertising ecosystem, are excluded from the scope.

597 Moreno Belloso and Petit (n 596) 21.

598 See Wolf-Posch (n 591) Article 5(9) and (10) DMA, para [209].

599 Wolf-Posch (n 591) Article5(9) and (10), para [209]; Sally Broughton Micova, 'DMA Transparency Requirements in Relation to Advertising' (CERRE 2022) 10.

600 Recitals 54–60 Directive 2019/790 of the European Parliament and of the Council of 17 April 2019 on copyright and related rights in the Digital Single Market and amending Directives 96/9 and 2001/29, OJ L 2019/130, 92.

601 Alexandre De Streel and others, 'Effective and Proportionate Implementation of the DMA' (CERRE 2023) 15; Broughton Micova (n 599) 11.

602 De Streel and others (n 601) 15.

The access right may also be exercised by third parties that have been authorised by the advertiser or publisher. However, it is questionable whether this authorisation needs to be specifically aimed at requesting access to the required data on behalf of the authorising party or whether it is sufficient that the third party is authorised to conclude advertising contracts on behalf of the advertiser or publisher. It has been argued that the fact that Recital 58 explicitly mentions advertising agencies as an example of an authorised third party would suggest that they can access the relevant data from the gatekeeper without additional and specific authorisation.[603]

Not addressed by the DMA is the situation that the authorisation obviously does not serve the purpose of evaluating the advertising performance, e.g. if a competing search engine is authorised by an advertiser. In these cases, the gatekeepers should be entitled to refuse the access request.[604]

6.3.3 Modalities

Article 6(8) DMA requires the gatekeeper to provide the data in a manner that enables advertisers and publishers to run their own verification and measurement tools in order to assess the performance of the core platform services provided by the gatekeepers. Arguably, this requires the gatekeeper to provide the data in a structured, machine-readable form. Moreover, it is set out that access needs to be provided free of charge. Hence, gatekeepers may not demand compensation for costs associated with the provision of this data, such as the labour involved in gathering the data or modifications with regard to the data format. Fees may only be charged if the advertiser or publisher requests access to data that is not covered by Article 6(8) DMA.[605]

Other than that, Article 6(8) DMA contains very limited guidance regarding the modalities of the access right. This vagueness, however, seems to be on purpose. Effective performance verification tools rely on data being provided in usable formats and through accessible interfaces, such as Application Programming Interfaces (APIs). These technical details can be highly specific and varied between different gatekeepers and the services they offer. It is thus expected that the Commission will make use of its

603 Wolf-Posch (n 591) Article 6(8) DMA, para [163].
604 Wolf-Posch (n 591) Article 6(8) DMA, para [163].
605 Wolf-Posch (n 591) Article 6(8) DMA, para [169].

powers under Article 8(2) DMA and adopt an implementing act in which the measures to be taken by the respective gatekeeper in connection are specified in more detail. During the regulatory dialogue, the Commission can take on board the technical expertise and feedback from the market and further tailor the gatekeeper's obligations in such a way that the regulatory purpose of Article 6(8) is achieved.[606]

6.3.4 Data covered by Article 6(8) DMA

With regard to the covered data, Article 6(8) DMA is similarly opaque. The provision only sets out that the gatekeeper has to provide access to aggregated and non-aggregated data necessary for the independent evaluation of the advertising inventory. Generally, this can include data that provides an overview of ad performance trends, audience demographics, and broader campaign success as well as more detailed data such as individual click rates or time spent on an ad. Since such data relates to the business activities of the advertiser or publisher, it qualifies as co-generated data.[607]

Although it does not follow directly from the wording of Article 6(8) DMA, data concerning the ads of other advertisers or publishers does not fall within the scope of the access right.[608] Otherwise the data access right may potentially harm the legitimate business interests of the other advertisers and publishers as it may reveal strategic information that could be exploited by competitors.

Where the data requested by the advertiser or publisher includes personal data, Article 8(1) DMA clarifies that the gatekeeper has to ensure compliance with the GDPR.[609] This may be done in two ways but with very different results for the advertisers and publishers. One method gatekeepers could employ to comply with the GDPR is stripping away personally identifiable information. Once redacted, the data ceases to be personal data and is no longer covered by the GDPR. While redaction ensures compliance, it also diminishes the usefulness of the data provided for advertisers and publishers, who may find non-personal data less valuable for analysis. Alternatively, the obligation of the gatekeepers to ensure compliance with

606 Wolf-Posch (n 591) Article 6(8) DMA, para [174]; König (n 593) 385.

607 See Neil Cohen and Christiane Wendehorst (n 119) Principle 18(1)(a).

608 Oles Andriychuk, 'The Digital Markets Act Proposal: Key Elements & Smart Features' (2022) 43 European Competition Law Review 112, 121.

609 Wolf-Posch (n 591) Article 6(8) DMA, para [172].

the GDPR could and should be interpreted as meaning that they make a serious effort that the affected individuals are informed about and agree to their data being used not just by the gatekeeper but also by advertisers or publishers. This would ensure that the gatekeepers cannot hollow out the access right by relying on their supposed obligations under the GDPR. If the affected individuals do not consent, redaction—as the only available option—is always permissible.

6.4 Portability of data provided by end users or generated through their activities (Article 6(9) DMA)

Article 6(9) DMA lays down a data portability right that is intended to 'complement' the RtDP set out in Article 20 GDPR (Recital 59 DMA). The provision requires gatekeepers to offer end users and third parties authorised by the end user the ability to transfer data, provided by the end user or generated through the end user's activity on the core platform service, in an effective free manner and free of charge. This includes providing complimentary tools to facilitate the smooth transfer of data and ensuring continuous and real-time access to that data. While it seems clear that the European legislator wanted to improve on the deficiencies of Article 20 GDPR and not repeat the same mistakes, there are some uncertainties surrounding the scope of Article 6(9) DMA. This concerns in particular the question of whether the portability right of the DMA refers only to observed data or also to derived and inferred data (6.4.4.2). Different views have also been expressed as to the legal nature of Article 6(9) DMA and its relationship to Article 20 GDPR (6.4.5.1). However, this subsection aims to show that this discussion has no real practical implications.

6.4.1 Objectives

As described above (3.1.1), platform services are particularly prone to creating large data silos due to indirect network effects and economies of scope. In theory, digital platform markets are less likely to be monopolised by one large player than 'traditional' markets with network effects (such as the telecommunications market or software markets), because the users of platforms can multi-home and use the services of different providers at the same time. For example, a person may actively use and maintain profiles on different social media platforms or shop simultaneously on various e-commerce platforms. In contrast, users typically only have one mobile phone contract or only use the office software of a single provider because the costs of multiple subscriptions or packages would be too high. This cost barrier makes multihoming less common in traditional markets, thereby potentially facilitating monopolistic market dynamics.[610]

However, undertakings that want to maintain a competitive advantage in a digital market, may forestall competition by hindering users to automatically move their data, such as files, settings, contacts, or preferences, to another platform. Integrating the data in the new platform manually would require users to invest time and effort, which could discourage them from switching platform provider and instead stay with their current platform provider even if the new platform offers better features or services. This creates a lock-in effect, which strengthens the position of the current platform provider and creates a significant advantage for them in the market. If a large number of users are discouraged from switching due to the lock-in effect, it can lead to the emergence of one dominant platform that monopolises the market. In such a scenario, the incentives for innovation may decrease, since the dominant platform provider faces less pressure to continuously improve and offer new features. A lack of competition also means less consumer choice, as users have limited options to switch to a different provider if the services of the dominant platform do not fully meet their needs or preferences.[611]

Article 6(9) DMA is the European legislator's attempt to respond to this issue. Consequently, the objective of the provision is twofold. On the one hand, fairness between gatekeepers and end users shall be ensured. On the other hand, by granting end users access to and portability of the data they themselves provide, the provision seeks to enable end users to switch providers or use multiple platforms simultaneously and break up the data silos of gatekeepers providing core platform services, which in turn should enhance competition and innovation.[612]

610 Schweitzer and others (n 205) 12.

611 Jacques Crémer and others, 'Fairness and Contestability in the Digital Markets Act' (2021) 3 Digital Regulation Project – Policy Discussion Paper 8; Schmidt (n 175) 476; Schweitzer and others (n 205) 12.

612 Wolf-Posch (n 591) Article 6(9) DMA, para [179].

6.4.2 Rightsholder and addressee

The DMA affords the portability right to so-called 'end users', which are defined as natural and legal persons that use core platform services other than for commercial or professional purposes. Article 6(9) DMA specifies that end users may also authorise third parties to exercise the portability right on their behalf. In line with the objective of Article 6(9) to safeguard and enhance competition in the digital sector by facilitating the switching of providers and the simultaneous use of multiple services, end users may also grant authorisation to competitors of the gatekeeper to access and transfer their data. This situation is also likely to occur in practice. Competitors of gatekeepers that want to attract new users have an inherent interest in facilitating the user's transfer of data from the gatekeeper's platform to their own platform. To achieve this, competitors may for example provide an interface that prompts users to provide a proxy authorisation: By doing so, users grant permission to the new provider to access and utilise the relevant data held by the gatekeeper.[613]

The fact that portability is not necessarily exercised on the initiative of the right holder, but on that of the company benefiting from the right, is one of the central points of criticism of the GDPR's RtDP (see 5.6.3).[614] Larger companies are often in a better position to take advantage of the RtDP under the GDPR than smaller players because they can proactively approach a large number of data subjects and encourage them to exercise the RtDP in favour of the large company. Moreover, these undertakings possess the technical and financial resources necessary to handle and seamlessly integrate different data formats on a larger scale. This can result in situations where the RtDP inadvertently facilitates the transfer of data from smaller companies to larger players, rather than the other way around, thereby reinforcing the data power of the latter.[615]

However, these concerns are not applicable to Article 6(9) DMA because, under the DMA, end users may only exercise their portability right against gatekeepers. This asymmetric nature of the DMA ensures that data is being transferred away from very large data holders to smaller players.

613 Wolf-Posch (n 591) Article 6(9) DMA, para [182].

614 Wendehorst, 'Konsument:innen in der Datenökonomie' (n 230) 225.

615 Datenethikkommission (n 114) 136; see also Thomas and others (n 494) 38.

6.4.3 Modalities

With regard to the modalities, the DMA's approach seems to reflect a deliberate effort by the European legislator to overcome the deficiencies of the GDPR's RtDP in order to make it a more efficient instrument for facilitating competition and empowering end users.[616] Article 6(9) DMA states that the portability shall be provided by the gatekeeper free of charge and in an effective manner, which includes the provision of continuous and real-time access. Thus, Article 6(9) DMA allows end users to combine the services of the gatekeeper with specific services from a third-party provider without entirely migrating all services (partial change of provider).[617]

Recital 59 DMA further clarifies that the gatekeeper should provide the data in a format that is structured, commonly used, and machine-readable and that, to ensure that users can port their data in real-time effectively, high-quality application programming interfaces (APIs) could be used. In contrast, under the GDPR, controllers are obliged to transmit data that has been provided by users directly from one controller to another only to the extent that it is technically feasible without defining any criteria or guidelines to determine such feasibility (see 5.3).

The initial proposal of the Commission was criticised for not laying down any standardisation of the data format or mechanisms to be used by gatekeepers when transferring data. Concerns have been expressed that gatekeepers may choose to comply with the DMA's data-sharing obligation by implementing interfaces and data formats, which are not compatible or interoperable with the systems used by other market participants. Since gatekeepers have strong commercial incentives to share as little data as possible with third parties in order to maintain their dominant position in the relevant market, they may opt to share data through APIs that are intentionally designed to prevent full interoperability with competitors' interfaces. Moreover, without standardisation regarding the data format, data may be transferred to competitors in a format that does not align with the specific needs and systems of the recipients, thereby diminishing the usefulness and value of the received data.[618]

Under the final text, Article 48 DMA entitles the Commission to mandate European standardisation bodies to facilitate the implementation of

616 Wendehorst, 'Konsument:innen in der Datenökonomie' (n 230) 228.
617 Wendehorst, 'Konsument:innen in der Datenökonomie' (n 230) 229.
618 Baschenhof (n 578) 116.

the obligations set out in the DMA by developing appropriate standards. This provision can be seen as a compromise between the arguments for standardisation and the counterarguments that specific standardisation may force market participants into using technologies that may become outdated shortly after they are adopted, increase compliance costs and hamper competition in innovation, as market players have no incentive to develop APIs that are more effective and user-friendly than the ones that follow the standard chosen for the whole market.[619]

Even if no standards have (yet) been adopted, the use of interfaces or data formats that are intentionally designed to prevent full interoperability with competitors' systems would be a breach of the gatekeeper's obligations under the DMA: while the DMA does not impose an obligation on gatekeepers to adapt APIs and data formats to those of the receiving platform,[620] Article 6(9) DMA specifically obliges gatekeepers to provide tools that 'facilitate the *effective* exercise' of the user's data portability right.

Moreover, like all obligations under Article 6 DMA, the gatekeepers' duty to provide effective portability is—although directly applicable—susceptible of being further specified. In principle, it is up to the gatekeeper to identify the appropriate measures to demonstrate compliance with the obligations under Article 6 DMA. However, Article 8(2) DMA entitles the Commission to further specify the obligations of a specific gatekeeper by way of an implementing act.[621] Hence, if the Commission finds that a gatekeeper is using APIs or data formats that impede data portability, it may prescribe the compliance with certain standards as a measure to ensure the gatekeeper effectively fulfils the obligation set out in Article 6(9) DMA.

6.4.4 Data covered by Article 6(9) DMA

Given the ongoing discussions surrounding the scope of data covered by Article 20 GDPR (see 5.1.4), it is remarkable that the DMA offers limited clarification as to the data to which the portability right applies. Article 6(9)

619 See also the suggestion by Baschenhof (n 578) 116'[T]his risk could arguably be addressed by the inclusion of a provision that would allow the Commission or a separate designated body to regularly revise the standardized formats and mechanisms to reflect the state of the art at a particular point in time.'; see also Michal Gal and Daniel Rubinfeld, 'Data Standardization' (2019) 94 New York University Law Review 737, 753.

620 Wolf-Posch (n 591) Article 6(9) DMA, para [192].

621 Herbers (n 578) 258; Akman (n 22) 97.

DMA only stipulates that end users may port 'data provided by the end user or generated through the activity of the end user in the context of the use of the relevant core platform service'.

6.4.4.1 Personal and non-personal data

At least with regard to one aspect the DMA's portability right provides for more legal clarity in practice. Unlike the GDPR, the DMA does not confine the scope of its portability right to personal data but simply refers to 'data', which is defined as 'any digital representation of acts, facts or information and any compilation of such acts, facts or information, including in the form of sound, visual or audiovisual recording' (Article 2(24) DMA).[622] Considering the broad notion of personal data (see 2.5.1.1), including non-personal data may not significantly expand the actual scope of the right to data portability under the DMA compared to the GDPR. However, this extension has the advantage that it is no longer necessary to determine whether certain data falls into the category of personal or non-personal data, which can be a very difficult task in practice (see 2.5.1).

6.4.4.2 Observed, derived and inferred data

Another noticeable difference between the portability right under the DMA and the GDPR is that Article 6(9) applies to data that is either 'provided by the end user' or 'generated through the activity of the end user in the context of the use of the relevant core platform service'. With regard to Article 20 GDPR there is an ongoing discussion whether 'provided by the data subject' covers only data that has been actively transmitted to the controller by the data subject, or also data that has been generated by observing actions or activities of an individual. This broader interpretation would include data, such as the online shopping history of end users as well as heart rate and sleeping rhythm measured by a smart watch (see above 5.1.4). Since Article 6(9) DMA stipulates that the portability right should also apply to 'data generated through the activity of the end user in the

622 Konstantina Bania, 'Fitting the Digital Markets Act in the Existing Legal Framework: The Myth of the "without Prejudice" Clause' (2023) 19 European Competition Journal 116, 132; Wolf-Posch (n 591) Article 6(9) DMA, para [184].

context of the use of the relevant core platform service', it is clear that the DMA also covers observed data.[623]

However, neither the blackletter nor the Recitals offer any further clarifications, which gave rise to a controversy as to whether Article 6(9) DMA also applies to inferred and derived data, i.e. data generated through the process of inference or contextualisation using provided and observed data.[624] An example of such data would be a user profile created by analysing the activities performed by the user on a particular platform. Already now, this discussion regarding the exact scope of Article 6(9) DMA seems to resemble the one under the GDPR. At first glance, the phrase 'generated through the activity of the end user' would suggest that it does not cover inferred and derived data because they are generated by the gatekeeper and not the end user. However, the European legislator did not use the wording 'generated *by* the activity of the end user' but 'generated *through* the activity of the end user'. This could be interpreted as encompassing data generated *on the basis* of the end user's data, which would include inferred and derived data.

An expansive reading of Article 6(9) DMA can be further supported by a teleological argument very similar to the one applied to Article 20 GDPR (see 5.1.4). End users will usually not have difficulties replicating provided data and—although to a lesser extent—observed data. Hence, a portability right that only allows end users to port 'their' data has a rather limited impact on achieving the DMA's goal of strengthening end users' control over their data and ensuring the competitiveness of the platform market. Recital 59 DMA explicitly states that the portability right should ensure 'that gatekeepers do not undermine the contestability of core platform services, or the innovation potential of the dynamic digital sector'. This speaks in favour of applying the portability right also to inferred and derived data, instead of allowing end users only to transfer data that they are able to replicate anyway.[625] Moreover, including derived and observed data limits the gatekeeper's possibilities to circumvent their obligations under Article

623 Wolf-Posch (n 591) Article 6(9) DMA, para [185]; Baschenhof (n 578) 115.

624 In favour of a narrow interpretation Wolf-Posch (n 591) Article 6(9) DMA, [185]; Konstantina Bania (n 622) 133; arguing for a broader notion Baschenhof (n 578) 115; Björn Lundqvist, 'An Access and Transfer Right to Data—from a Competition Law Perspective' [2022] Journal of Antitrust Enforcement 1, 6.

625 Baschenhof (n 578) 115; see also Konstantina Bania (n 622) 132.

6(9) DMA by deleting the provided and observed data and only keeping the slightly refined or derived data of the initial datasets.[626]

An argument that could be made against obliging gatekeepers to make inferred and derived data portable is that it could reduce their incentive to innovate because it allows others to benefit from their investments in time and technology without bearing the same costs. However, since the DMA's right to portability can be exercised only against gatekeepers, it only applies to markets that are subject to limited competition because they are dominated by one successful company. Barring effective competition, gatekeepers may have limited incentives to innovate. Conversely, a broad portability right would ensure that competitors are able to get access to data, without which they may not effectively contest digital markets in which gatekeepers are present. New competitors can leverage the data held by gatekeepers to develop innovative products and services, fostering greater competition and driving further innovation in the market.[627] Moreover, the incumbents are disadvantaged by Article 6(9) DMA only as long as they hold down a gatekeeper position. According to Article 4(1) DMA, gatekeepers may request a review of their gatekeeper status, if their position has substantially changed due to external circumstances, such as increased competition and market dynamics.[628]

It should also be noted that interpreting the phrase 'provided by or generated through the activity of the end user' as exclusively referring to observed data would be difficult to reconcile with the predominant understanding that Article 20 GDPR also covers observed data even though the latter provision only refers to 'data provided by'. Evidently, the European legislator consciously opted for broader language in the DMA as compared to Article 20 GDPR.[629] According to European legal methodology, the systematic interpretation of secondary legislation is not limited to the individual legislative act but extends to the EU's legal system as a whole, which includes other secondary legislation.[630] Therefore, when interpreting

626 See Wendehorst, 'Konsument:innen in der Datenökonomie' (n 230) 171.

627 Konstantina Bania (n 622) 132; Damien Geradin, Konstantina Bania and Theano Karanikioti, 'The Interplay between the Digital Markets Act and the General Data Protection Regulation' [2022] SSRN Electronic Journal 5 <https://www.ssrn.com/abstract=4203907> accessed 22 June 2023.

628 Sophie Gappa and Thorsten Käseberg, in Rupprecht Podszun (ed), *Digital Markets Act: Gesetz über digitale Märkte* (Nomos 2023) Article 4 DMA, para [4].

629 Article 20 GDPR only refers to 'personal data [...], which [the data subject] has provided to a controller' while Article 6(9) DMA uses the phrase

630 Riesenhuber (n 29) 261.

the DMA, it is necessary to consider its relationship with other relevant laws, such as the GDPR. The fact that the phrase 'provided by or' was added to the initial text of the DMA by the European Parliament during the Trilogue[631] seems to indicate a deliberate decision by the European legislator to emphasise that the scope of the DMA's portability goes beyond the ambit of the GDPR's RtDP. While this analysis does not directly resolve the question of whether the DMA encompasses only observed data or also encompasses derived and inferred data, it does imply that the scopes of the portability rights under the GDPR and the DMA differ and cannot be identical due to their divergent wording. Consequently, if one were to conclude that Article 6(9) DMA only covers provided and observed data, this would imply that Article 20 GDPR should be interpreted as being limited to data actively provided by the data subject. Otherwise, Articles 6(9) DMA and 20 GDPR would have the same scope despite the different wording of the two provisions.

A counterargument to the broad interpretation of including all inferred and derived data within the scope of Article 6(9) DMA is that it could impose an undue burden on gatekeepers, exceeding what is necessary to achieve the objectives of the DMA. However, this risk is mitigated by Article 8 DMA, which entitles the Commission to further specify the obligations outlined in Article 6 DMA if necessary. Hence, the Commission can limit the scope of the covered data if the Commission deems the inclusion of all data held by the gatekeeper, which was in some way deduced from the end users' activities or provided data, to be overly extensive. This flexibility to attain suitable outcomes in individual cases and to ensure that the scope of the covered data enables effective portability without overburdening the gatekeeper[632] can only be achieved with a broad interpretation of the scope of Article 6(9) DMA. This is because the Commission may narrow the scope by way of a delegated act but cannot go beyond what the DMA provides. Hence, if Article 6(9) DMA were to be understood as covering only provided and observed data, the Commission could not expand the scope based on Article 8 DMA.

631 Amendments adopted by the European Parliament on 15 December 2021 on the proposal for a regulation of the European Parliament and of the Council on contestable and fair markets in the digital sector (Digital Markets Act) (COM(2020)0842 – C9- 0419/2020 – 2020/0374(COD) TA/2021/0499, Amendment 130.

632 Wendehorst, 'Konsument:innen in der Datenökonomie' (n 230) 229.

6.4.5 Relationship to Article 20 GDPR

Article 6(9) DMA conveys the clear intention of the European legislator to introduce a data right that resembles Article 20 GDPR's RtDP (5) but with several improvements to make it a more efficient tool to facilitate competition and empower the rightsholders by enabling them to multi-home and switch provider. Recital 59 DMA even contains an explicit reference to Article 20 GDPR, stating that '[f]or the avoidance of doubt, the obligation on the gatekeeper to ensure effective portability of data under this Regulation complements the right to data portability under the Regulation (EU) 2016/679'.

6.4.5.1 A new data right

However, there is some doubt as to the legal nature of Article 6(9) DMA and its relationship to Article 20 GDPR. It has been argued that the DMA does not create a new data right but merely supplements the existing data portability right under the GDPR.[633] The wording of the Commission's original DMA proposal[634] did indeed strongly imply such an interpretation.[635] Article 6(1)(h) of the DMA proposal laid out that gatekeepers shall 'provide effective portability of data generated through the activity of a business user or end user and shall, in particular, provide tools for end users to facilitate the exercise of data portability, in line with Regulation EU 2016/679'. While the final text of the DMA lacks such an explicit reference in the binding provisions, the statement in Recital 59 that Article 6(9) DMA

633 Baschenhof (n 578) 114; less explicit Bostoen (n 22); see also Christina Etteldorf, 'DMA – Digital Markets Act or Data Markets Act?' (2022) 8 European Data Protection Law Review 255, 258 who describes the problem but remains undecided.

634 COM(2020) 842 final of 15 December 2020; regarding the Commissions's initial intentions see also European Commission, 'Data protection as a pillar of citizens' empowerment and the EU's approach to the digital transition – two years of application of the General Data Protection Regulation' COM(2020) 264 final, 8 in which the Commission states that the right to data portability has not yet reached its full potential, although individuals are increasingly aware of their rights under GDPR. The Communication emphasises the Commission's commitment to unlock the full potential of the data portability right, highlighting it as one of its key priorities for the preparation of the DMA proposal.

635 Baschenhof (n 578) 113.

'*complements*' the GDPR's RtDP might also suggest that the DMA does not create a separate legal basis.[636]

Drawing from a textual and systemic analysis of the DMA, more persuasive arguments can be made in favour of Article 6(9) DMA constituting a distinct data right rather than merely expanding the scope of the GDPR.[637] Firstly, a reference to Article 20 GDPR is made only in the Recitals but not directly in Article 6(9) DMA. It can be assumed that an extension of Article 20 GDPR would be explicitly laid down in the legislative text of the Regulation and not only in the nonbinding Recitals. Moreover, the reference to Article 20 GDPR was not included in the Recitals of the initial proposal,[638] which indicates that the Commission's intention was not to expand Article 20 GDPR but to introduce a new portability right. This argument can be reinforced by comparing the language used in Article 6(9) DMA with that of other data rights laid down in the DMA. Due to the resemblance in wording and structure between Article 6(9) DMA and Articles 6(8) and 6(11) DMA, which undisputedly afford new data rights, it can be assumed that Article 6(9) DMA does also introduce an additional ground for a data portability right.

In light of the foregoing, it can be concluded that the Recital 59 DMA simply clarifies that Article 6(9) DMA does not replace Article 20 GDPR but that the end user may choose which right they want to exercise. In its Guidelines on the RtDP, the Article 29 WP clarified that the GDPR's data portability provisions do not apply if it is clear from the data subject's request that they do not wish to exert their portability right under the GDPR, but rather, to invoke their rights under sectorial legislation.[639] Hence, in practice, it needs to be determined whether a person wants to exercise their portability right under the DMA or GDPR.[640] However, when a user of core platform services submits a request to transfer their data from a gatekeeper, it can be reasonably inferred that their intention is to exercise their right under Article 6(9) DMA. This is because the DMA's portability right covers not only personal data but all relevant data (see 6.4.4) and enables continuous and real-time transfers (see 6.4.3), making it

636 See Konstantina Bania (n 622) 131 who, however, concludes that Article 6(9) DMA is not a mere extension of Article 20 GDPR.

637 Konstantina Bania (n 622) 131; Wendehorst, 'Konsument:innen in der Datenökonomie' (n 230) 228; Wolf-Posch (n 591) Article 6(9) DMA, para [197].

638 COM(2020) 842 of 15 December 2020.

639 Article 29 Working Party, 'Guidelines on the Right to Data Portability' (n 479) 7.

640 Konstantina Bania (n 622) 135; see also Etteldorf (n 633) 258.

a more effective mechanism for switching service providers. Only in cases where the end user explicitly invokes Article 20 GDPR, or where this can be clearly deduced from the surrounding circumstances, the portability right under the GDPR should take precedence over Article 6(9) DMA.[641]

6.4.5.2 Practical implications?

At least at first glance, it may seem that the question of whether Article 6(9) DMA merely expands Article 20 GDPR or constitutes a new data right that derogates Article 20 GDPR is not only a matter of legal theory but also carries practical implications. This is because the GDPR contains provisions that limit the controller's obligation to a certain extent, while the DMA does not lay down any corresponding rules. Firstly, Article 12(5) GDPR allows controllers to either refuse or charge a fee if a portability request is excessive (5.6.1). Secondly, Article 20(4) GDPR stipulates that exercising the RtDP shall not adversely affect the rights and freedoms of others. Such a conflict between the RtDP and the rights and freedoms of others may, primarily, arise where the requested personal data relates not only to the requesting person but also to other data subjects (see 5.1.5).[642] If it is assumed that Article 6(9) DMA does not afford a separate and distinct data right to end users but only expands Article 20 GDPR, these GDPR provisions would also apply directly to portability requests that fall within the scope of the DMA.

In contrast, if Article 20 GDPR and Article 6(9) DMA are treated as distinct portability rights, Articles 12(5) and 20(4) GDPR would not be directly applicable to portability requests under the DMA. However, since these two rights are closely related, the GDPR provisions could be applied by way of analogy, but this would require demonstrating that there is a lacuna in the DMA.[643] For example, it could be argued that Article 6(9) of the DMA lacks a specific provision on how to deal with excessive portability requests and that this gap could be filled by Article 12(5) GDPR. After all, gatekeepers and controllers are in very similar positions, and the limitation

641 *Cf.* Steinrötter (n 515) 222 who applies the same argument to the relationship between Article 4 Data Act and Article 20 GDPR.

642 Strubel (n 499) 360.

643 ECJ, C-6/78, Union française de Céréales, EU:C:1978:154, para 4; Katja Langenbucher, 'Argument by Analogy in European Law' (1998) 57 The Cambridge Law Journal 481, 511.

on the exercise of the portability right serves the legitimate interests of preventing the misuse of the right and safeguarding the interests of the addressee. However, an application of the GDPR by analogy seems to be rather unlikely not only because it is difficult to prove a lacuna but also because the CJEU is quite reserved when it comes to analogies.[644]

A similar result as applying Articles 12(5) and 20(4) GDPR by analogy could be achieved if Article 6(9) DMA is interpreted consistently with fundamental rights and the general principles common to the laws of all Member States.[645] Afterall, Article 12(5) GDPR does nothing more than restricting the excessive use of the portability right in order to protect the legitimate interests of the data controller. However, it follows already from EU primary law that a right shall not be exercised in a way that unduly interferes with the fundamental rights of others.[646] On several occasions the CJEU has recognised this so-called abuse of rights doctrine in horizontal relations.[647] Accordingly, the right to an effective remedy under Article 47 of the Charter should not be used to deny or unnecessarily limit the opposing rights and freedoms of other parties.[648] Excessive portability requests based on Article 6(9) DMA could be considered to unnecessarily encroach the gatekeeper's fundamental right to conduct business and contractual

644 See Johannes Köndgen, in Karl Riesenhuber (ed), *European Legal Methodology* (2nd edn, Intersentia 2021) 143.

645 See Stefan Leible and Ronny Domröse, in Karl Riesenhuber (ed), *European Legal Methodology* (2nd edn, Intersentia 2021) 187.

646 A prohibition on the abuse of rights is laid down in Article 54 of the CFR. But even before the CFR was declared in 2000, the ECJ has repeatedly held, particularly in the context of fundamental freedoms, that 'the Community law cannot be relied on for abusive or fraudulent ends'. See ECJ, C-367/96, *Kefalas*, EU:C:1998:222, para 20 with further references to case law. On the discussion whether a general EU-specific principle of abuse of rights exists, see Norbert Reich (ed), 'An Emerging Principle of Good Faith and of a Prohibition of Abuse of Rights?', *General Principles of EU Civil Law* (Intersentia 2013) 209.

647 E.g. ECJ, C-110/99, *Emsland-Stärke*, EU:C:2000:695, paras 51 ff. and ECJ, C-321/05, *Kofoed*, EU:C:2007:408, para 38; in ECJ, C-489/07, *Messner*, EU:C:2009:502, the prohibition of abuse of rights was derived from the principle of good faith; see Reich (n 646) 210; Annekatrien Lenaerts, 'The General Principle of the Prohibition of Abuse of Rights: A Critical Position on Its Role in a Codified European Contract Law' [2010] European Review of Private Law 1121, 1138; Stefan Grundmann, 'The General Clause or Standard in EC Contract Law Directives – A Survey on Some Important Legal Measures and Aspects in EC Law' in Stefan Grundmann and Denis Mazeaud (eds), *General clauses and standards in European contract law: comparative law, EC law and contract law codification* (Kluwer 2006) 147.

648 Reich (n 646) 209.

freedom (Article 16 CFR). Thus, in light of the abuse of rights doctrine, Article 6(9) DMA must be interpreted in such a way that excessive requests are not permitted or only if the costs incurred are reimbursed.[649] Similarly, Article 20(4) GDPR merely sets out that the interests of the rights holder need to be balanced against the fundamental rights of others. However, since secondary law must be interpreted in conformity with higher-ranking primary law, including the CFR, the GDPR's RtDP and Article 6(9) DMA need to be interpreted as not permitting an unjustifiable encroachment of the fundamental rights of others anyway. Hence, Article 20(4) GDPR could be viewed as a mere reiteration of this general rule of interpretation that does not need to be applied by way of analogy but is inherent also in Article 6(9) DMA and can be inferred by interpretative means.

Based on the above considerations it can be concluded that the limitations set out by Articles 12(5) and 20(4) GDPR also apply to the portability right under Article 6(9) DMA, irrespective of whether it is considered to be a sperate data right or an extension of Article 20 GDPR. Hence, the discussion about the legal nature of Article 6(9) DMA and its relationship to the GDPR, whilst interesting from a legal theory perspective, has no real practical implications.

6.5 Access to data generated by the products and services of business users (Article 6(10) DMA)

Business users of core platform services provided by gatekeepers often encounter a situation similar to that of regular end users. They actively contribute to the generation of vast amounts of data through their interactions with these services. However, their access to this data is severely limited due to the gatekeeper's factual control over it. As a result of the gatekeeper's market power, business users typically lack the leverage to negotiate specific clauses regarding access to co-generated data in their contracts, but rather are confronted with standard contractual clauses drafted by the gatekeeper on a 'take it or leave it' basis.

By affording a right resembling Article 6(9) DMA to business users, the DMA acknowledges that business users face similar challenges in accessing co-generated data as end users. According to Article 6(10) DMA, the gatekeeper needs to provide business users upon their request 'free of

649 On the interpretation of secondary union law in conformity with higher ranking primary law, see Leible and Domröse (n 645) 187 with references to CJEU case law.

charge, effective, high-quality, continuous and real-time access to, and use of, aggregated and non-aggregated data, including personal data, that is provided for or generated in the context of the use of the relevant core platform services or services provided together with, or in support of, the relevant core platform services by those business users and the end users engaging with the products or services provided by those business users.'

6.5.1 Objectives

The portability right afforded by Article 6(10) DMA, needs to be seen in light of the concerns about possible data-related anti-competitive behaviour by large platform providers vis-à-vis businesses that rely on the platform services. Once a platform has reached a critical mass of users on both sides of the market, businesses often simply cannot afford not to use the services even if it means giving up control over valuable data and supplying it to the platform provider. Vertically integrated platforms, where gatekeepers do not only act as platform providers and intermediaries between business and end users but also as business users on their own platform in direct competition with other business users, are particularly prone to potentially abusive behaviour (see 3.1.1.1).

As intermediaries, gatekeepers have two ways of using their data power to their benefit and to the detriment of business users. On vertically integrated platforms, gatekeepers can collect and use the data of their business users (such as data on customers or products/services) to set up or intensify their own activities on the platform and compete with other business users (the most prominent example is the Amazon Marketplace constellation,[650] see 3.1.1.1). To address this problem, the DMA now prohibits gatekeepers already ex-ante from using any data that is generated or provided by business users and is not publicly available, including data generated or provided by the customers of the business users, in competition with those business users (Article 6(2) DMA). Gatekeepers can also harm business users by limiting their access to data generated by the business users and their customers. This restriction makes it challenging for business users to

650 Bundeskartellamt, 'Bundeskartellamt Initiates Abuse Proceeding against Amazon' <https://www.bundeskartellamt.de/SharedDocs/Meldung/EN/Pressemitteilungen/2018/29_11_2018_Verfahrenseinleitung_Amazon.html?nn=3591568> accessed 23 August 2023; Lundqvist, 'An Access and Transfer Right to Data—from a Competition Law Perspective' (n 624) 3.

effectively utilise the data for their own purposes and can impede their ability to switch to alternative platforms.[651]

Article 6(10) DMA aims to address the latter issue. By enhancing the business user's control over their data, the provision intends to facilitate provider switching and multi-homing, which in turn is supposed to protect and promote innovation in the digital sector. Enhancing the contestability of the platform market by creating an environment where new or non-dominant platform service providers can enter or expand within the market not only benefits the competitors of gatekeepers but also business users, as they gain more options and potentially better services as a result of increased competition. As in Article 6(9) DMA, the justification for interfering with the interests of gatekeepers resides not only in their market dominance but also in the idea that business users should have access to the data they have helped to generate. The business shall have an appropriate share in the economic value of data generated in the course of their activities.[652]

6.5.2 Rightsholder

The rightsholders and direct beneficiaries of the access right under Article 6(10) DMA are 'business users' of core platform services. These are defined in 2(21) DMA as 'natural or legal person acting in a commercial or professional capacity using core platform services for the purpose of or in the course of providing goods or services to end users.' It has been suggested that regarding the assessment whether a user acts in the course of their commercial or professional capacity recourse could be taken to the CJEU's case law on the definition of trader in EU consumer law.[653] Several Directives, such as the Consumer Rights Directive[654] or the Digital

651 Wolf-Posch (n 591) Article 6(10) DMA, para [205]; Wolfgang Kerber, 'Datenrechtliche Aspekte des Digital Markets Act – Datenwirtschaftsrecht I: Vorschlag einer Ex-ante-Regulierung von Gatekeeper-Plattformen' [2021] ZD 544, 546.

652 Wolf-Posch (n 591) Article 6(10) DMA, para [205]; Lundqvist, 'An Access and Transfer Right to Data—from a Competition Law Perspective' (n 624) 5.

653 Philipp Bongartz and Alexander Kirk, in Rupprecht Podszun (ed), *Digital Markets Act: Gesetz über digitale Märkte* (Nomos 2023) Article 2 DMA, para [103].

654 Article 2(2) Directive 2011/83/EU of the European Parliament and of the Council of 25 October 2011 on consumer rights, amending Council Directive 93/13/EEC and Directive 1999/44/EC of the European Parliament and of the Council and repealing Council Directive 85/577/EEC and Directive 97/7/EC of the European Parliament and of the Council, OJ L 2011/304, 64.

Contract Directive,[655] define trader as natural or legal person, who is acting for purposes relating to that person's trade, business, craft, or profession.[656]

According to some commentators, inspiration could be drawn from the non-exhaustive, non-exclusive criteria developed by the CJEU[657] in order to determine whether a person acts in a commercial or professional capacity qualifies as a 'trader'.[658] Since these criteria have been formulated with a classic sales relationship between retailer and consumer in mind, many of them cannot be applied directly. For example, criteria, such as 'whether the sale on the online platform was carried out in an organised manner' or 'whether the seller had technical information and expertise relating to the products which she offered for sale which the consumer did not necessarily have'[659] do not fit in the context of the DMA, because business users may not only sell products via a gatekeeper's platform but may also use it for advertising or other commercial purposes. However, if the criteria of the CJEU are abstracted and adapted, they can very well be used for determining whether a person qualifies as business user. Recourse could be taken, inter alia, to the following: whether a person pursues an activity on a regular basis and in an organised manner, for profit-making purposes, using a legal form enabling them to engage in the performance of commercial transactions, that is connected to other economic activates, or whether the person is subject to VAT.[660]

Just like end users, business users may authorise third parties that can exercise the right under Article 6(10) DMA on their behalf. This could include persons that act as processors of the relevant data for the business user (see Recital 60 DMA) or data intermediaries employed by the business user. Other providers of the platform services that compete with the gatekeeper could also be authorised to exercise the data right. The providers receiving the data are the indirect beneficiaries of the data right; they may receive highly valuable datasets but are dependent on the business user's willingness to exercise their right under Article 6(10) DMA (see 6.4.2).[661]

655 Article 2(5) Directive (EU) 2019/770 of the European Parliament and of the Council of 20 May 2019 on certain aspects concerning contracts for the supply of digital content and digital services, OJ L 2019/136, 1.

656 Bongartz and Kirk (n 653) Article 2 DMA, para [103].

657 ECJ, C-105/17, *Kamenova*, EU:C:2018:808, para 38.

658 Bongartz and Kirk (n 653) Article 2 DMA, para [103].

659 ECJ, C-105/17, *Kamenova*, EU:C:2018:808, para 38.

660 Bongartz and Kirk (n 653) Article 2 DMA, para [103].

661 Wolf-Posch (n 591) Article 6(10) DMA, para [210].

6.5.3 Modalities

Article 6(10) DMA—like Article 6(9) DMA—stipulates that the gatekeeper's access to the relevant data provided to business users or authorised third parties shall be 'free of charge, effective, high-quality, continuous and real-time'. Recital 60 DMA further specifies that gatekeepers should also ensure continuous and real-time access to the requested data by means of appropriate technical measures and mentions high-quality application programming interfaces or integrated tools for small-volume business users as examples of such measures. The DMA itself does not put forward any standardisation measures regarding the APIs or other interfaces. However, Article 48 DMA entitles the Commission to mandate European standardisation bodies to develop appropriate standards in order to facilitate the implementation of Article 6(10) DMA.[662]

Moreover, the terms 'effective and high-quality' are rather broad and leave much room for interpretation. In principle, it is the responsibility of the gatekeeper to evaluate whether their access modalities comply with the obligations set forth by Article 6(10) DMA. Should the legal uncertainty surrounding the access modalities, however, affect the effectiveness of the provision, the Commission can further specify the obligations of a specific gatekeeper by way of an implementing act (Article 8(2) DMA).[663] The possibility to offer early guidance to uncertainties is one of the advantages of the DMA's data rights in comparison to those of other pieces of legislation, as it allows both rightsholders and addressees to better adapt to the regulatory framework and develop according plans and strategies.[664] In contrast, although there are many uncertainties regarding the modalities of Article 20 GDPR (such as the 'technical feasibility', see 5.3), the CJEU has not had the opportunity to rule on any of these questions even years after the GDPR entered into force.

Since access must be provided 'free of charge', gatekeepers cannot demand compensation for costs directly linked to fulfilling their obligation under the DMA. This includes the investment that the gatekeeper has put into generating the requested data. Only if business users request additional measures that are not required by Article 6(10) DMA, the gatekeepers can

662 Wolf-Posch (n 591) Article 6(10) DMA, para [242].

663 Herbers (n 578) 258; Akman (n 22) 97.

664 See Wolf-Posch (n 591) Article 6(10) DMA, para [241] who believes that Article 8(2) DMA will play an important role in the implementation of the DMA's data rights.

charge a fee for the additional effort. For example, the DMA obliges the gatekeeper to only offer the requested data in a common format suitable for export. If the business wants to have the data transferred to a competing platform that uses a format that is not used by the gatekeeper and not customary in the sector, the gatekeeper can charge the business user for converting the data into that format.[665] Like Article 6(9) DMA and in contrast to the GDPR, Article 6(10) DMA does not explicitly allow gatekeepers to either refuse access requests or charge a fee if they are manifestly unfounded or excessive. However, as outlined above (6.4.5.2), it seems appropriate to allow gatekeepers to charge a reasonable fee to cover the administrative costs associated with processing excessive requests (or deny the request altogether).[666] Such a limitation of the business user's right could either be based on an analogous application of Article 12(4) GDPR, or on an interpretation of Article 6(10) DMA in line with fundamental rights and the general principles common to the laws of all Member States (see 6.4.5.2).

6.5.4 Data covered by Article 6(10) DMA

Article 6(10) DMA obliges gatekeepers to provide access to 'aggregated and non-aggregated data, including personal data, that is provided for or generated in the context of the use of the relevant core platform services or services provided together with, or in support of, the relevant core platform services by those business users and the end users engaging with the products or services provided by those business users.' The provision is aimed at enabling the business user to access the data generated by their own commercial activity.[667] This is based on the idea that the business user had a significant share in the generation of such data and should thus also be entitled to use it for its own purposes.[668] Article 6(10) DMA, however, does not only afford business users the right to access data that was generated solely by their own interactions with a gatekeeper's core platform service but also to access the data generated by end users engaging with the business user on the gatekeeper's platform. This data is generated not only by joint contributions from the business user and the gatekeeper

665 Wolf-Posch (n 591) Article 6(10) DMA, para [243].
666 See also Wolf-Posch (n 591) Article 6(10) DMA, para [226].
667 Wolf-Posch (n 591) Article 6(10) DMA, para [215].
668 See Neil Cohen and Christiane Wendehorst (n 119) Principle 18.

but also by those of the end users. In order to protect the interest of the end user, the DMA allows business users to access the personal data of end users only if the end users opt in to such sharing by giving consent (see 6.5.4.2).

6.5.4.1 Data provided or generated by the business user

For data to be covered by Article 6(10) DMA, there must be a connection between the gatekeeper's core platform service or supporting services that are inextricably linked to the core platform service[669] and the generation or provision of the data. The DMA does not give any indications as to what such supporting services may be, but the Commission's proposal mentions—albeit in a different context—'ancillary services' and lists payment services, fulfilment, identification, and advertising services as examples.[670] For example, if the business user of an online marketplace, which has core platform service status, uses the gatekeeper's payment and delivery services to process their customers' payments and deliver the products, the data generated in the context of those services also falls under Article 6(10) DMA even if the latter two services are not core platform services.

Different opinions have been expressed on the question of whether Article 6(10) DMA applies only to provided and observed data or also to data derived from such data.[671] The debate resembles the one on the material scope of Article 6(9) DMA (6.4.4.2). Since the wording of the two provisions is almost identical and they both have the objective of enabling users to switch providers or use different platform services simultaneously, similar arguments as for Article 6(9) DMA can also be made with regard to Article 6(10) DMA. In line with the portability right of end users, Article 6(10) DMA should be interpreted as also applying to derived and inferred data.

Regarding the argument that such a broad interpretation may place an undue burden on gatekeepers and could potentially disincentivise the

669 Recital 60 DMA.

670 Recital 14 COM(2020) 842 final of 15 December 2020.

671 Supporting a narrow interpretation Wolf-Posch (n 591) Article 6(10) DMA, para [216]; arguing that inferred data should also be made accessible Lundqvist, 'An Access and Transfer Right to Data—from a Competition Law Perspective' (n 624) 6; see also Polley and Konrad (n 582) 207 who, however, criticise the broad scope.

generation of data,[672] it should be pointed out that business users get access only to inferred data that relates to their own commercial activity. Hence, data on user behaviour aggregated across several users (e.g. sales, search, click and view data on certain products by all end users of the platform), which is particularly valuable for business users, is not covered by the access right.[673] Consequently, competitors of the gatekeeper cannot freeride on the investments the gatekeeper has made to draw inferences from the activities of different users on their platform.

6.5.4.2 Personal data of end users

Article 6(10) DMA gives business users the right to access data which were generated not only in the context of their own interaction with a gatekeeper's platform but also to the data generated by end users who engage with the products or services provided by business users on the gatekeeper's platform. Since this data is generated not only by joint contributions from the business user and the gatekeeper but also by those of the end users, it needs to be ensured that the interests of the latter are adequately safeguarded. The DMA aims to achieve this by (i) including only personal data that is directly connected with the use effectuated by the end users in respect of the products or services offered by the business user through the relevant core platform service (ii) and by requiring the end users' consent to the sharing of their personal data.[674]

While the phrase 'use of the business user's products and service' might suggest specific actions, such as making a purchase, it has been pointed out that the requirement should not be interpreted too narrowly. In particular, Article 6(10) DMA should not be understood as requiring that the data is generated or provided in connection with completed transactions. Rather, any connection to the use of the products and services offered by the respective business user via the core platform service should suffice. This means that Article 6(10) DMA should cover data on end user interactions in general, such as clicks on a business user's offer, even if the respective end users did not complete a transaction with the business user. The broad interpretation aligns with the objectives of Article 6(10)

672 Polley and Konrad (n 582) 203.

673 See Wolf-Posch (n 591) Article 6(10) DMA, para [215] who, however, argues that derived and inferred data are not covered by the data right.

674 Baschenhof (n 578) 117; Etteldorf (n 633) 259.

DMA. Since click-and-view data results from the interactions between the business user and their customers, business users have a legitimate interest in accessing this data irrespective of whether the customer has made an actual purchase. This data can be extremely valuable for business users, as it provides insights into the interests and preferences of end-users and enables business users to fine-tune their competitive strategies and improve their offerings. Allowing access to this data contributes to equitable business relationships and prevents gatekeepers from exerting undue control over valuable information. Moreover, the ability of business users to switch to the platform services of a provider competing with the gatekeeper or to engage in multi-homing hinges on their capacity to access and potentially transfer this data, because otherwise, business users would need to choose between switching to another platform and losing access to their customer data.[675]

Even under this broader understanding of Article 6(10) DMA, the business user's right does not extend to personal data that pertains to transactions between end users and other business users who use the same core platform service. For example, business users may access data on which of their products end users have viewed and for how long, but do not have the right to access data on whether and which product the end user purchased from another business user on the platform. Regarding the latter type of data, the required direct connection between the data and the business user's activities on the core platform service is missing. Rather, this transaction data is closely tied to the activities of other business users using the same core platform service. Consequently, the data falls within the scope of the access right that these other business users have against the gatekeeper.[676]

Ambiguities exist regarding the requirement that end users need to opt in to the sharing of their personal data by giving their consent. It is clear that the intention is to protect the legitimate interests of the end users, who are the subject of the accessed data. After all, the interest of business users to switch to a different provider and the public interest of ensuring the contestability of platform markets may not simply overrule the interest of the individual end users in protecting their personal data. However, it is uncertain whether Article 6(10) DMA allows business users to access the personal data of end users without consent if the processing of the request-

675 Wolf-Posch (n 591) Article 6(10) DMA, para [219].

676 Wolf-Posch (n 591) Article 6(10) DMA, para [220].

ed data would be lawful under another legal basis of the GDPR, such as the need to access the data for the performance of contractual obligations. According to the wording of Article 6(10) DMA that the end users need to 'opt in to such sharing by giving their consent' it would seem that the lawfulness on other grounds of the GDPR is not sufficient and that consent is always required. However, Recital 60 states gatekeepers should 'enable business users to obtain consent of their end users for such data access and retrieval, *where such consent is required* under Regulation (EU) 2016/679 [GDPR] and Directive 2002/58/EC [e-Privacy Directive][emphasis added].' The phrase 'where such consent is required' could be understood as suggesting that there are cases where the data may be accessed but consent is not required because another legal ground of the GDPR renders the processing lawful.[677] What seems more plausible, however, is that this wording was used because under the e-Privacy Directive consent may be necessary also for the processing of non-personal data[678] and the European legislator simply wanted to refer to all cases where consent is required.

Moreover, two different arguments can be brought forward as to why other legal grounds of the GDPR, and in particular the need to access data for the performance of contractual obligations (Article 6(1)(b) GDPR), are not sufficient to meet the requirements of Article 6(10) DMA. First, interpreting Article 6(10) DMA as allowing business users to access the data of end users without their consent, in case other legal grounds of the GDPR are present, would run counter to the explicit wording of the DMA and would therefore require strong teleological arguments. However, the requirement that end-users need to consent to the sharing of their data seems to be coherent with the legislator's intention to protect the legitimate interests of end-users by giving them a say in whether business users may access their personal data and transfer the data to a different provider. Secondly, relying on other legal grounds, and in particular, the need to access data for the performance of contractual obligations (Article 6(1)(b) GDPR, to justify access to and transfer of end users' personal data would also be incompatible with the GDPR. Either the gatekeeper, the business user or both are already processing the requested data based on one of the legal grounds of Article 6(1) GDPR. Transferring the data to the requesting

677 Wolf-Posch (n 591) Article 6(10) DMA, para [222]; Baschenhof (n 578) 117.

678 See Article 5 Directive 2002/58/EC of the European Parliament and of the Council of 12 July 2002 concerning the processing of personal data and the protection of privacy in the electronic communications sector, OJ L 2002/201, 37 (e-Privacy Directive).

undertaking is a form of processing that will, in most cases, not be compatible with the initial purpose of processing.[679] According to Article 6(4) GDPR, processing personal data for a purpose that is incompatible with the purpose for which the data was initially collected is lawful only if it can be based on the legal grounds of 'consent' (Article 6(1) lit a GDPR), 'legal obligation' (lit c) or 'performance of a task carried out in the public interest' (lit e). The other lawful bases listed in Article 6(1) GDPR, including the need to access data for the performance of contractual obligations, cannot legitimise further processing incompatible with the original purpose.[680] As for the remaining three legal grounds, only 'consent' seems to provide a sufficient justification for accessing the personal data of end users based on Article 6(10) DMA. Neither the gatekeeper nor the business user will perform a task in the public interest. While Article 6(10) DMA obliges the gatekeeper to allow business users to access end users' data, the provision explicitly requires the consent of the relevant end users. Thus, a legal obligation of the gatekeeper exists only once the affected end users have opted in. It can therefore be concluded that grammatical, systematic and teleological interpretation suggests that Article 6(10) DMA allows business users to access the personal data of end users only if they have given their explicit consent.[681]

6.5.5 Relation to the Platform2Business Regulation

The DMA is not the first European Instrument that addresses the relationship between business users and providers of platform services. Already in 2019, the European legislator passed the P2B Regulation,[682] which was aimed at promoting fairness and transparency for business users of online intermediation services. However, the P2B Regulation has a broader scope, as it is a symmetric piece of legislation that applies to all online platforms,

679 See Tombal (n 409) 351.

680 Article 29 Working Party, 'Opinion 03/2013' (n 161) 36; Heberlein (n 444) Article 6 para 51.

681 But see Baschenhof (n 578) 118, who argues that the consent requirement could undermine the effectiveness of the provision, as actors in the data economy often cite rights to privacy or the protection of personal data under the GDPR to refuse data access that is actually legitimate.

682 Regulation (EU) 2019/1150 of the European Parliament and of the Council of 20 June 2019 on promoting fairness and transparency for business users of online intermediation services, OJ L 2019/186, 57.

regardless of their size or market position. The DMA, on the other hand, focuses on addressing specific issues related to market dominance and the behaviour of gatekeepers, imposing strict obligations on them to ensure fair competition and protect the interests of end and business users.[683]

The two Regulations also diverge with regard to the type of obligations they place on online intermediation services. The P2B Regulation primarily places transparency requirements on platform providers in order to disclose whether they are involved in certain potentially unfair or anti-competitive practices. In contrast, under the DMA, platform providers designated as gatekeepers are obliged not to engage in these practices at all, rather than just being required to disclose them. In other words, the DMA places stricter, proactive obligations on gatekeepers to prevent unfair or anti-competitive practices, rather than merely demanding transparency about them.[684]

Since the P2B Regulation and the DMA take two very different approaches to achieve the same objective, they are, in principle, not in conflict with each other but are in a complementary relationship. In the initial DMA proposal, the Commission explicitly stated that the DMA shall 'build on the existing P2B Regulation, without conflicting with it.'[685] The transparency and fairness rules applicable to all online platforms regardless of their size or position introduced in the P2B Regulation shall serve as a baseline. The DMA is intended to complement these provisions where, due to the gateway function of a particular platform, the requirements of the P2B Regulation are insufficient to protect fairness in P2B relationships.[686]

The relationship between Article 6(10) DMA and Article 9(1) P2B Regulation is an example of how information duties and access rights can complement each other. Already in the P2B Regulation, the European legislator attempted to address the issue that business users often have only limited access to the data they or their end users generate while using the platform services. Article 9(1) P2B Regulation introduced an obligation for (all) platform providers to explain in their general terms and conditions the technical or contractual access, or lack thereof, to personal or other data provided or generated in connection with the use of the platform by the

683 Konstantina Bania (n 622) 119; Baschenhof (n 578) 129.
684 Konstantina Bania (n 622) 119; Baschenhof (n 578) 129.
685 COM(2020) 842 final of 15 December 2020, 3.
686 COM(2020) 842 final of 15 December 2020, 3; Konstantina Bania (n 622) 119.

business user or end users.[687] Article 6(10) DMA goes much further and requires gatekeepers to grant business users access to this data, subject to an appropriate level of anonymisation or end-user consent if personal data is concerned.[688] In markets where no gatekeeper is present, business users do not have an access right based on the DMA, but the transparency obligation of the P2B Regulation empowers business users by informing them about which data the platform provider collects, whether and which they can access, and how platform providers handle that data.[689] This reduces—at least to some extent—the information asymmetry between the platform providers and business users and can potentially increase competition, as users can inform themselves about which provider offers the most favourable data practices and choose the best deal.[690] Vis-à-vis gatekeepers, both obligations apply at the same time. In these constellations, Article 9(1) P2B Regulation informs business users already before they enter into a business relationship with a gatekeeper which data they can later access based on Article 6(10) DMA and about the data usage of the gatekeeper.[691] The situation is similar as under the GDPR, where Article 15(1) GDPR gives data subjects the right to request from the controller whether and how personal data of them is being processed. Based on this information, they can decide if they want to exercise their portability pursuant to Article 20 GDPR.[692]

In order for Article 6(10) DMA and Article 9(1) P2B Regulation to complement each other, the two provisions must also be interpreted coherently. This concerns, for example, the question of which data is covered by the transparency requirement and the right of access. Article 9(1) P2B Regulation and Article 6(10) DMA use very similar language to describe the covered types of data. Article 9(1) P2B Regulation stipulates that the transparency obligation applies to 'any personal data or other data, or both, which business users or consumers *provide for the use* of the online intermediation services concerned or which are *generated through the provision*

687 For a detailed analysis of the transparency obligation, see Podszun (n 246) Article 9 P2B Regulation.

688 Wolf-Posch (n 591) Article 6(10) DMA, para [252].

689 Podszun (n 246) Article 9 P2B Regulation, para [96].

690 Podszun (n 246) Article 9 P2B Regulation, para [7]; On the limited effect of Article 9 P2B Regulation on restoring the informational level playing field between platforms and users, see Martens and others (n 182) 27.

691 Cf Podszun (n 246) Article 9 P2B Regulation, para [128].

692 ECJ, C-434/16, *Nowak*, EU:C:2017:994, para 57; Dix (n 246) Article 15 GDPR, para [1].

of those services.' With regard to Article 6(10) DMA, it has been argued above (6.5.4.1) that 'generated in the context of the use of the relevant core platform services' should be interpreted as also covering derivative data to the extent that the data can reasonably be expected to be necessary for facilitating the transition of business users to alternative service providers. If—as is argued here—the transparency requirement is understood as an instrument to facilitate the subsequent exercise of the access right, the scope of application of the transparency requirement should be at least as broad as that of the DMA's access right. Since the wording of the provisions is quite similar and the transparency obligation encroaches on the interests of the data holder (i.e. the provider of intermediary services) to a much lesser extent, there do not seem to be any compelling reasons not to interpret Article 9(1) P2B as also covering derived data.[693]

6.6 Access to search engine data for third parties (Article 6(11) DMA)

Article 6(11) DMA is the European legislators' reaction to a growing consensus that Google/Alphabet has such a dominant position in the search engine market that it can hardly be challenged any more. In economic literature it is argued that the dominance of Google/Alphabet is rooted in their comprehensive collection and analysis of data, which encompasses detailed records of user search queries and the subsequent interactions users have with the search results.[694] This has created a major barrier to market entry, as competing search engines, especially newcomers or smaller competitors, may not have access to such comprehensive data, which makes it challenging for them to provide as effective and relevant search results.[695] To address this issue, Article 6(11) DMA obliges gatekeepers to 'provide to any third-party undertaking providing online search engines, at its request, with access on fair, reasonable and non-discriminatory terms

693 See Podszun (n 246) Article 9(1) P2B Regulation, paras [53], [70] who also seems to support a broad interpretation, but does not explicitly state whether derived data are covered by Article 9(1).

694 See Jens Prüfer and Christoph Schottmüller, 'Competing with Big Data' [2017] SSRN Electronic Journal 27 <http://www.ssrn.com/abstract=2918726> accessed 10 October 2023 with further references.

695 Kerber, 'Datenrechtliche Aspekte des Digital Markets Act – Datenwirtschaftsrecht I: Vorschlag einer Ex-ante-Regulierung von Gatekeeper-Plattformen' (n 651) 547; Simonetta Vezzoso, 'The Dawn of Pro-Competition Data Regulation for Gatekeepers in the EU' (2021) 17 European Competition Journal 391, 396.

to ranking, query, click and view data in relation to free and paid search generated by end users on its online search engines. Any such query, click and view data that constitutes personal data shall be anonymised.' This obligation is quite far-reaching. It mandates the direct sharing of data with competitors, enabling them to enhance their services and potentially challenge the dominant position of the gatekeeper in the market.[696]

6.6.1 Objective and rationale

In contrast to the data rights the DMA affords to end users and business users, Article 6(11) DMA has one clear goal: promoting the competitiveness of the online search engine market.[697] In comparison, Article 6(9) and (10) DMA have a twofold objective. On the one hand, these provisions want to protect the individual interests of the end users and business users by giving them access to data that is generated by their activities. On the other hand, the data rights are also supposed to promote the public interest of enhancing competition and innovation by enabling users to effectively switch from the platform of the gatekeeper to those of other providers.[698] Article 6(11) is an additional and more far-reaching measure to promote competition in one specific sector. Like traditional competition law, Article 6(11) is not intended to protect the interests of the individual competitors—to whom the right is afforded and who, of course, benefit from it—but to promote the public interest of enhancing consumer welfare by intervening against concentrations that impede effective competition.[699]

Another difference between Articles 6(9) and (10) DMA is that Article 6(11) DMA is not a cross-sectoral provision but only applies to the online search engine market. The reason why the European legislator deemed it necessary to introduce additional measures for this market, is that the network effects, which are typical for all platform markets, are particularly strong when it comes to search engines. This is because the operators of a search engine need aggregated datasets from the past on search queries and

696 Kerber, 'Datenrechtliche Aspekte des Digital Markets Act – Datenwirtschaftsrecht I: Vorschlag einer Ex-ante-Regulierung von Gatekeeper-Plattformen' (n 651) 547.

697 Recital 61 DMA; Wolf-Posch (n 591) Article 6(11), para [256].

698 See 6.4.1 and 6.5.1.

699 See Baschenhof (n 578) 118; Victoria Daskalova, 'Consumer Welfare in EU Competition Law: What Is It (Not) About?' (2015) 11 Competition Law Review 131, On the consumer welfare approach of EU competition law, see.

the interactions of users on the search results to improve their products and services.[700] As more users engage with the search engine, the search engine has more data to work with, which helps it improve its performance and provide more valuable results. This is particularly relevant with regard to less common queries (so-called 'tail queries'). A search engine that handles a large number of requests is more likely to have encountered infrequently entered search terms and is able to answer tail queries more effectively. The algorithms of smaller, competing search engines may not have had exposure to as many queries, especially less common ones. Consequently, newcomers and smaller players may struggle to provide satisfactory search results for users, particularly for tail queries. Over time, this leads to market tipping. Since the competing search engines cannot match the search result quality of the gatekeeper's search engine, users increasingly turn to the services of the gatekeeper. As a result, the competing search engines receive fewer search queries and thus have less data to improve their service, while the gatekeeper amasses more and more data and continues to solidify its position on the market.[701]

However, the assessment of the European legislator on the indisputability of the search engine market may have to be reconsidered in light of new developments. Even if not explicitly mentioned, the gatekeeper that is targeted by the obligation of Article 6(11) DMA is Google/Alphabet, which, over decades, has been able to maintain a consistent and largely undisputed market dominance.[702] In the Google Shopping case, the Commission demonstrated that Google has held a market share of over 80 % in all EEA markets for general search engines since 2008. By 2016, Google had reached a market share of well above 90 % in many of the EEA countries, while the share of its direct competitors, Yahoo and Bing, only ranged somewhere between 1 % and 9 %.[703] The Commission also observed that, since 2007, a number of operators have abandoned the business or confined themselves to a particular national market or language area.[704] However,

700 Kerber, 'Datenrechtliche Aspekte des Digital Markets Act – Datenwirtschaftsrecht I: Vorschlag einer Ex-ante-Regulierung von Gatekeeper-Plattformen' (n 651) 547.

701 Commission Decision AT.39740, Google Shopping, C(2017) 4444 final, paras 287 ff; Wolf-Posch (n 591) Article 6(11) DMA, para [256].

702 Kerber, 'Datenrechtliche Aspekte des Digital Markets Act – Datenwirtschaftsrecht I: Vorschlag einer Ex-ante-Regulierung von Gatekeeper-Plattformen' (n 651) 547.

703 Commission Decision AT.39740, *Google Shopping*, C(2017) 4444 final, paras 276, 280, 300.

704 Commission Decision AT.39740, *Google Shopping*, C(2017) 4444 final, paras 285 ff; EGC, T-612/17, *Google v Commission*, EU:T:2021:763, para 47.

the introduction of ChatGPT and the subsequent acquisition by Microsoft, which has integrated the generative AI model into its Bing search engine, has created a new competitive dynamic in the market. After ChatGPT set the record for the fastest-growing consumer application in history (100 Million users in two months),[705] Google declared a 'code red' emergency for the company[706] and raced to launch its own generative AI chatbot.[707] While it is impossible to make any credible predictions for the future, as of now, it seems like Google is still holding on to its dominant position. Nevertheless, the success of ChatGPT shows that digital markets can change very quickly and unexpectedly.

6.6.2 Relation to competition law

In terms of its objective and its modalities, Article 6(11) DMA is very closely related to the Essential Facility Doctrine (EFD) that the CJEU developed on the basis of Article 102 TFEU (4.2).[708] Like the EFD, the justification for the encroaching on the interests of the gatekeeper is that ranking, query, click and view data is considered an essential input for undertakings that want to enter or effectively compete on the search engines market.[709] Both under the DMA and competition law, the remedy is mandated access to the essential facility, i.e. the required data, based on FRAND terms (4.3.7). Moreover, Article 6(11) DMA and competition law afford the right directly to the competitors of the gatekeeper/dominant undertaking, even though they did not contribute to its generation.[710]

Looking at the issue that Article 6(11) DMA wants to address, through the lens of competition law it could be argued that the ranking, query,

705 Krystal Hu, 'ChatGPT Sets Record for Fastest-Growing User Base - Analyst Note' *Reuters* (2 February 2023) <https://www.reuters.com/technology/chatgpt-sets-record-fastest-growing-user-base-analyst-note-2023-02-01/> accessed 16 October 2023.

706 Nico Grant, 'Google Calls In Help From Larry Page and Sergey Brin for A.I. Fight' *The New York Times* (20 January 2023) <https://www.nytimes.com/2023/01/20/technology/google-chatgpt-artificial-intelligence.html> accessed 16 October 2023.

707 Cade Metz and Nico Grant, 'Racing to Catch Up With ChatGPT, Google Plans Release of Its Own Chatbot' *The New York Times* (6 February 2023) <https://www.nytimes.com/2023/02/06/technology/google-bard-ai-chatbot.html> accessed 16 October 2023.

708 See Lamping (n 283) 132.

709 Recital 61 DMA.

710 See Neil Cohen and Christiane Wendehorst (n 119) Principle 24.

click and view data constitutes a hypothetical big data market (i.e. the primary market), on which the gatekeeper has a dominant position (4.3.1.2.2). This data is an indispensable input for undertakings that want to enter the search engine market not because of the semantic information of the single data points but because of the size and diversity of the data, which cannot be replicated or substituted (4.3.3.3). Since access to such data is necessary to develop effective search engines that produce reliable results even for more unusual queries, the refusal to supply is liable to eliminate competition in the search engine market (i.e. the secondary market) (4.3.4).

While this theoretical analysis may suggest that it would be rather straightforward to rely on Article 102 TFEU to gain access to the ranking, query, click and view data, in reality, the application of the EFD to data refusal constellations is fraught with a number of uncertainties (see 4.3). First, there are several legal ambiguities, such as how to define the primary and secondary markets or whether the new product requirement is a relevant criterion also for refusals to share data. Secondly, even if these legal uncertainties were resolved, it can be very difficult for undertakings to factually prove that all the requirements of the EFD are actually fulfilled. Finally, competition law only provides for ex-post remedies. This means that even if a competitor were to take legal action and succeed, it could take several years for them to gain access to the required data (see 4.4). The resulting delay can be a significant obstacle because it might force competitors to abandon their plans to enter the search engine market before they even get access to the required data.

In this regard, Article 6(11) DMA has clear benefits vis-à-vis the EFD for undertakings seeking access to search engine data. As an ex-ante remedy, the DMA's data-sharing obligation is triggered by the designation of a company as a 'gatekeeper' alone. Hence, it is not necessary to demonstrate that the data collected by a dominant undertaking constitutes an 'essential facility' to which access is indispensable for competition so that denying competitors such access would constitute an abuse of a dominant position.[711] Rather, the DMA operates on the premises that the mere presence of a gatekeeper in the search engine market leads to competitive distortions that justify legal intervention. Departing from the case-by-case analysis of traditional competition law renders Article 6(11) DMA a much more effective and practicable remedy for competitors of the gatekeeper. Furthermore, it reduces 'false negatives', which occur when regulators or authorities fail to

711 Baschenhof (n 578) 119.

identify or act (timely) against market failures. The downside of the ex-ante approach is that it is more prone to 'false positives'. In this context, a 'false positive' means that the companies get access to search engine data even when it would not have any positive effects on competition.[712] However, there is a broad consensus among economists that, in the case of large dominant platforms, the potential costs associated with 'false negatives' can be significantly higher compared to the costs of 'false positives'.[713]

It should also be kept in mind that, at least to some extent, it is possible to adapt the effects of the DMA in case market conditions change. This is because the European legislators have granted significant regulatory power to the Commission. Should, for example, Google lose its dominance in the search engine market (6.6.1), the Commission could react by invoking its gatekeeper status. This would render the access right provided by Article 6(11) DMA ineffective, as there would be no addressee against whom the right could be exercised.

6.6.3 Addressee: gatekeeper offering search engine services

As with all other provisions of the DMA, only companies that are designated gatekeepers can be addressees of the obligation to provide access to search engine data. However, compared to the DMA's other data rights, Article 6(11) DMA has an even narrower scope because it only obliges gatekeepers that provide online search engines.[714] The DMA itself does not define what an 'online search engine' is, but refers in Article 2(6) to the definition of the P2B-Regulation. Article 2(5) P2B Regulation defines 'online search engine' as 'a digital service that allows users to input queries in order to perform searches of, in principle, all websites, or all websites in a particular language, on the basis of a query on any subject in the form of a keyword, voice request, phrase or other input, and returns results in any format in which information related to the requested content can be found.'

Since the definition refers to 'searches on all websites' specialised search engines that are designed to focus on specific topics, industries, or types

712 Jasper van den Boom, 'What Does the Digital Markets Act Harmonize? – Exploring Interactions between the DMA and National Competition Laws' (2023) 19 European Competition Journal 57, 64.

713 Crémer, de Montjoye and Schweitzer (n 170) 51; Kerber, 'Updating Competition Policy for the Digital Economy?' (n 202) 19.

714 Wolf-Posch (n 591) Aricle 6(11) DMA, para [258]; Baschenhof (n 578) 118.

of content and do not crawl the whole internet are not covered.[715] Hence, search engines that operate within a specific platform, website, or system, allowing users to search for information or products contained within that particular environment would be excluded from the scope.[716] This means that Article 6(11) DMA does not oblige gatekeepers operating an e-commerce marketplace or social media site to provide access to ranking, query, click and view data that is generated by their internal search engine.

The requirement for the search function to relate to searches 'on the basis of a query on any subject' excludes specialised search engines that although they search the whole internet, they focus only on a specific category or niche, such as travel, shopping, or health (so-called vertical search engines). Therefore, Article 6(11) DMA only applies to gatekeepers that provide general-purpose search engines, which can provide information or results on virtually any subject.[717]

6.6.4 Rightsholder

The DMA affords the right to access the ranking, query, click and view data generated by the gatekeeper's search engine to 'any third-party undertaking providing online search engines'. Since the term 'search engine' also refers to the definition of the P2B Regulation, Article 6(11) DMA only entitles companies that operate a general-purpose search engine. Undertakings that provide a website with an internal search engine or only offer specialised search services (i.e. vertical search engines)[718] would not have the right

715 Bongartz and Kirk (n 653) Article 2 DMA, para [40]; Luis MB Cabral and others, 'The EU Digital Markets Act: A Report from a Panel of Economic Experts' (Joint Research Centre 2021) JRC122910 23; Alexandre De Streel and others, 'Making the Digital Markets Act More Resilient and Effective' (CERRE 2021) 12 <https://cerre.eu/publications/european-parliament-digital-markets-act-dma-resilient-effective/> accessed 16 October 2023.

716 Wolf-Posch (n 591) Article 6(11) DMA, para [258].

717 Bongartz and Kirk (n 653) Article 2 DMA, para [39]; Cabral and others (n 715) 23; De Streel and others (n 715) 12.

718 But see Wolf-Posch (n 591) Article 6(11) DMA, para [260], who, with regard to vertical search engines, seems to contradict her own assessment under para [261]. There she states that the competitor must operate a search engine within the meaning of Article 2(5) of the P2B Regulation. As described above, the prevailing opinion, which is also held by two other authors in the same volume, is that vertical search engines do not fall under this definition. Therefore, an undertaking operating only

to request access to the search engine data.[719] This restriction aligns with the broader objective of fostering competition in the search engine market. Accessing search data solely for the purpose of improving the search functionality on their own websites, would neither improve the services of the existing competitors of the gatekeeper in the search engine market nor lead to new market entries.

Since Article 6(11) DMA is intended to enable the entry of new market participants, the provision is to be interpreted in such a way that the right of access to data can also be exercised by companies that do not yet operate a (general-purpose) search engine but are planning to enter the market.[720] This, of course, puts into perspective the restriction that companies, which only provide an internal or specialised search engine cannot exercise the access right. In order to invoke Article 6(11) DMA, they would only have to demonstrate that they intend to enter the general search engine market. However, the requesting undertaking would be allowed to use the accessed data only for the purpose of developing a general search engine and not to improve its internal or vertical search engine. As the DMA does not contain explicit provisions on data usage, this is not expressly provided for in the DMA, but follows from the purpose of Article 6(11) of the DMA and the abuse of rights doctrine.[721]

While it makes sense to also afford the access right to undertakings that are not yet active on the search engines market, it has been criticised that the DMA does not limit this right to undertakings that do not have gatekeeper status in another market.[722] Most of the companies that are going to have gatekeeper status are active in many digital markets and are direct competitors in some of them. Article 6(11) DMA does not put forward any restrictions that would prevent gatekeepers like Microsoft (operator of Bing) or Amazon (hypothetical operator of a general online search engine) from leveraging this DMA provision to request search data from Google. The intention of the DMA is that the obligation to share search data with

---

a vertical search engine would not be entitled to request access under Article 6(11) DMA.

719 Wolf-Posch (n 591) Article 6(11) DMA, para [261].

720 Wolf-Posch (n 591) Article 6(10) DMA, para [260]; Baschenhof (n 578) 119.

721 E.g. ECJ, C-367/96, *Kefalas*, EU:C:1998:222, paras 20 – 28; in ECJ, C-489/07, *Messner*, EU:C:2009:502, the prohibition of abuse of rights was derived from the principle of good faith; see Reich (n 646) 210; Grundmann (n 647) 147.

722 Baschenhof (n 578) 121; less critical Wolf-Posch (n 591) Article 6(11) DMA, para [261].

competing search engines shall primarily benefit smaller search engine providers, as they can use the data to enhance their services to attract more users. It is argued, however, that other gatekeepers are likely to benefit more from accessing search data compared to smaller search service providers. This is because many gatekeepers share similar business models that rely on monetising 'insights from user data'. Thus, they may be able to integrate the accessed data into their strategies for user engagement, advertising, and revenue generation with little effort. Moreover, gatekeepers have the financial resources, infrastructure, and expertise to manage, process, and store the data effectively. They can deploy advanced data analysis tools and employ skilled professionals to ensure that the data they receive from the search engine gatekeeper is effectively utilised. It is asserted that these capabilities allow gatekeepers to derive greater value from such data than smaller competitors, which ultimately contributes to the former's dominance and influence in the digital landscape[723]

How much value can be extracted from the data acquired via Article 6(11) DMA also depends on whether and to what extent the search engine data can be combined with other datasets.[724] On the surface, it would seem that at least in that regard, competing gatekeepers are in a worse position than other competitors because Article 5(1)(b) DMA prohibits gatekeepers from combing the personal data from their different business ventures, unless the users have given consent.[725] While the ranking, query, click and view data is typically personal data,[726] the second sentence of Article 6(11) DMA explicitly stipulates that such data shall be anonymised (regarding the details of this obligation, see 6.6.5). If anonymised the data is not covered by Article 5(1)(b) DMA and gatekeepers are free to combine the acquired data, increasing the volume and variety of the data they hold, which in turn renders the dataset more valuable.[727]

It has also been pointed out that the risk that Article 6(11) DMA may overly benefit large corporations also has a geo-strategic dimension. Since

723 Baschenhof (n 578) 121, 150.

724 Rubinfeld and Gal (n 227) 346.

725 Rupprecht Podszun, in Rupprecht Podszun (ed), *Digital Markets Act: Gesetz über digitale Märkte* (Nomos 2023) Article 5(2) DMA, para [14]; Rupprecht Podszun, 'Should Gatekeepers Be Allowed to Combine Data? – Ideas for Art. 5(a) of the Draft Digital Markets Act' [2021] SSRN Electronic Journal <https://www.ssrn.com/abstract=3860030> accessed 18 October 2023.

726 EDPS, 'Opinion 2/2021 on the Proposal for a Digital Markets Act' (2021) 12.

727 See Rubinfeld and Gal (n 227) 347.

the wording of the provision does not require that the requesting company offers an online search service in the EU, a Chinese company operating a search engine in the Chinese market could get access to the search engine data of the European market. Given the purpose of Article 6(11) DMA, the provision is to be limited to the effect that a company operating only outside of the EU cannot invoke the access right. The objective of promoting the contestability of online search engine markets in the EU presupposes that the access right can at least potentially have positive effects on competition in that market. However, a planned EU market entry by a foreign search engine provider can potentially influence competition in the EU and would thus be sufficient to trigger the access obligation.[728]

6.6.5 Data covered by Article 6(11) DMA

Gatekeepers are obliged to provide access to the 'ranking, query, click and view data in relation to free and paid search generated by end users on its online search engines.' The obligation is much broader than a potential access based on the Essential Facilities Doctrine, as competitors do not have to demonstrate that the data is indispensable (see 4.3.3) for operating a search engine. There is also no limitation to accessing only necessary or at least useful data. Only if the request can be deemed obviously unsuitable, constituting an abusive exercise of the right, the gatekeeper may refuse to provide access. The broad material scope of the obligation is in line with the rationale of Article 6(11) DMA, which aims to allow competitors unhindered access to data that is essential to improve their search engine functions by avoiding lengthy debates on the necessity of the accessed data in each individual case.[729]

Such data will typically constitute personal data that can provide deep insights into the private lives of individuals. Ranking, query, click and view data can be utilised to construct a comprehensive profile of an individual's preferences, and draw inferences about their status (including financial and health status) or their interests and convictions (including religious and political beliefs).[730]

---

728 Wolf-Posch (n 591) Article 6(11) DMA, para [260].
729 Wolf-Posch (n 591) Article 6(11) DMA, para [271].
730 EDPS, 'Opinion 2/2021 on the Proposal for a Digital Markets Act' (n 726) 12.

Due to the highly sensitive nature of this data, the access obligation of Article 6(11) DMA is subject to an anonymisation requirement. Gatekeepers have to redact all personal data before granting access to competitors. However, there is a tension between the need to protect the privacy of users and the goal to make valuable datasets available to competitors because anonymisation compromises the utility of the data for competing search engines. Once anonymised, the data may lose some of its original relevance or specificity, making it less valuable or effective for other search engines trying to use the data for their purposes.[731] In an attempt to strike a balance between these two competing interests, the European legislator added in Recital 61 that the anonymisation shall not 'substantially' degrade the 'quality or usefulness of the data'.

However, it has been pointed out it remains unclear how the 'usefulness' of data related to an individual can be maintained despite anonymisation. Moreover, no standard exists against, which the degradation is to be assessed. While a plain reading of the requirement could imply that degradation is measured against the quality and utility of the still-personal data held by the gatekeeper, this can hardly be the case. Personal data typically holds more value and versatility, being usable for various purposes, in comparison to anonymised data. Therefore, if the still-personal data were the standard for assessing degradation, any form of anonymisation could potentially be considered as substantially diminishing the quality of the data.[732]

Ultimately, Recital 61 DMA merely clarifies that the gatekeepers shall anonymise the required data as much as necessary to protect the privacy of its users but as little as possible in order to ensure that the data is still of value to competitors. In other words, gatekeepers may not render the requested data useless by applying overly extensive anonymisation measures. The assessment which anonymisation measures are the most appropriate to achieve this goal is left to the gatekeepers.[733] However, the Commission may —either at their own initiative or at the request of the gatekeeper—specify the anonymisation requirement (Article 8(2) DMA).

731 Kerber, 'Datenrechtliche Aspekte des Digital Markets Act – Datenwirtschaftsrecht I: Vorschlag einer Ex-ante-Regulierung von Gatekeeper-Plattformen' (n 651) 547.

732 Baschenhof (n 578) 118.

733 Wolf-Posch (n 591) Article 6(11) DMA, para [272].

6.6.6 FRAND-based access

Article 6(11) DMA obliges the gatekeeper to grant competitors 'access' to the relevant ranking, query, click and view data. The intent of the provision is to enable third-party undertakings to use the data to improve their online search engines. Hence, the gatekeeper needs to ensure that the third party is granted full control over the data and possesses the capability to integrate it seamlessly into their server infrastructure. Merely making the data visible would not fulfil the requirements of Article 6(11) DMA, because the third party will need to actively use and manipulate the data and not only observe it.[734]

Since Article 6(11) DMA affords an access right to parties that have not contributed to the generation of the accessed data, the gatekeeper is not obliged to grant its competitors free access to its search engine data.[735] Gatekeepers may charge fees, but the terms need to be fair reasonable and non-discriminatory (FRAND). In this regard the DMA draws inspiration from competition law.[736] As described above 4.3.7, in the EFD cases regarding IP rights, the dominant undertaking was obliged to conclude a contract for the transfer of the requested data on 'reasonable' and 'non-discriminatory' terms.

Originally, the concept of FRAND terms for access was developed by Standard Setting Organisations (SSOs) for so-called 'standard essential patents' (SEPs). SEPs are patents that implement a particular technology standard for a certain sector (for example, mobile communication standards, such as 4G and 5G).[737] The patented standard will often be crucial for ensuring interoperability and compatibility among devices or systems. The patent holder could potentially exploit this dependence of other companies by demanding exorbitant licensing fees and/or discriminating against certain competitors. Moreover, SEPs are typically very broad and may cover multiple different ways of implementing a standard, which can

734 Wolf-Posch (n 591) Article 6(11) DMA, para [273].

735 See Peter Georg Picht, 'Caught in the Acts: Framing Mandatory Data Access Transactions under the Data Act, Further EU Digital Regulation Acts, and Competition Law' (Max Planck Institute for Innovation and Competition Research Paper No 22-12 2022) 28 <https://papers.ssrn.com/sol3/papers.cfm?abstract_id=4076842>.

736 SWD(2017) 2 final of 10 January 2017 21.

737 Tim Pohlmann and Knut Blind, 'Landscaping Study on Standard Essential Patents' (European Commission 2016) 7; Jeffery Atik, 'The FRAND Ceremony and the Engagement of Article 102 TFEU in the Licensing of Standard Essential Patents' (2019) 42 Fordham Int Law J 949, 951.

make it difficult for implementers to determine whether their products infringe a SEP. In order to address these problems, many standard-setting organisations (SSOs) have adopted policies that require SEP holders to disclose their SEPs to the SSO and to commit to licensing their SEPs on FRAND terms.[738] The idea behind FRAND commitments is to strike a balance between the need for innovators to be rewarded for their inventions (by allowing them to license their SEPs) and the need for widespread adoption of technology standards. Furthermore, it prevents the abuse of market power by patent holders and promotes a level playing field for companies implementing standards.[739]

However, there is no universally accepted set of tests or criteria to definitively determine whether a licensing agreement fulfils a FRAND commitment. Hence, disputes regularly arise as parties disagree on what constitutes fair, reasonable, and non-discriminatory terms for licensing these essential patents. The same issue also exists in connection with Article 6(11) DMA, as the DMA does not further specify the FRAND requirement. Recourse to SEP case law, however, is only of limited help. In *Huawei/ZTE*[740]—the leading case on the application of FRAND conditions to SEPs—the ECJ did not provide any criteria for determining whether terms satisfy the FRAND requirement. Instead, it laid down a procedural framework that formalises the negotiation stage between potential licensees and licensors.[741] As further described below (6.6.6.1), the principles of the *Huawei/ZTE* framework can be used to develop an adapted negotiation scheme for finding a FRAND compensation under the Data Act and potentially also the DMA.[742]

An important source for the interpretation of the FRAND concept as set out in Article 6(11) DMA is the Data Act, which contains a rather

738 Benjamin Franz and Rupprecht Podszun, 'Nach Huawei/ZTE: Die kartellrechtliche Zwangslizenz im Patentverletzungsprozess' (2017) 15 205, 209.

739 Jeffery Atik (n 737) 950 ff; see also Mathew Heim and Igor Nikolic, 'A FRAND Regime for Dominant Digital Platforms' (2019) 10 JIPITEC 38, 44; Heiko Richter and Peter R Slowinski, 'The Data Sharing Economy: On the Emergence of New Intermediaries' (2019) 50 International Review of Intellectual Property and Competition Law 4, 18.

740 ECJ, C-170/13, *Huawei/ZTE*, EU:C:2015:477

741 Oscar Borgogno and Giuseppe Colangelo, 'Data Sharing and Interoperability: Fostering Innovation and Competition through APIs' (2019) 35 Computer Law & Security Review 1, 15.

742 Erik Habich, 'FRAND Access to Data: Perspectives from the FRAND Licensing of Standard-Essential Patents for the Data Act Proposal and the Digital Markets Act' (2022) 53 International Review of Intellectual Property and Competition Law 1343, 1364 ff.

detailed articulation of the different criteria. This connection is established through Article 12(1) DA, which extends the application of FRAND obligations delineated in Chapter III of the DA beyond those data rights laid down in the DA itself to all provisions of Union law or national legislation mandating b2b data sharing. Although the provisions of Chapter III do not apply retroactively but only to legislation that enters into force after 12 September 2025 (Article 50 DA), and thus are not directly applicable to the DMA, they should guide the interpretation of the FRAND criteria. This approach would ensure a harmonised understanding of the principles of fairness, reasonableness, and non-discrimination in the digital market and a uniform application in different contexts and access scenarios within the Union's legal framework. Hence, where the DMA does not contain specific or diverting obligations on data access, the substantive provisions of Chapter III DA should be instructive for the interpretation of the duties under the DMA.[743]

6.6.6.1 The *Huawei/ZTE* judgment

Recourse to SEP case law to determine the FRAND is only of limited help. In *Huawei/ZTE*[744]—the leading case on the application of FRAND conditions to SEPs—the ECJ did not provide any criteria for determining whether terms satisfy the FRAND requirement. Instead, it laid down a procedural framework that formalises the negotiation stage between potential licensees and licensors.[745] In the case, Huawei argued that ZTE, another Chinese telecommunications company, infringed one of Huawei's SEPs related to 3G and 4G wireless telecommunications standards. Huawei had made a commitment to the SSO that issued the SEP to grant third parties a licence on FRAND terms. Prior to the initiation of the lawsuit, the involved parties engaged in negotiations concerning the alleged patent infringement and the potential issuance of a license. However, no contractual offers were submitted by either party and the talks were ultimately unsuccessful. ZTE argued that the infringement action by Huawei constitutes an abuse under

743 Habich (n 742) 1352.

744 ECJ, C-170/13, *Huawei/ZTE*, EU:C:2015:477

745 Borgogno and Colangelo (n 741) 15.

Article 102 TFEU, asserting that Huawei had a dominant market position and is obliged to offer a license the SEP on FRAND terms.[746]

The ECJ ruled that the holder of the SEP, in this case Huawei, must inform the (alleged) infringer of the patent in question and the specific infringement before filing an action.[747] Furthermore, the SEP holder must submit a specific written offer to conclude a licence agreement on FRAND terms, which states the amount of the licence fee and its calculation method.[748] If the SEP holder does not adhere to this procedure, an infringement action against the party seeking access would constitute an abuse under Article 102 TFEU.[749] Conversely, the access seeker must respond to this offer carefully and without delaying tactics by accepting the offer or immediately submitting a counter-offer that complies with the FRAND conditions.[750]

Both the SEP holder and the access seeker have incentives to adhere to the specified procedural framework. The SEP holder is protected from antitrust measures, while the access seeker benefits from protection against the threat of injunctions.[751] This could also serve as inspiration for the DMA in case the gatekeeper and the requesting party are unable to reach an agreement. However, parties should not be constrained to follow this process exclusively, as they could well reach an agreement outside of this established framework.[752]

6.6.6.2 Fair

Among the three FRAND terms, 'fair' is the most elusive one, as it has received surprisingly little attention in both legal decisions and academic discussions. It can even be questioned whether fairness is a separate requirement. Especially in the US, the acronym RAND is often used instead of FRAND and scholars have asserted that there is no meaningful differ-

746 ECJ, C-170/13, Huawei/ZTE, EU:C:2015:477, paras 21-28; see also Ronny Hauck, '„Erzwungene" Lizenzverträge – Kartellrechtliche Grenzen der Durchsetzung standardessenzieller Patente' [2015] NJW 2767, 2769; Franz and Podszun (n 740) 211 ff.

747 ECJ, C-170/13, *Huawei/ZTE*, EU:C:2015:477, para 61.

748 ECJ, C-170/13, *Huawei/ZTE*, EU:C:2015:477, para 63.

749 ECJ, C-170/13, *Huawei/ZTE*, EU:C:2015:477, para 60.

750 ECJ, C-170/13, *Huawei/ZTE*, EU:C:2015:477, para 65.

751 Borgogno and Colangelo (n 741) 15; see also Habich (n 742) 1362.

752 Heim and Nikolic (n 739) 46.

ence between the two concepts.[753] In the US case *Apple, Inc. v. Motorola, Inc.*, the judge argued that the 'the word "fair" adds nothing to "reasonable" and "nondiscriminatory".'[754] Particularly with regard to the fee that the gatekeeper can charge for access, it is difficult to see what the difference between a fair and a reasonable price is. Or to put it another way, can a price be reasonable but not fair?

In the context of the DMA, however, 'reasonable' and 'fair' are not interchangeable but serve distinct roles within the FRAND framework. While 'reasonable' is specifically related to the pricing aspect, indicating an acceptable or justified cost (see 6.6.6.3), 'fair' introduces a (un)fairness test for other terms within the access agreement beyond just the price.[755] This fairness test entails a comprehensive evaluation of the various conditions and provisions governing the use and access of requested data to ensure an equitable and balanced relationship between the gatekeeper and the access seeker. After all, it is not only the price for the data but also the specifications and restrictions concerning modalities of access and types of permissible use, data formats, timing, data security, as well as further support required for effective access or use that determine whether an agreement reflects a fair balance of the parties' interest.[756]

The interpretation that the 'fairness' criterion introduces an 'unfairness test' can be derived from a combined reading of the DMA and Chapter III of the Data Act (DA). This Chapter applies to all provisions of Union law or national legislation mandating b2b data sharing and thus also to Article 6(11) DMA. The central provision of the DA's Chapter III is Article 8(1) DA, which stipulates that where Union law (or national legislation) obliges a data holder to make data available to a data recipient, the data holder shall agree with the data recipient on the arrangements for making the data available and shall do so under fair, reasonable and non- discriminatory terms and conditions. Article 8(2) DA further specifies that any terms of this agreement shall not be binding if they fulfil the conditions of the unfairness test laid down in Article 13 DA.[757] Although Article 13 DA is situated within Chapter IV of the DA, its scope of application does also go

753 Anne Layne-Farrar, 'The Economics of FRAND' in Daniel Sokol and Roger Blair (eds), *The Cambridge Handbook of Antitrust, Intellectual Property, and High Tech* (Cambridge University Press 2017) 58; Jorge L Contreras, 'A Brief History of FRAND' (2015) 80 Antitrust Law Journal 39, 39.

754 *Apple, Inc. v. Motorola, Inc.*, 869 F. Supp. 2d 901 (N.D. Ill. 2012).

755 *Cf.* Habich (n 741) 1354.

756 See Franz and Podszun (n 737) 222; *cf.* Thomas and others (n 494) 27.

757 Habich (n 742) 1352; Picht (n 735) 38.

beyond the boundaries of the DA. According to Article 1(2)(c) DA, Chapter IV, i.e. the unfairness test of Article 13 DA, applies to any private sector data accessed and used on the basis of contract between enterprises.

It can therefore be concluded that the 'fair' requirement introduces an unfairness test that is further specified by Article 13 DA. According to Article 13(7) DA, contractual terms related to the main subject matter or the price are excluded from the scope of the unfairness test. This dovetails well with the concept of FRAND-based access data obligations. The main subject matter, i.e. the data which the requesting undertaking receives, is defined directly by the provision itself. In the case of Article 6(11) DMA it is 'ranking, query, click and view data in relation to free and paid search generated by end users on its online search engines.' The adequacy of the price charged by the gatekeeper is assessed under the 'reasonableness' constraint. Moreover, the unfairness test applies only to unilaterally imposed contract terms. These are defined in Article 13(5) DA as terms, which have been supplied by one contracting party and the other contracting party has not been able to influence its content despite an attempt to negotiate it. The party that supplied the contractual term bears the burden of proving that it was not imposed unilaterally.[758]

In order to determine whether a clause used by the gatekeeper is unfair recourse can also be taken to Article 13 DA, which specifies the concept of 'unfairness' in three steps. Firstly, Article 13(3) DA introduces a blacklist with terms that are deemed unfair without the need for further assessment. Secondly, Article 13(4) DA lists several terms that are presumed to be unfair (so-called grey list). The presumption of unfairness attached to these terms can, however, be rebutted. To fall under either the black or grey list, a term merely needs to have, as its "object or effect," an outcome condemned by either list. This approach, influenced by competition law, departs from a strict focus on the term's success in generating unfair effects, emphasising instead its intended purpose or impact. In case a term is not covered by the black or grey list, it can still be deemed unfair under the general clause of Article 13(2) DA if the term's use 'grossly deviates from good commercial practice in data access and use, contrary to good faith and fair dealing.'[759] (for a more comprehensive analysis of Article 13 DA, see 7.9)

758 Picht (n 735) 38.
759 Picht (n 735) 39.

6.6.6.3 Reasonable

In the FRAND context, the 'reasonable' criterion is considered to refer to the compensation that the recipient must pay for receiving access.[760] Assessing the reasonableness of the remuneration that gatekeepers may charge requires a careful balancing act. On one hand, competitors should not face excessive fees that would render the access right ineffective because the high price creates another barrier that would stifle competition. On the other hand, the data holders deserve fair compensation for their investment in the generation of such data. While the DMA as such does not provide any specifications on how to determine the reasonableness of the remuneration, recourse can be taken to the EFD, in particular the *Microsoft* decisions, and the Data Act.

In the initial *Microsoft* case (see 4.3.7) the Commission ordered Microsoft to license interoperability information necessary for complementary services to third parties under non-discriminatory and reasonable terms.[761] In a follow-up decision, the Commission deemed Microsoft's pricing scheme for the information as being unreasonable[762] and imposed periodic fines, which were subsequently raised by the Commission in two additional decision.[763] Microsoft challenged the grounds for the penalty and argued, inter alia, that the Commission had failed to specify definitively what it meant by 'reasonable' and therefore the imposed obligation lacked sufficient clarity;[764] an argument which the EGC rejected (see also 4.3.7).

While neither the Commission nor the EGC provided Microsoft with an exact figure, they both referred to two abstract criteria on how to determine

760 Philipp Hacker, Johann Cordes and Janina Rochon, 'Regulating Gatekeeper AI and Data: Transparency, Access, and Fairness under the DMA, the GDPR, and Beyond' 19 <https://arxiv.org/abs/2212.04997> accessed 3 May 2023; see also Herbers (n 578) 256.

761 Commission Decision C-3/37.792, *Microsoft*, OJ L 2007/32, 23, paras 1005–1009.

762 Commission Decision C(2005) 4420 of 10 November 2005.

763 Commission Decision fixing the definitive amount of the periodic penalty payment imposed on Microsoft Corporation by Decision C(2005)4420 final and amending that Decision as regards the amount of the periodic penalty payment 6 September 2006; Commission Decision fixing the definitive amount of the periodic penalty payment imposed on Microsoft Coporation by Decision C(2005)4420 final 27 February 2008, C(2008) 764 final.

764 EGC, T-167/08, *Microsoft v Commission*, EU:T:2012:323, para 75; for a more detailed outlined of the case law, see Sophie Lawrance and Laura Peirson, 'The General Court's 2012 Microsoft Judgment: "Reasonable" Fines and "Reasonable" Licence Fees' (2013) 8 Journal of Intellectual Property Law & Practice 236.

the reasonableness of the remuneration, which can also be used in the context of the DMA. Firstly, the remuneration rate set must allow users to compete viably with Microsoft. Secondly, it should reflect only the 'intrinsic' value of the information to be licensed and must exclude any 'strategic' value stemming from Microsoft's market power.[765] The intrinsic value of the interoperability information was defined by the EGC as the value that lies in the innovative character of the technologies. While the strategic value is considered as the value that stems from Microsoft's ability to prevent competitors from interacting with its dominant operating systems.[766]

Transferring this line of argumentation to Article 6(10) DMA, a reasonable remuneration for accessing the search engine data may only reflect the inherent worth of the data derived from its core characteristics and capabilities, independent of any external factors or market dominance. This could, inter alia, include the comprehensiveness of the data, the technological investments necessary to collect the data, as well as the investments made in data organisation, accessibility and quality control. Any advantages gained from the gatekeeper position, such as lock-in effects or reduced competition, would need to be redacted.[767]

It is true that companies may be motivated to develop certain services, like search engines because of the potential gains to be made by collected data once the service is widely adopted.[768] However, the provisions of the DMA make it quite clear that the European legislators are more concerned about the negative effects resulting from a lack of competition than they are about gatekeepers potentially reducing their data investments because of access obligations.[769] Gatekeepers should use the data generated by their services to foster innovation and service quality enhancement, rather than as a tool to maintain their market dominance. Hence, it would run counter to the objectives of the DMA if gatekeepers could reap the benefits stemming from their gatekeeper position by charging competitors for the strategic value of ranking, query, click and view data.

765 EGC, T-167/08, Microsoft v Commission, EU:T:2012:323, para 85.

766 EGC, T-167/08, Microsoft v Commission, EU:T:2012:323, para 87; Lawrance and Peirson (n 764) 237; Lévêque (n 341) 87.

767 See Lévêque (n 341) 88 ff.

768 Lawrance and Peirson (n 764) 237.

769 Recital 61 DMA explicitly states that the European legislators consider the access by gatekeepers to ranking, query, click and view data a significant barrier to entry and expansion, which undermines the contestability of online search engine market.

The approach by the Commission and the EGC in *Microsoft* also aligns with the one pursued by the European legislators in the Data Act. Article 9 DA sets out that where data holders are obliged to make data available to a third party, they may charge a reasonable and non-discriminatory remuneration that may include a margin.[770] Recital 47 DA further outlines several factors to determine what the Commission has labelled the 'intrinsic value' of data. A reasonable compensation may cover various costs related to making data available to third parties. These costs include technical aspects such as data reproduction, electronic dissemination, and storage. Additionally, preparations necessary for data sharing, like formatting the data into a usable form, are also factored into these costs. The total cost can vary depending on several factors, including the amount of data involved and the specific terms of the data sharing arrangement. Long-term data sharing agreements, such as subscription models or the use of smart contracts, could streamline the process and potentially reduce costs, particularly in ongoing transactions. In addition to covering these direct costs, reasonable compensation might also incorporate a profit margin. This margin reflects the value added by the data holder and can vary based on various attributes of the data, like its volume, format, and type. The margin also takes into account the investment made by the data holder in collecting the data. For instance, if the data was collected by the holder primarily for their own business use without significant additional investment, the margin might be relatively small. On the other hand, if the data holder made substantial investments to collect the data specifically for their business needs, the margin could be correspondingly higher.

6.6.6.4 Non-discriminatory

The FRAND requirement of Article 6(11) DMA does not only stipulate that gatekeepers need to provide access to search engine data on fair terms and ensure that the compensation charged is reasonable but also that they do not discriminate among different recipients. The two criteria 'fairness' and 'reasonableness' leave gatekeepers with a certain degree of flexibility. Since there is not only one set of access conditions that can be considered fair and the notion of a reasonable price refers to a range of acceptable values, not a single figure, gatekeepers have some discretion as to terms they

770 See also Habich (n 742) 1356.

may apply.[771] The 'non-discrimination' leg adds another layer and limits the gatekeeper's flexibility to some extent, but it does not oblige gatekeepers to treat all recipients schematically equally. Rather it stipulates that like situations must be treated alike and different situations differently. This means that the gatekeeper must grant the same or similar terms to all similarly situated recipients.[772]

Already in the first *Microsoft* decision, the EGC held that the Commission's decision to license the information under reasonable and non-discriminatory terms does not mean that Microsoft must impose the same conditions on every undertaking seeking such licences. Instead, the EGC emphasised that these conditions could be tailored to the unique requirements of each entity seeking a license. Such customisation could depend on factors like the volume of information needed or the specific application of the data in various products.[773]

It is also important to stress that the non-discrimination requirement extends beyond mere pricing but also applies to other terms,[774] particularly those concerning access conditions. Hence, it is the entire agreement, rather than individual terms in isolation, that must be assessed in order to determine adherence to this requirement. This, on the one hand, means that a gatekeeper charging identical prices to similarly situated competitors might still be deemed discriminatory if the access conditions offered vary in quality or favourability. Such a situation could arise if a gatekeeper imposes more burdensome or restrictive conditions on some competitors, despite charging them the same price as others. On the other hand, the non-discrimination requirement does not prevent gatekeepers from offering a variety of pricing schemes. However, they have to ensure that all potential recipients are provided with the same range of options. The essence of non-discrimination in this context is not that every recipient should pay

771 See, Dennis W Carlton and Allan L Shampine, 'An Economic Interpretation of FRAND' (2013) 9 Journal of Competition Law & Economics 531, 542; Lévêque (n 341) 88.

772 Wolf-Posch (n 591) Article 6(11) DMA, para [267]; Yann Ménière, 'Fair, Reasonable and Non-Discriminatory (FRAND) Licensing Terms: Research Analysis of a Controversial Concept.' (Joint Research Centre 2015) JRC 96258 17; Carlton and Shampine (n 771) 546.

773 EGC, T-201/04 *Microsoft v Commission* EU:T:2007:289, para 811.

774 Cf *Unwired Planet International Ltd & Anor v Huawei Technologies Co Ltd & Anor [2017] EWHC 711 (Pat)* para 177.

the exact same royalty rate, but rather that they should all have an equal opportunity to select from the same set of terms and conditions.[775]

With regard to FRAND access to standard essential patents, there has been a debate about whether the non-discrimination clause prohibits (i) unequal treatment for similarly situated firms in general, or (ii) only those differences that are capable of distorting competition. The latter interpretation can be derived from competition law. Article 102(c) TFEU prohibits applying dissimilar conditions to equivalent transactions with other trading parties only if it places them at a competitive disadvantage.[776] Also with regard to the EFD, the Commission in its initial *Microsoft* decision stated that Microsoft had to disclose the interoperability information on a 'non-discriminatory basis. If it was otherwise, the remedy would discriminate against undertakings, thereby introducing new distortions of competition'. Due to the similarities between the EFD and Article 6(11) DMA (as pointed out above 6.6.2), it would seem reasonable to apply the competition law understanding of non-discrimination also to the DMA's access right.

However, as has already been pointed out in legal literature, competition law must not simply be copied to the realm of data law but needs to be critically assessed and refined.[777] At a closer look, it would run counter to the objectives of the DMA if the non-discrimination requirement would only prohibit differences capable of distorting competition. The DMA places obligations on gatekeepers irrespective of whether the conduct of the gatekeepers has a negative impact on competition.[778] In stark contrast to competition law, the DMA views the gatekeepers' dominance as such as problematic. The purpose of the DMA's ex-ante approach is to avoid the often lengthy and complex procedures to demonstrate whether a partic-

775 Gregory Sidak, 'Fair and Unfair Discrimination in Royalties for Standard-Essential Patents Encumbered by a FRAND or RAND Commitment' (2017) 2 Criterion Journal on Innovation 301, 321; see also Wolf-Posch (n 591) Article 6(11) DMA, para [268].

776 See also ECJ, C-525/16, *Meo*, EU:C:2018:270; para 25; ECJ, C-95/04 P, *British Airways v Commission*, EU:C:2007:166, para 144.

777 Picht (n 735) 27.

778 See Recital 11 DMA: 'This Regulation pursues an objective that is complementary to, but different from that of protecting undistorted competition on any given market, as defined in competition-law terms, which is to ensure that markets where gatekeepers are present are and remain contestable and fair, independently from the actual, potential or presumed effects of the conduct of a given gatekeeper covered by this Regulation on competition on a given market. This Regulation therefore aims to protect a different legal interest from that protected by those rules and it should apply without prejudice to their application.'

ular practice has anti-competitive effects (see 6.1), as they would delay the enforcement of fair market practices and allow gatekeepers to continue their potentially harmful behaviour until a decision is reached. This objective would be compromised if the assessment of possible anti-competitive effects is omitted at first but then has to be carried out at a later point in time—namely when assessing whether the access conditions fulfil FRAND criteria. Moreover, since an undertaking requesting access to search engine data does not initially have to prove (and may not be able to) that denied data access has anti-competitive effects, it may struggle to then demonstrate that different access conditions distort competition.[779] Hence, in the context of Article 6(11) DMA the non-discrimination leg of FRAND should be interpreted as prohibiting unequal treatment for similarly situated recipients in general, irrespective of the potential effects on competition.

Different contractual conditions for the provision of data by the gatekeeper do not, however, constitute unlawful discrimination, if these differences are justified by objective reasons.[780] Although the DMA does not expressly stipulate this for Article 6(11) DMA, it follows from the general principle of equal treatment that differentiation is permitted if objectively justified.[781] This Principle has also been applied to abusive discrimination cases dealt with under Article 102(c) TFEU.[782] Moreover, with regard to FRAND obligations under the DA, Recital 41 DA states that differing terms for data access do not amount to unfair discrimination if they are backed by objective justifications.

Under Article 102(c) (TFEU), there has been a reluctance by the courts to accept objective justifications for differential treatment.[783] This trend primarily stems from the nature of cases adjudicated under Article 102(c) TFEU, which predominantly involve forms of price discrimination related to the customer's nationality and therefore have direct implications on EU

779 *Cf. Habich (n 742) 1354.*

780 *Cf. Sidak (n 775) 304.*

781 For example, in ECJ, C-313/04, *Franz Egenberger*, EU:C:2006:454, para 33 the ECJ held that general principle of equal treatment 'requires that comparable situations must not be treated differently and different situations must not be treated alike *unless such treatment is objectively justified*'.

782 EGC, T-612/17, *Google v Commission*, EU:T:2021:763, para 180; ECJ, C-525/16, Meo, EU:C:2018:270, para 29; for a detailed analysis, see Lena Hornkohl, 'Article 102 TFEU, Equal Treatment and Discrimination after Google Shopping' (2022) 13 Journal of European Competition Law & Practice 99.

783 ECJ, C-27/76, *United Brands*, EU:C:1978:22, para 233

internal market integration.[784] One potential avenue for justification could be the argument that market circumstances have evolved between two similar access requests, thereby warranting different treatment.[785] For instance, if the market dynamics or cost structures have significantly changed since the initial access request, a gatekeeper might argue that these changes necessitate a revised approach in their contractual terms.

6.7 Summary

In total, the DMA introduces four different access and portability rights against gatekeepers. Two of them—Articles 6(9) and (10) DMA—have a rather broad scope and are afforded to the users of any core platform service. The other are more specific, as they only afford advertisers/publishers (Article 6(8) DMA) and the providers of search engines (Article 6(11) DMA) the right to access data from gatekeepers.

With Article 6(9) DMA the European legislator intended to overcome the deficiencies of the GDPR's RtDP and introduce an access and portability right that is more efficient in facilitating competition and empowering end users. Since the portability shall be provided by the gatekeeper continuously and in real-time, Article 6(9) DMA allows end users to combine the services of the gatekeeper with specific services from a third party provider without entirely migrating all services (partial change of provider). With regard to the data format, the DMA empowers the Commission to mandate European standardisation bodies to develop appropriate standards. Another reason why the portability right is more effective in addressing the lock-in situation of end users is that it explicitly applies to provided and observed data, irrespective of whether data qualifies as personal data or not. However, there is a debate whether Article 6(9) DMA also applies to inferred and derived data, as the wording of the provision is inconclusive on this matter. In light of the objectives of enabling effective switching to other providers and striking a fair balance between the competing interests, the provision should be interpreted as also covering inferred and derived data. If the Commission deems the inclusion of all data deduced from users'

784 Marco Botta and Klaus Wiedemann, 'To Discriminate or Not to Discriminate? Personalised Pricing in Online Markets as Exploitative Abuse of Dominance' (2020) 50 European Journal of Law and Economics 381, 392.

785 *Cf. Unwired Planet International Ltd & Anor v Huawei Technologies Co Ltd & Anor (Rev 1) [2018] EWCA Civ 2344* para 166 ff.

activities or provided data to be overly extensive, it can limit the scope of covered data through a delegated act. There has also been a debate regarding the legal nature of Article 6(9) DMA and its relationship to Article 20 GDPR. It has been demonstrated that this discussion is merely theoretical and has no practical implications. This is because the limitations outlined in Articles 12(5) and 20(4) GDPR also apply to the portability right provided under Article 6(9) DMA, irrespective of whether it is considered to be a separate data right or an extension of Article 20 GDPR.

Similarly to end users, business users also face challenges in accessing data they have co-generated with the gatekeeper. Therefore, Article 6(10) DMA provides business users with the right to access data that is generated by their own interactions with a gatekeeper's core platform service, as well as to the data that is generated by end users engaging with the business user on the gatekeeper's platform. However, since the latter data is generated by joint contributions from the business user, the gatekeeper, and the end users, business users may access the personal data of end users only if the end user has given consent by opting in to such sharing. In line with the portability right of end users, Article 6(10) DMA should be interpreted as also applying to derived and inferred data. The right, however, does not extend to personal data that pertains to transactions between end users and other business users who use the same core platform service. Gatekeepers have to provide access to the relevant data to business users or authorised third parties free of charge and continuous and real-time basis. Article 9(1) P2B Regulation complements the access right by informing business users, before entering into a business relationship with a gatekeeper, about which data they can later access based on Article 6(10) DMA, and also about the data usage of the gatekeeper.

Article 6(8) DMA affords advertisers and publishers the right to access the data needed for the independent verification of advertising inventory to enable them to cross-check the claims made by advertising platforms regarding the effectiveness and reach of gatekeeper's advertising services. Scope and modalities of this access right are not clearly defined, making it the most ambiguous provision of the DMA. It will therefore need to be further specified in delegated acts of the Commission. If the requested data includes personal data, the gatekeeper has to ensure compliance with the GDPR. However, since redacting the personally identifiable information would significantly reduce the usefulness of the data, the gatekeepers should primarily try to obtain consent from affected individuals that legitimises the use by advertisers or publishers.

Finally, Article 6(11) DMA mandates gatekeepers to allow third-party undertakings that provide online search engines to access the gatekeeper's ranking, query, click, and view data. Personal data must be anonymised as much as necessary to protect the privacy of the users of the gatekeeper but as little as possible in order to ensure that the data is still of value to competitors. The access right of Article 6(11) DMA is quite far-reaching, as it requires gatekeepers to share data directly with their competitors, enabling them to enhance their services and potentially challenge the gatekeeper's dominant position in the search engine market. In contrast to other data rights of the DMA, Article 6(11) DMA affords an access right to a person that has not contributed to the generation of the covered data. Hence, gatekeepers may charge fees for the access, but the terms need to be fair reasonable and non-discriminatory (FRAND). The FRAND criteria are not further specified in the DMA, but the interpretation may draw inspiration from the Data Act. Within the framework developed here, the 'reasonable' leg is specifically related to the pricing aspect. A reasonable fee covers expenses such as data reproduction, electronic dissemination, and storage. It may also include a margin that reflects the value added by the data holder, which varies based on factors such as the volume, format, and type of data, as well as the investment made in collecting the data. The 'fair' criterion, on the other hand, should be understood as introducing an unfairness test for other terms within the access agreement beyond just the price. Non-discrimination means that the gatekeeper must grant the same or similar terms to all similarly situated recipients.

7 Data Act, Chapters II to IV

The Data Act, which was adopted on 13 December 2023, is not only the centrepiece of the European Commission's data strategy but also holds significant relevance for this analysis. Chapter II of the DA introduces two novel data rights for the users of internet of things (IoT) devices regarding access, use and sharing of the data generated through their use of these devices. These rights intend to empower private individuals and companies by giving them control over data generated by the use of their connected ('smart') products (such as fitness trackers and smart TVs) and associated services (such as cloud-based smart TV platforms). Traditionally, this data is controlled by the device manufacturers, limiting the users' ability to utilise the data generated by their IoT devices independently or to share it with third-party service providers that offer complementary services. The rights laid down in Articles 4 and 5 (Chapter II) of the DA are applicable horizontally across all sectors. There is a consensus among commentators that these rights will have a significant impact on the digital economy, though opinions vary on whether this impact will be positive or negative.

The second significant aspect of the Data Act that is of direct relevance to this subject of this book is the provisions that are not limited to the data rights introduced by the DA, but that apply to any situation in which Union or national law mandates data sharing between companies.

Chapter III of the DA regulates the amount of the remuneration and the other contractual conditions for any legally required data exchange between companies. The scope of Chapter III is not limited to the data rights introduced by the DA but extends to any situation of statutory data sharing obligations between enterprises mandated by Union or national law that entered into force after 12 September 2025 (Article 50 DA). Moreover, Chapter VI, which only contains a single provision, namely Article 13 DA, lays down an unfairness test that applies to any private sector data accessed and used on the basis of a contract between enterprises concluded after 12 September 2025. Hence, the DA produces effects also with regard to other data access and portability rights of the *acquis*.

7.1 Product and related services

The objective of the DA's access and portability rights is to make available the data generated by IoT devices, which the DA refers to as 'connected product'. The central element of the DA's definition of a connected product is that it is an item that has the capacity to generate, collect, and transmit data. This capability can be realised through electronic means or via an integrated interface within the device, allowing for data extraction (Article 2(5) DA). Examples of connected products are smart home devices, connected vehicles, networked medical devices and networked production machines. These products have the ability to generate, collect, and transmit data as a core feature of their functionality. Devices whose main purpose is to store, process or transmit data on behalf of third parties are expressly excluded from the scope of the DA. This exclusion refers to devices such as servers or cloud infrastructures (see Recital 16 DA).[786]

However, the DA's scope extends beyond data directly generated by the physical device and also covers data that has been generated by 'related services'. Related services are defined as digital services that are integrated into a product or connected to it in a manner that the product cannot function properly without the service. These services may already be connected to the product at the time of purchase or added later by the product manufacturer or a third party. A typical example is companion apps that are designed to complement and enhance the functionality of a certain smart device. The definition of the DA for related services is aligned with that for goods with digital elements as set out in Article 2(5)(b) of the Sale of Goods Directive (SGD).[787] The DA also explicitly includes virtual assistants in the scope of its data access rights (Article 1(4) DA). Recital 22 clarifies that the access and portability rights shall only apply to data generated by the interaction between the user and a connected product or related service through the virtual assistant. Any data generated by the virtual assistant unrelated to product use is explicitly excluded.[788]

786 See Simon Assion and Lukas Willecke, 'Der EU Data Act: Die neuen Regelungen zu vernetzten Produkten und Diensten' [2023] MMR 805, 806.

787 Dirk Staudenmayer, 'Der Verordnungsvorschlag der Europäischen Kommission zum Datengesetz – Privatrechtsregeln für Datenzugangsrechte' [2022] EuZW 1037, 1039.

788 Louisa Specht-Riemenschneider, 'Data Act – Auf dem (Holz-)Weg zu mehr Dateninnovation?' [2022] ZRP 137, 138.

Related services can be a part of the purchase, rental, or lease agreement for the connected product. According to Recital 17 DA, in case of doubt, it shall be presumed that a service is provided as part of the purchase, rent or lease contract. This presumption mirrors that of Article 3(3) SGD. However, it is sufficient for the application of the DA if the related services are provided for products of the same type, and users may reasonably expect them to be provided in view of the nature of the product and taking into account any public statements made by the seller, lessor, landlord or others in earlier links of the contractual chain, including the manufacturer.[789]

It has been pointed out that it is not described how the concept of 'function' is to be understood and it can therefore be challenging to determine whether a service qualifies as 'related service'. An example that has been provided to illustrate this uncertainty is a map app on a smartphone. It has been argued that it is not clear whether the map app is essential for the smartphone's functionality or whether it is only an optional feature.[790] However, the alignment between the DA and the SGD allows for reference to the considerations outlined in the SGD when defining related services under the DA.[791] In the context of the SGD, it is argued that the determination of what constitutes a product's 'function' should depend on the type of use and the purposes of the goods as they would normally be used or as specified in the contract.[792] Applying this consideration to the example of the map app on a smartphone, it can be concluded that users typically expect to use a smartphone for the purposes of route finding, accessing traffic information, using public transport options, and finding local points of interest. Based on this typical use and purpose, the map app on a smartphone should qualify as a related service.

Digital services and digital content that do not fall within the definition of related services are excluded from the DA's scope. This exclusion cannot be justified by arguing that a synchronisation between SGD and DA should be established. This is because the concept of 'goods with digital elements' is not intended to avoid regulating digital content and digital services altogether, but to demarcate the scope of the SGD in relation to the DCD. Given the DA's relatively novel and far-reaching approach to data access

789 See Staudenmayer (n 787) 1040.

790 Assion and Willecke (n 786) 806.

791 See Staudenmayer (n 787) 1039.

792 Juliette Sénéchal, in Reiner Schulze and Dirk Staudenmayer (eds), *EU Digital Law: Article-by-Article Commentary* (First edition, Beck, Hart, Nomos 2020) Article 2, para [16].

and usage, the exclusion of digital services and content could be seen as a legal policy precaution and an effort to reach a relatively swift political agreement.[793] By focusing on data related to products and their related services, the legislators may have sought to circumvent potential industry resistance to regulating the broad area of data generated by digital content and services, which could have potentially derailed the entire piece of legislation.

7.2 User, data holder and data recipient

According to the envisioned concept of the DA, the users of connected products should play the central role with regard to data usage.[794] Or as the Recitals put it: 'The user bears the risks and enjoys the benefits of using the connected product and should also enjoy access to the data it generates.' Article 2(12) DA defines 'user' as a person that owns a connected product or to whom temporary rights to use that connected product have been contractually transferred, or that receives related services. Both legal persons and natural persons can be 'users' under the DA.[795] Recital 18 DA also clarifies that it is possible for multiple persons to be simultaneously users of one connected product. In such cases, all of these persons have user rights with regard to the generated data.[796]

The data rights of the user are directed against the data holder. The Commission's initial proposal makes it quite clear that the DA wants to address the person having de facto control over the data, which will typically be the manufacturer of the connected product. According to Article 2(6) of the DA proposal, a data holder was defined as a legal or natural person who has the right or obligation under the DA, under applicable Union law or under applicable national law implementing Union law to make data available and who is in a position to provide certain data by controlling the technical design of the product and related services.

793 Staudenmayer (n 787) 1040.

794 Axel Funk, 'Das Prinzip der Nutzerzentriertheit des Data Act – ein gravierender Strukturfehler — Untersuchung und Bewertung der zentralen Rolle des Nutzers in der Datenökonomie nach der Konzeption des Data Act.' (2023) 39 Computer und Recht 421, 423.

795 Assion and Willecke (n 786) 807.

796 Specht-Riemenschneider (n 788) 138.

However, it has been argued that basing the definition of data holder on the control over the product's technical design and the technical control over the data would be too narrow. Manufacturers who do not have technical and factual control over the data, or actors that control the data but do not control the technical design of the product would not have been addressed under this definition.[797] The final version of the DA significantly broadens the scope of who qualifies as data holder.[798] Article 2(13) DA, defines data holder as 'natural or legal person that has the right or obligation, in accordance with this Regulation, applicable Union law or national legislation adopted in accordance with Union law, to use and make available data, including, where contractually agreed, product data or related service data which it has retrieved or generated during the provision of a related service.' Especially the last part of this rather cryptic definition is not quite clear.[799] It would seem that the element of control over the data has been eliminated altogether, which dilutes the boundaries of the definition. The 'de facto control' is the defining element for who is to be considered data holder. Removing it may lead to situations where nearly any participant in the data processing chain could be labelled a data holder because they all have either rights or obligations with regard to the data.[800] This would overextend the intended reach of the DA's provisions and make it challenging to determine who exactly bears the responsibilities under DA.

However, the English version of the DA could also be understood as referring to persons that are in a position to either retrieve product data from a connected product or generate related service data in the course of providing a related service.[801] Hence, the data holder is not just any person that happens to have access to the data, but rather one that is

797 Specht-Riemenschneider (n 788) 138.

798 Funk (n 794) 423.

799 Assion and Willecke (n 786) 807.

800 See Schmidt (n 175) 77.

801 In the German version of Artice 2(13) DA both retrieve ('abgerufen') and generated ('generiert') refer only to to related services and not to the connected product. '„Dateninhaber" ist eine natürliche oder juristische Person, die nach dieser Verordnung, nach geltendem Unionsrecht oder nach nationalen Rechtsvorschriften zur Umsetzung des Unionsrechts berechtigt oder verpflichtet ist, Daten – soweit vertraglich vereinbart, auch Produktdaten oder verbundene Dienstdaten – zu nutzen und bereitzustellen, die sie während der Erbringung eines verbundenen Dienstes abgerufen oder generiert hat.' This seems to be a translation error resulting from the cumbersome wording.

in a position where they can actively manage, retrieve, or generate this data through their engagement with the product or service, i.e. have de facto control over the data.[802] Such an interpretation would ensure that the obligations outlined in the DA are directed at persons capable of fulfilling these responsibilities.[803]

7.3 Objectives and rationale

The underlying issue that the data rights introduced by the Data Act intend to address is that IoT devices, which are becoming ubiquitous both in our business and personal lives, generate an unprecedented amount of data. However, manufacturers can develop the technical design of their IoT products in such a way that they retain exclusive control over the data produced through device usage. Hence, end-users often find themselves without access to the data they have generated using their IoT devices. Other companies are unable to access this IoT data to provide complementary services and products, which harms consumer choice and innovation.[804] Article 20 GDPR is only of limited help because it only covers personal data and does not enable continuous, real-time access, which will usually be necessary for the use of complementary products and services (see 5.6.1).[805]

Affording users a right to access the usage data generated by their IoT device (Article 4 DA)—irrespective of whether it qualifies as personal or non-personal data—and to transfer it to third party (Article 5 DA) is intended to empower users by giving them more control over the data they have co-generated.[806] This shall ensure a more equitable distribution of the IoT data's value within the data economy.[807] Another objective is to prevent scenarios of data-based 'lock-ins', where users are confined to a single provider due to the provider's exclusive control over user-generated data. Enabling users to transfer the usage data to third parties, allows them to use data-dependent complementary services and products, thereby promoting

802 See Schmidt-Kessel (n 246) 77 who also points that qualifying a person as a data holder is unrealistic if there is no indication of actual or at least legally authorised access to the data.

803 See Assion and Willecke (n 786) 607.

804 Wolfgang Kerber, 'Governance of IoT Data: Why the EU Data Act Will Not Fulfill Its Objectives' (2023) 72 GRUR International 120, 120.

805 See Steinrötter (n 515) 222.

806 Recital 19 DA.

807 Recital 27 DA.

a more competitive aftermarket and stimulating the development of entirely novel services.[808]

Although increased competition in aftermarkets is one of the DA's objectives, its approach is different to traditional competition law, but also to the approach of the Digital Markets Act. The rationale of the DA is that data is often underutilised and that this inefficiency hinders innovation. Thus, unlike competition law the DA provides general data rights, regardless of whether the entity holding the data is dominant or if refusing access would constitute an abuse of dominance.[809] The main justification for introducing access and portability rights is that that the user has contributed to the generation of the data and should therefore have a say in how this data is used (see 10.1.1.1). This approach is proactive and aims to reshape the dynamics of data usage and access in a broader sense.[810]

7.3.1 Access based on the concept of co-generated data

Initially, the European Commission considered introducing an ownership right with regard to non-personal IoT data.[811] However, after many different commentators have demonstrated that a data ownership would not be a suitable tool to address the existing issues of user lock-in and unfair value distribution and could potentially introduce additional problems, the Commission changed course. The current approach of affording the users of IoT devices data rights with regard to usage data has been significantly influenced by the Principles of the Data Economy—a joint project of the ALI and ELI. While the DA is not the only instrument that lays down data rights in co-generated data (see 10.1.1 and 10.1.3), it is the first time that the European legislator explicitly refers to the concept of co-generated data and was visibly influenced by the suggestions of the Principles.

---

808 Recital 30 DA.

809 See Matthias Leistner and Lucie Antoine, 'IPR and the Use of Open Data and Data Sharing Initiatives by Public and Private Actors' (European Parliament 2022) 15 <https://www.europarl.europa.eu/thinktank/en/document/IPOL_STU(2022)732266> accessed 2 January 2024.

810 Axel Metzger and Heike Schweitzer, 'Shaping Markets: A Critical Evaluation of the Draft Data Act' [2023] ZEuP 42, 48.

811 Communication from the Commission to the European Parliament, the Council, the European Economic and Social Committee and the Committee of the Regions, "Building a European Data Economy" COM(2017) 9 final, 13.

In a nutshell, Part II, Chapter B of the Principles recommends that whoever has contributed to the generation of data should generally have some rights with respect to its use and the value it generates.[812] The Principles identify four different types of contributions to the generation of data.[813] Concerning IoT data, users primarily engage in the two forms that the Principles deem to be the most substantial. For much of the IoT data generated, the user is either the person who is the subject of the information (e.g. data about the shopping preferences of a natural person), or the owner or operator of the asset that is the subject of that information (e.g. data on the maintenance status of machinery). In instances where this is not the case, the user's contribution to the data generation process typically involves either carrying out an activity that generates the data or simply owning or operating a device that generates the data.

Affording data rights to parties that have co-generated data is intended to fulfil functions similar to those fulfilled by ownership with regard to traditional rivalrous assets. However, unlike intellectual property rights, rights in co-generated data do not afford their holder a clearly defined range of rights with *erga omnes*-effect, but should be tailored to a concrete situation and address the underlying issue.[814] The biggest difference between data ownership and data rights in co-generated IoT data is that the latter do not endow an exclusive position with regard to the data to either the manufacturer of the IoT device (i.e. data holder in the terminology of the DA) or the user. Rather the data holder and user, along with any third-party recipients, may use the data simultaneously for their respective purposes. This concurrent usage model aims to prevent the monopolisation of data and foster a more collaborative and open data environment.[815] Generally the co-generators are free to use the data for any lawful purpose, the Data Act does, however, impose certain constraints with regard to data usage where it is necessary to protect the legitimate interest of the other co-generating party. A notable example is Article 4(4) DA, which restricts users from utilising the data to develop a product that directly competes with the original product from which the data was generated (see 7.5.5.2). The foundational reasoning behind this limitation is also rooted in the concept of co-generation, as articulated in the Principles. Co-generation is not only

812 See Staudenmayer (n 787) 1041.

813 Neil Cohen and Christiane Wendehorst (n 119) Principle 18(1).

814 Neil Cohen and Christiane Wendehorst (n 119) Notes to Principle 16.

815 See Metzger and Schweitzer (n 810) 48.

a basis for justifying access to data but also entails a responsibility to refrain from data activities that could harm the interests of other co-generators.[816]

The fact that the data rights afforded by the Data Act revolve around the concept of co-generated data becomes even more evident when looking at Article 5 DA. One of the objectives of this provision is to make data available to third party providers in order to create opportunities for businesses to develop and offer additional products or services that complement or enhance the functionality of connected products. This is intended to stimulate innovation in aftermarkets, and promote the creation of entirely new services that make effective use of data from a variety of connected products and related services.[817] However, the data right does not afford an access right directly to third party providers, but gives the user the right to request a direct transfer from the data holder to the third party recipient. Hence, third party service providers are only indirect beneficiaries of the data right—their access depends on the willingness of the user to request a data transfer (see 7.6). This indirect access approach is consistent with the concept of co-generation. Since the third party has no specific relationship to the way in which the data was generated, granting a direct right of access to third parties could not be justified by co-generation, but would have to be based on an overriding public interest. A common public interest consideration in granting data rights to third parties is the promotion of undistorted competition.[818] However, as already pointed out above, the DA is a horizontal regime that applies to a variety of different sectors irrespective of whether a concrete market failure can be identified. Moreover, providing third parties with direct access rights could potentially conflict with another key objective of the Data Act: enhancing user control over data generated by their IoT devices. If third parties, who have not contributed to the generation of the data, were given direct access, it would undermine the user's authority and involvement in the decision-making process regarding 'their own' data.

816 See Neil Cohen and Christiane Wendehorst (n 119) Principle 21; See also Metzger and Schweitzer (n 810) 50 who state that the aim of the DA is to 'create a legal infrastructure of shared rights of data co- generators to use these data, and to use these data independently, but with respect for the legitimate interests of the other party.'

817 Recital 32 DA.

818 Neil Cohen and Christiane Wendehorst (n 119) Notes to Principle 24.

7.3.2 Recognising/strengthening the de facto control of manufacturers?

A central point of criticism of the DA's access approach is that the DA implicitly recognises—and even strengthens—the data holder's de facto control over the IoT data. Especially Article 11 DA, which gives the data holder the right to apply technical protection measures against the unlawful use of data is viewed as affording the manufacturer of an IoT device a position similar to that of the holder of an exclusive right.[819] Furthermore, it is asserted that the exclusive control of the data holders over the data is further strengthened by Article 4(11) DA, which stipulates that the user shall not use coercive means or abuse gaps in the technical infrastructure of a data holder which is designed to protect the data in order to obtain access to data.[820]

This critical view is not shared, for several reasons. First, the DA's recognition of the manufacturer's entitlement, in addition to that of the user, to utilise IoT data aligns with the concept of co-generation. After all, the manufacturer, having invested in the development of the product, is just as much a contributor to the generation of data as the user. This approach also supports the broader objective of enhancing data usage for various purposes.

The fact that the generated data typically remains on the servers, and thus under the control of the data holder, is not inherently problematic. The data generated by the IoT must be stored somewhere, and the manufacturer's infrastructure is the most appropriate option. Storage on the data holder's servers would only be problematic if the user's data rights were limited exclusively to accessing the data on the data holder's infrastructure (in-situ access) without the option to receive the data. With regard to the initial draft of the DA, this was argued by several commentators.[821] However, as shown under 7.5.4, the final version of the DA can and should

819 Specht-Riemenschneider (n 788) 137.

820 Kerber, 'Governance of IoT Data' (n 804) 124.

821 Kerber, 'Governance of IoT Data' (n 804) 124; Josef Drexl and others, 'Position Statement of the Max Planck Institute for Innovation and Competition of 25 May 2022 on the Commission's Proposal of 23 February 2022 for a Regulation on Harmonised Rules on Fair Access to and Use of Data (Data Act)' (2022) 26 <https://www.ip.mpg.de/fileadmin/ipmpg/content/stellungnahmen/Position_Statement_MPI_Data_Act_Formal__13.06.2022.pdf> accessed 2 January 2024; Louise Specht-Riemenschneider, 'Der Entwurf des Data Act: Eine Analyse der vorgesehenen Datenzugangsansprüche im Verhältnis B2B, B2C und B2G' [2022] MMR 809, 816.

be interpreted as allowing in-situ access upon user request, but not limiting access exclusively to this method.

If one adopts the viewpoint expressed, asserting that both the data holder and the user have a right to use the IoT data for any lawful purpose, it also makes sense to enable them to protect this data. Since unauthorised access is a shared concern of both data holders and users, the possibility to apply technical protection measures pursuant to Article 11 DA will typically be in the interest of both parties. If the user wants to access the data or share it with third parties, the provision explicitly stipulates that the technical protection measures may not hinder the exercise of the user's data rights. In all other scenarios, the user and data holder share a mutual interest in preventing unauthorised access to the co-generated data.

Without the DA, there have been no real limitations—besides data protection and IP law—to the de facto control of the manufacturer. The DA not only gives users the possibility to access and use the data generated by the IoT devices but also places certain limits on data usage. While some commentators may have hoped that the access right would be more extensive, it is difficult to see how these two measures strengthen and not weaken the de facto control of the manufacturer.

7.4 Overview of the contractual aspects of the DA

Another peculiarity of the DA is its strong emphasis on contractual relationships between the involved parties.

The first contractual relationship typically exists between the user and the person from which the user purchases, rents, or leases a connected product. This person could either be the manufacturer of the connected product (who will usually also qualify as data holder) but may also be a retailer. Article 3 DA establishes pre-contractual information duties, requiring the contractual partner (i.e. the retailer or manufacturer) to, inter alia, provide the user with essential information about the data that the connected product will generate and how the user can access this data.[822]

In most cases, a second contract between the data holder (typically the manufacturer of the connected product) and the user will come into play. This is because Article 4(13) DA specifies that a data holder can only use non-personal data generated by the connected product if there is a contract

822 See Schmidt-Kessel (n 246) 79.

in place with the user (see 7.5.6.1). Under the same contract or in an additional contract, the data controller and the users may determine the details of the data access on the basis of Article 4(1) DA and the subsequent use of the data by the product user.[823]

Finally, if a user decides to exercise their right to transfer data to third parties under Article 5 DA, two additional contracts will be concluded. The user will usually exercise their portability right if the third party recipient offers the user a contract through which the user receives a service or another type of economic benefit. According to Article 6(1) DA, the third party may process the data made available to it pursuant to Article 5 DA only for the purposes and under the conditions agreed in this contract. Another contract needs to be concluded between the data holder and the third-party recipient. Article 8 DA stipulates that the data holder must reach an agreement with the third-party recipient regarding the arrangements for making the data available. The contract between the data holder and the third-party recipient needs to outline the terms and conditions for data access, usage and sharing, and adhere to principles of fairness, reasonableness, and non-discrimination (see 7.6.2.1).[824]

Although the aforementioned contracts are generally subject to the contractual freedom of the parties, certain mandatory requirements are imposed by the DA. For instance, when a third party receives data under Article 5 DA, they are allowed to use the data for purposes agreed upon in the contract with the user. However, there is a restriction, as stipulated in Article 6(2)(b) DA, which prohibits the third-party recipient from using the received data for profiling unless it is deemed necessary to provide the service requested by the user. Additionally, unilaterally imposed clauses of some of the contracts are subject to an unfairness test. With regard to the b2b contracts between data holders and third party recipients, the criteria for assessing the unfairness test are established in Article 13 DA.[825] Contracts between the data holder and users relating to the use of non-personal data are subject to the Unfair Contract Terms Directive (see Article 1(9) and

823 See Metzger and Schweitzer (n 810) 62; Dirk Staudenmayer, 'Der Verordnungsvorschlag der Europäischen Kommission zum Datengesetz – Auf dem Weg zum Privatrecht der Datenwirtschaft' [2022] EuZW 596, 597.

824 Staudenmayer (n 823) 597.

825 Assion and Willecke (n 786) 809; Staudenmayer (n 823) 597 f.

Recitals 9, 29 DA) or, more precisely, its national implementing legislation (for a detailed analysis of the unfairness test, see 7.9).[826]

Despite the DA's strong emphasis on the contractual relationship between the different parties, it is important to highlight, that the access and portability rights of Articles 4 and 5 DA are non-contractual rights by nature. The user may enforce its right against the data holder even if no contract has been concluded.[827]

7.5 Horizontal access to data generated by the use of a product or related service (Article 4 DA)

According to Article 4(1) DA, data holders are obliged to make readily available data, as well as the relevant metadata necessary to interpret and use those data, accessible to the user. This has to be done without undue delay, easily, securely, free of charge, in a comprehensive, structured, commonly used and machine-readable format and, where relevant and technically feasible, continuously and in real-time.

However, users may only invoke the data access right set out in Article 4 DA if the manufacturer did not comply with its duty under Article 3 DA to design and manufacture IoT devices in a way that the user can access the relevant data directly from the connected product or related service (access by design). Article 3 DA bears a strong resemblance to the provisions of product safety law.

Compared to other data access and portability rights of the acquis, the DA contains relatively detailed explanations of the data covered and the conditions of access—though the bar was not set very high in this respect either. However, despite the addition of a significant number of provisions throughout the legislative process, the DA does not provide answers to key issues. For instance, it remains unclear whether Article 4 DA obliges the data holder to put the user in full control of the data, or if in-situ access is sufficient. Many questions regarding the delicate relationship between the DA and the GDPR are also left open. Moreover, the accelerated pace and intensity of activity during the legislative process have also led to the inclusion of some provisions whose content and underlying intentions are

826 Sebastian Schwamberger, 'Die Klauselkontrolle in Art. 13 Data Act' [2024] MMR 96, 98.

827 Metzger and Schweitzer (n 810) 47.

not entirely clear. A key issue, which warrants a dedicated sub-chapter, is the complex relationship between Articles 4 and 5 of the DA.

Unlike other regulations that primarily focus on access and portability rights, Articles 4 (and 5) DA also specify usage limitations for both the data holder and the user. These limitations contribute to the DA's overarching goal of challenging the data holder's de facto control over IoT data and redistributing the extraction of value from the generated data. By restricting how data holders can use the data, the DA further prevents data holders from maintaining exclusive control and sole discretion over data usage. The usage limitations of the user are intended to protect the legitimate interests of the data holder (see 7.5.5).

7.5.1 Data generated by the use of a product or related service

The access right of the user set out in Article 4(1) DA applies to data generated by the use of the connected product or the related service, irrespective of whether the generated data is personal or non-personal data (regarding the relationship to the GDPR, see 7.10).[828] While most data rights do not address the question whether they cover only provided data or also observed or even derived and inferred data (see e.g. 6.4.4.2), the DA contains quite specific instructions in that regard. According to Recital 15 DA, 'data generated by the use of the connected product or the related service' should be understood to cover both data recorded intentionally as well as data which results indirectly from the user's action.

Intentionally recorded data, which corresponds with the understanding of provided data, refers to data that users knowingly and actively record through their interactions with the connected product or related service. Examples include setting preferences in a smart home device, inputting information into a fitness tracking app, or scheduling tasks with a smart assistant. In contrast, indirect data is generated as a by-product of the operation of IoT devices, i.e. observed data.[829] For instance, a smartwatch collects environmental data such as temperature and altitude, as well as interaction data with other devices, all of which are indirect results of the user's actions. The Recitals also clarify that the access and portability rights should also cover data generated when the user is not actively using the

828 See Assion and Willecke (n 786) 806.
829 Kerber, 'Governance of IoT Data' (n 804) 125.

product. This would, inter alia, include data about the status of the product or its components, like battery levels and network connection, when in standby mode or switched off.[830]

The data that is to be shared or made accessible must be accompanied by relevant metadata, the time at which data was collected (timestamp) and the conditions under which it was generated (basic context). Including this data shall make the raw data meaningful and actionable for further usage.[831] For instance, a timestamp may help users or third-party services to sequence events and understand patterns over time and draw valuable inferences from the raw data.

7.5.1.1 Exclusion of inferred and derived data

Inferred or derived data, which is not directly generated by the connected product or related service but is instead deduced from the raw data by data analysis, does not fall within the scope of the DA, unless there exists an agreement between the user and the data holder stating otherwise (Recital 15 DA). This means that data holders that invest in advanced data processing techniques retain control over the fruits of their investments.[832] This limitation has been criticised by commentators. They argue that inferred and derived data will often be of greater importance for the creation of innovative products and services on secondary markets than raw data. For services of third party providers, it may not be sufficient to have only access to raw data.[833] Moreover, it has been asserted that derived data also contains a connection to the user, which would justify a data access right with regard to inferred and derived data, particularly in view of the DA's objective of ensuring a fair distribution of the value created from data.[834] With regard to the initial DA-proposal, concerns have been voiced that the exclusion of inferred and derived data would only leave genuinely raw data within the scope of the access right, because almost every meaningful and readable representation of data has already undergone some form of processing or conversion. Such raw data would likely be unusable for users,

830 See Specht-Riemenschneider (n 821) 815.
831 Andreas Wiebe, 'Der Data Act – Innovation oder Illusion?' [2023] GRUR 1569, 1570.
832 Recital 14 DA; see also Wiebe, 'Der Data Act – Innovation oder Illusion?' (n 831) 1570.
833 Kerber, 'Governance of IoT Data' (n 804) 127.
834 Specht-Riemenschneider (n 821) 815.

especially if they are consumers.[835] With regard to the final draft, however, the Recitals make it clear that the legislator did not intend the scope of application to be that narrow.[836] Recital 15 states that the data access right covers not only raw but also pre-processed data. Raw data, or source data, is collected directly by the device without any further modification. Pre-processed data, on the other hand, has undergone initial treatment to render the data comprehensible and ready for further analysis.

The general criticism of the exclusion of derived and inferred data is not shared. The restriction of the scope of application is consistent with the concept of co-generated data, which justifies the users' right to access the IoT data. Inferred data still contains a contribution of the user, but the user's role in generating inferred data is less pronounced, while the data holder's role is more substantial, as they invest in the analytical processing of the raw data. Hence, it would require additional circumstances that justify a right to access that data. The Principles for a Data Economy rightly point out that the share which a party had in the generation of the data is the only factor that needs to be considered in determining whether it is appropriate to afford an access right to a party. Another important factor is the imbalance of bargaining power between the parties.[837] With regard to Articles 6(9) and (10) DMA, which afford users the right to access and port data generated during the use of a gatekeeper's core platform services, it is argued in this work that these rights should also cover inferred and derived data. However, there is a decisive difference between the DA and DMA. The DMA affords data rights against data holders with significant market power, while the DA grants access and portability rights regardless of the data holder's market position. Third party data recipients may even be economically more powerful players than the data holders from which they receive the data. Moreover, if a data holder can derive valuable insights from IoT data through their investments and algorithms, it raises the question of why third-party service providers should not be able to do the same, provided they are willing to make similar investments. In light of these considerations, excluding inferred and derived data from the scope of the DA seems justified. To address potential gaps, the general access and portability rights under the DA could be complemented by

835 Rupprecht Podszun, *Der EU Data Act und der Zugang zu Sekundärmärkten am Beispiel des Handwerks* (Nomos 2023) 44.

836 See Wiebe, 'Der Data Act – Innovation oder Illusion?' (n 831) 1570.

837 Neil Cohen and Christiane Wendehorst (n 119) Principle 19.

sector-specific and more far-reaching access and portability rights that also apply to derived and inferred data.[838]

7.5.1.2 'Readily available data' only

The final text of the DA has limited the scope of the access and portability rights to 'readily available'. According to Article 2 (17) DA, 'readily available' data refers to the data that the data holder, can access without disproportionate effort, meaning that retrieving this data should not require more than a 'simple operation'. This limitation seeks to ensure that data holders are not required to store or transfer data that they do not use in the ordinary course of their operations or that the connected product is not designed to retain (Recital 20 DA). The DA does not want to impose an obligation on data holders to create new or additional means of data storage simply to fulfil a request for access under the DA.[839] For example, a smart thermostat might measure and adjust room temperature in real-time, but it may not store historical temperature data because the collected data has no further use once the immediate purpose is served. Since this data is not intended to be stored by the manufacturer and is not used beyond its initial purpose, the manufacturer is not obliged to store the data solely to satisfy a potential future access request.

Limiting the scope to 'readily available data' also ensures compliance with data protection law. An obligation to store all data generated by a connected product would be in conflict with the GDPR's principle of data minimisation, which requires a reduction in the amount of personal data processed.[840]

838 Recital 27 DA explicitly states that 'Union or national law may be adopted to address sector-specific needs and objectives'; see also Rupprecht Podszun and Clemens Pfeifer, 'Datenzugang nach dem EU Data Act: Der Entwurf der Europäischen Kommission' [2022] GRUR 953, 960.

839 See Assion and Willecke (n 786) 807; Wiebe, 'Der Data Act – Innovation oder Illusion?' (n 831) 1571.

840 On the principle of data minimisation, see e.g. Stephan Pötters, in Peter Gola and Dirk Heckmann (eds), *Datenschutz-Grundverordnung, Bundesdatenschutzgesetz: DS-GVO / BDSG* (3rd edn, Beck 2022) Article 5 GDPR, para [22 ff.].

7.5.2 Data format and quality

The DA mandates that data provided to users must be in a commonly used and machine-readable format. These requirements for the data format were missing from the original draft of the DA, which led to justified criticism from commentators.[841] After all, in the public consultation on the Data Act, 69 % of respondents cited technical hurdles, including the challenge posed by divergent data formats and the absence of uniform standards, as obstacles to b2b data sharing.[842] As requested by commentators, the legislators added a data format requirement that aligns with that of Article 20 GDPR, which ensures consistency between the two data rights.[843] Since Article 4 DA and Article 20 GDPR use the exact same wording, reference can be made to comment on the data format requirement under the GDPR (5.4).

With regard to data quality, Article 4 DA sets out that the quality of the data made available to the user must be on par with the quality of the data available to the data holder, as far as technically feasible. This means that the data should not be degraded or altered in a way that diminishes its accuracy, relevance, or usefulness. The purpose is to ensure that the user receives data that is as valuable and functional as it is for the data holder. Conversely, however, this also means that recipient-friendly preparation of the raw data is not required.[844]

7.5.3 Access conditions

Access to IoT data must be granted 'without undue delay, free of charge, and, where applicable, continuously and in real-time'. By obliging the data holder to provide access on a continuous basis and in real-time, the right of access under Article 4(1) DA goes well beyond the GDPR's RtDP in terms of data access modalities. It has already been pointed out above that

841 Podszun, *Der EU Data Act und der Zugang zu Sekundärmärkten am Beispiel des Handwerks* (n 835) 67; Steinrötter (n 515) 222; Drexl and others (n 821) 27.

842 Data Act Proposal, COM(2022) 68 final, 10.

843 Podszun, *Der EU Data Act und der Zugang zu Sekundärmärkten am Beispiel des Handwerks* (n 835) 68; Drexl and others (n 821) 27.

844 Torsten Gerpott, 'Vorschlag für ein europäisches Datengesetz — Überblick und Analyse der Vorgaben für vernetzte Produkte' (2022) 38 Computer und Recht 271, 275.

the lack of real-time and continuous access is considered one of the most central deficits of Article 20 GDPR. This is because a continuous and real-time stream of data will often be necessary for the use of complementary services of third parties that build upon the functionality provided by the original service or product.[845]

While both the GDPR and the DA mandate timely access to the requested data, the DA imposes more stringent requirements on data holders. Under the GDPR, data controllers are required to comply with data access requests 'within one month of receipt of the request.' This period can be extended by two additional months if necessary, considering the complexity and number of the requests. Article 4(1) DA stipulates that the data holder needs to provide access without undue delay, i.e. the provision of data should happen as quickly as reasonably possible. This difference reflects the DA's emphasis on facilitating broader and more efficient data sharing and portability for the IoT sector.[846]

The right of the user to access the data generated by the IoT device is explicitly stated to be free of charge. This is the same under the GDPR. However, Article 12(5) GDPR allows the data controller to either charge an appropriate fee or refuse to take action at all in case the access request is manifestly unfounded or excessive. Such an explicit restriction is not provided for in the DA. However, as argued above 6.4.5.2, based on the abuse of rights doctrine, which follows from primary law,[847] Article 4(1) DA should be interpreted in such a way that excessive requests are not permitted or only if the costs incurred are reimbursed in order to protect the data holder's fundamental right to conduct business and contractual freedom.

---

845 Gill and Metzger (n 563) 229; Graef, Husovec and van den Boom (n 485) 13; Furman and others (n 563) 68.

846 See Steinrötter (n 515) 221.

847 A prohibition on the abuse of rights is laid down in Article 54 of the CFR. But even before the CFR was declared in 2000, the ECJ has repeatedly held, particularly in the context of fundamental freedoms, that 'the Community law cannot be relied on for abusive or fraudulent ends'. See ECJ, C-367/96, *Kefalas*, EU:C:1998:222, para 20 with further references to case law. On the discussion whether a general EU-specific principle of abuse of rights exists, see Reich (n 646) 209.

7.5.4 In situ access or full control?

A key question is whether Article 4(1) DA puts users in full control of the IoT data or whether it only affords the right to process the data on the data holder's servers. The latter form of access is referred to as 'in situ access', which is based on the idea that the algorithms are brought to the data instead of transferring the data to the person that wants to process the data. This approach offers the advantage of mitigating the risks associated with data transfers, such as security breaches or privacy concerns. Moreover, in situ access eliminates the need for redundant data transfers, particularly when the data does not require modification but merely needs to be read or analysed. For users that only require simple, read-only access to data, in situ access will typically be the preferred approach, as it simplifies the user experience by providing instant access to data without the complexities and delays associated with data transfer and external processing.[848] However, in situ access also means that data holders retain technical control over the data. Consequently, the modalities for data access and sharing under in-situ access do not involve actual data transfer or allow users the flexibility to freely and easily combine the data with other datasets.[849] The extent to which Article 4(1) DA empowers the user (and encroaches the data holder's de facto control) depends quite significantly on whether the user gets full access or in situ access only. It is, therefore, all the more surprising that the DA does not explicitly address this matter, but rather gives vague indications that can be interpreted in both ways.

Root of the controversy is Recital 21 of the initial DA-Proposal (Recital 22 in the final DA), which states that connected products 'may be designed to permit the user or a third party to process the data on the product or on a computing instance of the manufacturer.' Some commentators have interpreted this section of the Recitals as implying that the data holder is not obligated to transfer a copy of the data to the user in order to fulfil their data availability requirement. Instead, it would be sufficient for the data holder to grant access to the data on their own servers or those of a cloud provider of their choice.[850] It was criticised that a mere in-situ

848 Podszun, *Der EU Data Act und der Zugang zu Sekundärmärkten am Beispiel des Handwerks* (n 835) 69.

849 See Kerber, 'Governance of IoT Data' (n 804) 124; Wiebe, 'Der Data Act – Innovation oder Illusion?' (n 831) 1571.

850 Kerber, 'Governance of IoT Data' (n 804) 124; Drexl and others (n 821) 26; Specht-Riemenschneider (n 821) 816.

access without specific prerequisites is an inadequate measure to challenge the data holder's factual control over the data and ensure a fair value distribution of data.[851]

Other commentators have challenged the narrow interpretation of the DA-proposal and argued that the DA should be read as allowing in-situ access at the user's request but does not restrict access exclusively to this mode.[852] While they acknowledge that Recital 21 DA proposal may suggest that in situ access is sufficient to comply with Article 4(1) DA, they have pointed out that the telos and systematic of the DA speak against such a narrow interpretation. The whole purpose of Article 4 (and 5) DA is to empower users with more substantial control over the data, enabling them to manage, process, and utilise the data in ways that extend beyond mere viewing or limited interaction within the data holder's infrastructure. Moreover, Article 4(10) DA (Article 4(4) DA Proposal), which restricts users from utilising accessed data to develop products that compete with those of the data holder, implies that users must have the capability to obtain a copy of the data.[853]

While the ambiguity of the initial proposal certainly left enough room for both interpretations, the final version of the Data Act reinforces the argument in favour of allowing in-situ access upon user request, without making it the exclusive mode of access.[854] Recital 22 DA added to the initial statement of Recital 21 DA-Proposal that connected products 'may be designed to permit the user or a third party to process the data on the connected product or on a computing instance of the manufacturer' the phrase 'or within an information and communications technology (ICT) environment chosen by the user or the third party.' This addition indicates that data holders cannot unilaterally dictate the type of access, but that the ultimate choice lies with the users (or, in the context of Article 5 DA, the third party). Moreover, Article 4(2) DA states that users and data holders may contractually restrict or prohibit further data sharing if it could undermine the security requirements of the connected product. The use of the term 'further sharing' (translated as 'erneute Weitergabe' in German

851 Specht-Riemenschneider (n 821) 816.

852 Podszun, *Der EU Data Act und der Zugang zu Sekundärmärkten am Beispiel des Handwerks* (n 835) 70 f; Steinrötter (n 515) 222; See also Wiebe, 'Der Data Act – Innovation oder Illusion?' (n 831) 1571, who, however, referrers to final text of final trilogue version.

853 Podszun, *Der EU Data Act und der Zugang zu Sekundärmärkten am Beispiel des Handwerks* (n 835) 70; Steinrötter (n 515) 222.

854 See Wiebe, 'Der Data Act – Innovation oder Illusion?' (n 831) 1571.

and 'partage ultérieur' in French) suggests that there has already been an initial transfer of data to the user. This implies that under Article 4(1) DA the user is, generally, put in full control of the data, and only specific circumstances, like security risks as outlined in Article 4(2) DA, could justify contractual limitations on how this data is handled or shared after it has been transferred to the user.

7.5.5 Usage limitations of the user

Article 4(1) DA establishes the principle that users can utilise the accessed data for any purpose (Recital 29 DA), without the need to inform the data holder about the specific intended use. This is an essential element in achieving the DA's goal of fostering competition and innovation. By allowing users (and third parties) to use data without disclosing their business plans, the DA aims to prevent data holders from gaining an unfair advantage by pre-emptively knowing the intentions and strategies of potential competitors.[855]

While the DA promotes the independent use of data, it also recognises the need to protect the data holder's legitimate interests. Article 4(6) DA stipulates that trade secrets may be protected and disclosed only on the condition that data holders and users agree on appropriate technical and organisational measures to ensure the confidentiality of the shared data. Another usage limitation is set out in Article 4(10) DA. The provision prohibits the user from utilising the data obtained to develop a connected product that competes with the connected product from which the data originate or share the data with a third party with that intent. Furthermore, the data may not be used to derive insights about the economic situation, assets and production methods of the manufacturer or, where applicable the data holder.[856] The prohibition of accessing, using or further sharing data in a way that could compromise the security of connected products (Article 4(2) DA) is a protective measure for both the user and the data holder.[857] Users are protected from potential harms such as privacy breaches, identity theft, and other cyber threats that could arise from compromised device security, while data holders are shielded against reputational damage and legal liabilities.

855 Kerber, 'Governance of IoT Data' (n 804) 124; Metzger and Schweitzer (n 810) 55.

856 See Metzger and Schweitzer (n 810) 56.

857 Schmidt-Kessel (n 246) 81.

7.5.5.1 Protection of trade secrets

Where the data covered by the access rights of Article 4(1) DA falls under the protection of the Trade Secret Directive, it creates a situation where the conflicting interests of the data holder and the user become even more pronounced. On one hand, data holders have a legitimate interest to protect their trade secrets and avoid, in particular, the disclosure to potential competitors. If, however, the mere assertion by data holders that the requested data is covered by trade secret protection were sufficient to deny access to data, Article 4(1) DA would remain largely ineffective.[858] From a regulatory standpoint, the challenge is that in advance of any legal proceedings, it is very difficult to determine whether specific data sets held by data holders qualify as trade secrets.[859]

The primary concern of the European legislators seems to have been that companies could cite trade secrets as a pretext for refusing to disclose data. Hence, the DA generally prioritises data access over the protection of trade secrets.[860] However, in order to protect the interests of the data holders, Article 4(7) sets out that the trade secrets shall be disclosed only if all 'specific necessary measures are taken to preserve the confidentiality of trade secrets in particular with respect to third parties'. The necessary measures are to be set out in contracts between data holders and product users. Examples of such protective measures include confidentiality agreements, access restrictions or technical standards. The data holder has to specify the data that they consider to be protected as a trade secret, including relevant metadata. In case no agreement can be reached on 'appropriate' protective measures or if the user does not comply with the agreed protective measures, the data holder can refuse to disclose the data identified or suspend the sharing (Article 6(8) DA). Moreover, should the user not implement the agreed-upon measures to protect trade secrets, any resulting use or disclosure of the trade secrets would be considered unlawful under Article 4(3) Trade Secrets Directive.[861]

---

858 Metzger and Schweitzer (n 810) 75.

859 Kerber, 'Governance of IoT Data' (n 804) 124; Drexl and others (n 821) 101.

860 Wiebe, 'Der Data Act – Innovation oder Illusion?' (n 831) 1573; Sabine Grapentin, 'Datenzugangsansprüche und Geschäftsgeheimnisse der Hersteller im Lichte des Data Act' [2023] RDi 173, 176; Moritz Hennemann and Björn Steinrötter, 'Data Act – Fundament des neuen EU-Datenwirtschaftsrechts?' [2022] NJW 1481, 1484.

861 Schweitzer and Metzger (n 246) 75.

While under the original proposal the data holder would always have had to disclose trade secrets—provided that appropriate measures were taken—a right to refuse disclosure for exceptional cases was added in the course of the legislative process.[862] According to Article 4(8) DA, a data holder who holds trade secrets can refuse a specific request for access to data if they can demonstrate that there is a high likelihood of suffering significant economic damage from disclosing those trade secrets, despite the user having implemented the technical and organizational measures specified in paragraph 6 of Article 4 DA. The data holder must objectively substantiate their assertion, demonstrating the concrete risk of serious economic damage expected to result from a specific data disclosure and the reasons why the measures taken to safeguard the requested data are not considered to be sufficient. Factors that may be cited include the enforceability of the protection of trade secrets in third countries, the degree of confidentiality of the requested data, the uniqueness and novelty of the associated product and other relevant elements. However, the threshold is rather high,[863] as Recital 31 clarifies that 'economic damage implies serious and irreparable economic loss'.

For cases in which the data owner refuses to disclose data because either no agreement can be reached on suitable protective measures (Article 6(7) DA) or serious economic damage is highly likely (Article 6(8) DA), the DA stipulates formal requirements in addition to the substantive conditions.[864] The data holder must communicate their refusal and the reasons for it in writing to the user. In addition, they are required to inform the designated competent authority as outlined in Article 37 DA. This notification acts as a tool for ensuring oversight and transparency in the decision-making process, verifying the legitimacy of the refusal.

It is clear that the DA cannot resolve the inherent conflict between the objective of facilitating data access and the protection of trade secrets, but can only try to strike a balance between the opposing interests. However, it seems that this is a task that will inevitably attract criticism. The initial version of the DA faced scrutiny because it supposedly failed to take sufficient account of the importance of protecting trade secrets.[865] The response to grant data holders a right to refuse access under exceptional circumstances,

862 Wiebe, 'Der Data Act – Innovation oder Illusion?' (n 831) 1573; Grapentin (n 860) 176.

863 Grapentin (n 860) 177.

864 See Assion and Willecke (n 786) 1574.

865 Specht-Riemenschneider (n 821) 816; Grapentin (n 860) 176, 180.

did not go far enough for some,[866] while others feared it might dilute the DA's effectiveness in ensuring data access.[867]

At this stage, the practical implications of the DA's provisions on trade secrets and data access rights are uncertain. On paper, however, the general approach of establishing a preference for data sharing, while empowering the data holder to oblige the user to accept confidentiality requirements and allowing for exceptions in cases where disclosure could cause significant economic harm seems to be a balanced approach to address the tension between data access and trade secret protection.[868] However, as has been pointed out by other commentators, the DA's provisions on trade secret protection will not immediately result in legal certainty for stakeholders. Determining whether specific data sets qualify as trade secrets involves complex considerations and may vary case by case. Courts will play a crucial role in interpreting and clarifying the obligation under DA's provisions over time, particularly the conditions under which data access can be refused.[869]

7.5.5.2 Not develop competing products

The DA's prohibition to use the accessed data for developing a competing connected product underscores its aim to foster competition and innovation in the aftermarkets and not in the primary IoT market. The rationale is that data access is necessary to stimulate the development of novel products or services (in particular, but not only, maintenance, repair and other aftermarket services or products), which will liberate aftermarkets and other new markets. However, the data shall not be used to create direct product competitors. This does not preclude the use of data in aftermarkets, where competition can lead to improved services and products for consumers, even if the data holder is also active in these aftermarkets.[870] The underlying assumption is that to encourage data holders to continue equipping their products with advanced data collection and processing capabilities, it is essential to protect their competitive advantages derived

866 Grapentin (n 860) 176, 177.
867 Wiebe, 'Der Data Act – Innovation oder Illusion?' (n 831) 1573.
868 Metzger and Schweitzer (n 810) 75; Drexl and others (n 821) 101.
869 Metzger and Schweitzer (n 810) 75.
870 Kerber, 'Governance of IoT Data' (n 804) 124.

from this data in the primary market.[871] This approach is very similar to the one of the EFD doctrine. The EFD intends to address cases where the denial of access to an essential facility has a market leveraging effect and allows the dominant undertaking to expand its position into related but economically self-contained, secondary or downstream markets to gain an unjustified competitive advantage in that market (see 4.2.1.2). To prevent such leveraging competitors are afforded access to essential resources, so they can effectively compete in the secondary or downstream markets. The key difference, is of course, that Article 4 DA not only applies to data holders that have a dominant position in the (primary) IoT market.

Recital 32 of DA provides guidance on how to determine whether two related products compete in the same product market and refers to the established principles of Union competition law for defining the relevant product market. Typically, the relevant product market is defined by assessing whether products are seen by consumers as interchangeable or substitutable based on their characteristics, prices, and intended use. The methodology used by the Commission for the analysis of this demand substitutability is the so-called SSNIP (small but significant and non-transitory increase in price) test (see 4.1.3.1).[872]

It can be questioned, though, whether the application of the SSNIP test results in a product definition that could be too broad for the purposes of the DA. With a view to promoting innovation in the secondary market, it should be possible to use data to improve the original product. However, the demand substitutability test (see 4.1.3.1) might result in a product market definition, where both the initial product and the improved version are treated as part of the same market, which could impede innovation. With regard to the initial proposal, it had been suggested that the new product requirement of the EFD, as interpreted in the *Microsoft* decision, could be used (4.2.1.4).[873] According to the EGC, the applicant company may not simply duplicate the initial product but it is sufficient to prove that access to the requested data is suitable for bringing technical developments to the market.[874] However, the final text of the DA no longer allows for this narrower interpretation. The explicit reference in Recital 32 to the

---

871 Metzger and Schweitzer (n 810) 61; Drexl and others (n 821) 34; Leistner and Antoine (n 809) 14.

872 Also referred to as 'hypothetical monopolist test' or '5 % test'.

873 Podszun, *Der EU Data Act und der Zugang zu Sekundärmärkten am Beispiel des Handwerks* (n 835) 84.

874 EGC, T-201/04 Microsoft v Commission EU:T:2007:289, para 647; Rousseva (n 352) 123.

'established principles of Union competition law for the definition of the relevant product market' essentially rules out the possibility of using the more flexible EFD-based approach.

7.5.6 Usage limitations of the data holder

The DA curtails the data holder's exclusive de facto control not only by affording access and portability rights to the user but also by imposing specific limitations on data holders regarding the use of data. Article 4(13) DA sets out that data holders may only use non-personal, readily available data based on a contractual agreement with the user. Moreover, the DA further restricts data holders from using data in a manner that would allow them to gain insights into the user's economic situation, assets, production methods, or any other aspect that could influence the user's economic position in the markets they operate in. Late in the legislative process, an additional restriction was added. Article 4(14) DA stipulates that data holders may not make non-personal product data available to third parties for commercial or non-commercial purposes other than the fulfilment of their contract with the user. Where appropriate, data holders must also contractually oblige third parties not to further share the received data.

7.5.6.1 Contract for the use of non-personal data

The requirement that non-personal data may only be processed on the basis of a contract with the user is an interesting one, as commentators have evaluated this provision very differently. Some have argued that a regime where data holders, in order to make use of the collected data, would need to enter into contracts with every user would be excessively burdensome.[875] This rule would impose more stringent restrictions on the use of non-personal, machine-generated data than on the use of personal data. Under the GDPR, consent—not even a fully-fledged contract—is just one of several legal bases for the processing of personal data (Article 6(1)(a)–(f)

875 Wiebe, 'Der Data Act – Innovation oder Illusion?' (n 831) 1571; Drexl and others (n 821) 20 ff; Leistner and Antoine (n 809) 92, 97.

GDPR).[876] Commentators have asserted that such a restrictive regime could stifle the very innovation the DA seeks to encourage. Since both, the data holder and user, have contributed to the generation of the data, both should have the right to use that data for their own purposes without needing the consent of the other party, as long as such use does not adversely affect the other party's legitimate interests. This symmetrical approach is considered to better serve the DA's objectives of fostering innovation and competition in secondary and related markets.[877]

Others have rightly pointed out that the DA only appears to impose strict requirements on the use of non-personal data, but in reality represents a hurdle that can easily be overcome by data holders.[878] This is because, in contrast to the GDPR, the DA does not provide for a prohibition of coupling or tying. Article 7(4) GDPR stipulates that the performance of a contract shall not be made dependent upon the consent of the data subject to the processing of personal data which is not needed for the performance of that contract. A comparable limitation is notably absent in the DA. As a result, it is anticipated that data holders, who are typically the manufacturer of the connected product, will likely link the use of their products to the conclusion of a contract that allows the data holder to use the generated non-personal data; essentially presenting users with a take it or leave it scenario.[879] For example, when purchasing an IoT device, such as a fitness tracker, the initial setup may require the user to agree to clauses that grant the manufacturer broad rights to collect, use, and potentially share the non-personal data generated by the device. The software may be set up in such a way that users have no choice but to accept these terms in their entirety if they wish to activate and use the product. The user's formal agreement in such situations does not reflect freely given consent.[880] Since users have no real choice, the DA will not achieve its objective of giving users real sovereignty over their non-personal data.[881] It has therefore been argued that the formal requirement for contractual agreements will not

876 Metzger and Schweitzer (n 810) 55; David Bomhard and Marieke Merkle, 'Der Entwurf eines EU Data Acts: Neue Spielregeln für die Data Economy' [2022] RDi 168, 174.

877 Metzger and Schweitzer (n 810) 55.

878 Steinrötter (n 515) 219; Specht-Riemenschneider (n 821) 816.

879 Steinrötter (n 515) 219; Podszun and Pfeifer (n 838) 956; Specht-Riemenschneider (n 821) 817.

880 Kerber, 'Governance of IoT Data' (n 804) 132.

881 Podszun, *Der EU Data Act und der Zugang zu Sekundärmärkten am Beispiel des Handwerks* (n 835) 56.

significantly alter the power dynamics between data holders and users with regard to non-personal data generated by the device of the users.[882]

However, both sides of the argument miss the crucial point. It is not the contract as such that imposes the usage limitation on the data holder but the subsequent unfairness control set out in Article 13 DA.[883] The underlying problem that the Commission was trying to solve with Article 4(13) DA is that although the user and the data holder may (but do not necessarily) have a contractual relationship through the purchase of the connected product, the specifics regarding the use of the data generated by these products are usually not regulated in this contract. From the data holder's perspective, negotiating and agreeing to terms regarding the use of the co-generated data would curtail their control and flexibility. This is because the restrictions on the processing of non-personal data mandated by law are relatively limited. Without contractual limitations, data holders who possess de facto control over the data due to their ownership of the product's server infrastructure are thus generally free to use the data for their purposes. Consequently, there is little incentive for data holders to proactively seek agreements that define their data usage rights. The problem that a manufacturer with a more dominant bargaining power has control over the data co-generated by the user, and uses that data in a manner that is unfair vis-à-vis the user will usually not be rooted in the contractual terms but rather in their absence.[884]

In the European Law Institute's response to the public consultation of the DA, it was pointed out that the unfairness test of contractual terms, as envisioned by the Commission, would run empty in these scenarios where data holders use the data based on their de facto control, rather than explicit contractual agreements. To address this gap, the authors of the ELI's response therefore suggested expanding the scope of the unfairness test to include unfair practices.[885] The Commission, however, took a different approach. By requiring the data holder to conclude a contract with

---

882 See Podszun, *Der EU Data Act und der Zugang zu Sekundärmärkten am Beispiel des Handwerks* (n 835) 56 ff; Specht-Riemenschneider (n 821) 817.

883 But see Drexl and others (n 821) 21; Specht-Riemenschneider (n 821) 817 ,who criticise that business users (e.g. a farmer) are better protected than consumers because Article 13 only b2b relationships. However, what is overlooked here is that the Unfair Contract Terms Directive (Directives 93/13/EEC) applies between a data holder and a consumer as user of a connected product (Recital 28 DA) and the level of protection is therefore just as high in b2c relations (see 7.9.3).

884 See Thomas and others (n 494) 26.

885 Thomas and others (n 494) 25.

the user if they want to use the co-generated data, any data usage by data holders is always subject to an unfairness assessment. The contract also introduces a layer of transparency for users. It ensures that the processing of co-generated data is not conducted in an opaque manner but is based on terms that the user has had the opportunity to review and agree to in advance. By informing the users about how their data is used, their understanding and control over data usage is enhanced. Whilst it is true that it will not be difficult for data holders to conclude a contract with users, this is precisely the point. Article 4(13) DA wants to address unfair data usage practices without imposing undue burdens on data holders or granting users quasi-exclusive control over the data. This also explains why non-personal data may 'only' be used on the basis of a contract and there are no 'other legal grounds for the processing of the non-personal data similar to those of the GDPR: it would defeat the purpose of creating a contractual legal relationship between user and data holder that is subject to the unfairness test.

It has been argued that the DA should have provided for provisions that prevent linking product or service usage to contractual consent for data use and that establish cancellation options and time limits.[886] However, this would significantly restrict the data holder's ability to dispose of the data and would, in fact, impose stricter requirements on the use of non-personal data than on personal data. It would also run counter to the basic idea of the DA that all co-generators should be free to use the co-generated data for their own purposes as long as such use does not unfairly affect the other parties.[887] Embedding the use of data in a contractual framework that is subject to an unfairness test is a convincing approach to reconciling the protection of users with the interests of data holders.

However, it must be criticised that this interaction between the unfairness test and the contractual requirements for the use of non-personal data is not something that is obvious when reading the DA—as demonstrated by the many different interpretations of the commentators.[888] The extensive Recitals of the DA (over 30 pages!) could have been used to clarify the

886 Specht-Riemenschneider (n 821) 817.

887 See Metzger and Schweitzer (n 810) 55.

888 For example Kerber, 'Governance of IoT Data' (n 804) 132; and Podszun, *Der EU Data Act und der Zugang zu Sekundärmärkten am Beispiel des Handwerks* (n 835) 56 ff argue that the Data Act does not address the market failure that manufacturers will only leave consumers with the choice of either buying the IoT device and accepting the exclusive use of their data by the data holders or not buying it at all ('take it or leave it'). This suggests that they assume that Article 13 DA does not

intended relationship between Articles 4(13) and 13 DA and avoid misunderstandings and legal uncertainty.

7.5.6.2 Not make data available to third parties

Article 4(14) DA restricts data holders from making non-personal product data available to third parties, except when it is necessary for fulfilling their contract with the user. As this provision was introduced relatively late in the legislative process, very little has been written about it in academic literature.

The problem with this provision is that it is not clear to which contract the phrase 'other than for the fulfilment of their contract with the user' refers to. Grammatically, the word 'their' refers to the data holder but it is not clear whether Article 4(14) means the contract through which the user acquired the connected product, or the contract governing the data holder's use of the non-personal data. However, this distinction is crucial as it determines the extent of the limitation on the data holder. If the phrase refers to the initial contract under which the user acquired the connected product, this would imply a significant limitation on the data holder. The data could only be shared with third parties if it were necessary to deliver the connected product or related service. Hence, data sharing would only be possible in the interest of the user and not for the purposes of the data holder even if such sharing could not harm the legitimate interests of the user. Conversely, if Article 4(14) DA refers to the contract governing the use of non-personal data, which is concluded due to the requirement in Article 4(13) DA, data holders would be able to define the purposes for data sharing within this contract. Hence, in this case, the limitation would be more about ensuring transparency rather than restricting data usage. It has been pointed out that Article 4(14) DA may also be understood as referring to the contract concluded between the third-party recipient and the user.

The wording of Article 4(14) DA would suggest that Article 4(14) DA does not refer to the data usage contract. This is because it is not entirely clear what 'fulfilment' would entail in the context of a contract that is established solely to authorise the use of non-personal data, as the data usage itself does not constitute a deliverable in the same way that a product

apply to the contract between the user and the controller, as an unfairness test is the traditional regulatory response to the problem that terms are unilaterally imposed by a stronger party.

or service does. The use of the phrase 'necessary for fulfilling their contract' in Article 4(14) would be an awkward fit for referring to a contract that exists primarily to grant permissions for data use. One would rather expect a wording like 'the data holder may only use the data for purposes specified in the contract with the user'.

The most convincing interpretation of Article 4(14) DA is that it addresses situations not explicitly covered by the data usage contract. Where the right to share data with third parties for specific purposes was not included in the contract on data use between data holder and user, Article 4(14) DA clarifies that data holders are permitted to share data with third parties when necessary for fulfilling their contractual duties to the user. According to this interpretation, Article 4(14) DA refers to any contract between the data holder and the user that involves data usage. This includes contracts such as sales, leases, or rentals, provided that fulfilling the contract necessitates sharing data with third parties. For instance, if a user leases a connected device from the manufacturer (i.e. data holder), and the lease contract requires ongoing maintenance that necessitates data sharing with a third-party service provider, Article 4(14) DA permits this sharing despite it not being explicitly covered in a data usage agreement. In case the data is shared based on Article 4(14) DA, the second sentence of the provision requires the data holders to contractually bind the third-party recipient not to further share the data. This ensures that, in case there is no data usage contract between data holder and user, the data is shared and used only for the purpose of fulfilling the contractual obligation.[889]

It needs to be pointed out that Article 4(14) DA is, in contrast to Article 4(13) DA, limited to 'product data' and does not cover data that has been generated by 'related services'. Hence, the data holder may share related services data only based on a data usage agreement within the meaning of Article 4(13) DA but not without such agreement under Article 4(14) DA. However, it has been argued that in exceptional cases where the sharing of related services data is critical for fulfilling the data holder's contractual duties to the user, Article 4(14) DA needs to be applied by analogy.[890]

---

889 Christiane Wendehorst, 'Model Contractual Terms for Mandatory Data Sharing: Challenges and Considerations' in Sebastian Lohsse, Reiner Schulze and Dirk Staudenmayer (eds), *Private Law and the Data Act: Münster Colloquia on EU Law and the Digital Economy VIII* (Nomos (forthcoming)) IV.2.c).

890 Wendehorst, 'Model Contractual Terms for Mandatory Data Sharing: Challenges and Considerations' (n 889) IV.2.c).

7.6 Right to share data with third parties (Article 5 DA)

While the DA is built on the concept that the user is the central actor when it comes to controlling and utilising the data generated by IoT devices, it also recognises that in many instances it is not the users themselves who want to process this data because they lack the technical expertise, interest, or resources to utilise the generated data effectively.[891] Users may rather have an interest in transferring the data to third party providers who offer complementary services or products and enhance user experience. This applies in particular to users who are consumers but may also hold true for business users. From a macroeconomic perspective, it also makes sense to give third party providers access to the IoT data, as they may be in a better position to extract value from this data, e.g. to develop new services or improve existing ones. This in turn can foster innovation and competition, potentially leading to greater consumer benefits and efficiencies within downstream markets.[892]

However, since the DA's regulatory framework is constructed on the notion of co-generation (see 2.5.3), third party providers are not afforded a direct right to access the IoT data. Instead, Article 5(1) DA gives users the right to share the data generated by the connected product with third parties. Upon the request of a product user or a third party acting on the user's behalf, the data holder is mandated to give the third party access without the data first being transmitted to the user.[893] By making data sharing contingent upon a user's request, the DA gives users a say in whether the data they have co-generated is shared with third parties.[894] This approach is an attempt to ensure that the public interest in facilitating a competitive aftermarket does not override the individual interest of users in controlling the data they have helped to generate (see 10.1.3.2).

Regarding scope and access modalities, Article 5(1) DA mirrors those of Article 4(1) DA. It covers provided and inferred data, and the access must be provided promptly, free of charge to the user, continuously, in real-time, and with the same level of quality as the data holder has access to.[895] Hence, reference can be made to the remarks under 7.5.1, 7.5.2 and 7.5.3.

891 Metzger and Schweitzer (n 810) 51.

892 See Metzger and Schweitzer (n 810) 58.

893 Assion and Willecke (n 786) 808; Metzger and Schweitzer (n 810) 51, 55.

894 Podszun, *Der EU Data Act und der Zugang zu Sekundärmärkten am Beispiel des Handwerks* (n 835) 62.

895 Schmidt-Kessel (n 246) 80.

The position of the third party recipient, however, differs from that of the user in two aspects. Firstly, Article 6 DA imposes additional data use restrictions on the third party recipient to which users are not subject due to their role in generating the data. The second difference is that the data controller may charge the third party recipient a reasonable and non-discriminatory fee for receiving the data.

7.6.1 Usage limitations of the third-party recipient

While the user is in principle free to use the co-generated data for any lawful purpose, Article 6(1) DA imposes a purpose limitation on third party recipients for the processing of data received under Article 5 DA. According to Article 6(1) DA, the third party may process the data made available to it pursuant to Article 5 DA only for the purposes and under the conditions agreed with the user in this contract. It has already been pointed out (7.4) that there will be a contractual relationship between the user and the third party because the user will exercise their right under Article 5 DA only if they want to use a complementary service or product that requires access to the data generated by the IoT device. Following the completion of the agreed purpose, the third party is required to erase the data. This provision ensures that the data does not remain indefinitely with the third party, potentially subject to misuse or unauthorised sharing.[896]

The third party is also prohibited from making the data available to another third party, unless the data is made available on the basis of a contract with the user and the subsequent third party undertakes to maintain the confidentiality of any trade secrets in accordance with the measures agreed between the original data holder and the third party. Moreover, Article 6(2)(h) DA shall prevent third parties from monopolising the received data by contractually preventing users from making the same data available to other parties. This clause ensures that users retain the freedom to share their data with multiple third parties if they so wish, thus promoting competition and preventing the creation of data silos.[897] According to Article 2(14) DA, only the third party that receives data from the data holder based on Article 5-request of the user is considered a data recipient. Hence, if the user decides to first access the data based on Article 4 DA and then shares

896 Schmidt-Kessel (n 246) 80; Metzger and Schweitzer (n 810) 59.
897 Schmidt-Kessel (n 246) 80; Metzger and Schweitzer (n 810) 59.

data with another party, the restrictions of Article 6 DA do not apply (this issue is further discussed under 7.11.2).[898]

The mandatory character of these obligations has been criticised. It has been argued that their underlying assumption that there is a structural imbalance of bargaining power or an asymmetry of information between users and third party recipients does not necessarily hold true in all cases. There are instances where large users of products, which may be corporations with substantial resources and expertise, engage with smaller companies or start-ups as third parties. In such scenarios, the power dynamics could be reversed, or at least not as imbalanced as the act presupposes. Some of the provisions, such as Article 6(1) DA, which mandates the deletion of data when it's no longer necessary for the agreed purpose, along with Article 6(2)(c) and (f) DA, which dictate restrictions on sharing data with third parties and preventing users from freely sharing received data, reflect reasonable default rules for contracts, but should not be mandatory.[899]

However, the criticism does not take into account that the purpose of the mandatory nature of these provisions is not (only) to protect the interests of the user, but also those of the data holder. The data holder has also contributed to the generation of the data but is not involved in the contract negotiations between user and third party. The mandatory character of rules laid down in Article 6 DA ensures that when users and third parties enter into contractual negotiations, the data holder's interests are also safeguarded. For example, requiring the deletion of data when no longer necessary prevents the data holder's data from being retained indefinitely without purpose, protecting the data holder from potential misuse or exploitation of their data assets. Similarly, restrictions on sharing data with third parties prevent unauthorised or excessive dissemination of data.

7.6.2 Contract between data holder and the third party

Once the user has made the request that the data holder shall share the data with a third party, Article 8(1) DA stipulates that the data holder shall agree with the data recipient on the concrete arrangements for making the data available. The conditions under which data is shared must adhere to

898 See Wiebe, 'Der Data Act – Innovation oder Illusion?' (n 831) 1572.
899 Metzger and Schweitzer (n 810) 59.

principles of fairness, reasonableness, and non-discrimination. This obligation only applies to b2b relationships.

While the user can both access the product data under Article 4 DA and request the data's transfer based on Article 5 DA free of charge, the data holder is permitted to impose a reasonable and non-discriminatory fee on the third-party recipient (Article 9 DA). The difference in treatment is based on the idea that the third party did not contribute to the data's generation and should therefore compensate the data holder for investing in the generation of the data. The compensation should cover the various costs related to making data available to third parties, but it may also include a margin except for SMEs and not-for-profit research organisations. This margin reflects the value added by the data holder and can vary based on various attributes of the data, like its volume, format, and type. (see 6.6.6.3).[900] While the DA lists several factors that may be taken into account, it does not specify a specific method to calculate a reasonable price. However, Article 9(7) DA stipulates that the data controller shall provide the data recipient with information setting out the basis for the calculation of the compensation in such detail that the data recipient can assess whether the requirements of Article 9 DA are met. Moreover, the Commission may issue guidelines for calculating the appropriate compensation. These guidelines should take into account the assessment of the European Data Innovation Board (Article 9(5) DA). The DA is silent on the legal quality of these guidelines, but it can be assumed that they are not binding. They can, however, facilitate negotiations between the parties and serve as a benchmark for the assessment of the dispute settlement bodies that Member States are required to set up pursuant to Article 10 DA and courts.[901]

These obligations are not limited to the sharing of data based on Article 5 DA. Article 12(1) DA extends the scope of Chapter III DA to encompass any requirement imposed by Union national legislation adopted in accordance with Union law, that compels a data holder to provide data to a data recipient. This extension applies to obligations in b2b relationships that enter into force after 12 September 2025 (Article 50 DA). Although the provisions of Chapter III DA do not apply to already existing FRAND obligations, they may guide the interpretation (see 7.6.2.1).

900 See Leistner and Antoine (n 809) 101; Sebastian Louven, 'Vorschriften im Data Act zur Ausgestaltung und Kompensation von Datenbereitstellungspflichten' [2024] MMR 82, 82.

901 Louven (n 900) 86 f.

It is important to stress that Articles 8 and 9 DA do not create a new data-sharing obligation but presuppose that such an obligation already exists. The role of these articles is to set out the conditions under which mandated data sharing should occur. Hence, they do not address the question of whether data is to be shared but how it is to be shared.[902]

7.6.2.1 The FRAND concept of the Data Act

Even before the final version of the Data Act was published, the analysis advanced here argued that 'fair' within the FRAND framework denotes a broad unfairness test, encompassing all contractual clauses except for the price (6.6.6.2), while the 'reasonable' criterion refers to the appropriateness of the pricing within the contract (6.6.6.3). The 'non-discrimination' applies to both the price and other terms of the contract in order to ensure that no party is unjustly favoured or disadvantaged either through the pricing structure or other contractual clauses (6.6.6.4).

Initially, this interpretation might seem challenging to reconcile with the Data Act since Articles 8 and 9 DA both outline (F)RAND criteria. Article 8 DA stipulates that the data holder 'shall agree with a data recipient the arrangements for making the data available and shall do so under fair, reasonable and non-discriminatory terms and conditions'. Article 9 DA sets out that 'any compensation agreed upon between a data holder and a data recipient for making data available in business-to-business relations shall be non-discriminatory and reasonable'. At first glance, it may appear that these provisions introduce two different sets of requirements: one for the price (Article 9 DA) and one for all the other terms and conditions (Article 8 DA).

On closer inspection, however, the understanding of FRAND developed here is compatible with the DA. The 'reasonable' criterion in Article 8(1) DA can be understood as a reference to Article 9 DA, which addresses the pricing aspect in more detail. This is supported by the fact that Article 8(2) DA specifies the 'fairness' aspect by setting out that a term should not be binding if it is 'an unfair contractual term within the meaning of Article 13', and Article 8(3) DA further describes the 'non-discrimination' criterion. However, the 'reasonable' element is not mentioned in Article 8 DA. Only Article 9 DA lists the factors that should be taken into account when

902 Louven (n 900) 83.

calculating a reasonable price. Moreover, the understanding of the fairness criterion as a reference to an unfairness test encompassing all clauses apart from the price is reinforced by the fact that only Article 8—and not Article 9 DA, which only deals with the remuneration—mentions 'fair' as one of the requirements.

7.6.2.2 Transfer without contract

Concerns have been raised that the requirement for the data holder and data recipient to negotiate and agree on a reasonable remuneration before making the data available under Article 5 DA could potentially hinder efficient data sharing and create barriers to access for third parties. The ex-ante negotiation process will usually delay the data sharing process or could even be exploited as a means to delay or obstruct access to data by third parties. Since the data recipient can only deliver the services requested by the user, once they have access to data, they find themselves under considerable pressure to agree to the terms proposed by data holders. This pressure could lead to the acceptance of an unfavourable remuneration. The problem is even elevated in cases where the data recipient is a small player and in a weaker bargaining position vis-à-vis the data holder.[903] It is asserted that the requirement to negotiate a contract effectively assigns control of the data to the data holder, thereby reinforcing their de facto position rather than breaking it up as intended by the DA.[904] Critics suggest third parties should be given immediate and free access once the user has requested the data transfer, without having to negotiate with the data holder.[905]

The issues described arise only if one assumes that the contract between the data holder and data recipient needs to be concluded before the data is transferred. However, the DA does not explicitly mandate that the data may only be transferred once a contract pursuant to Article 8 DA has been concluded. It has rightly been pointed out that the obligation of the data

903 Podszun, *Der EU Data Act und der Zugang zu Sekundärmärkten am Beispiel des Handwerks* (n 835) 61 f; Leistner and Antoine (n 809) 104; Drexl and others (n 821) 28.

904 Podszun, *Der EU Data Act und der Zugang zu Sekundärmärkten am Beispiel des Handwerks* (n 835) 62; see also Kerber, 'Governance of IoT Data' (n 804) 134.

905 Podszun, *Der EU Data Act und der Zugang zu Sekundärmärkten am Beispiel des Handwerks* (n 835) 64; Drexl and others (n 821) 29.

holder to make data available to a third party, upon the user's request, should be viewed as distinct from and independent of the data holder's right to receive compensation from the data recipient.[906] Hence, the data holder would be required to share the data, even if the data holder and data recipient have not yet been able to agree on the conditions for FRAND compensation.

Support for this interpretation is drawn from Article 5(1) DA, which specifies that data must be made available without undue delay. This would mean that the transfer of data should not be made dependent on the prior agreement on compensation. Furthermore, regarding personal data, Article 5(7) DA stipulates that disagreements over data transmission arrangements between the data holder and the third party should not impede the rights of data subjects under the GDPR, particularly the right to data portability. Since Article 5(7) DA does not explicitly address non-personal data, it could be argued that the data holder could refuse access to non-personal data until an agreement on the compensation is reached. However, typically it will be challenging to distinguish between personal and non-personal data, especially in cases where the data types are intermixed or cannot be clearly delineated. Prioritising the portability right over the right to FRAND compensation only with regard to personal data would result in unnecessary legal uncertainty, as data holders would need to navigate the blurred lines between personal and non-personal data to avoid a violation of either the DA or the GDPR.[907] Moreover, the objective of giving the user control over their data and enable them to use the connected services or products of third parties would be undermined if the data transfer would be dependent on the agreement between data holder and recipient on the compensation. The benefits of Article 5 DA for users will be significantly diminished if they cannot access and use third-party services in a timely manner. Conversely, the question of what constitutes appropriate remuneration can still be assessed after the data has been made available to the third party. Finally, the argument that compensating data holders for sharing data with recipients does not necessarily motivate data holders to enhance their data collection efforts, strengthens the argument that the users' right to data portability should be decoupled from the compensation mechanism between data holders and recipients. If the right to compensation does not serve to incentivise the collection of data, then restricting access to

906 Habich (n 742) 1360.
907 Habich (n 742) 1359.

data until compensation is settled does not protect any legitimate incentive function of the data holder.[908]

The fact that the data holder must transfer the data does not mean that the recipient can use the data without restrictions. If the data holder submits a contractual offer, and the recipient rejects the offer due to the fee's inappropriateness or a term's discriminatory nature but proceeds to use the data, the recipient should still be bound by the other contractual clauses of the initial offer.[909] Hence, the data recipient must adhere to any restrictions on how the data can be used, shared, or processed, outlined in the contractual offer made by the data holder.

The interests of the data holders could be further protected if a negotiation procedure similar to the one established by the ECJ in the *Huawei/ZTE* decision (see 6.6.6.1) were applied. Under such a scheme, the data recipient would be required to respond promptly to the data holder's initial offer, either by accepting it or by immediately submitting a counteroffer.[910] In case the data recipient fails to comply with this obligation, the data holder would have the right to refuse the transfer of data. However, despite calls from academia to incorporate such a mechanism into the final text of the DA,[911] the legislators did not do so. While it is conceivable that by way of judicial development, the CJEU will establish a Huawei/ZTE-like negotiation procedure also for the DA, the existence of such a mechanism cannot be inferred from the DA through interpretative means.

7.7 Waiving the access right

Given the DA's objective of enabling competition on aftermarkets based on user data, it was widely assumed that the data access and portability rights afforded to the user are of a mandatory nature. Otherwise, the data holder could circumvent the DA's objectives by having the users sign an unlimited waiver of all future access rights when the sale, rental or lease agreement is concluded. While the DA-proposal did not explicitly state that the access

908 Habich (n 742) 1360.

909 See Habich (n 742) 1369.

910 *Cf.* ECJ, C-170/13, *Huawei/ZTE*, EU:C:2015:477, para 65.

911 See Habich (n 742) 1364 ff. who has described in much detail how such a mechanism could work.

and portability rights are of a non-waivable nature, it was the prevalent interpretation among commentators.[912]

The final version of the DA, however, created much confusion regarding the waivability of user rights under Articles 4(1) and 5(1) DA. Initially, it would seem that Article 7(2) DA settled the matter and explicitly clarifies that the access and portability rights are non-waivable—as was recommended by commentators.[913] The provision stipulates that any contractual term which, to the detriment of the user, excludes the application of, derogates from or varies the effect of the user's rights under Chapter II shall not be binding on the user. However, additionally to Article 7(2) DA, a passage was added in Recital 25 DA stating that the DA 'does not prevent users, in the case of business-to-business relations, from making data available to third parties or data holders under any lawful contractual term, including by agreeing to limit or restrict further sharing of such data, or from being compensated proportionately, for example in exchange for waiving their right to use or share such data.' This appears to directly conflict with Article 7(2) DA.

The only way to reconcile Recital 25 and Article 7(2) DA is if it is assumed that, in b2b contexts, it is not to the detriment of the users if they receive compensation for waiving their data access and portability rights. Such an understanding can at least partly draw on support in the literature suggesting to reconsider the mandatory nature of access rights in the DA proposal.[914] This is based on the argument that allowing waivers of data access rights could sometimes benefit both parties, particularly in cases where data holders require exclusivity to justify significant long-term investments.[915] By granting data holders temporary exclusive use of data, such waivers could incentivise innovation and encourage investment in products or functions that might otherwise be financially untenable. However, the proponents of this view also concede that even in b2b relationships waving the access rights afforded by the DA may be the result of asymmetric information. Especially in tightly oligopolistic markets, where all manufacturers request a waiver, or when buying long-lasting products, users may be cut-off from taking advantage of future data-driven business

912 Kerber, 'Governance of IoT Data' (n 804) 123; Metzger and Schweitzer (n 810) 56; Drexl and others (n 821) 32.
913 Drexl and others (n 821) 32.
914 Metzger and Schweitzer (n 810) 58.
915 Metzger and Schweitzer (n 810) 51.

opportunities, which would undermine the overall objectives of the DA.[916] It thus had been suggested that in the absence of significant power imbalances waivers should be permissible, but only under the condition that users retain the right to revoke the waiver after a specified period (e.g., 2–3 years).[917] However, the DA's putative approach of allowing the waiver of access rights against payment in all b2b situations would go far beyond this recommendation and ignore the problem of information asymmetries that can affect both SMEs and larger market players.

The interpretation that the waiver of access rights against payment is not permitted under the DA could only be supported by arguing that Recital 25 DA is an editorial mistake. Article 7(2) DA as well as the overall objectives of the DA quite strongly support the interpretation that the DA's access rights cannot be waived. For an exception to the mandatory nature of the right of access to be valid, it would have to be provided for in the binding part of the DA and could not be laid down in the non-binding Recitals.[918] Since the Articles are the legally binding components of the Regulation, any contradiction between a Recital and an Article resolves in favour of the latter.[919] Hence, it can be argued that the data rights afforded by Articles 4(1) and 5(1) DA are mandatory and cannot be waived by agreement.[920] Recital 25 DA, which might suggest otherwise, is not supported by the operative part of the DA and thus may not alter the mandatory nature of the rights set out in these Articles.

916 Metzger and Schweitzer (n 810) 57.

917 Metzger and Schweitzer (n 810) 58.

918 In ECJ, C-290/12, Della Rocca, EU:C:2013:235 the ECJ stated that ‚the preamble to a European Union act has no binding legal force and cannot be relied on either as a ground for derogating from the actual provisions of the act in question or for interpreting them in a manner clearly contrary to their wording'

919 See Riesenhuber (n 29) 268.

920 But see Wendehorst, 'Model Contractual Terms for Mandatory Data Sharing: Challenges and Considerations' (n 889) 85 who argues that the blackletter of the DA's regulatory text does not mention the user's 'right' to pass data retrieved via Article 4 DA on to third parties, but only offers the Article 5 DA mechanism for instances where users wish to share data with third parties. This, according to Wendehorst, means that the user's 'right' to pass data on is not a 'right' strictly afforded by the DA. Hence, the user can therefore waive this right also vis-à-vis the data holder, as long as the Article 5 DA mechanism remains available to the user. However, in order to pass the unfairness test under Article 13 DA, such a waiver would only be possible against proportionate compensation.

7.8 The 'Robin Hood approach'

A central feature of the DA is that companies of different sizes are treated differently: While gatekeepers within the meaning of the DMA shall not benefit from the access and portability rights, micro and small enterprises, to a certain extent also medium-sized enterprises (SMEs) are privileged in various aspect.[921] This approach is intended to address the inherent imbalances in digital markets and ensures that the benefits of data access lead to more competitive market and not entrench existing monopolies or oligopolies.[922]

According to Article 5(3) DA, gatekeepers are not eligible third-party recipients and may therefore not receive data based on the portability rights set out in Article 5(1) DA. Even if the user has obtained the pursuant to a request under Article 4(1) DA this data may not be passed on to gatekeepers (Article 5(3)(c) DA). Moreover, gatekeepers are not only restricted from being recipients of data but are also prohibited from advertising or promoting the transfer of product and service data to themselves (Article 5(3)(a) and (b) DA. Additionally, pursuant to Article 6(2)(d) DA any third party that receives data under Article 5(1) DA may not onward transfer this data to gatekeepers. These measures are aimed at avoiding further concentration of power and control over data, which could potentially stifle competition and innovation in the digital marketplace. Excluding gatekeepers from the DA's scope of beneficiaries reflects the strategic intent to safeguard the European IoT industry from the dominance of large, primarily non-European digital conglomerates, such as Alphabet, Meta, and Amazon.[923]

For data that is generated by products or services manufactured by micro or small enterprises, as defined in Article 2 of the Annex to Commission Recommendation 2003/361/EC,[924] Article 7 DA introduces a blanket exemption from the obligation to make data available pursuant to Article 4(1) and 5(1) DA. For medium-sized enterprises, the same exemptions apply only under specific conditions. Medium-sized enterprises are exempt from the obligation for one year after surpassing the medium-sized threshold. Moreover, connected products are exempted for one year after the date

921 Podszun and Pfeifer (n 838) 956.

922 Recital 40 DA; see Podszun, *Der EU Data Act und der Zugang zu Sekundärmärkten am Beispiel des Handwerks* (n 835) 27.

923 Podszun and Pfeifer (n 838) 957; but see Metzger and Schweitzer (n 810) 59, who are critical of the exemption of gatekeepers.

924 Commission Recommendation 2003/361/EC of 6 May 2003 concerning the definition of micro, small and medium-sized enterprises, OJ L 2003/124, 36.

on which they were placed on the market by a medium-sized enterprise. The exemption from the obligation to share data pursuant to Chapter II DA does not apply if the micro or small-sized enterprises have a partner enterprise or a linked enterprise within the meaning of Article 3 of the Annex to Recommendation 2003/361/EC that does not qualify as a micro enterprise or a small enterprise and is subcontracted to manufacture or design a connected product or to provide a related service.

If SMEs receive data from a data holder due to an Article 5 DA-request of the user, SMEs that do not have partner enterprises or linked enterprises that do not qualify as SMEs as well as for non-profit research organisations are only required to pay for the costs directly related to and attributable to the provision of the data they request. Hence, contrary to the situation where the data recipient is not an SME, data holders may not charge a margin or any additional charges beyond the actual costs incurred by the data holder. This is intended to ensure that smaller entities can access the data they need without facing financial barriers that could impede their ability to innovate and compete effectively.[925]

The regulatory measures outlined above have a certain redistributive effect with regard to IoT data. If gatekeepers manufacture connected products or provide related services, they must make the product data available to third parties at the request of users but may not receive any data from other manufacturers or providers. SMEs may get access to this data and do not even have to pay a profit margin but only the actual costs for accessing the data. The SMEs themselves, however, do not have to provide access to the data generated by their products. Hence, they only benefit from the DA but are not burdened by it. The regulatory measures are reminiscent of the tale of Robin Hood in that they redistribute resources (in this case IoT data) from the 'rich' (gatekeepers with significant market power and data control) to the 'poor' (SMEs with limited resources and market influence). Hence, it seems fitting to describe this form of asymmetric regulation as the 'Robin Hood approach', highlighting its intent to foster a more balanced and equitable data economy.

925 Podszun, *Der EU Data Act und der Zugang zu Sekundärmärkten am Beispiel des Handwerks* (n 835) 27; Podszun and Pfeifer (n 838) 957.

7.9 Unfairness Test

Chapter IV of the DA, which consists solely of Article 13, sets out an unfairness test for contractual terms concerning access to and the use of data or liability and remedies for the breach or the termination of data-related obligations that have been unilaterally imposed by one enterprise on another enterprise. Any clause that is unfair shall not be binding to the other party (Article 13(1) DA). However, not the entire contract is rendered void. The remaining contract will continue to be valid if it can exist without the unfair clause (Article 13(7) DA).

7.9.1 Scope of application

In principle, the unfairness test applies to contracts concluded after the DA entered into force. However, contracts concluded on or before the DA's date of entry into force do fall within the scope if they are of indefinite duration or expire at least 10 years after the DA entered into force (Article 50 DA).

Article 13(1) DA applies to all contractual relationships between two businesses that contain terms concerning access to and the use of data or liability and remedies for the breach or the termination of data-related obligations. The provision can thus be applicable to several of the contracts related to IoT data. Importantly, the unfairness test applies to the contractual relationship between the data holder and the user pursuant to Article 4(13) DA, which authorises the data holder to use non-personal data generated by the connected product. As has already been pointed out, the unfairness test and not the obligation to conclude a contract for the use of non-personal data as such constitutes the usage limitation for the data holder. This is because the data holder, as manufacturer of the connected device, will usually be able to impose any contractual terms on the user. Article 13 DA ensures that these terms do not unfairly disadvantage the user (see 7.5.6.1). Moreover, provided that the contract under which the user buys rents or leases the connected product contains provisions on the access or use of the generated data, these terms are also subject to the unfairness control. Finally, Article 13 DA is applicable to the contract that is concluded between the data holder and a third party recipient after the user has requested the data transfer pursuant to Article 5 DA.[926]

926 See Schwamberger (n 826) 97.

According to Article 13(7) DA, contractual terms defining the main subject matter of the contract or the adequacy of the price are excluded from the scope of the unfairness test. Since the exclusion of the core terms corresponds to Article 4(2) UTD, the existing case law interpreting the UTD can be applied to the DA.[927] The CJEU regards as clauses relating to the main subject matter of the contract those that 'lay down the essential obligations of the contract and, as such, characterise it'.[928] For this assessment, the entire system and provisions of the contract, as well as the contract's legal and factual context need to be taken into account.[929] However, a central difference between the UTD and DA is that clauses on the main performance fall under the UTD's unfairness test if they are not in plain intelligible language. Article 13 DA does not contain such a transparency requirement.[930]

7.9.2 Rationale for the unfairness control

Generally, there are two different rationales for subjecting standard terms to judicial control: to address unequal bargaining power or to correct a market failure arising from an information asymmetry.[931] Typically, one rationale is predominant over the other when justifying the need for an unfairness test in standard contracts.

In the DA proposal, the unfairness test was only applicable to terms that have been unilaterally imposed on micro, small and medium-sized enterprises. Thus, initially, the DA proposal seemed to be predicated on the 'unequal bargaining power' rationale. The unfairness test was intended to protect SMEs, which despite having the formal freedom to negotiate terms, have little to no actual influence over the contractual terms due to their weaker bargaining position.[932]

However, in the final version of the DA, the unfairness test is no longer limited to clauses that are imposed on SMEs but applies irrespective of the

927 Schwamberger (n 826) 98; Staudenmayer (n 823) 601.

928 ECJ. C-28/13, Kasler, EU:C:2014:282, 43.

929 Staudenmayer (n 823) 601.

930 Schwamberger (n 826) 98; Staudenmayer (n 823) 602.

931 Hein Kötz, *European Contract Law* (2nd edn, Oxford University Press 2017) 132; Phillip Hellwege, 'It Is Necessary to Strictly Distinguish Two Forms of Fairness Control!' [2015] EuCML 129, 131.

932 See Staudenmayer (n 823) 600.

enterprise's market power. The broader scope of the unfairness test suggests that the primary concern is not the unequal bargaining power but the fact that it is too time-consuming and cost-intensive to go through all standard terms that have been unilaterally imposed by one party. The result is an information asymmetry where only the party supplying the standard terms is familiar with their content. This may lead to a lack of competition on the quality of the terms themselves, as there is no market recognition or reward for providing fairer terms. Since those who use standard terms to their own advantage, and to the detriment of their contractual partners, gain a competitive edge, companies are incentivised to include more unfavourable terms.[933] To stop this so-called race to the bottom and to prevent market failure, it is necessary to subject standard terms to judicial control.[934]

7.9.3 Relationship to the Unfair Terms Directive

Article 13 DA applies only to b2b relations while consumer contracts remain covered by the Unfair Terms Directive (UTD).[935] It has been criticised that only business and not consumers benefit from the updated and data-specific unfairness tests and that consumers thus may, with regard to IoT data, be less protected than businesses.[936] However, as has been rightly pointed out that even though Article 13 DA, in particular its grey and black list, is not directly applicable to B2C contracts, the established criteria can still be considered when evaluating unfair terms under the UTD.[937] The unfairness test under the general clause of the UTD assesses whether the clause deviates from the national law that would apply in the absence of an agreement to such an extent that a fair and equitable seller could not reasonably assume that a consumer would have agreed to such term in individual negotiations.[938] However, as there are no default rules

933 The reasoning is based on the economic theory of market failures of George A Akerlof, 'The Market for "Lemons": Quality Uncertainty and the Market Mechanism' (1970) 84 The Quarterly Journal of Economics 488, 489 ff.

934 Akerlof's lemons market theory may also be applied to standard terms, see Michael Schillig, in James Devenney and Mel B Kenny (eds), *The transformation of European private law : harmonisation, consolidation, codification or chaos?* (Cambridge University Press 2013) 263.

935 Article 1(9) DA; Recital 9 and 28 DA.

936 Drexl and others (n 821) 45.

937 Schwamberger (n 826) 98.

938 ECJ, C-415/11, Aziz, EU:C:2012:700, para 74.

for data-related obligations, it is indicated to use the DA's black and grey list as well as the model contractual clauses developed by the Commission as a benchmark for the unfairness assessment. This approach would bridge regulatory gaps and ensure that consumers enjoy the same level of protection as businesses.

7.9.4 Unilaterally imposed terms

Subjects of the unfairness test are only terms that have been unilaterally imposed. Article 13(6) DA specifies that a provision is deemed unilaterally imposed if it is introduced by one party to the contract, and the other party is unable to influence its content despite making an attempt to negotiate it. The party introducing the contractual term bears the burden of proof to demonstrate that it was not imposed unilaterally. In take-it-or-leave-it situations, where one party holds significant power and dictates the terms of the contract, it will usually be fruitless for the weaker party to attempt to negotiate the term. However, in order to benefit from the unfairness test, the party would need to engage in pro forma negotiations, making an effort to negotiate even when it is understood that there is no real possibility of influencing the terms.[939] This requirement is also inconsistent with the rationale of Article 13 DA unfairness test set out by the DA.[940]

As argued above, the justification for the assessment of data related standard terms seems to be that parties accept standard terms not (only) because of their weak bargaining power but because the high efforts necessary to review standard terms presented by the other party make it economically unreasonable to go through all of them. However, if the economic unreasonableness of reviewing and negotiating standard terms is the justification for intervening with the private autonomy, then requiring parties to negotiate each clause imposes a burden that the rationale of the provision seeks to mitigate.

For b2c contracts, the scope of the unfairness test is broader. The UTD applies to terms that have not been individually negotiated and specifies that a term shall always be regarded as not individually negotiated where it has been drafted in advance and the consumer has therefore not been able to influence the substance of the term (Article 3(2) UTD). This means that

---

939 Drexl and others (n 821) 45; see also Schwamberger (n 826) 98.

940 See Drexl and others (n 821) 45.

consumers, who simply accept the provided terms without attempting to negotiate them benefit from the UTD's unfairness test, while business users would not fall under the protection of Article 13(1) DA.[941]

7.9.5 General clause

The heart of the unfairness test is the general clause laid down in Article 13(3) DA, which stipulates that a contractual term is unfair if 'its use grossly deviates from good commercial practice in data access and use, contrary to good faith and fair dealing'. Regarding the gross deviation from good business practice—the first of the two cumulative elements of the unfairness test—it has been pointed out that DA primarily wants to respect the contractual freedom of the parties (Recital 61 DA). Thus, the mere fact that a contractual term favours one of the parties does not render the clause non-binding, as such an advantage is an inherent part of commercial dealings and is not necessarily abusive. It is not enough for the terms to merely reflect an imbalance; the imbalance must go significantly beyond what can be considered a good business practice.[942]

Typically, the benchmark for determining what constitutes 'good business practice' is the default terms established by national law, as they serve as a baseline for evaluating the fairness of contractual provisions.[943] However, when it comes to data-specific obligations, existing national law provides limited guidance. A key source for establishing a benchmark for the unfairness test will be the non-binding model contract terms for data access and use, once they are adopted by the Commission.[944] Moreover, the terms of the black and grey list (Article 13(4) and (5) DA) are, according to Recital 62 DA, also intended to serve as a yardstick to interpret the general unfairness provision.[945] Soft law instruments, such as the ALI/ELI Principles for a Data Economy[946] or the UNCITRAL's Default Rules for Data

941 Drexl and others (n 821) 45; see also Podszun, *Der EU Data Act und der Zugang zu Sekundärmärkten am Beispiel des Handwerks* (n 835) 81.

942 Staudenmayer (n 823) 599.

943 ECJ, C-415/11, Aziz, EU:C:2012:700, para 71 ff.

944 Schwamberger (n 826) 99.

945 Leistner and Antoine (n 809) 107.

946 Neil Cohen and Christiane Wendehorst (n 119).

Provision Contracts[947] can also play an important role in that regard.[948] It is important to note that the existing business practice may not simply be used as a benchmark because it does not necessarily reflect a 'good' business practice. The prevailing industry practice may, for example, be abusive due to the dominance of a quasi-monopolist within the sector.[949]

The criterion 'deviation from good commercial practice' should not be equated with the UTD's criterion of a 'significant imbalance in the parties' rights and obligations to the detriment of the consumer.' While the two wordings would generally be interchangeable, the threshold for determining when a clause constitutes a deviation from good commercial practice is higher, as businesses are presumed to have more experience, resources, and understanding of commercial practices than consumers.[950]

The second cumulative element of the general clause pertains to the breach of the requirement of 'good faith and fair dealing'. Since the concept of 'good faith' is also used in Article 3 UTD, the interpretation of this requirement can be based on the case law of the CJEU on the UTD. Hence, a contractual clause is deemed acceptable only if the party proposing it could reasonably expect that the other party would agree to it after fair and equitable negotiations. The reference to 'fair dealing' in Article 13 DA underscores the standard in business dealings is, again, higher than in consumer contracts. The case law of the CJEU must therefore be adapted accordingly to the expected behaviour in b2b contracts.[951]

7.9.6 Black and grey list

Additionally, to the general clause, the DA sets out a black (Article 13(4) DA) and a grey (Article 13(5) DA) list. Terms that fall within the blacklist are always unfair within the meaning of Article 13(3) DA. The three terms on the blacklist—(a) exclusion or limitation of liability for intentional acts or gross negligence, (b) exclusion of remedies in case of non-performance or of liability for contractual obligations and (c) unilateral determination of conformity or interpretation of any term—pertain more to general contract

947 UNCITRAL's ongoing work can be followed here <https://uncitral.un.org/en/working_groups/4/electronic_commerce> accessed 21 March 2024.
948 Schwamberger (n 826) 99.
949 Staudenmayer (n 823) 599.
950 Staudenmayer (n 823) 599; see also Leistner and Antoine (n 809) 107.
951 Staudenmayer (n 823) 599.

law concerns rather than addressing data-specific issues. However, despite the lack of a direct data-specific focus, the fact that parties may not avoid their liability and obligations under the contract may indirectly contribute to improving data quality.[952]

Terms that fall under the so-called grey list of Article 13(5) DA are only presumed to be unfair. The imposing party can rebut the presumption by demonstrating that in the specific context of the agreement, the term is not unfair.[953] Some clauses on the grey list also relate to matters of general contract law, but the list also contains clauses that relate to data-specific issues. In particular, a term is presumed to be unfair if it has the effect or objective of allowing the imposing party to use the co-generated data in ways that harm the other's interests, especially if the data are sensitive or protected (b); preventing a party from using the data provided or generated data during the contract, or significantly limit their ability to manage or derive value from their data (c); restricting a party from obtaining copies of data they provided or generated during or within a reasonable period after the termination of the contract (e).

7.10 Data protection of third parties

When providing personal data based on Article 4(1) or 5(1) DA, this must be done in accordance with data protection law and therefore requires a legal basis for the processing. If a user requests access to personal data concerning themselves, this poses no problem, as the request also constitutes implicit consent to the necessary processing.[954] However, there may also be situations where the user is not the data subject of the generated data or where the data relates to the user as well as other natural persons.[955] For instance, a business user might want to access IoT data that could indirectly identify employees or customers.[956] In such cases, user consent is a not

952 Leistner and Antoine (n 809) 107.

953 Schwamberger (n 826) 99; Leistner and Antoine (n 809) 108; Staudenmayer (n 823) 598.

954 Specht-Riemenschneider (n 821) 810; Metzger and Schweitzer (n 810) 77; Steinrötter (n 515) 223; Wiebe, 'Der Data Act – Innovation oder Illusion?' (n 831) 1574.

955 Drexl and others (n 821) 110; Metzger and Schweitzer (n 810) 77; Steinrötter (n 515) 223.

956 Metzger and Schweitzer (n 810) 77.

sufficient legal basis, because the processing affects the data protection rights of individuals who are not the user.[957]

Hence, an alternative legal ground needs to be found. Obtaining consent from all affected individuals might not be a suitable option, especially in real-time access scenarios, due to difficulties in contacting all relevant parties and delays in obtaining their consent.[958] One might assume that the access rights afforded by the DA would constitute legal obligations within the meaning of Article 6(1)(c) GDPR.[959] However, Recital 7 DA explicitly states that where the user is not the data subject, the DA does not create a legal basis for providing access to personal data or for making personal data available to a third party.[960]

This leaves only recourse to Article 6(1)(f) of the GDPR, which allows processing based on legitimate interests pursued by the data controller or a third party. However, this introduces significant legal uncertainties, as, in principle, case-by-case analysis would be necessary.[961] It could be argued though that because the EU legislator created these access rights in the DA, there is an implied intention that the interest in processing the data is generally considered legitimate outweighing the interests of the affected data subjects. Only in exceptional cases would the data protection interests of third parties prevail and preclude the data rights of the DA.[962] For sensitive data, the legitimate interests pursued by the controller or a third party do not constitute a legal basis for the processing. In this case, the explicit consent of affected data subjects (Article 9(2)(a) GDPR) would be the only way to legitimise the access to sensitive data.[963]

In conclusion, if a user seeks to exercise their data rights under the DA with regard to data concerning other individuals, the permissibility of such a request under the GDPR remains uncertain. This legal ambiguity significantly undermines the effectiveness of access rights, as it enables data holders to potentially reject access requests on the grounds of protecting the data rights of third parties.[964]

---

957 A similar situation can arise with regard to the portability right under Article 20 GPR in so-called multi-data subject constellations, see 5.1.5.

958 Drexl and others (n 821) 110.

959 See Specht-Riemenschneider (n 821) 811.

960 Steinrötter (n 515) 223.

961 Steinrötter (n 515) 223; Wiebe, 'Der Data Act – Innovation oder Illusion?' (n 831) 1574.

962 Specht-Riemenschneider (n 821) 811; sceptical Steinrötter (n 515) 223.

963 Steinrötter (n 515) 223.

964 Drexl and others (n 821) 111.

7.11 Overlaps undermining the DA's obligations

One of the biggest shortcomings of the DA is that there are several overlaps between the different obligations that not only create legal uncertainty, making it challenging for the involved parties to understand their obligations and rights, but may also inadvertently counteract the DA's intended objectives. This is true both for the relationship between Articles 3 and 4 DA and for the relationship between Articles 4 and 5 DA.

7.11.1 Relationship between Articles 3 and 4 DA

As described above 7.5.5, Articles 4(6)-(9) DA and Article 6(11) DA impose restrictions on the user regarding the use and onward transfer of the data obtained from the data holder based on a request pursuant to Article 4(1) DA. These restrictions pertain to the handling of trade secrets and the use of the accessed data for developing a competing connected product. However, it has been pointed out that similar restrictions do not exist for Article 3 DA. This means that in case the manufacturer does not comply with their primary (!) obligation to design and manufacture connected products and related services in such a manner that the product data and related service data is easily accessible by the user, more restrictions on how the user can use the data apply.[965] If the data obtained directly from a connected product is subject to fewer restrictions compared to data obtained under Article 4(1) DA, this regulatory imbalance could incentivise manufacturers to design their products in such a way that the data is not 'directly' accessible. It would therefore seem appropriate to apply the restrictions of Article 4 DA also to data obtained directly from the product.[966]

7.11.2 Relationship between Articles 4 and 5 DA

The essential difference between Articles 4 and 5 DA is that the user may obtain the data generated by IoT products free of charge, while the third party recipients that receive data based on Article 5 DA have to financially

965 Schmidt-Kessel (n 246) 80.

966 See Grapentin (n 860) 177; but see Schmidt-Kessel (n 246) 80, who argues that there is no lacuna and that an analogous application of the restrictions is therefore not possible.

compensate the data holder. The rationale is that the user had a significant share in the generation of the data and should thus have the right to access the data and use it for their own purposes without having to pay for it. In contrast, the third party recipient obtains the data without having contributed to its generation and should therefore pay a remuneration for receiving the data.

The issue, however, is that the DA does not consistently maintain this distinction. Article 4 DA does not set out any limitations on the onward transfer of the received data. Hence, data recipients can circumvent the obligations and costs associated with access based on Article 5(1) DA by having users request data directly from data holders under Article 4(1) DA and then pass it on to the recipients indirectly.[967]

In general, there are arguments both in favour of and against the obligation of third-party recipients to compensate the data owner for the data received. One objection to a remuneration duty is that the DA is based on the idea that users should enjoy a certain autonomy over the data they have co-generated and the users should therefore be free to decide whether to use the data internally within their organisation or externally through third-party services. For example, an industrial user needing data access to repair a manufacturing machine may opt to delegate the repair to its own maintenance unit (Article 4 DA) or outsource maintenance to an external service provider (Article 5 DA). The decision whether to outsource should not affect the data holder's entitlement to compensation. Mandating compensation for third-party data access could even create competitive imbalances disadvantaging smaller competitors. Small commercial users are typically more dependent on external services due to a lack of in-house capabilities. Small users may therefore be indirectly charged for data usage, because the third-party provider has to pay compensation to the data holder and will usually pass these costs on to the user.[968] Larger commercial users with resources to establish efficient in-house services would not be affected. The argument extends to consumers, who will always need to rely on external services.[969] Furthermore, the fact that the third party did not co-generate the data does not necessarily mean that third parties who receive the data must compensate the data holder. This is because the access

967 Specht-Riemenschneider (n 821) 822; Wendehorst, 'Konsument:innen in der Datenökonomie' (n 230) 233.

968 Drexl and others (n 821) 29; see also Kerber, 'Governance of IoT Data' (n 804) 133.

969 Drexl and others (n 821) 29.

right is not afforded directly to the third party but to the user, who decides whether and who receives the data; the third party recipient is only an indirect beneficiary. Moreover, the DA intends to facilitate competition in secondary markets and not in the primary IoT market.[970] Hence, requiring third-party recipients to compensate data holders for data access is not essential for protecting the competitive position of data holders in the primary market, as the primary market dynamics are distinct from the value creation and competitive interplays in secondary markets.

On the other hand, if the transfer to third party recipients is free of charge, manufacturers or data holders will need to anticipate widespread data sharing and may factor the potential loss of revenue (from what they could have charged third parties for data access) into the initial pricing of their products or services. This means that the cost of the device or service could be higher to reflect the expected 'free' data access by third parties. As a result, all users of the product or service will bear these higher costs, regardless of whether they intend to share the data with third parties or not. Users who do not share their data are ultimately cross-subsidising those who do, as the initial higher price includes the cost of providing data access to third party provider, which only some users take advantage of.[971]

The EU legislators' policy decision is to be criticised in that they have not committed to either providing IoT data to third-party recipients at no cost or requiring them to compensate the data holder. Instead, they have opted for an approach that combines the unfavourable aspects of both options. Essentially, the DA has inadvertently replicated the issue of the GDPR, where larger players might disproportionately benefit from the data access provisions (see 5.6.3). Large companies, due to their existing user base and market presence, could more effectively encourage users to exercise their Article 4(1) DA right in favour of the company, thereby gaining access to IoT data free of charge.[972] This dynamic might reinforce existing market imbalances because larger entities can consolidate their dominance by leveraging broader data access. Even if this turns out not to be true, the DA may introduce new competitive imbalances. The distinction between third party recipients who are required to pay for data access and those who are not is completely arbitrary, depending solely on whether users decide to

970 See Recitals 6, 27 and 30 DA.

971 Wendehorst, 'Konsument:innen in der Datenökonomie' (n 230) 233.

972 *Cf.* Wendehorst, 'Konsument:innen in der Datenökonomie' (n 230) 225; Datenethikkommission (n 114) 136; see also Thomas and others (n 494) 38.

exercise their rights under Articles 4 or 5 DA, instead of following a clear or equitable rationale.

It is completely unclear why Article 4(1) DA affords users the right to access and forward data in real-time and on a continuous basis when they do have a portability right pursuant to Article 5(1) DA. If the objective were to enable users to switch providers of IoT devices a one-time data supply would be sufficient to facilitate provider transitions effectively (see 10.2.2). Situations, where the users themselves require continuous and real-time access to the data generated by the IoT device, are hardly conceivable because most users do not develop or provide the complementary service themselves. Even if the users need such access, restrictions that they may not pass on the data continuously and in real-time to third parties should have been introduced. Without such limitations, the policy decision of Article 5(1) DA that third party recipients shall remunerate the data holder for receiving access is thwarted.

7.12 Summary

Articles 4 and 5 DA give users the right to access and transfer the data generated by the use of IoT devices to third parties in order to empower users, ensure a fairer distribution of data value, promote a competitive aftermarket, and stimulate the development of new services. The critique that the DA does not achieve its objective and may even strengthen the data holder's de facto control over the IoT data is not shared. Without the DA, there would be no real limitations—besides data protection and IP law—to the de facto control of the manufacturer. The DA not only gives users the possibility to access and use the data generated by the IoT devices but also places limits on the data holder's data usage.

In case the manufacturer fails to design IoT devices in a way that allows direct access to the IoT data, Article 4(1) DA gives users the right to access the data generated by the use of the IoT device including the relevant metadata, irrespective of whether the generated data is personal data or not. The explicit exclusion of derived and inferred data from the scope of the DA seems justified. While inferred data involves some user contribution, the data holder's role in the generation is rather limited, warranting additional justification for user access rights. Under the DMA the inclusion of inferred and derived data can be justified by the significant market power of gatekeepers. The DA, however, grants access and portability rights irrespective of the data holder's market position, potentially involving economically stronger third-party data recipients. The DA does not address the essential question of whether Article 4(1) DA puts users in full control of the IoT data or only affords the right to process the data on the data holder's servers. However, the fact that Article 4(2) DA states that users and data holders may contractually restrict or prohibit *further data sharing* suggests that there has already been an initial transfer of data to the user. This supports the interpretation that Article 4(1) DA puts the user in full control of the data.

Article 5(1) DA allows users to request that the data generated by the connected product be transferred directly to a third-party recipient. Concerns have been raised that the requirement for the data holder and data recipient to negotiate and agree on a reasonable remuneration before making the data available under Article 5 DA could potentially hinder efficient data sharing and create barriers to access for third parties. However, the fact that Article 5(1) DA stipulates that the data must be made available without undue delay suggests that the transfer of data should not be made dependent on the prior agreement on compensation.

Recital 25 DA appears to imply that users have the option to waive their rights under Articles 4(1) and 5(1) DA. However, Article 7(2) DA as well as the overall objectives of the DA suggest that the rights afforded by Articles 4(1) and 5(1) are mandatory and cannot be waived through agreement. As the legally binding components of the regulation, Articles override Recitals in case of any contradiction. Therefore, any exception to the mandatory nature of access rights would have need to be explicitly provided for in the binding part of the DA and not only in the non-binding Recitals.

Much debate also revolves around the requirement that the data holder may process non-personal data generated by the IoT device only on the basis of a contract with the user. The analysis tried to demonstrate that the objective of this requirement is to subject the data use of the data holder to the unfairness test set out in Article 13 DA.

Legal uncertainties arise in situations where the user requests access to the data generated by their IoT product, but this includes data related to other individuals. The data sharing obligation of the DA itself does not constitute legal obligations within the meaning of Article 6(1)(c) GDPR that would justify the processing of such personal data. Moreover, obtaining consent from all affected individuals might not be a suitable option, especially in real-time access scenarios, due to difficulties in contacting all relevant parties and delays in obtaining their consent. This leaves only recourse to Article 6(1)(f) GDPR, which, however, requires that the interests of the user are balanced against those of the affected data subjects on a case-by-case basis.

Finally, the overlaps between Articles 3 and 4 DA and Articles 4 and 5 DA create legal uncertainties and possibly counteract the intended objectives. If the user obtains data based on Article 4(1) DA certain usage limitations are imposed by Articles 4(6)-(9) DA and Article 6(11) DA. However, these restrictions do not apply if the user has accessed the data directly from the device because the manufacturer has complied with its duty to ensure access by design. As this would give the wrong incentives the restrictions that apply to data access based on Article 4 DA should also apply to data obtained directly from the product. Concerning the relationship between Articles 4 and 5 DA, the problem is that Article 4 DA does not impose any limitations on the user regarding the onward transfer of the received data. This allows third parties to bypass the obligations and costs associated with receiving the data based on Article 5(1) DA by having users request data from data holders under Article 4(1) DA and then passing it on to the third party. This practice undermines the regulatory intent of the DA that users should access the data free of charge because they had a significant share in generating the data, while third-party recipients, which have not contributed to the data's generation, should pay for receiving the data.

8 Data Act, Chapter VI

In Chapter VI, the DA lays down another portability right, which entitles the customers of data processing services to have their data and digital assets ported to another provider. Article 25(2)(a) DA mandates that the contract between the customer and the initial provider, which is referred to as source provider, shall include a contractual clause that allows the customer, upon request, to switch to a data processing service offered by a different provider of data processing services (destination provider) or to port all exportable data and digital assets to an on-premises ICT infrastructure. In addition, Article 23 DA obliges the data processing service providers to eliminate and refrain from imposing pre-commercial, commercial, technical, contractual and organisational obstacles, which inhibit customers from switching providers. Article 29 DA sets out a gradual withdrawal of so-called switching charges (Article 29 DA), while Article 30 DA lays down technical interoperability requirements.

8.1 Scope of Application

The obligations laid down in Chapter VI DA apply to data processing services, which shall be understood as referring in particular to cloud computing and edge computing services.[973] A rather technical definition provides Article 2(8) DA, according to which a data processing service is a 'digital service that is provided to a customer and that enables ubiquitous and on-demand network access to a shared pool of configurable, scalable and elastic computing resources of a centralised, distributed or highly distributed nature that can be rapidly provisioned and released with minimal management effort or service provider interaction'. Recital 80 further describes the technical aspects of this definition.

While the initial proposal of the DA excluded online content services as defined in the Cross-Border Portability Regulation,[974] in particular audio-

973 See Recital 78 DA.

974 Regulation (EU) 2017/1128 of the European Parliament and of the Council of 14 June 2017 on cross-border portability of online content services in the internal market, OJ L 2017/168, 1.

visual media streaming services such as Netflix and Spotify, from its scope, this exemption was not maintained in the final version. Commentators had been rightly pointing out that the Cross-Border Portability Regulation—contrary to what the name would suggest—does not deal with portability in the sense of switching providers but deals with cross-border availability of online content services between member states, so-called 'geo-portability'.[975]

According to Article 31(1) DA, data processing services tailored to the specific needs of an individual customer, either because the majority of their main features have been custom-built or all components have been developed for a singular customer, should be exempt from certain obligations related to service switching. However, services that are offered on a broad commercial scale by the provider via its service catalogue are not covered by this exemption (Recital 98 DA). The reason for this is that complying with the switching provision is more burdensome for providers of these customised services. Beta versions that are provided for testing and evaluation purposes and for a limited period of time are excluded from all obligations (Article 32(2) DA). In case the services fall under one of these exemptions, the provider has to inform prospective customers of such services, prior to the conclusion of a contract, that obligations laid down in this Regulation do not (fully) apply to the relevant services (Article 32(3) DA).[976]

8.2 Objective: facilitating provider switching

Chapter VI DA is the regulatory response to vendor lock-ins in the data processing services market. Customers of data processing services often do not have the contractual right to transfer their data to another service and/or they also lack the technical means to do so.[977] Moreover, switching

975 Geiregat (n 20) 30; see also Gregor Lienemann and Marie Wienroeder, in Moritz Hennemann and others (eds), *The Data Act Proposal – Literature Review and Critical Analysis* (University of Passau Institute for Law of the Digital Society 2023) 2.

976 see also Carlo Piltz and Johannes Zwerschke, 'Cloud Switching nach dem Data Act aus der Beratungsperspektive' (2024) 40 Computer und Recht 153, 154.

977 EY, 'Study on the Economic Detriment to Small and Medium-Sized Enterprises Arising from Unfair and Unbalanced Cloud Computing Contracts' (European Commission 2018) 46 ff; Björn Lundqvist, 'Cloud Services as the Ultimate Gate(Keeper)' (2019) 7 Journal of Antitrust Enforcement 220, 234.

cloud services, especially for small and medium-sized enterprises (SMEs), can incur significant costs, including data transfer fees, license expenses, potential downtime, and the need for overlapping services during the transition. Additionally, customers are not always informed about the process and costs of switching or exiting their services before they enter the contract. Without this information, the initial low costs and easy entry into cloud services may lure customers into a lock-in situation.[978] Due to the combination of contractual obligations, economic burdens, and technical barriers, customers may find it challenging to change provider essentially trapping the customers with their current service provider.[979]

Initially, the European legislator wanted to tackle this problem with the Regulation on the Free Flow of Non-Personal Data[980] under which self-regulatory Codes of Conduct, so-called SWIPO (Switching Cloud Providers and Porting Data),[981] were developed. However, the European legislator conceded that they have not been widely adopted by service providers and that voluntary measures alone have not been effective in addressing the issues of vendor lock-in and ensuring interoperability among different cloud services (Recital 79 DA).[982]

Given these challenges, the Commission opted for a more far-reaching regulatory intervention. Chapter VI intends to facilitate the process by which customers can switch from one service provider to another while retaining a baseline level of functionality even after transitioning to a new service provider. This approach aims to preserve service continuity and minimise disruption for customers. Enhancing consumer choice shall lower the entry barrier for providers thereby stimulating innovation and preventing market concentration that could stifle competition (Recital 78 DA).

---

978 Commission, 'Impact Assessment Accompanying the Proposal for a Regulation of the European Parliament and of the Council on a framework for the free flow of non-personal data in the European Union' SWD(2017) 304 final, 11; Lundqvist, 'Cloud Services as the Ultimate Gate(Keeper)' (n 977) 233.

979 Commission, 'Proposal for a Regulation of the European Parliament and of the Council
on harmonised rules on fair access to and use of data', SWD(2022) 34 final, 19 f.

980 Regulation (EU) 2018/1807 of the European Parliament and of the Council of 14 November 2018 on a framework for the free flow of non-personal data in the European Union, OJ L 2018/303, 59.

981 'About SWIPO – SWIPO' <https://swipo.eu/about-2/> accessed 11 April 2024.

982 Commission, 'Impact Assessment Accompanying the Proposal for a Regulation of the European Parliament and of the Council on harmonised rules on fair access to and use of data', SWD(2022) 34 final, 19 f; see also Gregor Lienemann and Marie Wienroeder (n 975) 1; Leistner and Antoine (n 809) 112.

8.3 Legal nature: contractual right to port data

The regulatory approach chosen by the legislator in Chapter VI differs considerably from that of Articles 4 (1) and 5 (1) DA, but also from that of the DMA and GDPR. In the latter instances, the law affords the rightsholder a statutory, i.e. self-standing and immediately enforceable subjective right, to access the data or have the data ported to a third party, irrespective of a contractual relationship to the data holder.[983] Conversely, Article 25 DA stipulates minimum content for the contractual agreement between customer and source provider with regard to switching to a new (destination) service. Instead of mandating that the customer of a data processing service provider shall be able to port data to a different provider, Article 25(2)(a) DA sets out that the contract between the customer and the provider shall include a contractual clause that allows the customer to do so. The focus on the contractual aspect is understandable because there will always be a contract between the customer and the provider, and the contractual partner will also be the person controlling the relevant data. This may not be the case in IoT situations, where the user buys the product from a retailer, but the data is stored on the servers of the manufacturer.

However, the regulatory approach of Chapter VI DA has raised the question whether it affords a subjective right to customers of data processing services.[984] As long as the providers comply with their duty under Article 25(2)(a) DA and include a clause that allows the user to switch providers, the situation is unproblematic because the customer could invoke their contractual rights in civil law proceedings. However, if the service provider fails to incorporate such a clause into the contract, it is questionable whether customers can demand portability directly from the provider and seek legal recourse through civil courts to enforce this right.[985] It has been argued that, despite the terminological difference to Articles 4(1) and 5(1) DA, Article 25 DA, when interpreted teleologically, should be

983 For the DA, see Metzger and Schweitzer (n 810) 79; and Wiebe, 'Der Data Act – Innovation oder Illusion?' (n 831) 1577; regarding the DMA, see Rupprecht Podszun, Philipp Bongartz and Alexander Kirk, 'Digital Markets Act – Neue Regeln für Fairness in der Plattformökonomie' NJW 3249, 3253; and Christian Karbaum and Max Schulz, '„Antitrust Litigation 2.0" – Private Enforcement beim DMA?' [2022] NZKart 107, 111.

984 Gregor Lienemann and Marie Wienroeder (n 975) 3.

985 Geiregat (n 20) 39 f.

understood as directly bestowing a self-standing, immediately enforceable subjective right on costomers.[986]

Whilst agreeing that public enforcement by the competent authority alone would fall short in remediating the switching-related obstacles faced by customers,[987] the difference in language between Chapter II and Chapter VI matters in terms of the parties' rights and remedies.[988] As Chapter VI DA regulates the contractual relationship between customer and provider—not only with Article 25 DA but also with the duty of good faith (Article 27 DA)—national contract law should give effect to the duty laid down in Article 25(2)(a) DA. The objective of Chapter VI DA is that providers and customers enter into contracts that allow the latter to port their data to another provider.[989] How to achieve this goal effectively is left to the applicable national law.[990] It is conceivable that a national court could derive a mandatory contractual rule for data processing service contracts from Article 25(2)(a) DA or regard the porting obligation as an implied term. The porting of the relevant data could then be enforced by relying directly on the contract. Similarities can be drawn to the Unfair Terms Directive. Under the UTD, consumers have the right not to be bound by unfair terms but leaves it to the Member States to determine the legal consequences of unfairness in their national legal orders (absolute or relative nullity).[991]

8.4 Switching and portability

Under the clause that Article 25(2)(a) requires to be included in the contract, the customer has actually two rights: they may request that the data and digital assets be transferred to a new provider ('switching'), or retrieve the data and digital assets on a device of their choice ('port to an on-premises ICT infrastructure').[992] Once the customer requests to switch

---

986 Geiregat (n 20) 40.
987 Gregor Lienemann and Marie Wienroeder (n 975) 4; Drexl and others (n 821) 67.
988 *Cf.* Olha O Cherednychenko, 'Rediscovering the Public/Private Divide in EU Private Law' (2020) 26 European Law Journal 27, 34.
989 Drexl and others (n 821) 61.
990 This follows from the effet utile, which requires member States are to take all the measures necessary to ensure that EU law is fully effective, in accordance with the objective it pursues. ECJ, C-350/03, *Schulte*, EU:C:2005:637, para 69; see also Riesenhuber (n 29) 272.
991 Cherednychenko (n 988) 35.
992 Geiregat (n 20) 34.

to the services of another provider or have the data and digital assets transferred to an on-premises ICT infrastructure, a notice period for initiating of the switching process is triggered. The parties need to agree on such a period in the contract, but it may not exceed two months. After this notice period has lapsed, the provider has to complete the switching process and transfer the data without undue delay but at the latest at the end of a mandatory maximum transitional period of 30 days.

In order to ensure a smooth transition and reduce barriers to switching, the DA obliges providers to support the switching process in a reasonable manner (Article 25(2)(a)(i) DA) and continue to provide the contractually agreed functions or services (Article 25(2)(a)(ii) DA). Hence, the customer may still use the old services until the process of transitioning to the destination provider is completed.[993]

The contract with the source provider is terminated with the successful completion of the switching process (Article 25(2)(c)(i) DA, or, in case the customer wants to retrieve their data, at the end of the notice period. However, the source provider needs to keep the data and digital assets of the customer for a retrieval period of at least 30 days that starts after the transitional period (max 30 days), which again starts after the notice period (max two months). After this period has expired, the provider has to guarantee full erasure of all exportable data and digital assets generated directly by the customer or relating to the customer directly (Article 25(2)(h) DA).

8.4.1 Covered data: exportable data and digital assets

The porting obligation applies to all exportable data and the digital assets of the customer. According to Article 2(38) DA, exportable data should include, at a minimum, input (e.g. files the customer uploads) and output data (e.g. results or reports generated by the service), including metadata, directly or indirectly generated or cogenerated, by the customer's use of the data processing service. Digital assets are defined as digital elements including, in particular, software applications and the corresponding metadata related to settings configurations, security parameters, and rights for access and control management. Customers may only request the transfer

993 Leistner and Antoine (n 809) 115; Gregor Lienemann and Marie Wienroeder (n 975) 10; Bomhard and Merkle (n 876) 175.

of digital assets if they have the right to use them independent of the contractual relationship with the data processing service it intends to switch from (Article 2(32) and Recital 83 DA). This rather broad scope, which also includes the relevant metadata, is intended to ensure that the destination provider can provide the customer with a functionally equivalent service.[994]

Data or assets that are protected by intellectual property rights of others or constitute trade secrets of the service provider or third parties are excluded. Additionally, data related to the integrity and security of the service is also excluded, if transferring such data would create cybersecurity risks.

The contract between provider and customer needs to specify the types of data and digital assets that can be ported during the switching process. The categories of data that are excluded from the portability right because a risk of breach of trade secrets of the provider exists also need to be described in the contract.

8.4.2 Switching charges

The vendor lock-in of customers may not only be the result of the outright denial to port the relevant data but may also be caused by charging high fees for the retrieval of data and their onward transfer (data egress charges) and/or for specific support actions during the switching process (switching charges).[995] While providers would argue that switching services and migrating the data and digital assets is a highly complex, burdensome and cost-intensive task and therefore these costs are justified,[996] the DA wants to gradually fade out these costs (Recital 88 DA). Chapter VI DA introduces a transitional period of three years starting on 11 January 2024 during which providers are still allowed to charge for switching services (Articles 25(2)(i) and 29(2) DA). However, these charges must be reduced to such an extent that they only cover the direct costs associated with the switching process (Article 29(3) DA). After the three-year transitional period, Article 29(1) DA mandates the complete abolition of switching charges.

---

994 Leistner and Antoine (n 809) 115.

995 Recital 88 DA; Gregor Lienemann and Marie Wienroeder (n 975) 13; Daniel Schnurr, 'Switching and Interoperability between Data Processing Services in the Proposed Data Act' (CERRE 2022) 15.

996 Benjamin Jenkins, 'Why Cloud Data Egress Is Expensive' (*The New Stack*, 15 November 2022) <https://thenewstack.io/why-cloud-data-egress-is-expensive/> accessed 11 April 2024.

The standard service charges that customers pay for the ongoing provision of data processing services are not subject to the withdrawal (Article 29(4) DA).[997] Moreover, Recital 89 DA specifies that the customer shall be able to request the provision of additional services that go beyond the provider's switching obligations laid down in Chapter VI DA and that the provider may charge for these requested services if the customer agrees to the price in advance. This means that Article 29 DA applies only to the switching charges for specific support actions during the switching process that the provider has to provide under the DA or performs without the customer having requested it.

Cancellation fees for the early termination of the contract remain permissible, provided they clearly inform potential customers about these fees before concluding the contract (Article 29(4) DA). These types of fees are irrelevant for customers who use services that are based on the so-called pay-as-you-go model where the service charges for the use of cloud services are based solely on consumption and there is no obligation for the customer to purchase certain quantities of computing services. Hence, once the customer stops using the services, they do not have to pay. However, services may also be based on the commitment model where the customer receives a kind of volume discount but in return, they must purchase a certain amount of computing power per year from the provider. When the customer wants to terminate the contract during the commitment period, they must pay the cloud provider a cancellation fee agreed in advance.[998]

With regard to the DA proposal, commentators have raised concerns that the total withdrawal of switching charges would particularly burden smaller cloud service providers, as they may have difficulties compensating for the loss of intermediary fees through other sources of revenue. In order to address this, it was suggested to allow SMEs to continue to claim reduced switching charges even after the transitional period has ended.[999] Comparisons were drawn to Chapters II and III where SMEs only benefit from the access and portability rights but are not burdened by it (see 7.8).[1000] However, this suggestion was not picked up by the legislator and

997 Jacek Lagoni, 'Cloud Switching gemäß Data Act: Die Abschaffung von Switching Charges — Was ist ein Wechselentgelt und welche Wechsel sind betroffen?' (2024) 40 Computer und Recht 91, 92.

998 Lagoni (n 997) 94.

999 Gregor Lienemann and Marie Wienroeder (n 975) 14; Schnurr (n 995) 15.

1000 Gregor Lienemann and Marie Wienroeder (n 975) 15.

the withdrawal of switching charges applies to all providers despite the asymmetries in the financial capabilities of differently sized enterprises.

8.4.3 One-off supply and ongoing data transfers

Article 25(2)(c)(i) DA, which stipulates that the contract with the source provider is terminated with the successful completion of the switching process, creates the impression that the act of invoking portability rights is inherently linked to the termination of the contractual relationship with the provider. This would mean that customers can exercise their portability rights only once, specifically when they express their intention to terminate their contract with the current provider.[1001] The provision of a one-off portability right aligns with the overarching objective of Chapter VI to facilitate competition on the data processing service market by enabling customers to switch provider.

However, Article 34(1) DA stipulates that the obligations to facilitate data transfers 'apply *mutatis mutan*dis [...] for the purposes of in-parallel use of data processing services.' This addition, which is introduced at a rather surprising place in the DA, as Article 34 DA does not belong to Chapter VI but to Chapter VIII, is quite significant. It changes the one-off portability right that only enables the switching between providers of data processing services, to a portability right to continuous real-time data transfers that also facilitate in-parallel use of multiple data processing services with complementary functionalities. Hence, customers do not have to terminate their contract and may still request that the data be transferred to a different provider. However, since facilitating the in-parallel use of services will usually be an ongoing activity, in contrast with the one-off egress required as part of the switching process, Article 34(2) DA allows providers to impose data egress charges, not exceeding the costs incurred, for the purposes of in-parallel use even after the transition period set out in Article 29(2) DA has lapsed.

While the objective of promoting multihoming and not just a complete change of provider can be supported, the regulatory implementation must be criticised. Not only is the extension to multihoming constellations arguably in the wrong chapter, but it will also be burdensome for providers to fulfil this obligation. As explained above, Article 25(2) DA does not

1001 Geiregat (n 20) 34.

confer self-standing rights but obliges the provider to include clauses in the contract that allow the customer to terminate the contract and transfer the data. However, these contractual clauses do not simply apply *mutatis mutandis* to situations that they do not address. Rather, the provider must include additional clauses that deal with the situation that the user wants to keep using the services of the source provider and simultaneously use those of other providers. Apparently, the European legislator did not want to go to the trouble of formulating guidance on how the rules in Article 25(2) DA can be adapted to take account of multihoming, leaving this to the providers.

8.4.4 Technical feasibility

According to Article 25(4) DA, providers are exempted from the obligation to facilitate effective switching or data retrieval within the maximum transitional period of 30 days, if meeting this deadline is technically unfeasible for the provider. In this case, the provider needs to give the customer a detailed report justifying the technical unfeasibility within 14 days after the request and propose an alternative timeline for completing the switching process, which may not exceed seven months. Although the burden to prove the technical unfeasibility is on the provider, commentators have raised concerns that the vagueness of the term 'technical feasibility' could potentially allow providers to exploit this exemption delay compliance with their switching and portability obligations and jeopardise the objective of smooth transitions for customers.[1002]

Since Data processing services can vary widely in complexity, from straightforward applications to highly complex systems involving large volumes of data and intricate dependencies, it is conceivable that technical challenges could indeed prevent compliance within the standard timeframe of 30 days. Arguably, the exception is necessary to leave enough room to accommodate the technical challenges inherent in complex data processing services.

The question has been raised as to how the extension of the transition period affects the customer's obligation to pay remuneration.[1003] Generally,

1002 Drexl and others (n 821) 65 f.; Geiregat (n 20) 36.

1003 David Bomhard, 'Auswirkungen des Data Act auf die Geschäftsmodelle von Cloud-Anbietern' [2024] MMR 109, 111.

Recital 89 DA is quite clear on that matter. It provides that the standard service fees remain applicable until the contract for the provision of the relevant services ceases to apply. Hence the customer would need to pay until the contract ends, which is when the transition process is complete. However, it has been argued that Article 25(4), sentence 2 of the DA, which requires the provider to ensure continuity of the service during an extended transition period, could be interpreted as a unilateral obligation placed on the provider that does not necessitate reciprocal compensation from the customer.[1004] This understanding is quite far-fetched. The second sentence of Article 25(4) states that the service continuity shall be ensured '*in accordance with paragraph 1*' of Article 25 DA. This reference to paragraph 1 would suggest that the intention of the second sentence of Article 25(4) DA is to clarify that the provider's obligation to continue providing the service does not cease after the standard 30-day transition period but extends into the longer alternative transition period that applies in case of technical unfeasibility. It needs to be noted, however, that there seems to be an editorial mistake in the DA: service continuity was initially addressed in paragraph 1 in the proposal stage but is found in paragraph 2 in the final version of the DA.

8.5 Relationship to the DMA and Chapter II of the DA

There may be cases where the data processing services are provided by a provider that is considered a gatekeeper under the DMA. In these situations, customers not only have the option to invoke their rights outlined in Chapter VI DA but can also exercise their access and portability rights under DMA, particularly Articles 6(9) and 6(10) DMA.[1005] Additionally, there may be constellations where the manufacturer of an IoT product offers cloud services for storing the data generated by the product, leading to the questions how Article 24 DA interacts with Articles 4(1) and 5(1) DA.

The most important difference is that under the DMA and Chapter II DA user can access and transfer their data on a continuous basis and in real-time, free of charge. Hence, they may continue to use the services of the gatekeeper/the IoT product while utilising the co-generated data for their own purposes, or have it transferred to third party providers that offer

1004 Bomhard (n 1003) 111.
1005 Leistner and Antoine (n 809) 113.

complementary services or products. In contrast, under Article 24(2)(a) DA the customer may port the data and digital asset for free only once when terminating the contract.[1006] For a continued transfer of data, the provider may charge additional fees (8.4.3).

However, the scope of Article 24 DA is broader than those of access and portability rights of the DMA and Chapter II DA, as it also covers digital assets, which includes software applications and the corresponding metadata related to settings, configurations, security parameters, and rights for access and control management.[1007] The Articles 6(9) and 6(10) DMA only apply to data provided by the user or generated through the activity of the user; digital assets are not mentioned. Chapter II DA even explicitly excludes content from its scope of application. Since the transfer of digital assets is typically necessary for maintaining the continuity and integrity of the service experience post-switch, the access and portability of the DMA and Chapter II are not suitable instruments for a complete migration to a new provider.

8.6 Summary

Chapter VI of the DA addresses the challenges, such as contractual obligations, economic burdens, and technical barriers, that prevent or make it difficult for customers of cloud services (data processing services) to change provider. One of the measures to achieve this is Article 25(2)(a) DA, which requires that contracts between customers and data service providers include clauses for data portability.

The question has been raised whether Article 25(2)(a) DA grants a subjective right to customers that can be directly enforced if such a clause is absent. In this analysis, it is argued that the terminological difference to other data rights matters in terms of the remedies and that Article 25(2)(a) DA does not lay down a self-standing, immediately enforceable subjective right for customers. Rather, it is for national contract law to ensure the effective implementation of the duty set out in Article 25(2)(a) DA. A national court might, for example, derive a mandatory contractual rule for data processing service contracts from Article 25(2)(a) DA or treat the porting obligation as an implied term. In these cases, the portability of relevant data could be enforced directly through the contract.

1006 See Leistner and Antoine (n 809) 113.
1007 See Leistner and Antoine (n 809) 113.

The porting obligation under Article 25(2)(a) DA applies to all exportable data and the customer's digital assets. Digital assets encompass digital elements like software applications and related metadata (settings configurations, security parameters, access and control rights). In contrast, Articles 6(9) and 6(10) DMA apply only to data provided by the user or generated through the user's activity, excluding digital assets. Chapter II of the DA explicitly excludes content from its scope. Since transferring digital assets is often crucial for maintaining service continuity and integrity after switching providers, the access and portability provisions in the DMA and Chapter II are inadequate for a complete migration to a new provider.

It has been pointed out that Article 25(2)(c)(i) DA creates the false impression customers can exercise the portability right only when they intend to end their contract with the source provider. This is because the important addition, set out in Article 34(1) DA, that the obligations to facilitate data transfers also apply for the parallel use of data processing services is located in Chapter VIII instead of Chapter VI, where such a provision would logically belong.

For such continuous access, the provider may charge additional fees from the customer. In contrast, under the DMA and Chapter II DA, users can access and transfer their data continuously and in real time at no cost.

9 Sector-specific data rights

This Chapter explores some of the data access and portability rights that can be found in a range of sector-specific Regulations and Directives. These legislative instruments are typically very technical pieces of legislation that contain a variety of very different rules with data access and portability rights only being one small part. Examples are the Payment Services Directive II, the Electricity Directive or the Reach Regulation. Given the extensive range of sector-specific Regulations and Directives that incorporate access and portability rights, a comprehensive analysis of each would go beyond the scope of this work. Instead, this Chapter will selectively detail some of the more prominent examples that best illustrate the diversity of these rights. By highlighting key instances rather than providing an all-encompassing catalogue, this chapter aims to underscore the varied applications of data access and portability rights and their tailored implementation in addressing distinct sectoral needs.

9.1 Payment Services Directive II (Payment Services Regulation)

In the banking sector, the Payment Services Directive II[1008] introduced a data portability right, which is commonly referred to as the 'access-to-account' or XS2A rule. The objective of this portability right is to enable payers (i.e. the customers of banks[1009]) to use 'payment initiation services' (PIS) and 'account information services' (AIS) of third parties. Third-party payment initiation service providers (PISP) position themselves as inter-

1008 Directive (EU) 2015/2366 on payment services in the internal market, OJ L 2015/337, 35 (PSD II).

1009 The PSD II does not use the term bank but 'account servicing payment service providers' (ASAP), which it defines as credit institutions including branches thereof that are located within the EU, irrespective of whether the head office of these branches is based on EU territory, that maintain a payment account for a payer (Article 4(17), 4(11) and 1(1) PSD II). However, such ASPSPs will usually be banks, see Alan Brener, 'Payment Service Directive II and Its Implications' in Theo Lynn and others (eds), *Disrupting Finance: FinTech and Strategy in the 21st Century* (Springer 2019) 111. In order to avoid the rather cumbersome term 'account servicing payment service provider', they are referred to as 'banks' in the following.

mediaries between payers and merchants on the side, and ASPSPs on the other in order to facilitate transactions between online traders and their customers.[1010] For example, the webshop of a merchant that has integrated a PIS, prompts its customers to choose their bank and then redirects them to their bank's login page to confirm the payment. After the payment has been validated, the PISP will access the account and initiate the transaction on behalf of the payer, who is then transferred back to the merchant's site.[1011] 'Account information service providers' (AISP) offer software solutions that give a consolidated and user-friendly overview of different financial accounts.[1012] This information can be used to employ services, such as financial management programs, creditworthiness assessments or comparison tools.

Following a review of the PSD II in 2022, the European Commission determined that a revision was necessary. Consequently, the Commission has proposed two distinct legislative acts: a new directive on payment services and electronic money services (PSD III)[1013] and a new regulation on payment services (PSR).[1014] The provisions on data access are not included in the PSD III proposal but are detailed in Chapter 3 of the PSR proposal. However, as of the completion of this manuscript, the PSR has not yet en-

1010 Oscar Borgogno and Giuseppe Colangelo, 'Data, Innovation and Competition in Finance: The Case of the Access to Account Rule' [2020] European Business Law Review 573, 579.

1011 'PSD2' (*Bundesbank*) <https://www.bundesbank.de/en/tasks/payment-systems/psd2/psd2-775954> accessed 27 February 2023; 'Account Information Services and Payment Initiation Services' (*Banco de Portugal*) <https://www.bportugal.pt/en/page/account-information-services-and-payment-initiation-services> accessed 27 February 2023; An example of a PISP is the company 'KEVIN EU, UAB', see Adelina Kiskyte, 'What Is Payment Initiation Service (PIS)?' (*Kevin.*, 15 April 2022) <https://www.kevin.eu/blog/payment-initiation-service/> accessed 27 February 2023.

1012 'PSD2 - Third Party Payment Service Providers: What Effect Does PSD2 Have on Services Such as Sofort, IDeal and Trustly? | Payment Services Law Blog | GÖRG' <https://payment-law.eu/psd2-third-party-payment-service-providers-what-effect-does-psd2-have-on-services-such-as-sofort-ideal-and-trustly> accessed 30 April 2020.

1013 Proposal for a Directive of the European Parliament and of the Council on payment services and electronic money services in the Internal Market amending Directive 98/26/EC and repealing Directives 2015/2366/EU and 2009/110/EC (COM(2023) 366 final).

1014 Proposal for a Regulation of the European Parliament and of the Council on payment services in the internal market and amending Regulation (EU) No 1093/2010 (COM(2023) 367 final).

tered the trialogue stage. Therefore, this the 'old' access to account (XS2A) provisions of PSD II will be outlined and potential changes highlighted.

9.1.1 The XS2A rule

Article 66 PSD II lays down the payer's right to have its data transferred to the provider of payment initiation services. When the payer gives its explicit consent for a payment to be executed, the bank shall immediately after receipt of the payment order from a PISP, provide or make available all information on the initiation of the payment transaction and all information accessible to the bank regarding the execution of the payment transaction to the PISP.[1015] Article 67 PSD II contains a similar rule for payers that want to use account information services. With the payer's explicit consent, the account information service provider (AISP) may access information from designated payment accounts and associated payment transactions.[1016] Contrary to a suggestion supported by the banking industry, it is not necessary that the bank and the third-party service provider conclude a contract before the XS2A rule can be exercised. The contractual approach of the banking industry raised concerns about undermining its objectives, as it would have left the ultimate decision on the access to the required data to the account servicing PSPs and not to the account owner.[1017] Although established banks raised concerns about the XS2A rule, it should be pointed that incumbents offering PIS or AIS may also benefit from the PSD II's regime, as Articles 66 and 67 PSD II are not limited to market entrants or SMEs.[1018]

The bank only has to transfer the data needed for a payer to make use of either payment initiation or account information services, irrespective of whether it is personal or non-personal data. The purposes for which the receiving controller (i.e. the PISP or AISP) may use the data are also explicitly limited by the PSD. According to Article 66(3)(g) PSD II, the receiving controller may not use, access or store any data for purposes other than for the provision of the payment initiation service as explicitly requested by the

1015 Article 66(4)(b) PSD II
1016 Article 67(1)(a) and (d) PSD II.
1017 SWD(2013) 288 final, 64.
1018 Borgogno and Colangelo (n 1010) 586.

payer. The provider may, however, not store any sensitive data of payers[1019] and must ensure that the personalised security credentials of the payer are not shared with other parties.[1020] Such sensitive payment data is data, including personalised security credentials, which can be used to commit fraud. Moreover, PISPs may transfer the received data only to the natural or legal person who is the intended recipient of the payment transaction but not to any other third parties. The PSD II requires banks to transfer the required data directly to PISPs and AISPs in real time. Furthermore, the PSD II does not limit the duty to enable direct portability to what is technically feasible, but requires banks to set up access interfaces in accordance with the technical guidelines of the European Banking Authority[1021] to facilitate access for PISPs and AISPs.[1022]

9.1.2 Regulatory objective: facilitating the uptake of payment services

The intention of the XS2A rule is to address the difficulties for third-party payment service providers to launch innovative, safe and easy-to-use digital payment services and to provide consumers and retailers with effective, convenient and secure payment methods.[1023] FinTech companies that want to offer payment solution will regularly be depended on the willingness of established banks to grant access to the data that is necessary to perform such services. In an ideal competitive market where consumers are well-informed and there are no switching costs, banks would be motivated to provide a variety of complementary services to attract potential customers. However, informational market failures and lack of customer engagement hamper the functioning of the banking market.[1024]

1019 For some reason, the European legislator uses the terms 'payer' and 'payment service user' interchangeably in Article 66(3), which unnecessarily complicates the already confusing terminology of the PSD II.

1020 Article 66(3)(b) and (e) PSD II.

1021 Commission Delegated Regulation (EU) 2018/389 of 27 November 2017 supplementing Directive (EU) 2015/2366 of the European Parliament and of the Council with regard to regulatory technical standards for strong customer authentication and common and secure open standards of communication, OJ L 2018/69, 23.

1022 Heike Schweitzer and Robert Welker (n 567) 123; Krämer, Senellart and de Streel (n 536) 32.

1023 Recital 4 PSD II.

1024 Heike Schweitzer and Robert Welker (n 567) 124.

Research has shown that customers generally find it difficult to properly evaluate financial products. One of the reasons is that personal current accounts are complex products consisting of a bundle of services such as account management, processing of transfers and direct debits, and overdraft facilities. In order for customers to choose the best account for them, they need to combine information about the different account fees, eligibility criteria and premiums as well as the complex fee structures for overdrafts with detailed knowledge about their own account usage.[1025] Due to this information asymmetry, customers are not responsive to variations in price and quality and are generally very reluctant to switch banks.[1026] If customers pay little attention to whether their account is compatible with innovative services of third-party providers, banks have no real incentives to compete on complementary services. Rather, they are tempted to vertically integrate and monopolise the customers' access to their own payment solutions or limit access to selected partners in order to maintain market power and increase profits.[1027] With the introduction of the XS2A rule, the PSD2 took a decisive step towards opening up the retail payments market to eligible new entrants, marking the departure from the previous situation, where banks were the sole custodians of payment data.[1028]

9.1.3 The regulatory technical standards (RTS) for common and secure communication

In order to ensure that the XS2A rule is implemented in an effective and customer-friendly way without sacrificing the security of account data transfers, Article 98 PSD II confers a mandate to the European Banking Authority (EBA) to draft regulatory technical standards (RTS) that specify common and secure open standards for the communication between

1025 Simonetta Vezzoso, 'Fintech, Access to Data, and the Role of Competition Policy' in Vicente Bagnoli (ed), *Competition and Innovation* (2018) 33 <https://www.ssrn.com/abstract=3106594> accessed 15 March 2023; CMA, 'Retail Banking Market Investigation Final Report' (2016) para 70.

1026 The UK Competition and Markets Authority has found that only 8% of customers have switched their main bank account to another bank in the last three years and more than a third have been with the same bank for more than twenty years. For comparison, switching rates in the last three years for savings products or energy were 13% and 30% respectively. See CMA (n 1025) paras 64 ff.

1027 Heike Schweitzer and Robert Welker (n 567) 124.

1028 Borgogno and Colangelo (n 741) 8.

banks, PISPs, AISPs, payers and payees. Based on the draft provided by the EBA, the Commission has adopted these RTS by way of a delegated act.[1029]

Before the PSD2 and the RTS went into force, PISPs would use a method called 'screen-scraping', where they access the customer accounts to provide the relevant services. This process involved using software that impersonates the payer and gives third party providers access to all the payer's account data. Since access is not limited to the data necessary to perform the requested action, this method does not meet the requirements set out by Articles 66 and 67 PSD II.[1030] In order for PISPs and AISPs to provide their service in compliance with the PSD II, they depend on the bank to offer an adequately functioning interface.[1031]

Hence, Article 33 RTS requires banks to offer at least one interface based on international or European communication standards that allows PISPs and AISPs to access payment account information and initiate payments. In the initial draft RTS of the EBA foresaw access through a dedicated interface for third-party service providers as the only access option.[1032] This policy choice was met with concerns by PISPs and AISPs that banks do not have any incentives to develop the best possible dedicated interface, as this interface is only used by third party providers, i.e. competitors of the bank.[1033] As a response, the Commission has amended the rule to allow banks to choose whether to develop dedicated interfaces for third-party providers or to adapt their customer-facing interface to allow third-party access. Should the bank decide to develop a dedicated interface, they would still need to provide access via their customer interface as fallback option

1029 Commission Delegated Regulation (EU) 2018/389 of 27 November 2017 supplementing Directive (EU) 2015/2366 of the European Parliament and of the Council with regard to regulatory technical standards for strong customer authentication and common and secure open standards of communication, OJ L 2018/69, 23.

1030 Borgogno and Colangelo (n 1010) 588; Markus Demary and Christian Rusche, 'Strengthened Competition in Payment Services' (German Economic Institute 2018) 4; Fernando Zunzunegui, 'Digitalisation of Payment Services' [2018] Ibero-American Institute for Law and Finance Working Paper 24 <https://www.ssrn.com/abstract=3256281> accessed 8 March 2023; European Banking Authority, 'Opinion on the Amended Text of the RTS on SCA and CSC' (2017) EBA-Op-2017-09 8.

1031 Pieter Wolters and Bart Jacobs, 'The Security of Access to Accounts under the PSD2' (2019) 35 Computer Law & Security Review 29, 35.

1032 European Banking Authority, 'Draft Regulatory Technical Standards on Strong Customer Authentication and Common and Secure Communication under Article 98 of Directive 2015/2366' (2017) EBA/RTS/2017/02 Article 28.

1033 See European Banking Authority (n 1030) 7.

in case the dedicated interface is unavailable (Article 33(4) RTS). The duty to have a fallback interface is intended to ensure that any unavailability or insufficient performance of the dedicated interface does not impede the ability of payment initiation services while the customer-facing interface is operating smoothly, enabling the bank to continue offering its own payment services and fighting off competition by third-party providers.[1034]

However, the EBA has criticised this rule since the fallback obligation for increasing compliance costs for banks.[1035] Banks cannot simply open the user interface to PISPs and AISPs, but need to modify the interface to ensure that the providers identify themselves and their access is limited to the information that is necessary for the provision of the payment services. The additional costs could prompt banks not to develop dedicated interfaces altogether, which could jeopardise the development of standardised APIs.[1036] In a compromise, an additional provision was included in the RTS that allows national authorities to exempt banks from the fallback obligation if they are able to provide sufficient assurances with regards to the functioning of the interface and third-party providers had the opportunity to check the reliability of the banking interfaces and review their quality (Article 33(6) RTS).[1037] In the proposal for the PSR, the Commission changed its approach and eliminated the requirement for banks to maintain a permanent fallback interface, except in authorised exceptional cases.[1038]

9.1.4 Access based on non-discriminatory terms (and for remuneration?)

PSD II stipulates that banks must not discriminate against payment orders and data requests transmitted through the services of a third-party provider unless there are objective reasons.[1039] With regard to PIS, Article 66(4)(c) PSD II further states that this non-discrimination obligation applies in particular to 'timing, priority or charges vis-à-vis payment orders transmitted

1034 See Recital 24 Commission Delegated Regulation (EU) 2018/389 of 27 November 2017 supplementing Directive (EU) 2015/2366 of the European Parliament and of the Council with regard to regulatory technical standards for strong customer authentication and common and secure open standards of communication, OJ L 2018/69, 23.

1035 See European Banking Authority (n 1030) 7.

1036 Wolters and Jacobs (n 1031) 35.

1037 Borgogno and Colangelo (n 1010) 589.

1038 COM(2023) 367 final, Article 35(1).

1039 Articles 66(4)(c) and 67(3)(b) PSD II.

directly by the payer'. The provision, however, is unclear with regard to the question of whether banks are entitled to charge a fee from PISPs and AISP for accessing the account information. The phrase 'without any discrimination vis-à-vis payment orders transmitted directly by the payer' can either mean that no additional charges should be imposed at all, or it may suggest that no additional charges should be imposed on the customers.[1040]There is agreement that Article 66(4)(c) PSD II prohibits banks from charging the payers for the use of payment initiation services provided by third-party providers beyond the regular charges for payment services provided by the bank unless there are any objective reasons.[1041]

Different opinions, however, have been expressed as to whether banks can charge a fee from PISPs and AISPs in exchange for granting access to the account data. According to some, the XS2A obliges banks to provide the required data free of charge.[1042] If Article 66(4)(c) applies not only to the bank-customer but also to bank-PISP relationship, banks would need to apply the same modalities as for payment orders transmitted directly by the account holder. Hence, they need to grant access to PISPs and AISPs without additional fees, unless it is objectively justified.[1043] Others have expressed the opinion that the non-discrimination obligation does not have any effects on the legal relationship between bank and PISPs. They argue that banks are free to negotiate fees within the general limits of fairness, reasonableness and non-discrimination (FRAND), drawing inspiration from the CJEU's essential facility case law and.[1044]

1040 Jörg Hoffmann, 'Safeguarding Innovation in the Framework of Sector-Specific Data Access Regimes' in Bundesministerium der Justiz und für Verbraucherschutz and Max-Planck-Institut für Innovation und Wettbewerb (eds), *Data Access, Consumer Interests and Public Welfare* (Nomos 2021) 374.

1041 Hoffmann (n 1040) 374; Borgogno and Colangelo (n 1010) 587; The Netherlands Authority for Consumers & Markets, 'Fintechs in the Payment System: The Risk of Foreclosure' 35.

1042 Fabiana Di Porto and Gustavo Ghidini, '"I Access Your Data, You Access Mine": Requiring Data Reciprocity in Payment Services' [2020] International Review of Intellectual Property and Competition Law 307, 312; Wolters and Jacobs (n 1031) 31; Miguel de la Mano and Jorge Padilla, 'Big Tech Banking' (2018) 14 Journal of Competition Law and Economics 494, 503.

1043 Hoffmann (n 1040) 374; Graef, Husovec and van den Boom (n 485) 11.

1044 Amanda Cliffe, 'To What Extent Does European Law Ensure a Level Playing Field for Fintechs in the Payment Services Sector?' (2022) 18 European Competition Journal 168, 185; Hoffmann (n 1040) 375; Borgogno and Colangelo (n 1010) 587; Heim and Nikolic (n 739) 51.

Proponents of the view that the XS2A rule allows banks to charge fees for providing access to account data also base their interpretation on teleological arguments. They argue that banks might be disincentivised from competing or innovating on the quality of this data and its API if the portability right is free of charge.[1045] Moreover, the PSD2 also enables digital conglomerates to enter the market with innovative payment services and may therefore put the incumbent banks at an overly burdensome competitive disadvantage. This in turn may enable digital conglomerates to re-shape traditional retail banking and payment markets with the risk of further monopolisation in the long run.[1046]

However, it can also be argued that European legislators intentionally did not introduce a remuneration scheme for the XS2A rule because the account and transaction data that is the subject of the portability right is a mere side product of the bank's activities. Since this kind of data is created anyways there is no need to create any monetary incentives for its generation. Moreover, granting access to the required data free of charge clearly contributes to the PSD II's objective of effectively placing third-party service providers at a level playing field with the bank's vertically integrated payment services solutions.

Finally, the legitimate concerns that the XS2A rule is not asymmetrical enough and may therefore favour other powerful market players or put small and innovative banks at a disadvantage cannot be denied.[1047] However, these concerns are rooted in the overall configuration of the XS2A and cannot be sufficiently remedied by payment modalities. If digital conglomerates want to use the XS2A account rule to enter the banking and payment market and challenge incumbent banks, they are not going to be stopped by the fact that they would have to pay a reasonable fee to get access to the relevant data. Finally, the view that banks are allowed to charge fees based on FRAND terms would presuppose that they conclude a contract with the PISPs and AISPs. However, Articles 66(5) and 67(4) PSD II explicitly clarify that no contractual relationship between the bank and third-party provider is required. Hence, the view that the XS2A rule sets out an obligation to enter into a contract based on FRAND terms, similar to the remedy provided for in EFD cases, is difficult to reconcile with the wording of the PSD II.

1045 Cliffe (n 1044) 185; Hoffmann (n 1040) 376.

1046 Hoffmann (n 1040) 377; Vezzoso (n 1025) 35; The Netherlands Authority for Consumers & Markets (n 1041) 35.

1047 Hoffmann (n 1040) 386; de la Mano and Padilla (n 1042) 512.

If the PSR proposal is adopted this matter would be clarified. Recital 56 of the PSR proposal explicitly states that access by account information and payment initiation service providers to payment account data, regulated under the PSR, is without a requirement for a contractual relationship and thus without charging fees.

9.2 Electricity Directive

Access and portability rights covering data on energy consumption are laid down in the Electricity Directive (ED).[1048] By affording electricity customers access to data collected through connected 'smart' meters, the ED intends to facilitate more informed decision-making and smoother transitions between electricity suppliers. This empowerment of customers shall enhance the competitiveness of the electricity market.[1049]

9.2.1 Regulatory objective: liberating the metering market

The background for the legislative intervention is that traditionally grid operators have also provided the process of meter operation (installation, operation and maintenance of meters) as well as the process of meter reading (data retrieval and data processing).[1050] Grid operators manage the infrastructure needed to distribute electricity from producers to consumers and are often considered a natural monopoly. This is because of the high costs necessary to build and maintain the required infrastructure, such as power lines and transformers, and the inefficiency of having multiple redundant networks built by competing companies.[1051] Despite efforts to liberalise the metering market by opening up the market to third party providers in order to put competitive pressure on grid operators to reduce the fee charged for meter reading,[1052] grid operators have remained a very

1048 Directive (EU) 2019/944 of the European Parliament and of the Council of 5 June 2019 on common rules for the internal market for electricity and amending Directive 2012/27/EU (recast), OJ L 2019/944, 125.

1049 Feasey and de Streel (n 227) 50; Tombal (n 409) 162.

1050 Heike Schweitzer and Robert Welker (n 567) 121; Stephan Schmitt and Matthias Wissner, 'Die Liberalisierung des Messwesens – Verhindert das Abrechnungsentgelt freien Wettbewerb?' (2015) 39 Zeitschrift für Energiewirtschaft 171, 172.

1051 Heike Schweitzer and Robert Welker (n 567) 121.

1052 Schmitt and Wissner (n 1050).

large market share.[1053] Where access to metering data is controlled by entities with significant market power there is a risk of data being used to distort competition or manipulate market conditions. This prompted the European legislator to introduce the mandatory rights to access and port metering data.

9.2.2 Customer access and portability

Article 20(e) ED stipulates that at the request of the customer, they shall get access to data on the electricity they feed into the grid and their electricity consumption. This data access is to be provided through a standardised communication interface, ensuring that data is accessible in a consistent and user-friendly manner across different systems. Moreover, Article 20(e) ED provides the data shall be made available to the customer through remote access and in a format that is easy for consumers to understand facilitating the comparison of different electricity offers on a like-for-like basis. By having transparent access to their electricity data, consumers can make more informed choices and take advantage of competitive offers. This is intended to enhance customer empowerment and market fluidity by making it easier to switch between electricity suppliers.[1054] Article 23(2) ED further expands the access right by allowing final customers to have metering and consumption data as well as data required for customer switching, demand response and other services transferred to an eligible third party.

Articles 20(e) and 23(2) ED address a typically co-generation situation, as the covered data has been generated by the customer's activities and/or relates to the customer's activities but is held by the electricity provider. The customer needs this data for legitimate purposes such as switching providers or using complementary services, like smart home devices and energy management systems that help customers to optimise their energy usage. Third parties can only provide these services if they have access to the necessary data.[1055] Which third party providers are 'eligible parties' within the meaning of the ED to receive the relevant data at the request of the customer is left to the Member States (Article 23(1) ED).[1056]

1053 Heike Schweitzer and Robert Welker (n 567) 121.
1054 Heike Schweitzer and Robert Welker (n 567) 122.
1055 See Heike Schweitzer and Robert Welker (n 567) 122.
1056 Graef, Husovec and van den Boom (n 485) 10.

9.2.3 Charges for eligible third parties and access modalities

Access to the relevant data or requesting the transfer to eligible parties shall, according to Article 23(5) ED, be free of charge for the customer. However, reasonable and duly justified charges may be imposed on the eligible third parties that receive the data at the request of the customer.[1057] In line with the Article 6(11) DMA and Article 9 DA, a reasonable compensation should be understood as covering the direct costs of the data generation and transfer as well as a profit margin (see 6.6.6.3 and 7.6.2.1). Moreover, Article 23(2) ED provides that the eligible parties should receive access in a non-discriminatory manner. This does not mean that all recipients need to be treated equally but that similarly situated recipients should receive the data under the same or similar terms.

Regarding access modalities, Article 24(2) ED mandates the Commission to establish interoperability requirements and non-discriminatory and transparent procedures for access to data through an implementing act.[1058] Member States are then responsible for ensuring that electricity undertakings operating within their jurisdiction comply with the interoperability requirements and data access procedures established by the Commission.[1059] The interoperability requirements shall ensure that different energy services and systems can work together seamlessly and that customers may use complementary services offered by third parties.[1060]

9.3 Type Approval Regulation

Another prominent example of a sector-specific data access right can be found in the automotive sector. Article 61(1) Type Approval Regulation (TAR)[1061] obliges car manufacturers to grant independent maintenance and

1057 Graef, Husovec and van den Boom (n 485) 10.

1058 See Commission Implementing Regulation (EU) 2023/1162 of 6 June 2023 on interoperability requirements and non-discriminatory and transparent procedures for access to metering and consumption data, OJ L 2023/154, 10.

1059 Graef, Husovec and van den Boom (n 485) 11.

1060 See Heike Schweitzer and Robert Welker (n 567) 122.

1061 Regulation (EU) 2018/858 of the European Parliament and of the Council of 30 May 2018 on the approval and market surveillance of motor vehicles and their trailers, and of systems, components and separate technical units intended for such vehicles, amending Regulations (EC) No 715/2007 and (EC) No 595/2009 and repealing Directive 2007/46/EC, OJ L 2018/151, 1.

repair service providers access to the technical data necessary to perform these services in a non-discriminatory way for fees that are reasonable and proportionate. The rationale of this access right is that due to the complexity of today's vehicles, independent repair service providers, as well as spare part producers, can only offer their services and products if they have access to the necessary technical data.

The data access right in the automotive sector is directly afforded to the independent service providers, even though they do not contribute to the generation of the data covered by Article 61(1) TAR. In contrast, under the PSD or ED, the data covered by the access and portability rights is generated by contributions from both the payer/customer and the data holder (i.e. the bank or the electricity provider). Hence, the interference with the contractual freedom of car manufacturers, as well as their freedom to conduct business (Article 16 CFR), cannot be legitimised by the notion of co-generation, but needs to be justified by an overriding public interest.[1062]

9.3.1 Regulatory objective: preventing market failure in the aftermarket

The public interest in this context is to prevent a market failure in the aftermarket. In the automotive sector, access to technical data, such as diagnostic data, repair procedures, and parts specifications, is crucial for independent repair service providers and spare part producers to provide their services. However, the relevant data is typically held by the car manufacturers, which has led to significant challenges for independent service providers. This is because aftermarket services, including repairs, maintenance, and spare parts, represent a lucrative revenue stream for car manufacturers. By denying independent repair shops and spare part producers access to crucial technical data, car manufacturers can promote their network of authorised dealers and repairers. Such practices stifle competition, making it difficult for independent service providers to operate and compete effectively. Consumers face reduced choices and potentially higher prices for repair services and spare parts.[1063]

1062 See Neil Cohen and Christiane Wendehorst (n 119) Principle 24.

1063 Wolfgang Kerber and Daniel Gill, 'Access to Data in Connected Cars and the Recent Reform of the Motor Vehicle Type Approval Regulation' (2019) 10 JIPITEC 244, [5].

This issue was addressed already in 2007 with the first Type Approval Regulation.[1064] Article 6 of Regulation (EC) 715/2007 mandated that vehicle manufacturers must provide independent repairers with access to repair and maintenance information. Car manufacturers were required to provide the information in a standardised format. However, it did not specify that the information must be in an electronically processable format. This led to manufacturers providing information in formats that were not practical for third party providers. For example, instead of providing easily usable software solutions, manufacturers sometimes supplied the information through cumbersome web forms, which rendered the data unusable for independent service providers.[1065] In the revised version of the Type Approval Regulation this problem was rectified. Article 61(1) TAR (Regulation (EU) 2018/858) explicitly requires car manufacturers to grant independent service providers access to the necessary technical information in an easily accessible manner in the form of machine-readable and electronically processable datasets.[1066]

9.3.2 RAND-based fees for access

Article 63(1) of the Type Approval Regulation grants car manufacturers the right to charge 'reasonable and proportionate fees' for providing access to vehicle repair and maintenance information. This provision aims to balance the need for fair access with the manufacturers' legitimate interest in recovering their investment costs. The TAR specifies that a fee is not considered reasonable or proportionate if it discourages access by failing to consider the extent to which the independent operator uses the information. Hence, the fees must reflect the actual usage by independent operators, ensuring that smaller, less frequent users are not unfairly burdened with high costs. Moreover, manufacturers are required to provide unrestricted and non-discriminatory access to the technical data. This means

1064 Regulation (EC) No 715/2007 of the European Parliament and of the Council of 20 June 2007 on type approval of motor vehicles with respect to emissions from light passenger and commercial vehicles (Euro 5 and Euro 6) and on access to vehicle repair and maintenance information, OJ L 2007/171, 1.

1065 Rupprecht Podszun, *Handwerk in der digitalen Ökonomie: Rechtlicher Rahmen für den Zugang zu Daten, Software und Plattformen*, vol 5 (Nomos 2021) 95.

1066 Podszun, *Handwerk in der digitalen Ökonomie: Rechtlicher Rahmen für den Zugang zu Daten, Software und Plattformen* (n 1065) 96.

that all independent repairers, regardless of size or frequency of access, should have the same opportunity to obtain the necessary data without facing undue barriers[1067] Beyond this, the TAR does not provide any further guidance on how to assess whether the charged fee is reasonable and non-discriminatory. However, as the concept of reasonable and non-discriminatory fees for data access has become one that has been repeatedly used by the European legislator for very similar access constellations, it should, as further elaborated under 10.1.2.3, be interpreted consistently across the different instruments.

9.3.3 Time-based subscriptions for data access

Article 63(2) TAR mandates that manufacturers must make this information available on various time-based subscriptions, including hourly, daily, monthly, and yearly access options. The fees for accessing the information should vary according to the chosen period. Providing multiple access periods allows independent operators to select the duration that is most cost-effective for their specific requirements.[1068] For example, a repair shop might only need short-term access for a specific repair, while another might benefit from a long-term subscription for ongoing access, which entails a longer commitment period but also a lower price.

9.4 REACH Regulation

Another access right can be found in the chemicals sector. The Registration, Evaluation, Authorisation and Restriction of Chemicals (REACH) Regulation,[1069] which aims to ensure the safe use of chemicals, improve environmental and human health protection, and enhance the competitiveness of the EU chemicals industry, stipulates that a chemical substance may

---

1067 See Graef, Husovec and van den Boom (n 485) 10.

1068 See Graef, Husovec and van den Boom (n 485) 10.

1069 Regulation (EC) 1907/2006 of the European Parliament and of the Council of 18 December 2006 concerning the Registration, Evaluation, Authorisation and Restriction of Chemicals (REACH), establishing a European Chemicals Agency, amending Directive 1999/45/EC and repealing Council Regulation (EEC) No 793/93 and Commission Regulation (EC) No 1488/94 as well as Council Directive 76/769/EEC and Commission Directives 91/155/EEC, 93/67/EEC, 93/105/EC and 2000/21/EC, OJ L 2006/396, 1.

only be manufactured or placed on the market in the EU if it has been previously registered in accordance with the regulation (Article 5 REACH). This registration process involves the submission of detailed information about the chemical, including its properties, uses, and potential risks.

9.4.1 Access to testing data

Article 27(1) REACH gives manufacturers, who want to register a chemical substance (potential registrant), a right against manufacturers, who have already registered such a substance (previous registrant), to access the relevant testing data.[1070] The access right laid down in Article 27(1) REACH addresses two different situations. In case the necessary data involves tests on vertebrate animals, the potential registrant must file a request for accessing the data. By requiring companies to request data access, the regulation seeks to minimise the duplication of tests, particularly those involving animals, thereby promoting ethical research practices (Recital 47 REACH).[1071] Where the data does not involve tests on vertebrate animals, the potential registrant may exercise the right to request the data, but they do not have to. In this scenario, the rationale for the data access provision is primarily economic rather than ethical. The burden of generating extensive safety data shall be split among actors to increase efficiency and reduce costs.

Article 10 REACH Regulation specifies the data shall include detailed summaries of toxicological and ecotoxicological studies that have been conducted on the substance as well as comprehensive reports that assess the risks associated with the substance and outline measures to manage these risks. This information has significant economic value, as it involves considerable investment in research and testing. To ensure that the potential registrant is not freeriding on the investments of the previous registrant, Article 27(4) REACH stipulates that the previous registrants shall receive

1070 See Podszun, *Handwerk in der digitalen Ökonomie: Rechtlicher Rahmen für den Zugang zu Daten, Software und Plattformen* (n 1065) 99; Drexl, 'Designing Competitive Markets for Industrial Data – Between Propertisation and Access' (n 17) 289.

1071 Podszun, *Handwerk in der digitalen Ökonomie: Rechtlicher Rahmen für den Zugang zu Daten, Software und Plattformen* (n 1065) 100; Drexl, 'Designing Competitive Markets for Industrial Data – Between Propertisation and Access' (n 17) 290.

a fair, transparent and non-discriminatory compensation for making the testing data available to the potential registrant.[1072]

9.4.2 Dispute resolution mechanism

In contrast to other pieces of legislation that lay down an obligation to agree on a reasonable and non-discriminatory remuneration for accessing data, the REACH Regulation provides for a dispute resolution mechanism.[1073] According to Article 27(3) REACH both the previous and potential registrants must strive to determine the cost of sharing information fairly and transparently, following the guidance developed by the European Chemicals Agency (ECHA).[1074] If an agreement cannot be reached, the potential registrant must notify the ECHA. Within one month of receiving the notification, the ECHA shall grant the new registrant permission to access the data required for their registration dossier, provided the potential registrant shows that they have paid the previous registrant a proportionate share of the cost incurred for generating the requested data. The calculation of this proportionate share can be facilitated by the guidance adopted by the ECHA in accordance with Article 77(2)(g) REACH, ensuring fairness and consistency. If the previous registrant makes all the necessary data available to the potential registrant, the previous registrant has a legal claim against the potential registrant for an equal share of the cost incurred. This claim can be enforced through national courts, ensuring that the previous registrant is compensated fairly for their investment.

While the dispute resolution rules of the REACH Regulation are very context-specific, the European legislators may need to consider adopting similar mechanisms in other regulatory contexts to address potential stalemates and promote fair negotiations for FRAND-based access.[1075] As pointed out under 7.6.2.2, another source of inspiration for resolving such disputes would be the *Huawei/ZTE* decision of the ECJ. However, the procedure outlined by the Court is much less specific and does not involve

1072 Podszun, *Handwerk in der digitalen Ökonomie: Rechtlicher Rahmen für den Zugang zu Daten, Software und Plattformen* (n 1065) 100.

1073 Heim and Nikolic (n 739) 46.

1074 European Chemicals Agency, 'Guidance on Data-Sharing' (2017).

1075 See also Heim and Nikolic (n 739) 47; Drexl, 'Designing Competitive Markets for Industrial Data – Between Propertisation and Access' (n 17) 290.

a third party, like the ECHA, that oversees the process of reaching an agreement.

10 A Taxonomy of European Data Rights

The previous Chapters have shown that, over the past years, the European legislator has introduced a plethora of different access and portability rights between private parties. Some of these rights are very sector specific and address very concrete market failures related to data access while others are broad clauses that pursue more general objectives. The regulatory subject of the Regulations and Directives in which data rights can be found ranges from competition law (DMA) over technical legislation (Type Approval Regulation) to data protection law (GDPR). Due to the variety of subjects, different units within the European Commission have been responsible for drafting the initial proposal of these Regulations and Directives. Hence, it is not surprising that the wording and structure of the existing data rights differ significantly. The complexity and diversity of data rights and their configurations have created a dense and tangled jungle that can be difficult to navigate.

10.1 Three types of access and portability rights

However, by ignoring the many differences between the instruments described and focusing on the underlying similarities, it is possible to identify three different types of data rights: (i) access rights in co-generated data (CGD), (ii) access rights in the public interest, and (iii) data portability rights.[1076] The terms 'portability rights' and 'access rights' are widely used by legislators and legal scholars but not in a consistent manner and sometimes even synonymously. Identifying overarching conceptual and systematic connections between the data rights of the same category may help transform the jungle of data access and portability rights into a nicely groomed garden.

Establishing a classification for access and portability rights is not an end in itself but is intended to provide a better overview and understanding of them, facilitate a coherent interpretation and help identify overlaps between the different instruments. It is hoped that the framework will ulti-

1076 This categorisation builds on the work of Neil Cohen and Christiane Wendehorst (n 119) Chapter 3.

mately contribute to a more systematic, transparent and coherent approach to data rights.

10.1.1 Access rights in co-generated data

Direct access rights in co-generated data are intended to address the following situation: Two persons have made a substantial contribution to the generation of the data. However, the person with the stronger bargaining power manages to store the data on its servers and gain exclusive control over the co-generated data. In case the other person wants to access the data for their own purposes, the data holder can either charge high fees for access or deny access altogether due to de facto control.[1077]

For example, energy consumption data is typically held by the person operating the electricity meters, and customers would have to rely on their goodwill if they wanted to access the data. The situation is similar for advertisers and publishers who provide their advertising services via online platforms, which control the data necessary to measure the performance of their advertising activities. Hence, advertisers are dependent on the platform provider if they want to assess the effect of their ads. Another example is the use of platform services by end users and business-users, which generates substantial amounts of data held by the platform provider. By collecting data on user activity, such as the frequency and duration of user interactions, the nature of the content engaged with, and the identities of the communication partners, the provider is not only able to improve the platform's features but may also provide personalised ads and identify new trends and opportunities. However, a business user that sells products or services through an online platform and wants to understand the characteristics of its customers, such as their preferences, behaviours, and demographics, to better target its marketing efforts and develop more effective products has to rely on the willingness of the platform provider if they want to use the data for their purposes. End users may require data access to analyse their social media usage patterns and enhance their online presence or migrate to a different provider.

1077 Neil Cohen and Christiane Wendehorst (n 119) Principle 20; see also Martens and others (n 182) 9.

10.1.1.1 Contribution to the generation of data

What distinguishes direct access rights in CGD from direct access rights in the public interest is that access rights CGD are afforded to persons that in some way have contributed to the generation of the data.[1078] As pointed out under 2.5.3, the Principles for a Data Economy have identified four different forms of contributions to co-generation of data: (a) being subject of the data, or the owner or operator of an asset that is the subject of data; (b) pursuing an activity by means of which data has been produced; (c) assembling or structuring existing data in a way that creates something of a new quality; and (d) having produced or developed a product or service, which was used to generate the data.[1079]

Until now, EU law has only afforded access rights in CGD to individuals or entities that have generated the relevant data through the first two forms of contribution. For example, the right to retrieve and transmit personal data under Article 20(1) of the GDPR is given to the person who is the subject of the personal data. The access right of advertisers vis-à-vis gatekeepers under DMA applies to data, which was generated by the advertising activities of the rightsholder. The data covered by Article 20(f) ED is generated by a combination of the first two forms of contribution. Energy consumption data not only relates to the specific customer but is also generated by its activities. The same applies to the data covered by Articles 6(9) and (10) DMA (access rights of end users and business users); the data generated in the context of the use of core platform service will usually also relate to the end users and business users. The notion of co-generation also implies that the access rights in CGD extend only to data to generation of which the rightsholder has directly contributed. For example, Article 6(8) DMA applies only to data relating to the ads placed by the requesting advertiser or publisher. It does not extend to data about ads placed by other advertisers or publishers.

10.1.1.2 Two-person relationship

Another feature of direct access rights is that they establish a legal relationship between two persons: the rightsholder and the data holder, who is the addressee of the obligation. By establishing a direct relationship between

1078 Neil Cohen and Christiane Wendehorst (n 120) *cf.* Chapter B and Chapter C.
1079 Article 18 Neil Cohen and Christiane Wendehorst (n 119).

the rightsholder and the data holder, access rights in CGD aim to create a more equitable distribution of data control and usage. Granting access rights to persons who have made significant contributions to data creation and allowing them to use the data for their own purposes provides them with the opportunity to participate in the benefits of the data. This two-person relationship is what distinguishes access rights in CGD from Portability rights in the narrower sense. The latter involve a transfer from the initial data holder to a third-party recipient initiated by the rightsholder (see 10.1.3). In contrast, the holder of a data access right in CGD is also the recipient of the relevant data.

However, if the access right puts the rightsholders in full control of the data (i.e. does not stipulate usage restrictions), they may transfer the data to a third party once they have received it. This approach is commonly referred to as indirect portability and can be more closely linked to the category of data access rights in the CGD or to direct portability rights, depending on whether the data right only allows for a one-off provision or a continuous flow of data. Examples of the former are, Article 20(1) GDPR and Article 20(f) ED, which allow the data subject/customer to retrieve the data that the data holder controls at the time of the request and then pass it on to another party. The retrieval and subsequent transmission of the relevant data allows the rightsholder to switch completely from the services or products of the original data holder to those of a third party and enables multihoming. However, since these rights do not provide for continuous and real-time data exchanges between the original data holder and the third party, they are not capable of freeing the rightsholder from being tied to the product/service ecosystem of the data holder by enabling them to use complementary services (see 10.2.1).

There are, however, also access rights in CGD, such as Article 6(9) and (10) DMA and Article 4(1) DA, that allow the rightsholder to receive their data continuously and in real-time from the data holder and may also transfer the data to third parties. In these instances, access rights in CGD are very similar to direct portability rights because the rightsholder may set up a technical infrastructure where the data received from the data holder is immediately and continuously forwarded to third parties. Hence, the effects are very similar to direct portability rights (see 10.1.3). The only difference is that indirect portability rights do not create a direct legal relationship between the initial data holder and the third-party recipient. The rightsholder receives the data from the initial data holder based on the access right and then enters into a separate data transaction with a third party.

10.1.1.3 Justification: co-generation plus legitimate interest of the rightsholder

All data access and portability rights interfere with the interest and rights of the data holder, in particular its right to conduct business (Article 16 CFR), which also protects the freedom of contract,[1080] and therefore need to be justified. With regard to access based on Article 102 TFEU, this is done by applying the exceptional circumstances test (4.2.1). Concerning access rights in CGD, the Principles for a Data Economy have rightly pointed out that contributing to the generation of the relevant data is one ground of justification, but additional factors should be considered when granting access to co-generated data.[1081] In other words, just because a person has contributed to the generation of data does not automatically mean they should have access to the co-generated data.

The different grounds of justification described by the Principles can be divided into two broader categories: (i) individual interests of the rightsholder and (ii) overarching public interests. Examples of the first group are the grounds put forward by Principle 20 of the Principles for a Data Economy, such as access is necessary for using, maintaining, or reselling a product or service, or for rightfully switching supplier of a product or service. But also the weak bargaining power vis-à-vis the data holder is to be considered a legitimate individual interest that may justify an access right. Overarching public interests are, inter alia, ensuring a functioning and competitive market or promoting innovation.[1082]

1080 Explanations Relating to the Charter of Fundamental Rights OJ C 2003/303, 17.

1081 Neil Cohen and Christiane Wendehorst (n 119) Principle 19 defines the following five grounds: (1) The share a party had in generating the data, (2) the weight of grounds put forward by the party seeking data access; (3) the weight of any legitimate interests the controller or a third party may have in denying the data right; (4) any imbalance of bargaining power; and (5) any public interest including the interest to ensure fair and effective competition.

1082 Principle 19(2)(e) Neil Cohen and Christiane Wendehorst (n 119); see also Drexl, 'Legal Challenges of the Changing Role of Personal and Non-Personal Data in the Data Economy' (n 442) 21 who argues that these four objectives need to be considered: (1) establishing a functioning and competitive market for the data economy; (2) promoting innovation; (3) protecting consumer interests with a

The legal analysis of the different instruments shows that at least one ground of justification from each of the two categories will usually be present in both data access rights in CGD and access rights in the public interest. The difference, however, is that the individual interests of the rightsholder are the primary policy consideration for introducing data access rights in CGD while it is the other way around for access rights in the public interest (see 10.1.2.1). For example, Article 20(1) GDPR gives individuals more control over their personal data, strengthens their informational self-determination and enables them—to some extent at least—to escape 'lock-in' situations. Releasing more data for the data economy and increasing competition are side effects but not the primary objectives. For example, Article 20(1) GDPR neither addresses a concrete market failure nor ensures that the data is transferred to market entrants. Under the DMA, the access rights for advertisers, end users and business users are justified by their weak position vis-à-vis the gatekeeping platform. An additional ground of justification is to facilitate switching and multihoming and enable advertisers and business users to monitor and improve the quality of their services and products. The overarching public interest is to ensure that gatekeepers do not limit innovation by undermining the contestability of the platform market and adjacent markets. However, the DMA's access rights in CGD benefit competitors of gatekeepers only indirectly, as there is no guarantee that users will actually switch to the services of another platform provider even if they have the right to retrieve and transmit their data. Similar considerations also apply to the access right under the ED. Electricity customers have a weak barging position, and they need access to their metering data to monitor their consumption and be able to evaluate whether to switch suppliers. The indirect effect on the public interest is that increased transparency enables energy suppliers to compete effectively with incumbents by offering better terms. The resulting competition leads to lower prices and thus also benefits those energy customers who have not made use of their right of access.

10.1.1.4 Modalities: free of charge and full control

Another common characteristic of existing data access rights in CGD is that, generally, the rightsholder may exercise them free of charge. For

particular focus on protecting the privacy of natural persons; (4) promoting additional public interests.

instance, Article 12(5) GDPR clarifies that the data subject may retrieve and transmit their personal data for free, unless their access request is manifestly unfounded or excessive, in particular due to their repetitive nature. Similarly, Article 23(5) ED stipulates that no additional costs shall be charged to final customers for access to their data. Advertisers, business users and end users may also exercise their access rights under the DMA free of charge. Moreover, none of the access rights above do place any limitations on the rightsholder's data use and even explicitly allow the transmission of the retrieved data to third parties.

Existing data rights are free of charge and give full control to the rightsholder, because so far, the European legislator has only introduced access rights to data that are justified by the two strongest forms of contribution, namely being the subject of the data or engaging in an activity that generates the relevant data. These two types of contributions not only provide a strong ground of justification for curtailing the interests of the data holder but also invalidate the traditional argument for charging for data access. Granting free data access is believed to allow freeriding on the economic investments of data holders, which reduces the incentives for data holders to invest in data generation, leading to less data and consequently less innovation. However, persons that either are the subject of the data or generate it through their activities have had a significant share in the data's generation and are not freeriding if they use the co-generated data for a legitimate purpose (the situation, of course, is different for third party recipients of the data, see 10.1.3.3).

In the case of Article 20 GDPR, the data subjects have even provided the personal data themselves. Hence, there is no risk that an access right could discourage the generation of this type of data. Article 20(e) ED also does not pose a risk of disincentivising data generation. Data on electricity customers fed into the grid and their electricity consumption data are generated as part of the normal operation of the electricity grid and metering systems and are necessary for monitoring and controlling electricity distribution as well as for regulatory purposes. Finally, platform providers have a vested interest in collecting data that their users provide or generate through their activities, as it allows them to improve their algorithms and services and gain insights into user preferences, behaviour and trends. This interest, and therefore the incentive to generate such data, is not diminished if users are allowed to access this co-generated free of charge.

It should be clarified that these considerations do not suggest that access rights in CGD with data limitations or against remuneration are not conceivable and may never exist. For example, an access right afforded to a person that only had a minor share in the generation and which would enable the rightsholder to engage in direct competition with the data holder may warrant usage restrictions and/or an appropriate fee. However, the current tendency of the European legislator is to afford access rights in CGD only to persons whose share in the generation was quite significant. This, combined with individual and overriding public interests (see 10.1.1.3), will usually justify free access to the co-generated data. The lack of remuneration under the existing access rights in CGD is also a significant point of difference to access rights in the public interest, which always require the rightsholder to pay a fee.

10.1.2 Access rights in the public interest

As the name suggests, the central feature of data access rights in the public interest is that they are introduced by the European legislator when they are deemed to be a necessary and proportionate tool to achieve an objective in the public interest. In stark contrast to rights in CGD, the access right is not afforded to a person that had a share in the generation of the data but to a third party. Often the public interest is the prevention of a market failure, but there are also other public interests that existing instruments seek to promote.

The Principles for a Data Economy of the ALI and ELI, refer to these types of data rights as data rights in the public interest.[1083] They point out that such data rights follow more of a public law logic. The law does not attempt to strike a balance between competing private interests but encroaches the interests of the holder if they are outweighed by a public interest.[1084]

10.1.2.1 Justification: public interest

The justification for the interference with the rights and interests of the data holder is not the actions of the rightsholders or their individual interests but a public interest. In other words, access to the data is not granted

1083 See Neil Cohen and Christiane Wendehorst (n 119) Chapter C.
1084 See Neil Cohen and Christiane Wendehorst (n 119) Principle 24.

to the rightsholder for their own benefit or personal gain, but rather to benefit society as a whole.[1085] This rationale is similar to the consumer welfare approach in competition law.[1086] The primary objective of ex post competition law remedies, such as mandatory data sharing based on EFD, is to promote consumer welfare by ensuring that markets remain competitive. The protection of competitors against abusive behaviour by dominant undertakings is a means to achieve this goal; the individual interests of the competitors, however, are not the justification for legislative intervention.

The strong connection between competition law and sectoral data access rights in the public interest is highlighted by the fact that several of those access rights are designed to address some kind of market failure that would lead to higher prices, lower quality of services, less innovation, and less choice for consumers. For example, Article 61 Type Approval Regulation grants an access right to independent repair and maintenance service providers in order to address the market failure tendencies in the aftermarkets of the automotive sector. Similarly, Article 6(11) DMA obliges gatekeepers to provide access to ranking, query, click and view data in relation to free and paid search generated by consumers on online search engines to other undertakings to ensure the contestability of the online search engines market. Without access to this data, new market entrants may struggle to improve their services and compete effectively against gatekeepers. This can lead to a lack of competition in the market, which can result in higher prices for consumers and fewer choices for both end users and business users.[1087]

However, access rights in the public interest have a broader scope than competition law, because they can also be introduced for the protection of other public interests. Article 27 REACH Regulation, for example, grants a registrant seeking to register a chemical substance the right to access testing data from manufacturers who have already registered such a substance, in order to avoid duplicating tests that harm the environment and animals.

Another difference between data access rights in the public interest and access based on competition law is that the former intend to avoid unnecessary duplication of the generation of data. The EFD is much stricter in this regard. According to the *Bronner* decision, the requesting undertaking

---

1085 Neil Cohen and Christiane Wendehorst (n 119) Principle 24.

1086 On the consumer welfare approach see Daskalova (n 699).

1087 Recital 61 DMA.

would need to demonstrate that it is unable to replicate the dataset with a similar investment as the requested undertaking (see 4.2.1.2).[1088]

An example of an access right in the public interest is the one afforded by Article 6(11) DMA to search engine providers. The justification for granting competitors this data right lies solely in the fact that gatekeepers' access to ranking, query, click and view data constitutes an important barrier to entry and expansion, which undermines the contestability of online search engines.[1089] In contrast, the rights afforded by Articles 6(9) and 6(10) DMA to business users and end users is based on the idea that users of the core platform service contribute to the generation of the data and should thus have a right to access and transfer this data.

10.1.2.2 Two-person relationship

Data access rights in the public interest establish a two-person relationship between the initial data holder and a third party that did not contribute to the generation of the data. In contrast to data portability rights, the third-party recipients are put in a very strong position because they are the rightsholder and can exercise the access right at their convenience. Under portability rights, the third-party recipient is only an indirect beneficiary because their access to the required data is dependent on the decision of another person.

Typically, when affording access rights in the public interest only two interests need to be balanced against each other: the rights of the data holder versus the public interest. For example, under the Type Approval Regulation, the public interest to prevent a market failure of aftermarkets in the automotive sector outweighs the contractual freedom of car manufacturers and their freedom to conduct business (Article 16 CFR). However, there may also be situations where not only the data holder but also other persons had a share in the generation of the accessed data. This is, inter alia, the case if the accessed data is personal data relating to someone who is not the data holder. Affording an access right to a third party also affects the rights and interests of the co-generators, such as the right to privacy and data protection. In the DMA, the European legislator resolved this issue by obliging the data holder to remove the contribution of other parties.

1088 Drexl, 'Designing Competitive Markets for Industrial Data – Between Propertisation and Access' (n 17) 270.

1089 Recital 61 DMA.

According to Article 6(11) DMA, the gatekeeper shall anonymise the query, click and view data that constitutes personal data.

However, data access rights in the public interest are not an appropriate policy tool if the removal of the contribution is not possible without defeating the purpose of the access right, and the public interest does not outweigh the interests of the co-generators.[1090] In such cases, the data holder cannot serve as the sole access point for the necessary data for the public interest objective. The solution of the European legislator is to afford a direct data portability right to the party that co-generated the data. By doing so, the decision whether to transfer the data to a third party is left to the discretion of those persons who are affected by the access right. While this approach ensures that the interests of the co-generators are taken into account, the effectiveness of achieving the goal in the public interest is more limited (see 10.1.3.2).

10.1.2.3 Modalities: access based on FRAND conditions

Regarding access conditions, data access rights in the public interest have drawn inspiration from the competition law concept of 'fair, reasonable and non-discriminatory' (FRAND) access.[1091] For example, Article 6(11) DMA obliges gatekeepers to provide access on 'fair, reasonable and non-discriminatory' (FRAND) terms. Articles 27(3) and 30(1) REACH Regulation stipulate that data holders shall make every effort to ensure that the costs of sharing are determined in a 'fair, transparent and non-discriminatory way.' According to Article 61 Type Approval Regulation, car manufacturers shall provide non-discriminatory access but may charge reasonable and proportionate fees. Ensuring consistency between access rights in the public interest and access based on the EFD makes sense because both instruments address a situation where the data recipient has not contributed to the generation of the required data (see 10.1.2.1).

The fee charged for providing access to the data is intended to compensate the data holder for the investments they made in generating the data. Without this fee, the third-party recipients would unduly benefit from the data holder's investments. Moreover, providing free access to the data generated solely by the efforts of the data holder could potentially disincen-

1090 See Heike Schweitzer and Robert Welker (n 567) 134.

1091 See also the recommendation by Neil Cohen and Christiane Wendehorst (n 119) Principle 25(1).

tivise data holders from generating the required data. The requirement of non-discriminatory access ensures that all third-party recipients have equal access to the data, regardless of their status or relationship with the data holder. This prevents data holders from distorting competition by providing an unfair advantage to certain recipients.

Granting certain third parties access rights in the public interest can help avoid lengthy court proceedings because ex ante access provides more legal certainty for both data holders and potential recipients than ex post remedies imposed by competition law. In theory, the concept of FRAND-based access is well aligned with the intentions and objectives of data access rights in the public interest. However, if the parties cannot agree on what constitutes a fair and reasonable fee, it can also be a weak point in practice, as disagreement on this issue could embroil the parties in lengthy court proceedings. So far, the only instrument that addresses this issue is the REACH Regulation. Articles 27 and 30 REACH provide for rules on cost-sharing if there is no agreement found between the parties, as well as a dispute resolution mechanism. Commentators have argued that the approach of the REACH Regulation should serve as guidance for other access rights in the public interest.[1092] Surprisingly, the DMA provides for alternative dispute settlement only for access to software application stores, online search engines and online social networking services but not for access to ranking, query, click and view data. This runs somewhat counter to the objectives of ensuring swift and reliable data access and avoiding court proceedings.

10.1.3 Portability rights in the narrower sense

Portability rights in the narrower sense show traits of both access rights in CGD and access rights in the public interest and thus fall somewhere between the other two categories. The data covered by direct portability rights is co-generated by the data holder and the rightsholder. However, the co-generated data is not transmitted to the rightsholder, but directly to a third-party recipient designated by the rightsholder.

Due to the direct legal relationship between the data holder and the third-party recipient, direct portability rights can enable real-time and/or continuous data transfers. This feature renders Portability rights in the nar-

1092 Drexl, 'Designing Competitive Markets for Industrial Data – Between Propertisation and Access' (n 17) 290; see also Heim and Nikolic (n 739) 47.

rower sense an efficient measure to free customers from being locked into a provider's digital product or service ecosystem, as continuous and real-time data flows are usually required to use data-dependent complementary products and services (see 10.2.1). The analysis of the existing instruments also shows that enabling continuous and real-time data transfers to a third party is a characteristic of all of the examined direct portability rights have in common—with the notable exception of Article 20(2) GDPR (see 5.6.1).

However, the obligation to enable real-time and continuous data transfers also entails a more severe interference with the interests of the data holder. Implementing direct portability in real time and on a continuous basis will usually require the data holder to make significant investments in technology and IT infrastructure, such as adopting new software, hardware, or network components and implementing appropriate APIs and data transfer protocols.

10.1.3.1 Three-person relationship

A characteristic feature of Portability rights in the narrower sense is that they establish a three-person relationship. The right to initiate the data transfer is afforded to a person that had a share in the generation of data. At the request of the rightsholder, the data holder has to allow a third party to access the relevant data. Due to this three-person constellation, Portability rights in the narrower sense produce a twofold effect: On the one hand, the rightsholder gains control over data they have co-generated but are not holding. This data empowerment enables rightsholders, inter alia, to use data-dependent complementary services and products or to switch to a different provider without data loss. On the other hand, the third parties to which the data is transferred get access to data they may otherwise not have, which can lower market entry barriers and/or strengthen their competitive power vis-à-vis the initial data holder. The enhanced competition in the market may lead to better prices and/or quality and therefore also benefits consumers in general. However, these effects are dependent on whether the rightsholder decides to exercise its portability right. Hence, the rightsholder is the direct beneficiary, while third-party recipients and consumers in general only benefit indirectly from direct portability rights.

Some instruments leave it completely up to the rightsholder who should receive the data. For example, according to Article 6(9) and (10) DMA, gatekeepers shall provide access to 'third parties authorised by an end user/business user.' Similarly, Article 5(1) DA provides that the data holder shall make the data available to the third party as requested by the user. Other Instruments define the group of potential recipients and thus restrict the rightsholder's freedom of choice. Under the PSD II XS2A rule, payers may have their account data transferred only to providers of either payment initiation services or account information services. The ED provides that the data of electricity customers (metering and consumption data as well as data required for customer switching, demand response and other services) can be transferred to 'eligible parties', which are to be specified by the Member States.

10.1.3.2 Justification: individual interests of the rightsholder and public interests

Like data access rights, direct portability rights are justified by a combination of i) individual interests of the right holder and ii) overriding public interests. However, it varies from legal act to legal act which of the two grounds carries more weight. In contrast, access rights in the public interest are justified primarily by the latter and access rights in CGD are justified primarily by individual interests. Hence, it can be argued that access rights in CGD and access rights in the public interest represent opposite ends of a spectrum, with direct portability rights lying somewhere in between.

Some of the existing direct portability rights, such as Article 20(2) GDPR, are more closely related to access rights in CGD. Article 20(2) GDPR intends to enhance the data subjects' control over their personal data increasing their personal autonomy and therefore relies primarily on the individual interests of the data subject as justification.

Conversely, the PSD II's XS2A rule is geared more towards achieving a goal in the public interest, which renders it more closely related to access rights in the public interest. While the XS2A rule strengthens the payer's control over its account data enabling the use of AIS and PIS of third-party providers, arguably the primary goal is addressing the difficulties for third-party payment service providers to launch innovative, safe and easy-to-use digital payment services. By affording a portability right to the payer instead of allowing AISPs and PISPs to access the required data directly, the PSD II tries to ensure that the interests of the payer, who co-generated the account data, are sufficiently protected. Making the data transfer dependent on the actions of the payer, guarantees that the interest of the general public in more innovative payment services does not overrule the interest of individual payers, who might prefer the protection of their privacy over new ways of transferring their money.

The portability rights granted to end users and business users under Article 6(9) and (10) DMA are justified to a more or less equal extent by both public and individual interests. On the one hand, users of core services are put in control of the data they have co-generated enabling them to switch suppliers and multi-home. Business users might want to have their data transferred to a designated third party, that analyses website traffic, social media engagement, email open rates, and conversion rates to provide insights into the business users' operations. On the other hand, Articles 6(9) and (10) DMA also serve public interests by promoting competition and innovation in digital markets. The DMA's portability rights were introduced in response to gatekeepers' anti-competitive behaviour of tying their users to their services by limiting access to data generated by users' activities on the platform. Making it easier for users to switch to alternative services or use complementary services reduces barriers to entry for competitors and encourages competition among service providers. This helps to prevent gatekeepers from creating monopolies in digital markets, which can stifle innovation and limit consumer choice. However, in contrast to Article 6(11) DMA, competitors and providers of ancillary services do not have the possibility to access the data themselves under Articles 6(9) and (10) DMA, but depend on platform users exercising their right to portability.

10.1.3.3 Modalities: two types of legal relationships

The twofold effect of portability rights and the fact that they have features of both access rights in CGD and access rights in the public interest is also reflected with regard to the access modalities. It has already been established that EU law affords portability rights to persons that have had a share in the generation of the relevant data. Hence, the legal relationship between the rightsholder and the data holder is similar to the one established by access rights in CGD, with the exception that under the latter rights, the data is transferred to the rightsholder and not directly to a third party. Consequently, and in line with the observations made under 10.1.1.4, all of the analysed portability rights allow rightsholders to exercise their portability right free of charge.[1093]

The relationship between the data holder and the third-party recipient (i.e. the person that the rightsholder wants to receive the data) has similarities to access rights in the public interest. In both cases, a third party receives data without making any contribution to generating of that data. Furthermore, the data transfer is justified not by the individual interests of the third-party recipient but by the interests of the rightsholder and public interests. However, the position of the third-party recipient is weaker under data portability rights than under access rights in the public interest. This is because the decision whether the third party receives the data depends on the actions and choices of the right holder, whereas access rights in the public interest are granted directly to the third-party recipient. Another reason why under data portability rights the risk of third parties freeriding on the investments of the data holder is lower than under access rights in the public interest is that the data covered by portability rights is co-generated by the data holder and the rightsholder. Hence, third parties who receive access to this data under portability rights are not solely benefiting from the data holder's investments but also from the actions and contributions of the person who exercises the portability right and wants the data transferred to the third party.

Nonetheless, the third-party recipients benefit, at least to some extent, from the data holder's investment, as they gain control over the data that they might not otherwise have, which increases their competitive strength vis-à-vis the original data holder. Hence, some of the existing portability rights allow the data holder to charge third party recipients. For example, Article 23 ED stipulates that the individual Member States can decide whether the eligible parties have to pay a fee for receiving the data. According to some commentators, the PSD II also allows banks to charge PISPs for receiving the account data. However, as outlined above (9.1.3), Article 66 PSD II is rather unclear on this point and also allows for a different interpretation. Others, such as Article 6(9) and (10) DMA, do not require the third-party recipient to pay for receiving data from the gatekeeper based on a request from the user. However, with the adoption of the DA, the European legislator has made the decision that per default, any third party recipient shall pay a reasonable remuneration to the data holder. The remuneration requirement of Article 9(1) DA, which lays down the obligation

1093 See Articles 6(9) and (10) DMA; Article 20 ED; Article 12(5) GDPR; Article 66(4) (c) PSD II.

to agree on a reasonable and non-discriminatory compensation with the data holder, does not only apply to data received under Article 5(1) DA but also under any Union legislation entering into force after 12 September 2025 (Articles 12(1) and 50 DA). Hence, under future portability rights, the third party recipient will always have to remunerate the data holder unless it is explicitly provided that the portability right shall be free of charge for the recipient and as well as for the rightsholder.

10.2 Different rights for the different access scenarios

While the previous section aimed to find commonalities in the many different data rights that already exist in EU law in order to create overarching categories with shared characteristics principles, this section takes a different perspective. It does not focus on the access and portability rights but on the various contexts in which these rights are afforded. The situations that data rights intended to address are as diverse as each of access and portability rights. However, as scholars have rightly pointed out, by focusing on these underlying market failures, different data access scenarios that transcend the specifics of a particular sector or regulatory framework can be established.[1094] The objective of this Chapter is to demonstrate that the data rights of the established categories are tools to address the market failures of the defined access scenarios.

10.2.1 First scenario: complementary products and services

In the first scenario, the user of a data-generating product or service, such as an IoT product, social network or search engine, wants to use the complementary services of a third-party provider. In order to provide these services, the third-party provider requires access to the data generated during the use of the product or service by its potential customer. However, although the user has contributed to the generation of that data, the data is under the exclusive control of the manufacturer or services provider. Thus, the user has no possibility to make the data available to

1094 Heike Schweitzer and Robert Welker (n 567) 115 ff; Crémer, de Montjoye and Schweitzer (n 170) 75 f; Schweitzer (n 486) 572 f.

the providers of their choice.[1095] This situation leads to lock-in effects for users, as they become tied to complementary services and products of the primary provider. Such data-induced lock-ins are not only a problem for the individual end users but may also lead to competitive distortions. By denying data access, data holders can block companies from entering the aftermarkets or offering complementary services (such as GPS or diagnostic services for IoT devices), which may lead to less innovation and/or higher prices in these markets.[1096] Market newcomers must overcome the incumbent's advantage in personalisation, which often requires significant quality or price improvements to attract customers. In an ideal market scenario with sufficient competition and well-informed consumers, manufacturers and service providers would be under pressure to offer customer-friendly contracts and open access to data so that customers do not end up in a 'lock-in' situation.[1097] However, the competitive mechanisms do not always work as they should. Due to information asymmetries, users may choose a product for its immediate benefits, such as ease of use or a lower price, without considering the compatibility with third-party services and products. This is particularly problematic when purchasing expansive and long-lasting products or services. Moreover, users may also be unaware of what services they want or need in the aftermarket in the future, leading to an underestimation of data availability. Another reason competition might not lead to optimal outcomes is market dominance by one provider or because all service providers have opted for the same practice of refusing data access.[1098]

Particularly in b2c constellations, the appropriate regulatory instrument to address the market failure of this access scenario is to afford the user a data portability right. The users are freed from the lock-in situations if they can port the data to a third party that offers the complementary services or products they want to use. Merely allowing users to access and retrieve the data in a one-off instance would not be sufficient in this scenario because the user wants to continue using their primary product or service while taking advantage of third-party complementary services. To ensure a seamless interaction between complementary service and primary product, the data right needs to support the direct transfer to the third

1095 Schweitzer and Metzger (n 246) 338; Heike Schweitzer and Robert Welker (n 567) 115; Crémer, de Montjoye and Schweitzer (n 170) 75.
1096 Heike Schweitzer and Robert Welker (n 567) 116.
1097 Heike Schweitzer and Robert Welker (n 567) 116.
1098 Heike Schweitzer and Robert Welker (n 567) 117 f.

party continuously and in real-time.[1099] Typical examples are the XS2A rule of the PSD II or Article 5(1) DA.

In general, the same reasoning also applies to business users. The only difference, however, is that in contrast to consumers, some business users might not depend on the complementary services or products of third parties because they are able to develop or provide these services themselves.[1100] Hence, the DA affords users a portability right (Article 5(1) DA) and an access right (Article 4(1) DA) that enables users to rely on internal solutions instead of using the complementary services of third parties. However, when business users leverage data access rights to develop in-house services, these solutions typically remain internal and are not offered to the broader market. Consequently, if the goal of the regulatory intervention is to facilitate competition in complementary markets, an access right that allows users to utilise the data for their in-house services does not directly contribute to this objective. While the development of in-house services can lead to innovation, this innovation does not extend beyond the company's boundaries. The potential for these innovations to stimulate broader market advancements, such as more tailored services, better prices, higher quality or more consumer choice. Moreover, introducing both portability rights and access rights can create overlaps that introduce new competitive imbalances and/or undermine the effectiveness of the other right (one example is the relationship between Articles 4 and 5 DA, see 7.11.2).

10.2.2 Second scenario: changing provider

Another access scenario is that of a user of a data-dependent product or service who wants to switch to another provider or use the services of several providers in parallel (multi-homing). However, by denying the user to retrieve the data generated by the product or service the initial provider creates switching costs that deter users from transitioning to a new provider. For example, the user of a smartwatch who contemplates switching to the products of a different manufacturer after several years of using their watch may hesitate to make the transition if all their historical training

1099 Wendehorst, 'Konsument:innen in der Datenökonomie' (n 230) 220; Heike Schweitzer and Robert Welker (n 567) 119.

1100 Drexl and others (n 821) 29; see also Kerber, 'Governance of IoT Data' (n 804) 133.

data, performance profiles, and other metrics accumulated over the years will become inaccessible or lost.[1101] By incurring these switching costs, the original provider effectively creates barriers to market entry for competitors. Even if new entrants offer better quality or more competitive prices, they may find it difficult to gain traction because potential customers are put off by the inconvenience and potential loss associated with transferring their data. This environment benefits the established providers, as they can maintain their customer base and market share without necessarily having to perform better in terms of quality, innovation or price.[1102]

There is a certain similarity to the first scenario, as both constellations involve lock-in effects.[1103] However, in the first scenario, the lock-in affects the ecosystem surrounding the primary product, stifling innovation and reducing consumer choice in complementary markets. In this scenario, the lock-in directly impacts the primary market, making it challenging for new entrants to compete and for consumers to benefit from potentially superior alternatives.

Like in the first scenario, the appropriate response to the second scenario is affording the user of the service or product a portability right that enables them to request a direct transfer of the relevant data from the initial provider to the new provider.[1104] The essential difference to the first scenario, however, is that the transfer does not necessarily need to be in real-time and on a continuous basis, but that a one-time data transfer is sufficient to address the lock-in on the primary market. This is because switching in the primary market means a full transition to a competitor, while complementary services are used in conjunction with the primary service. Once the data is transferred and the user has fully migrated to the new service, there is no need for an ongoing data exchange with the initial provider. Hence, in order to break the lock-in in the primary market an access right to first retrieve the data and then transmit the data to the new provider (indirect portability) could be afforded to the user instead of a

1101 Wendehorst, 'Konsument:innen in der Datenökonomie' (n 230) 218; Schmidt (n 175) 476; Duch-Brown, Martens and Mueller-Langer (n 180) 43.

1102 Wendehorst, 'Konsument:innen in der Datenökonomie' (n 230) 218; Schmidt (n 175) 476; Paal and Hennemann (n 230) 25; Monopolkommission (n 230) 109; Graef, Verschakelen and Valcke (n 223) 57 f.

1103 See Schweitzer (n 486) 573 who refers to both constellations under the same access scenario.

1104 Wendehorst, 'Konsument:innen in der Datenökonomie' (n 230) 218; Heike Schweitzer and Robert Welker (n 567) 119; Elfering (n 487) 52; Datenethikkommission (n 114) 136; Schweitzer (n 486) 574; Monopolkommission (n 230) 10.

portability right. Article 20 GDPR is an example of a regulatory measure that only enables the data subject to switch suppliers but does not enable the use of complementary services.[1105]

Typically, portability rights that allow continuous and real-time data transfers have a dual function as they are capable of addressing the lock-in issues in both primary and complementary markets. Users can easily switch their primary service provider without losing valuable, up-to-date data. At the same time, the portability right ensures that users can use a variety of complementary services that extend the core functionality of their primary service, as these third-party services can access real-time data to provide personalised and coherent experiences. For example, Articles 6(9) and 6(10) DMA allow end users of core platform services to use complementary services, such as social media management tools, as well as to migrate the relevant data to a different platform for multi-homing or complete switching (see 6.4.1 and 6.5.1).

However, portability rights can also be designed in such a way that they facilitate the use of complementary services without enabling the user to change the primary providers. For instance, under the XS2A rule bank customers may only request data transfer from their bank to providers of payment initiation or account information services. Moreover, the portability right is limited to the data necessary for providing these services, and the providers of payment initiation or account information services are restricted to using the data solely for this purpose (see 9.1.1). Due to these specifics, the XS2A rule only facilitates the use of payment services but does not enable customers to migrate their bank accounts, complete with transaction histories and other banking data, to a different banking institution.

10.2.3 Third scenario: internal purposes of the co-generator

The third scenario arises when persons who have contributed to the generation of data but do not have control over it, seek access to the co-generated data for legitimate internal purposes, such as improving services, understanding customer behaviour, or enhancing product offerings. However, the controlling party's commercial practices or contractual arrangements limit

1105 Wendehorst, 'Konsument:innen in der Datenökonomie' (n 230) 219; Heike Schweitzer and Robert Welker (n 567) 119.

this access, thereby restricting the contributor's ability to leverage the data for their purposes.[1106] In contrast to the first two scenarios, this scenario centres not around transferring data to third parties.

An illustration of this scenario can be found in the platform economy. Traders use online platforms to distribute their services or products and facilitate transactions. In the process, a significant amount of data is generated, capturing detailed transaction histories, customer interactions, and buyer preferences. This data can offer invaluable insights into market trends, customer behaviour, and the effectiveness of various sales strategies. However, although the traders have contributed to the generation of the data, the control typically lies with the platform and traders may find themselves with limited or no access to this data.[1107] Traders often accept the limited access to data because of the imbalance in bargaining power between traders and platforms and the lack of alternatives. This is because once a platform has reached a critical mass, for many traders the platform becomes an almost indispensable tool to reach customers. In an ideal market, traders who are dissatisfied with the terms of one platform could switch to another with more favourable terms. However, when a few platforms dominate the market and each exerts similar control over data, traders have few, if any, viable alternatives. Hence, traders may find themselves in a position where they must accept restricted access to transaction data and customer information imposed by the platform.[1108] Similar challenges are faced by advertisers and publishers who rely on online platforms for ad distribution, as the data required to measure the performance of their advertising measures is controlled by the platform providers. Hence, advertisers and publishers have limited insights about the effect and performance of their advertising. This dependency on platforms for performance metrics constrains advertisers' ability to make informed decisions and optimize their advertising strategies.[1109]

Since the core issue revolves around an imbalance in data usage rights between parties involved in data co-generation and not the inability to have

1106 See Neil Cohen and Christiane Wendehorst (n 119) Principle 20.

1107 Wolf-Posch (n 591) Article 6 (10) DMA, para [205]; Kerber, 'Datenrechtliche Aspekte des Digital Markets Act – Datenwirtschaftsrecht I: Vorschlag einer Ex-ante-Regulierung von Gatekeeper-Plattformen' (n 651) 546; Demary and Rusche, 'Data Sharing im E-Commerce: Rechtliche und ökonomische Grundlagen' (n 192) 8.

1108 Schweitzer and others (n 205) 8, 42; Khan (n 213) 780 f.

1109 Wolf-Posch (n 591) Article 6(8) DMA, para [173]; Competition and Markets Authority (n 594) 410 f.

data transferred to a third party, the appropriate remedy is to afford a data access right in co-generated data to the non-controlling party. For instance, Article 6(8) DMA affords advertisers and publishers free of charge access to the data, including aggregated and non-aggregated data, necessary for advertisers to carry out their own independent verification of the provision of the relevant online advertising services. The essence of access rights is to establish a more equitable distribution of data access and control, by acknowledging that the data is generated collectively and that all who contribute should have a share in the benefits. This not only benefits the individual co-generators involved but also enhances the overall value proposition for end-users, who stand to gain from lower prices and/or the improved services and products that result from a more equitable data access regime.[1110] There may also be instances where an access right is combined with a portability right. Article 6(10) DMA is a prime example of such an approach. It grants business users not only the ability to access and utilise data for their internal purposes but also the right to request the direct transfer of this data to a third party in order to address lock-in issues.

Granting only an access right in CGD and not combining it with a right to portability has the advantage that a broader scope of access, including data that the controlling party has derived or inferred from the original data, can be justified more easily. This is because the ability to transfer data to third parties allows third parties that did not have a share in generating the data to freeride on the investments and efforts of the controlling party in processing and analysing the data to create derived and inferred insights. Exposing the data to wider use could potentially result in competitive disadvantages but may also lead to privacy and data security concerns. However, it needs to be kept in mind that an access right in CGD that puts the co-generating party in full control also enables them to onward transfer the data to third parties. Therefore, if the regulatory objective is to permit the co-generator to access the inferred and derived data while preventing third-party freeriding, limitations on the onward transfer of this data would need to be implemented.

1110 Neil Cohen and Christiane Wendehorst (n 119) Principle 20.

10.2.4 Fourth scenario: third party access

In the fourth scenario, access is sought by a party that has not contributed to the generation of the data. The requesting party may either be a direct competitor of the data holder or offer services or products in an adjacent market.[1111] This scenario differs significantly from the others in several aspects. In the first two scenarios, the services or products that the third party wants to offer depend on data that is generated by the user of a product or service but controlled by the provider or manufacturer. Since the usage data, irrespective of whether it is personal or not, is attributable to the user, the users should have the autonomy to decide who can use their data and for what purposes. The third party should not be able to access the data from the controlling party directly but rather persuade potential customers to share their usage data, so the third party can provide their data-dependent services or products.[1112]

In contrast, scenario four represents a situation where the requesting party needs access to data that is not co-generated data, meaning that it has no impact on the interests of parties other than the controlling party, or where co-generated data is needed on such a large scale that it is not possible to contact each co-generating party. In the latter case, it may be necessary to exclude the contribution of the parties concerned in order to protect their interests. If this is done, the constellation is actually similar to the first case, as the data no longer relates to the co-generators and thus the potential impact on their interests is mitigated. An example of the first constellation is mobility platform providers that require access to real-time data regarding train departures and delays from railway operators in order to provide their services. The request from providers of search engines to access anonymised ranking, query, click and view data from the dominant search engine provider would be an example of the second constellation.[1113] The value of this data results from the fact that it relates to a large number of individual actions by many different users. Given the vast number of individuals that have contributed to the generation of that data, it would be impossible to contact each of the affected individuals and persuade them to exercise a portability right regarding their search engine data in favour of the third party. However, by stripping the data of personally identifiable in-

1111 Neil Cohen and Christiane Wendehorst (n 119) Principle 24; Crémer, de Montjoye and Schweitzer (n 170) 75.
1112 Heike Schweitzer and Robert Welker (n 567) 134.
1113 Heike Schweitzer and Robert Welker (n 567) 134 f.

formation, the data can be shared with third-party search engine providers without compromising user privacy.

The regulatory measure to address this scenario is to afford the third party an access right in the public interest.[1114] Typically, this intervention is justified by the public interest of rectifying competitive distortions. In well-functioning markets, data holders would provide access to the necessary datasets at a fair price that reflects the market value. However, dominant data holders may charge unreasonable prices or completely deny access to maintain their market position and limit competition on the primary and/or adjacent markets.[1115] This constellation could also be addressed by Article 102 TFEU but only with significant drawbacks. The complex legal and factual questions that need to be addressed when invoking the EFD lead to lengthy and costly litigation and data access may only be granted at the end of such procedures (see 4.3.7). It has also been pointed out that besides addressing competitive distortions, there are also other grounds that could justify an access right of a party that has not contributed to the generation of the data, such as more efficient use of research money or the reduction of testing that could harm the environment (see 9.4).[1116]

10.3 Access and portability rights as pillars of EU data law

The previous sections allow for the conclusion that data access and portability rights have evolved from isolated legislative measures within a specific regulatory domain to cornerstones of EU data regulation transcending sectoral boundaries. Similarities can be drawn to the developments and discussions that happened in the field of European private law. This shall further substantiate the finding of previous sections that overarching principles and characteristics can be identified for the different categories of data rights.

1114 Neil Cohen and Christiane Wendehorst (n 119) Principle 24; Heike Schweitzer and Robert Welker (n 567) 137.
1115 Heike Schweitzer and Robert Welker (n 567) 136.
1116 Neil Cohen and Christiane Wendehorst (n 119) Principle 24.

10.3.1 Regulatory silos

Regarding the rights and obligations between private parties introduced by EU Regulations and Directives it has been argued that their primary objective is internal market integration rather than balancing the interests of the parties based on principles of autonomy and fairness.[1117] After all, the EU has no formal competence in the field of private law, and the legal basis for European private law regulation is ensuring the functioning of the internal market (Article 114 TFEU). Against this background, European private law has been referred to as Regulatory Private Law[1118] and conceptualised as merely a component of regulatory 'silos', which are relatively closed units following their own rationale and designed to regulate a certain sector or problem.[1119] The individual silos have little regard for each other, and private law concepts are guided by the logic of the respective silo rather than by an overarching rationale. In these silos, private law serves a concrete regulatory objective (removing a barrier to trade in the internal market) and is not primarily an instrument of corrective justice.[1120] Moreover, European private law is not necessarily enforced by private parties in front of civil courts but may also be publicly enforced by administrative agencies.[1121] The view of European private law as separate compartments is reinforced when considering that within the European Commission, the task of proposing new private law rules is not in the hands of a particular Directorate-General. Rather, various Directorates-General make use of private law if they deem it an effective tool to regulate their policy area.

1117 Hugh Collins, 'The Revolutionary Trajectory of EU Contract Law towards Post-National Law' in Sarah Worthington, Andrew Robertson, and Graham Virgo (eds), *Revolution and Evolution in Private Law* (Hart 2018) 321; Hans-W Micklitz, 'The Transformation of Private Law Through Competition' (2016) 22 European Law Journal 627, 629; Micklitz, 'Europäisches Regulierungsprivatrecht: Plädoyer für ein neues Denken' (n 34) 256 ff.

1118 E.g. Micklitz, 'Europäisches Regulierungsprivatrecht: Plädoyer für ein neues Denken' (n 34); Wendehorst, 'Methodenlehre und Privatrecht in Europa' (n 34) 829.

1119 Hans-W Micklitz, Yane Svetiev and Hans-W Micklitz, 'The Transformation(s) of Private Law' in Yane Svetiev and Guido Comparato (eds), *EUI Working Papers: European Regulatory Private Law – The Paradigms Tested* (European University Institute 2014) 78.

1120 Micklitz, Svetiev and Micklitz (n 1119) 76 ff.; Hans-W Micklitz, 'The Visible Hand of European Regulatory Private Law' (European University Institute) Law Working Papers 2008/14 12 ff.

1121 Cherednychenko (n 988) 29.

This descriptive account of European private law could also be used to describe the earlier Directives and Regulations that introduced data access and portability rights. The PSD II, the Type Approval Regulation and ED are all sector-specific instruments that introduce a variety of different obligations—most of which belong to the realm of public law—in order to promote market integration. They have not been adopted with the intention of establishing a data (private) law that follows overarching principles but are guided by the objective of the specific sector.

10.3.2 Pillars of EU data law

However, it has been pointed out that the silo account does not provide a full picture of European private law. It has been argued that consumer law does not (or no longer) correspond to the model regulatory silos reflecting the specific logic of a particular market sector but has emerged into a loosely coherent system built around three main pillars: withdrawal rights, unfair term control, and nonconformity.[1122] These three instruments apply to all sectors and resolve most of the legal disputes between sellers on the internal market and their customers. An example of this evolution is withdrawal rights. Initially, the European legislators implemented withdrawal rights for doorstep sales, which were subsequently expanded to include timeshare agreements, distance selling, and consumer credit arrangements. These rights were further harmonised through legislative revisions and ultimately broadened to encompass all online and off-premise contracts under the Consumer Rights Directive.[1123]

A similar development can be observed with regard to data law. Prior to 2020, the only horizontal instrument dealing with data was the GDPR, albeit with a focus primarily on regulating data protection and not the data economy—with the notable exception of Article 20 GDPR. However, within three years after 2020, the European legislator adopted three Regulations that represent a remarkable shift towards a more integrated approach to regulating the data economy: the DGA, the DMA and DA. The fact that two of those Regulations, the DMA and DA, introduce several horizontal data access and portability aimed at addressing various problems within the data economy suggests that data access and portability rights are be-

1122 Martijn W Hesselink, 'Private Law, Regulation, and Justice' (2016) 22 European Law Journal 681, 685.

1123 Hesselink (n 1122) 486.

coming one pillar of European data law. The DA, in particular, signals the European legislator's intent to move away from a piecemeal, sector-specific approach to data regulation towards a more cohesive and integrated framework of data rights. Article 12 DA explicitly states that Chapter III of the DA, which deals with the obligations of data holders that have to make data available in b2b situations, shall also apply to future Union law or national legislation adopted in accordance with Union law mandating data sharing with third parties. This harmonisation underscores the growing importance of data access and portability rights as foundational elements and reflects a departure from regulating data rights within isolated sectors to establishing a comprehensive and integrated legal framework that spans the entire data economy. The unfairness test of terms concerning data-related obligations laid down in Article 13 DA may become a second pillar, as it will apply to any private sector data accessed and used on the basis of a contract between enterprises (Article 1(1)(c) DA) and thus play a role across the entire data economy.

11 Findings

To conclude the findings of this analysis, data access and portability have become central regulatory tools in European law to address the de facto control over data and regulate its allocation. These rights can be found in various Directives and Regulations, ranging from highly sector-specific instruments, such as the ED (Energy Efficiency Directive) and REACH (Registration, Evaluation, Authorisation and Restriction of Chemicals) Regulation, to more general, horizontal instruments like the GDPR (General Data Protection Regulation) and the Data Act (DA).

Given the extensive array of existing data access and portability rights, it was not attempted to provide an exhaustive catalogue of all such rights but instead, focused on some of the more prominent examples that highlight the diversity of different data access and portability rights. This selective approach allowed for a more detailed analysis of the functioning of these rights, providing valuable insights into their effectiveness, challenges, and potential areas for improvement.

The analysis reveals a number of uncertainties in how these rights operate, including issues related to the scope of data covered, the modalities of access, the remuneration for access, and the interrelationships among these rights. The following section summarises the most important findings on these issues.

11.1 The Essential Facility Doctrine

The CJEU has significantly broadened the scope of the Essential Facility Doctrine (EFD), which has been developed on the basis of Article 102 TFEU to address cases of denied access to physical infrastructures. The Court has clarified that an essential facility may not only be a physical infrastructure but can also include information protected by intellectual property rights. These IP rights cases demonstrate that the exceptional circumstances test is flexible enough to be applied to cases where a dominant undertaking refuses to supply data. However, due to the special characteristics of data, it may be difficult for the undertaking seeking access to demonstrate that all the requirements of the exceptional circumstances test are present. This difficulty results in lengthy procedures, with compulsory data access only being granted at the end of such processes. Consequently, the EFD cannot provide swift and reliable relief to companies needing data access.

Typically, the requested data is used internally and not traded on an existing data market, which makes it necessary to define a hypothetical primary market. Substitutability on the demand side must be assessed based on the data's qualitative characteristics. In the case of 'single source data', factors such as semantic content or timeliness are decisive in determining the qualitative characteristics of the requested data. In the case of 'big data', the size, diversity and representativeness of the data set determine the quality of the data.

In order to demonstrate the indispensability of big data, the requesting undertaking has to prove that the data set cannot be duplicated or replaced due to its size and diversity. The requesting undertaking must prove that the costs of replicating the data would exceed the investment made by the original data owner.

If an undertaking seeks access to personal data, Article 20 GDPR may affect the indispensability test. The requesting undertaking could potentially duplicate the requested personal data by contacting the data subjects and urging them to exercise their data portability right under Article 20 GDPR. However, the mere fact that the requested data is covered by Article 20 GDPR does not allow conclusions as to the actual possibility of duplicating the requested data. Competition authorities or courts must evaluate whether market conditions and the limited scope of portability allow the undertaking to get access to the required data on the basis of Article 20 GDPR.

The dominant undertaking does not have to be active on the secondary market in order to meet the requirement of the exceptional circumstances test that the dominant undertaking's conduct excludes competition on the secondary market. It suffices if the undertaking plans to enter the downstream market soon or aims to prevent new disruptive markets that could weaken its primary market position.

The new product requirement should be dropped if market failures like network effects or switching costs render competition on innovation impossible, in order to allow competition by imitation. Where no such failures exist, the new product condition should be applied to promote competition in innovation.

The legal basis for a dominant undertaking to transfer the requested personal data is the decision of a competition authority or court to provide access to the requesting undertaking. The processing activities of the requesting undertaking (i.e. the recipient) must be based on Article 6(1)(f) GDPR, which requires that the objective of restoring effective competition outweighs the legitimate interests of the data subject.

11.2 The RtDP of data subjects (Article 20 GDPR)

The GDPR's RtDP is not a data protection norm in the strict sense, as it does not restrict the use of personal data but enables data subjects to access their personal data and transfer it to third parties, which facilitates the flow of personal data.

In light of Article 20 GDPR's objective to enhance the control of data subjects over their personal data and enable data subjects to switch providers, Article 20 GDPR needs to be interpreted as applying to both provided and observed data.

A conflict between the RtDP and the rights and freedoms of others may arise where the requested personal data also relates to other data subjects. If these other data subjects are either unwilling to give their consent or are unreachable, Article 6(1)(f) GDPR may provide a legal basis for the data transfer. In case the new controller processes the data for the same purposes as the original controller, it is unlikely that the interests of the other data subjects will outweigh the interests of the individual requesting data portability.

The RtDP only enables a one-off supply of data. Hence, Article 20 GDPR is not capable of tackling lock-ins within a provider's digital ecosystem, as data-driven ancillary services typically require real-time and/or continuous access to data.

Article 20 GDPR does not cover data processed based on Article 6(1)(f) GDPR. This could potentially allow data controllers to bypass their responsibilities under Article 20 GDPR by justifying data processing under the 'legitimate interests' provision rather than relying on consent or contract.

Article 20 GDPR may potentially benefit large companies more than smaller ones, which can solidify competitive imbalances. Companies that provide widely used services or products are better positioned to engage with a significant number of data subjects and encourage them to exercise their Right to Data Portability (RtDP) in favour of the company. Additionally, larger companies are more likely to have the resources to integrate different data formats and effectively analyse large datasets compared to small and medium-sized enterprises (SMEs).

Article 15(3) GDPR is a modality of the information duty provided for in Article 15(1) GDPR. The main purpose of Article 15(3) GDPR is to ensure transparency. It does not, however, specifically facilitate data portability or reuse as the controller is not required to provide the data in a machine-readable format.

The GDPR's RtDP falls short of achieving its objective of truly empowering data subjects in the data economy and addresses lock-ins due to its limited scope and modalities. However, some of the identified gaps have been closed by the access and portability rights afforded by Articles 6(9) and (10) DMA and Articles 4(1) and 5(1) DA.

11.3 Access right of advertisers and publishers (Article 6(8) DMA)

The scope and access modalities of the access right for advertisers and publishers afforded by Article 6(8) DMA are ambiguous, necessitating further specification through delegated acts by the Commission.

When advertisers or publishers seek access to personal data, gatekeepers must ensure that they provide the data in compliance with the GDPR. While redacting personally identifiable information is one option, it can reduce the data's utility and value. Therefore, gatekeepers should prioritise obtaining consent from affected individuals that also covers the use of the data by advertisers and publishers.

11.4 Portability right of end users of core platform services (Article 6(9) DMA)

The right afforded by Article 6(9) DMA to end users of core platform services is more effective in promoting competition and empowering end users than GDPR's RtDP. Article 6(9) DMA allows for continuous and real-time access and portability, enabling end users to integrate the services of the gatekeeper with specific services from a third-party provider (partial change of provider). Additionally, the DMA empowers the Commission to require European standardization bodies to develop appropriate standards for data formats. Furthermore, the portability right under DMA applies to both provided and observed data, regardless of whether the data qualifies as personal data, making it more effective in addressing end users' lock-in situations.

The wording of Article 6(9) DMA is inconclusive as to whether the portability right also applies to inferred and derived data. In light of the objective of enabling effective switching to other providers, the provision should be interpreted as also covering inferred and derived data. While this interpretation results in a broad scope of application, the burden on gatekeepers is mitigated by Article 8 DMA. If the Commission deems the inclusion of all data deduced from users' activities or provided data to be overly extensive, it can restrict the scope through a delegated act.

The DMA's Article 6(9) introduces a distinct and independent data right, rather than simply extending the data portability right outlined in Article 20 GDPR. End users have the option to exercise their right under either the DMA or the GDPR. If an end user does not explicitly specify the right they are invoking against a gatekeeper, it can be presumed that they intend to exercise their right under Article 6(9) DMA, as it encompasses all relevant data and facilitates continuous, real-time transfers.

It follows from the interpretation of Article 6(9) DMA in accordance with the fundamental rights and general principles common to the laws of all Member States that similar restrictions to those in Article 12(5) and Article 20(4) GDPR also apply to the right to portability under Article 6(9) DMA. In line with the abuse of rights doctrine, Article 6(9) DMA must be interpreted in such a way that excessive requests are not allowed or only if the costs incurred are reimbursed. Furthermore, Article 6(9) DMA must be interpreted in such a way that it does not allow unjustified interference with the fundamental rights of others. Article 20(4) GDPR is nothing more than a reiteration of this general rule.

11.5 Access right of business users of core platform services (Article 6(10) DMA)

Business users of core platform services face similar challenges in accessing co-generated data as end users. They actively contribute to the generation of vast amounts of data through their interactions with these services. However, their access to this data is severely limited due to the gatekeeper's factual control over it. As a result of the gatekeeper's market power, business users typically lack the leverage to negotiate specific clauses regarding access to co-generated data in their contracts, but rather are confronted with standard contractual clauses drafted by the gatekeeper on a 'take it or leave it' basis. The DMA addresses this issue by affording business users a data right similar to that of end users.

In accordance with the portability right of end users, Article 6(10) DMA should be interpreted to encompass derived and inferred data.

When determining whether a business user is acting in their commercial or professional capacity, recourse can be taken to the CJEU's case law on the definition of 'trader' in EU consumer law. These criteria were originally created for the relationship between traders and consumers, so some are not relevant in the context of the DMA and others need some adjustments. Key criteria to consider include: whether the person carries out an activity on a regular basis and in an organised manner for profit-making purposes; uses a legal structure that allows them to engage in commercial transactions; is connected to other economic activities; or is subject to VAT.

Business users have the right to access data generated from end users interacting with their products or services. This includes data generated when end users use the products and services offered by the business user through the core platform service, such as click-and-view data, even if the end users have not completed a transaction with the business user. However, this right does not extend to data related to transactions between end users and other business users on the same core platform service, as there is no direct connection between that data and the business user's activities on the platform.

Business users may access the personal data of end users only with the end users' consent and not based on any other legal grounds provided by the GDPR.

11.6 Access right of search engine providers (Article 6(11) DMA)

The European legislators have introduced Article 6(11) DMA in response to Google's strong position in the search engine market. Many economic experts argue that Google's dominance is primarily due to its extensive collection and analysis of user data, including detailed records of search queries and user interactions with search results. This has created a significant barrier for new or smaller search engine competitors, as they do not have access to similarly comprehensive data, hindering their ability to offer similarly effective and relevant search results.

Article 6(11) DMA affords a data access right not only to companies already operating in the search engines market but also to those that plan to enter the market. However, companies that have a gatekeeper status in another market are not excluded from the scope of this access right. These gatekeepers may benefit more from the data accessed based on Article 6(11) DMA than smaller companies because of their financial resources, infrastructure, and expertise to effectively use the accessed data. This could, contrary to the objectives of the DMA, strengthen the dominance of these gatekeepers.

If the requested ranking, query, click, and view data constitutes personal data, the gatekeeper must anonymise the data as much as necessary to protect the privacy of the affected users but as little as possible in order to ensure that the data is still of value to the requesting competitors.

The DMA does not provide clear guidance on how to interpret the requirement that access should be provided under fair, reasonable, and non-discriminatory (FRAND) conditions. However, recourse can be taken to the Data Act. The 'reasonable' criterion relates to the price charged by the gatekeeper for accessing the data. A reasonable fee may encompass costs such as data reproduction, electronic dissemination, and storage, and can also include a margin that reflects the added value provided by the data holder. The 'fair' requirement introduces an unfairness test regarding access terms other than the price. The 'non-discrimination' aspect requires that the gatekeeper offers the same or similar terms to similarly situated recipients.

11.7 Access and portability rights of IoT product users (Articles 4 and 5 DA)

Articles 4 and 5 DA grant users the right to access and transfer data generated by IoT devices to third parties in order to empower users, ensure a fairer distribution of data value, promote a competitive aftermarket, and stimulate the development of new services. Some critics argue that the DA fails to achieve its objectives and may even strengthen the data holder's control over IoT data because it legitimises their de facto control. However, the DA not only allows users to access and use the data generated by IoT devices but also imposes restrictions on the data holder's data usage. Without the DA, there would be no real limitations to the de facto control of the manufacturer, besides those provided by data protection and IP law. Hence, this criticism is not shared.

Excluding derived and inferred data from Articles 4 and 5 DA makes sense because users contribute little to generating this data, and the DA does not tackle a specific market failure. Unlike the DMA, which targets gatekeepers with significant market power, the scenarios addressed by the DA do not necessarily involve an inherent imbalance in bargaining power.

It is uncertain whether Article 4(1) DA grants the user full control over the data or only the right to access the data on the data holder's servers (in situ access). The interpretation favoured here supports the view that it grants full control. This view is reinforced by Article 4(2) DA, which states that users and data holders can contractually limit or prevent further data sharing, implying that the user has already been put in full control of the data.

The data holder is required to transfer the data requested by a user under Article 5(1) DA, even if the data holder and third-party recipient cannot agree on a reasonable fee. If the recipient rejects the data holder's contractual offer because they consider the fee unreasonable but still use the data, the recipient is nonetheless bound by the other terms of the initial offer and must abide by all usage, sharing, and processing restrictions outlined in the offer.

Recital 25 of DA suggests that users may have the option to waive their rights under Articles 4(1) and 5(1) DA. However, Article 7(2) DA states that any contractual term which, to the detriment of the user, excludes the application of, derogates from or varies the effect of the user's rights shall not be binding. This provision clearly indicates that the rights provided under Articles 4(1) and 5(1) DA are mandatory and users cannot waive these rights through a contractual agreement. Any exceptions to the mandatory nature of the access rights would have had to be explicitly stated in the legally binding part of the DA, not only in the non-binding Recitals.

The requirement that data holders may only process non-personal data generated by IoT devices on the basis of a contract with the user (Article 4(13) DA) aims to improve transparency regarding data use and make the data holder's usage subject to the unfairness test established in Article 13 DA.

When a user requests access to data from their IoT device that includes data related to other individuals, the data access and portability rights of the DA do not constitute a legal obligation within the meaning of Article 6(1)(c) GDPR that would justify the processing of such personal data. Particularly in situations where real-time access to the data is needed, it may not be feasible to obtain consent from all the affected individuals. In such cases, the only option is to base the processing on Article 6(1)(f) GDPR, which requires balancing the user's interests with those of the affected individuals on a case-by-case basis.

The restrictions on the user's data use provided for in Article 4(6) to (9) and Article 6(11) DA should not only apply when the data is accessed on the basis of Article 4(1) DA but also when the user has been able to access the data directly from the device because the manufacturer has fulfilled its obligation under Article 3 DA to ensure access by design. Otherwise, the DA would create a false incentive for the data owner: More usage restrictions would apply to the user if the data holder does not fulfil its primary obligation to design the product in such a way that direct access is possible.

Article 4 DA does not restrict users from passing on the data they receive to other parties. This means that third parties can circumvent the obligations and costs of obtaining data on the basis of Article 5(1) DA by asking users to request the data on the basis of their right under Article 4(1) and then pass it on to them. This creates a loophole that undermines the intention of the DA that users who have contributed to the generation of the IoT data should be able to access the data for free, while third parties who have not contributed to the generation of the data should pay for receiving the data.

11.8 Portability right of cloud customers (Article 25 DA)

Chapter VI of the Data Act focuses on the difficulties that hinder customers of cloud services from switching providers, such as contractual obligations, economic burdens, and technical barriers. A measure to address this is Article 25(2)(a) DA, which mandates that contracts between customers and data service providers contain clauses for data portability. However, Article 25(2)(a) DA does not lay down a self-standing, immediately enforceable subjective right for customers to port their cloud data. The effective implementation of the duty set out in Article 25(2)(a) is a matter of national contract law.

The porting obligation under Article 25(2)(a) DA is broader than those in Article 6(9) and (10) DMA and Article 5 DA. This is because Article 25(2)(a) DA applies not only to all exportable data but also to the customer's digital assets, which include digital elements such as software applications and the associated metadata (settings, configurations, security parameters, access and control rights).

Article 25(2)(c)(i) DA creates the false impression customers can exercise the portability right only when they intend to end their contract with the source provider. The important addition that the obligation to facilitate data transfers also applies to the parallel use of data processing services is set out in Article 34(1) DA, located in Chapter VIII. To avoid confusion, such a provision should have been placed in Chapter VI instead.

11.9 Categories of access and portability rights

Based on their characteristics, the broad variety of existing access and portability rights can be categorised into three different categories of data rights: (i) access rights in co-generated data (CGD), (ii) access rights in the public interest, and (iii) data portability rights.

Access rights in co-generated data are afforded to persons who have contributed to the generation of the data but are not in control of that data. They establish a legal relationship between the rightsholder and the data holder to create a more equitable distribution of data control and usage. The primary justification for affording an access right and encroaching the interests of the data holder is the individual interests of the rightsholder. Public interests only play a subordinate role. Since rights in CGD are usually afforded to persons that have a strong entitlement to the data due to their significant contributions to the data's generation, the rightsholder, typically, receives full control of the data and may exercise the right in CGD free of charge.

Unlike rights in CGD, data access rights in the public interest are afforded to third parties and not to persons involved in generating the data. These rights are not for the direct benefit of the individual rightsholder but aim to benefit the general public. The justification for interfering with the data holder's rights and interests often stems from the need to prevent market failure. As the rightsholders do not contribute to the generation of the accessed data, data access rights in the public interest allow the data holder to charge a fee, but it is required that the conditions of access are fair, reasonable, and non-discriminatory. This fee compensates the data holder for their investment in generating the data. Without reasonable remuneration, the recipient would unfairly benefit from the data holder's investments, potentially discouraging data generation. Non-discriminatory access ensures all third-party recipients have equal opportunities, preventing data holders from giving unfair advantages and distorting competition.

Portability rights in the narrower sense establish a three-person relationship. The person who contributed to the data generation has the right to initiate the transfer of the data. At the request of this person, the data controller must transfer the data directly to a third party designated by the rightsholder. Access rights in CGD and access rights in the public interest represent the opposite ends of a spectrum: Rights in CGD primarily serve individual interests, while rights in the public interest primarily benefit society as a whole. Direct portability rights lie in the middle and serve both individual and public interests to varying degrees, depending on the specific legal context. The rightsholder can exercise the right to direct portability free of charge because they have contributed to the generation of the data. The third party receives the data without having contributed to its creation, but compared to access rights in the public interest, their position is weaker as it depends on the actions of the rightsholder whether the third party receives the data. Thus, under some direct portability rights, the third party receives the data free of charge. In most cases, however, the recipient must pay a fee to cover the costs of the data provider's investment.

List of References

'About SWIPO – SWIPO' <https://swipo.eu/about-2/> accessed 11 April 2024

Abrams M, 'The Origins of Personal Data and Its Implications for Governance' [2014] SSRN Electronic Journal <http://www.ssrn.com/abstract=2510927> accessed 11 November 2021

'Account Information Services and Payment Initiation Services' (*Banco de Portugal*) <https://www.bportugal.pt/en/page/account-information-services-and-payment-initiation-services> accessed 27 February 2023

Ackoff R, 'From Data to Wisdom' (1989) 16 Journal of Applied Systems Analysis 3

Ahlborn CE, 'The Logic & Limits of the Exceptional Circumstances Test in Magill and IMS Health European Union' (2004) 28 Fordham Int Law J 1109

Akerlof GA, 'The Market for "Lemons": Quality Uncertainty and the Market Mechanism' (1970) 84 The Quarterly Journal of Economics 488

Akman P, 'Regulating Competition in Digital Platform Markets: A Critical Assessment of the Framework and Approach of the EU Digital Markets Act' (2021) 47 European Law Review 85

Alexy R, *Begriff und Geltung des Rechts* (3rd edn, Karl Alber 2016)

Amstutz M, 'Dateneigentum' (2018) 218 AcP 438

Andriychuk O, 'The Digital Markets Act Proposal: Key Elements & Smart Features' (2022) 43 European Competition Law Review 112

Apel K, *Die kartellrechtliche Zwangslizenz im Lichte des europäischen Wettbewerbsrechts* (Nomos 2015)

Article 29 Working Party, 'Guidelines on the Right to Data Portability' (2016) WP 242 rev.01

Article 29 Working Party, 'Opinion 03/2013 on Purpose Limitation' WP 203

Article 29 Working Party, 'Opinion 4/2007 on the Concept of Personal Data' WP 136

Article 29 Working Party, 'Opinion 05/2014 on Anonymisation Techniques' WP 216

Article 29 Working Party, 'Opinion 06/2014 on the Notion of Legitimate Interests of the Data Controller under Article 7 of Directive 95/46/EC' WP 217

Assion S and Willecke L, 'Der EU Data Act: Die neuen Regelungen zu vernetzten Produkten und Diensten' [2023] MMR 805

Barbero M and others, 'Study on Emerging Issues of Data Ownership, Interoperability, (Re-)Usability and Access to Data, and Liability: Final Report' (Deloitte 2018)

Bar-Hillel Y, 'An Examination of Information Theory' (1955) 22 Philosophy of Science 86

Baschenhof P, 'The Digital Markets Act (DMA): A Procompetitive Recalibration of Data Relations?' [2022] Journal of Law, Technology and Policy 101

Baskarada S and Koronios A, 'Data, Information, Knowledge, Wisdom (DIKW): A Semiotic Theoretical and Empirical Exploration of the Hierarchy and Its Quality Dimension' (2013) 18 Australasian Journal of Information Systems 5

Becker M, 'Lauterkeitsrechtlicher Leistungsschutz für Daten' [2017] GRUR 346

Bezemek C (ed), *Rechtsdogmatik – Stand und Perspektiven* (Manz 2023)

Bishop S and Baldauf M, 'Theoretische Grundlagen und praktische Anwendung wettbewerbsökonomischer Methoden in Bezug auf die Abgrenzung des relevanten Marktes' (RBB Economics 2006)

Blanke H-F and Mangiameli S (eds), *Treaty on the Functioning of the European Union – A Commentary* (Springer 2021)

Bomhard D, 'Auswirkungen des Data Act auf die Geschäftsmodelle von Cloud-Anbietern' [2024] MMR 109

Bomhard D and Merkle M, 'Der Entwurf eines EU Data Acts: Neue Spielregeln für die Data Economy' [2022] RDi 168

Bongartz P and Kirk A, in Rupprecht Podszun (ed), *Digital Markets Act: Gesetz über digitale Märkte* (Nomos 2023)

Borgogno O and Colangelo G, 'Data Sharing and Interoperability: Fostering Innovation and Competition through APIs' (2019) 35 Computer Law & Security Review 1

Borgogno O and Colangelo G, 'Data, Innovation and Competition in Finance: The Case of the Access to Account Rule' [2020] European Business Law Review 573

Bostoen F, 'Understanding the Digital Markets Act' (2023) 68 The Antitrust Bulletin 263

Botta M and Wiedemann K, 'To Discriminate or Not to Discriminate? Personalised Pricing in Online Markets as Exploitative Abuse of Dominance' (2020) 50 European Journal of Law and Economics 381

Breuvart C, Chassaing É and Perraut A-S, 'Big Data and Competition Law in the Digital Sector: Lessons from the European Commission's Merger Control Practice and Recent National Initiatives' [2016] Concurrences 41

Brillouin L, *Scientific Uncertainty, and Information* (Elsevier 1964)

Brink S and Eckhardt J, 'Wann ist ein Datum ein personenbezogenes Datum?' [2015] ZD 205

Broughton Micova S, 'DMA Transparency Requirements in Relation to Advertising' (CERRE 2022)

Buchner B, 'Datenschutz im vernetzten Automobil' (2015) 39 Datenschutz und Datensicherheit 372

Bundeskartellamt, 'Bundeskartellamt Initiates Abuse Proceeding against Amazon' <https://www.bundeskartellamt.de/SharedDocs/Meldung/EN/Pressemitteilungen/2018/29_11_2018_Verfahrenseinleitung_Amazon.html?nn=3591568> accessed 23 August 2023

Bundesministerium der Justiz und für Verbraucherschutz and Max-Planck-Institut für Innovation und Wettbewerb (eds), *Data Access, Consumer Interests and Public Welfare* (Nomos 2021)

Busch C (ed), *Verordnung (EU) 2019/1150 zur Förderung von Fairness und Transparenz für gewerbliche Nutzer von Online-Vermittlungsdiensten (P2B-VO): Kommentar* (Beck 2022)

Bydlinski F, *Juristische Methodenlehre Und Rechtsbegriff* (2nd edn, Verlag Österreich 2011)

Cabral LMB and others, 'The EU Digital Markets Act: A Report from a Panel of Economic Experts' (Joint Research Centre 2021) JRC122910

Caillaud B and Jullien B, 'Chicken & Egg: Competition among Intermediation Service Providers' (2003) 34 RAND Journal of Economics 309

Capurro R, *Information* (Saur 1978)

Carlton DW and Shampine AL, 'An Economic Interpretation of FRAND' (2013) 9 Journal of Competition Law & Economics 531

Cattaneo G and others, 'The European Data Market Monitoring Tool' (IDC & Lisbon Council 2020)

Chaffey D and Wood S, *Business Information Management: Improving Performance Using Information Systems* (Prentice Hall 2005)

Cherednychenko OO, 'Rediscovering the Public/Private Divide in EU Private Law' (2020) 26 European Law Journal 27

Chomsky N, 'Three Models for the Description of Language' (1956) 2 IRE Transactions on Information Theory 113

CIPL, 'Comments by the Centre for Information Policy Leadership on the Article 29 Data Protection Working Party's "Guidelines on the Right to Data Portability" Adopted on 13 December 2016' (2017)

Cliffe A, 'To What Extent Does European Law Ensure a Level Playing Field for Fintechs in the Payment Services Sector?' (2022) 18 European Competition Journal 168

CMA, 'Retail Banking Market Investigation Final Report' (2016)

Colangelo G and Maggiolino M, 'Big Data as Misleading Facilities' (2017) 13 European Competition Journal 249

Competition and Markets Authority, 'Online Platforms and Digital Advertising: Market Study' (2020)

Contreras JL, 'A Brief History of FRAND' (2015) 80 Antitrust Law Journal 39

Cotter T, 'The Essential Facilities Doctrine' [2008] SSRN Electronic Journal <https://ssrn.com/abstract=1125368> accessed 9 March 2022

Craig P and de Búrca G (eds) *The Evolution of EU Law* (3rd edn, OUP)

Crémer J and others, 'Fairness and Contestability in the Digital Markets Act' (2021) 3 Digital Regulation Project – Policy Discussion Paper

Crémer J, de Montjoye Y-A and Schweitzer H, 'Competition Policy for the Digital Era' (2019)

Damien Geradin, 'Limiting the Scope of Article 82 EC: What Can the EU Learn from the U.S. Supreme Court's Judgment in Trinko in the Wake of Microsoft, IMS, and Deutsche Telekom' (2004) 41 Common Market Law Review 1519

Daskalova V, 'Consumer Welfare in EU Competition Law: What Is It (Not) About?' (2015) 11 Competition Law Review 131

Data Governance Working Group, 'A Framework Paper for GPAI's Work on Data Governance' (GPAI 2020)

Data Governance Working Group, 'The Role of Data in AI' (GPAI 2020)

Datenethikkommission' 'Gutachten der Datenethikkommission' (Bundesministerium des Innern, für Bau und Heimat; Bundesministerium der Justiz und für Verbraucherschutz 2019)

David Ritchie, *Information* (Sage Publications 1991)

de la Mano M and Padilla J, *'Big Tech Banking'* (2018) 14 Journal of Competition Law and Economics 494

De Franceschi A (ed), *European Contract Law and the Digital Single Market* (Intersentia 2016)

De Franceschi A and Schulze R (eds), *Digital Revolution – New Challenges for Law: Data Protection, Artificial Intelligence, Smart Products, Blockchain Technology and Virtual Currencies* (Beck; Nomos 2019)

De Streel A and others, 'Making the Digital Markets Act More Resilient and Effective' (CERRE 2021) <https://cerre.eu/publications/european-parliament-digital-markets-act-dma-resilient-effective/> accessed 16 October 2023

De Streel A and others, 'Effective and Proportionate Implementation of the DMA' (CERRE 2023)

Demary M and Rusche C, 'Strengthened Competition in Payment Services'

Demary V and Rusche C, 'The Economics of Platforms' (Institut der deutschen Wirtschaft 2018) IW-Analysen, No. 123

Demary V and Rusche C, 'Data Sharing im E-Commerce: Rechtliche und ökonomische Grundlagen' (Institut der deutschen Wirtschaft 2019)

Denker and others '„Eigentumsordnung" für Mobilitätsdaten?' (Bundesministerium für Verkehr und digitale Infrastruktur 2017) <https://www.uni-kassel.de/fb07/index.php?eID=dumpFile&t=f&f=4043&token=5408d0e9eac3fa0fda9271f06e5d67cc84b646e8>

Derclaye E, 'Eudemonic Intellectual Property: Patents and Related Rights as Engines of Happiness, Peace, and Sustainability' (2012) 14 Vanderbilt Journal of Entertainment & Technology Law 495

Determann L, 'No One Owns Data' (2018) 70 Hastings Law Journal 1

Deuring S, *Datenmacht: Zugang als Herausforderung* (Nomos 2021)

Dewenter R, Rösch J and Terschüren A, 'Abgrenzung zweiseitiger Märkte am Beispiel von Internetsuchmaschinen' [2014] NZKart 367

Dewenter R and Lüth H, 'Datenhandel und Platformen' (ABIDA – ASSESSING BIG DATA 2018)

Di Porto F and Ghidini G, '"I Access Your Data, You Access Mine": Requiring Data Reciprocity in Payment Services' [2020] International Review of Intellectual Property and Competition Law 307

'DMA Designated Gatekeepers' <https://digital-markets-act.ec.europa.eu/gatekeepers_en> accessed 21 April 2024

Dommering EJ and Hugenholtz PB, *Protecting Works of Fact* (Springer 1991)

Drexl J, 'Intellectual Property and Antitrust Law IMS Health and Trinko – Antitrust Placebo for Consumers Instead of Sound Economics in Refusal-to-Deal Cases' (2004) 35 International Review of Intellectual Property and Competition Law 788

Drexl J, 'Designing Competitive Markets for Industrial Data – Between Propertisation and Access' (2017) 8 JIPITEC 257

Drexl J, 'Neue Regeln für die Europäische Datenwirtschaft? (Part 1)' [2017] NZKart 339

Drexl J, 'Neue Regeln für die Europäische Datenwirtschaft? (Part 2)' [2017] NZKart 415

Drexl J, 'Data Access and Control in the Era of Connected Devices' (BEUC 2018)

Drexl J, 'Position Statement of the Max Planck Institute for Innovation and Competition of 26 April 2017 on the European Commission's "Public Consultation on Building the European Data Economy"' (Max Planck Institute 2017)

Drexl J, 'Position Statement of the Max Planck Institute for Innovation and Competition of 25 May 2022 on the Commission's Proposal of 23 February 2022 for a Regulation on Harmonised Rules on Fair Access to and Use of Data (Data Act)' (2022) <https://www.ip.mpg.de/fileadmin/ipmpg/content/stellungnahmen/Position_Statement_MPI_Data_Act_Formal__13.06.2022.pdf> accessed 2 January 2024

Druey JN, *Information als Gegenstand des Rechts : Entwurf einer Grundlegung* (Schulthess, Nomos 1995)

Duch-Brown N, Martens B and Mueller-Langer F, 'The Economics of Ownership, Access and Trade in Digital Data' (2017) Digital Economy Working Paper 2017–01

EDPB, 'Guidelines 01/2022 on Data Subject Rights – Right of Access' (2023)

EDPS, 'Privacy and Competitiveness in the Age of Big Data: The Interplay between Data Protection, Competition Law and Consumer Protection in the Digital Economy' (2014) <https://edps.europa.eu/sites/edp/files/publication/14-03-26_competititi on_law_big_data_en.pdf.>

EDPS, 'Comments of the EDPS on a Proposal for a Regulation of the European Parliament and of the Council on a Framework for the Free-Flow of Non-Personal Data in the European Union' (2018)

EDPS, 'Opinion 2/2021 on the Proposal for a Digital Markets Act' (2021)

Ehmann E and Selmayr M (eds), *DS-GVO: Datenschutz-Grundverordnung: Kommentar* (2nd edn, Beck 2018)

Ehlermann C-D and Atanasiu I (eds), *European Competition Law Annual 2005: The Interaction Between Competition Law and Intellectual Property Law* (Hart Publishing 2007)

Elfering S, *Unlocking the Right to Data Portability* (Nomos 2019)

Hagemann E, 'Essential Facilities, Essential Patents, and the Essential Oversight of Qualcomm' [2021] SSRN Electronic Journal <https://papers.ssrn.com/sol3/papers.cfm?abstract_id=3893771>

Etteldorf C, 'DMA – Digital Markets Act or Data Markets Act?' (2022) 8 European Data Protection Law Review 255

European Banking Authority, 'Draft Regulatory Technical Standards on Strong Customer Authentication and Common and Secure Communication under Article 98 of Directive 2015/2366' (2017) EBA/RTS/2017/02

European Banking Authority, 'Opinion on the Amended Text of the RTS on SCA and CSC' (2017) EBA-Op-2017–09

European Chemicals Agency, 'Guidance on Data-Sharing' (2017)

Evans D and Schmalensee R, *Matchmakers: The New Economics of Multisided Platforms* (Harvard Business Review Press 2016)

EY, 'Study on the Economic Detriment to Small and Medium-Sized Enterprises Arising from Unfair and Unbalanced Cloud Computing Contracts' (European Commission 2018)

Ezrachi A and Maggiolino M, 'European Competition Law, Compulsory Licensing, and Innovation' (2012) 8 Journal of Competition Law and Economics 595

Farmelo G (ed), *It Must be Beautiful: Great Equations of Modern Science* (Granta 2002)

Feasey R and De Streel A, 'Data Sharing for Digital Markets Contestability' (CERRE 2020)

Fiedler H and Ullrich H (eds), *Information als Wirtschaftsgut* (Otto Schmidt 1997)

Filistrucchi L and others, 'Market Definition in Two-Sided Markets: Theory and Practice' (2014) 10 Journal of Competition Law & Economics 293

Franz B and Podszun R, 'Nach Huawei/ZTE: Die kartellrechtliche Zwangslizenz im Patentverletzungsprozess' (2017) 15 205

Forgó N and Krügel T, 'Der Personenbezug von Geodaten' [2010] MMR 17

Funk A, 'Das Prinzip der Nutzerzentriertheit des Data Act – ein gravierender Strukturfehler — Untersuchung und Bewertung der zentralen Rolle des Nutzers in der Datenökonomie nach der Konzeption des Data Act.' (2023) 39 Computer und Recht 421

Furman J and others, 'Unlocking Digital Competition: Report of the Digital Competition Expert Panel' (HM Treasury 2019)

G8, 'Open Data Charter' (2013)

Gal M and Rubinfeld D, 'Data Standardization' (2019) 94 New York University Law Review 737

Geiregat S, 'The Data Act: Start of a New Era for Data Ownership?' [2022] SSRN Electronic Journal <https://www.ssrn.com/abstract=4214704> accessed 8 April 2024

Geradin D, Bania K and Karanikioti T, 'The Interplay between the Digital Markets Act and the General Data Protection Regulation' [2022] SSRN Electronic Journal <https://www.ssrn.com/abstract=4203907> accessed 22 June 2023

Gerpott T, 'Vorschlag für ein europäisches Datengesetz — Überblick und Analyse der Vorgaben für vernetzte Produkte' (2022) 38 Computer und Recht 271

Gill D and Metzger J, 'Data Access Through Data Portability' (2022) 8 European Data Protection Law Review 221

Gola P and Heckmann D (eds), *Datenschutz-Grundverordnung, Bundesdatenschutzgesetz: DS-GVO / BDSG* (3rd edn, Beck 2022)

Graef I, 'Market Definition and Market Power in Data: The Case of Online Platforms' (2015) 38 World Competition 473

Graef I, *EU Competition Law, Data Protection and Online Platforms: Data as Essential Facility* (Kluwer 2016)

Graef I, 'Rethinking the Essential Facilities Doctrine for the EU Digital Economy' [2019] SSRN Electronic Journal <https://papers.ssrn.com/sol3/papers.cfm?abstract_id=3371457> accessed 24 June 2022

Graef I, Gellert R and Husovec M, 'Towards a Holistic Regulatory Approach for the European Data Economy' [2018] SSRN Electronic Journal <https://www.ssrn.com/abstract=3256189> accessed 9 November 2021

Graef I, Husovec M and Purtova N, 'Data Portability and Data Control: Lessons for an Emerging Concept in EU Law' (2018) 19 German Law Journal 1359

Graef I, Husovec M and van den Boom J, 'Spill-Overs in Data Governance: The Relationship Between the GDPR's Right to Data Portability and EU Sector-Specific Data Access Regimes' [2020] EuCML 3

Graef I, Tombal T and De Streel A, 'Limits and Enablers of Data Sharing. An Analytical Framework for EU Competition, Data Protection and Consumer Law' [2019] SSRN Electronic Journal <https://www.ssrn.com/abstract=3494212> accessed 20 April 2020

Graef I, Verschakelen J and Valcke P, 'Putting the Right to Data Portability into a Competition Law Perspective' [2013] Law: The Journal of the Higher School of Economics, Annual Review 53

Graef I, Wahyuningtyas SY and Valcke P, 'Assessing Data Access Issues in Online Platforms' (2015) 39 Telecommunications Policy 375

Grant N, 'Google Calls In Help From Larry Page and Sergey Brin for A.I. Fight' *The New York Times* (20 January 2023) <https://www.nytimes.com/2023/01/20/technology/google-chatgpt-artificial-intelligence.html> accessed 16 October 2023

Grapentin S, 'Datenzugangsansprüche und Geschäftsgeheimnisse der Hersteller im Lichte des Data Act' [2023] RDi 173

Grinlinton D and Taylor P (eds), *Property Rights and Sustainability* (Brill, Nijhoff 2011)

Grothe N, *Datenmacht in der kartellrechtlichen Missbrauchskontrolle* (Nomos 2019) <https://www.nomos-elibrary.de/index.php?doi=10.5771/9783748903437> accessed 13 May 2021

Grundmann S and Mazeaud D (eds), *General clauses and standards in European contract law: comparative law, EC law and contract law codification* (Kluwer 2006)

Gumm H and Sommer M, *Einführung in die Informatik* (9th edn, De Gruyter Oldenbourg 2011)

Habich E, 'FRAND Access to Data: Perspectives from the FRAND Licensing of Standard-Essential Patents for the Data Act Proposal and the Digital Markets Act' (2022) 53 International Review of Intellectual Property and Competition Law 1343

Hacker P, Cordes J and Rochon J, 'Regulating Gatekeeper AI and Data: Transparency, Access, and Fairness under the DMA, the GDPR, and Beyond' <https://arxiv.org/abs/2212.04997> accessed 3 May 2023

Harbour PJ and Koslov TI, 'Section 2 In A Web 2.0 World: An Expanded Vision of Relevant Product Markets' (2010) 76 Antitrust Law Journal 769

Hauck R, „Erzwungene" Lizenzverträge – Kartellrechtliche Grenzen der Durchsetzung standardessenzieller Patente' [2015] NJW 2767

Heath G, 'Origins of the Binary Code' (1972) 227 Scientific American 76

Heim M and Nikolic I, 'A FRAND Regime for Dominant Digital Platforms' (2019) 10 JIPITEC 38

Heldrich A and others (eds), *Festschrift für Claus-Wilhelm Canaris zum 70. Geburtstag* (Beck 2007)

Hellwege P, 'It Is Necessary to Strictly Distinguish Two Forms of Fairness Control!' [2015] EuCML 129

Hennemann M and Sattler A (eds), *Immaterialgüter und Digitalisierung: Junge Wissenschaft zum Gewerblichen Rechtsschutz, Urheber- und Medienrecht*, vol 2 (1st edn, Nomos 2017)

Hennemann M and Steinrötter B, 'Data Act – Fundament des neuen EU-Datenwirtschaftsrechts?' [2022] NJW 1481

Hennemann M and others (eds), *The Data Act Proposal – Literature Review and Critical Analysis* (University of Passau Institute for Law of the Digital Society 2023)

Herbers B, 'Der Digital Markets Act (DMA) kommt – neue Dos and Don'ts für Gatekeeper in der Digitalwirtschaft' [2022] RDi 252

Hesselink MW, 'Private Law, Regulation, and Justice' (2016) 22 European Law Journal 681

Heuzeroth T, 'Spotify: Hier versagt die DSGVO' (*Die Welt*) <https://www.welt.de/wirtschaft/webwelt/article176720143/Spotify-Hier-versagt-die-DSGVO.html> accessed 22 January 2023

Hilty R and Liu K-C (eds), *Compulsory Licensing* (2015)

Hoeren T, 'Dateneigentum. Versuch einer Anwendung von § 303a StGB im Zivilrecht' [2013] MMR 491

Hornkohl L, 'Article 102 TFEU, Equal Treatment and Discrimination after Google Shopping' (2022) 13 Journal of European Competition Law & Practice 99

Hornung G and Goeble T, '„Data Ownership" im vernetzten Automobil' (2015) 31 Die rechtliche Analyse des wirtschaftlichenWerts von Automobildaten und ihr Beitrag zum besseren Verständnis der Informationsordnung 265

Hou L, 'The Essential Facilities Doctrine: What Was Wrong in Microsoft?' (2012) 43 International Review of Intellectual Property and Competition Law 451

Hu K, 'ChatGPT Sets Record for Fastest-Growing User Base – Analyst Note' *Reuters* (2 February 2023) <https://www.reuters.com/technology/chatgpt-sets-record-fastest-growing-user-base-analyst-note-2023-02-01/> accessed 16 October 2023

Idot L, 'The Future of Regulation No. 1/2003: New Relations Between EU and National Laws' (2020) 11 Journal of European Competition Law & Practice 409

Jabloner C and others (eds), *Vom praktischen Wert der Methode, Festschrift für Heinz Mayer zum 65. Geburtstag* (Manz 2011)

Jaeger T and Stöger K (eds), *EUV/AEUV*

Jahnel D, Mader P and Staudegger E (eds), *Handbuch IT-Recht* (Verlag Österreich 2020)

Janal R, 'Data Portability – A Tale of Two Concepts' (2017) 8 JIPITEC 59

Janal R, 'Data Portability under the GDPR: A Blueprint for Access Rights?' in Bundesministerium der Justiz und für Verbraucherschutz and Max-Planck-Institut für Innovation und Wettbewerb (eds), *Data Access, Consumer Interests and Public Welfare* (Nomos 2021)

Japanese Ministry of Economy, Trade and Industry (METI), 'Contract Guidelines on Utilization of AI and Data: Data Section' (2018)

Jeffery Atik, 'The FRAND Ceremony and the Engagement of Article 102 TFEU in the Licensing of Standard Essential Patents' (2019) 42 Fordham Int Law J 949

Jenkins B, 'Why Cloud Data Egress Is Expensive' (*The New Stack*, 15 November 2022) <https://thenewstack.io/why-cloud-data-egress-is-expensive/> accessed 11 April 2024

Jülicher T, Röttgen C and v Schönfeld M, 'Das Recht auf Datenübertragbarkeit – Ein datenschutzrechtliches Novum' [2016] ZD 356

Kapusta I, 'Pflichten von Gatekeepern im Digital Markets Act' (2023) 20 83

Karbaum C and Schulz M, '„Antitrust Litigation 2.0" – Private Enforcement beim DMA?' [2022] NZKart 107

Kathuria V and Globocnik J, 'Exclusionary Conduct in Data-Driven Markets: Limitations of Data Sharing Remedy' (2020) 8 Journal of Antitrust Enforcement 511

Katja Langenbucher, 'Argument by Analogy in European Law' (1998) 57 The Cambridge Law Journal 481

Kerber W, 'A New (Intellectual) Property Right for Non-Personal Data? An Economic Analysis' [2016] GRUR International 989

Kerber W, 'Governance of Data: Exclusive Property vs. Access' (2016) 47 International Review of Intellectual Property and Competition Law 759

Kerber W, 'Updating Competition Policy for the Digital Economy? An Analysis of Recent Reports in Germany, UK, EU, and Australia' [2019] SSRN Electronic Journal <https://www.ssrn.com/abstract=3469624>

Kerber W, 'Datenrechtliche Aspekte des Digital Markets Act – Datenwirtschaftsrecht I: Vorschlag einer Ex-ante-Regulierung von Gatekeeper-Plattformen' [2021] ZD 544

Kerber W, 'Governance of IoT Data: Why the EU Data Act Will Not Fulfill Its Objectives' (2023) 72 GRUR International 120

Kerber W and Gill D, 'Access to Data in Connected Cars and the Recent Reform of the Motor Vehicle Type Approval Regulation' (2019) 10 JIPITEC 244

Khan L, 'Amazon's Antitrust Paradox' (2017) 126 Yale Law Journal 710

Khan LM, 'The Seperation of Platforms and Commerce' (2019) 119 Columbia Law Review 973

Kim D, 'No One's Ownership as the Status Quo and a Possible Way Forward: A Note on the Public Consultation on Building a European Data Economy' (2018) 13 Journal of Intellectual Property Law & Practice 154

Kiskyte A, 'What Is Payment Initiation Service (PIS)?' (*Kevin.*, 15 April 2022) <https://www.kevin.eu/blog/payment-initiation-service/> accessed 27 February 2023

Kloepfer M, *Informationsrecht* (Beck 2002)

König C, in Björn Steinrötter (ed), *Europäische Plattformregulierung: DSA, DMA, P2B-VO, DGA, DA, AI Act, DSM-RL* (Nomos 2023)

Körber T, 'Konzeptionelle Erfassung digitaler Plattformen und adäquate Regulierungsstrategien' [2017] ZUM 93

Körber T, Schweitzer H and Zimmer D (eds), *Immenga/Mestmäcker Wettbewerbsrecht* (6th edn, Beck 2019)

Konstantina Bania, 'Fitting the Digital Markets Act in the Existing Legal Framework: The Myth of the "without Prejudice" Clause' (2023) 19 European Competition Journal 116

Kötz H, *European Contract Law* (2nd edn, Oxford University Press 2017)

Kralj JM and others, 'Optical Recording of Action Potentials in Mammalian Neurons Using a Microbial Rhodopsin' (2012) 9 Nature Methods 90

Krämer J, Senellart P and De Streel A, 'Making Data Portability More Effective for the Digital Economy' (CERRE 2020)

Krause R, 'Meet The New Digital Conglomerates: Google, Facebook, Amazon ... And Apple? | Stock News & Stock Market Analysis – IBD' (*Investor's Business Daily*, 11 June 2016) <https://www.investors.com/news/technology/google-facebook-amazon-apple-digital-conglomerates/> accessed 15 January 2022

Kuebler-Wachendorff S and others, 'The Right to Data Portability: Conception, Status Quo, and Future Directions' (2021) 44 Informatik Spektrum 264

Kühling J and Buchner B (eds), *Datenschutz-Grundverordnung/BDSG: Kommentar* (2nd edn, Beck 2018)

Kühling J and Martini M, 'Die Datenschutz-Grundverordnung: Revolution oder Evolution im europäischen und deutschen Datenschutzrecht?' [2016] EuZW 448

Kuner C and others (eds), *The EU General Data Protection Regulation (GDPR): A Commentary* (Oxford University Press 2020)

Lagoni J, 'Cloud Switching gemäß Data Act: Die Abschaffung von Switching Charges — Was ist ein Wechselentgelt und welche Wechsel sind betroffen?' (2024) 40 Computer und Recht 91

Lambrecht A and Tucker C, 'Can Big Data Protect a Firm from Competition?' [2015] SSRN Electronic Journal <https://ssrn.com/abstract=2705530> accessed 20 April 2022

Larenz K, *Methodenlehre der Rechtswissenschaft* (6th edn, Springer 2013)

Lawrance S and Peirson L, 'The General Court's 2012 Microsoft Judgment: "Reasonable" Fines and "Reasonable" Licence Fees' (2013) 8 Journal of Intellectual Property Law & Practice 236

Le N, 'What Does "Capable of Eliminating All Competition" Mean?' (2005) 26 European Competition Law Review 6

Leistner M and Antoine L, 'IPR and the Use of Open Data and Data Sharing Initiatives by Public and Private Actors' (European Parliament 2022) <https://www.europarl.europa.eu/thinktank/en/document/IPOL_STU(2022)732266> accessed 2 January 2024

Lenaerts A, 'The General Principle of the Prohibition of Abuse of Rights: A Critical Position on Its Role in a Codified European Contract Law' [2010] European Review of Private Law 1121

Lerner AV, 'The Role of "Big Data" in Online Platform Competition' [2014] SSRN Electronic Journal <http://www.ssrn.com/abstract=2482780> accessed 15 January 2022

Lévêque F, 'Innovation, Leveraging and Essential Facilities: Interoperability Licensing in the Microsoft Case' (2005) 28 World Competition 71

Lim Y, 'Tech Wars: Return of the Conglomerate – Throwback or Dawn of a New Series for Competition in the Digital Era?' (2017) 19 Journal of Korean Law 47

Lipsky A and Sidak G, 'Essential Facilities' (1998) 51 Stan L Rev 1187

Liu K-C, 'Rationalising the Regime of Compulsory Patent Licensing by the Essential Facilities Doctrine' (2008) 39 International Review of Intellectual Property and Competition Law 757

Lobinger T, 'Perspektiven der Privatrechtsdogmatik am Beispiel des allgemeinen Gleichbehandlungsrechts' (2016) 216 Archiv für die civilistische Praxis 28

Loewenheim U and others (eds), *Kartellrecht: Kommentar zum deutschen und europäischen Recht* (4th edn, Beck 2020)

Lohsse S, Schulze R and Staudenmayer D (eds), *Trading Data in the Digital Economy: Legal Concepts and Tools: Münster Colloquia on EU Law and the Digital Economy III* (Nomos; Hart Publishing 2017)

Lohsse S, Schulze R and Staudenmayer D (eds), *Private Law and the Data Act: Münster Colloquia on EU Law and the Digital Economy VIII* (Nomos (forthcoming))

Louven S, 'Braucht es mehr materielles Kartellrecht für digitale Plattformen?' (2019) 17 ZWeR 154

Louven S, 'Vorschriften im Data Act zur Ausgestaltung und Kompensation von Datenbereitstellungspflichten' [2024] MMR 82

Lundqvist B, 'Cloud Services as the Ultimate Gate(Keeper)' (2019) 7 Journal of Antitrust Enforcement 220

Lundqvist B, 'An Access and Transfer Right to Data—from a Competition Law Perspective' [2022] Journal of Antitrust Enforcement 1

Lundqvist B, 'Study on the Digital Services Act and Digital Markets Act and Their Possible Impact on Research.' (European Commission 2022) <https://data.europa.eu/doi/10.2777/751853> accessed 31 May 2023

Lynn T and others (eds), *Disrupting Finance: FinTech and Strategy in the 21st Century* (Springer 2019)

Martens B, 'An Economic Policy Perspective on Online Platforms' (Joint Research Centre 2016)

Martens B, 'Business-to-Business Data Sharing: An Economic and Legal Analysis' (Joint Research Centre 2020)

Martin S, *Bits, Bytes, and Big Brother: Federal Information Control in the Technological Age* (Praeger 1995)

Ménière Y, 'Fair, Reasonable and Non-Discriminatory (FRAND) Licensing Terms: Research Analysis of a Controversial Concept.' (Joint Research Centre 2015) JRC 96258

Metz C and Grant N, 'Racing to Catch Up With ChatGPT, Google Plans Release of Its Own Chatbot' *The New York Times* (6 February 2023) <https://www.nytimes.com/2023/02/06/technology/google-bard-ai-chatbot.html> accessed 16 October 2023

Metzger A and Schweitzer H, 'Shaping Markets: A Critical Evaluation of the Draft Data Act' [2023] ZEuP 42

Micklitz H-W, 'Europäisches Regulierungsprivatrecht: Plädoyer für ein neues Denken' (2009) 6 Zeitschrift für Gemeinschaftsprivatrecht 254

Micklitz H-W, 'The Transformation of Private Law Through Competition' (2016) 22 European Law Journal 627

Micklitz H-W, 'The Visible Hand of European Regulatory Private Law' (European University Institute) Law Working Papers 2008/14

Monopolkommission, 'Wettbewerbspolitik: Herausforderung digitale Märkte' (2015) Sondergutachten 68

Moreno Belloso N and Petit N, 'The EU Digital Markets Act (DMA): A Competition Hand in a Regulatory Glove' [2023] SSRN Electronic Journal <https://www.ssrn.com/abstract=4358589> accessed 4 September 2023

Morris C, *Signs, Language, and Behavior*, vol 56 (Prentice-Hall 1946)

Narayanan A and Shmatikov V, 'How to Break Anonymity of the Netflix Prize Dataset' (2006) abs/cs/0610105 CoRR <http://arxiv.org/abs/cs/0610105>

Neil Cohen and Christiane Wendehorst, 'Principles for a Data Economy (ELI Final Council Draft)' (ALI/ELI 2021) <https://www.principlesforadataeconomy.org/fileadmin/user_upload/p_principlesforadataeconomy/Files/Principles_for_a_Data_Economy_ELI_Final_Council_Draft.pdf>

Neil Cohen and Christiane Wendehorst, 'Principles for a Data Economy' (ALI/ELI 2023) <https://europeanlawinstitute.eu/fileadmin/user_upload/p_eli/Publications/ALI-ELI_Principles_for_a_Data_Economy.pdf>

Newman N, 'Search, Antitrust, and the Economics of the Control of User Data' (2014) 30 Yale Journal on Regulation 401

Nimmer RT and Krauthaus PA, 'Information as a Commodity: New Imperatives of Commercial Law' (1992) 55 Law and Contemporary Problems 103

Nöth W, *Handbook of Semiotics* (Indiana University Press 1990)

Notter M and others (eds), *Europäische Idee und Integration – mittendrin und nicht dabei? liber amicorum für Andreas Kellerhals* (Schulthess 2018)

OECD, 'Recommendation of the Council for Enhanced Access and More Effective Use of Public Sector Information' (2008)

OECD, 'Data-Driven Innovation: Big Data for Growth and Well-Being' (2015)

OECD, 'Enhancing Access to and Sharing of Data: Reconciling Risks and Benefits for Data Re-Use across Societies' (2019)

Paal B and Pauly D (eds), *Datenschutz-Grundverordnung* (3rd edn, Beck 2021)

Paal B and Hennemann M, 'Big Data as an Asset' (ABIDA – ASSESSING BIG DATA 2018)

Pahlen-Brandt I, 'Datenschutz braucht scharfe Instrumente Beitrag zur Diskussion um „personenbezogene Daten"' (2008) 32 DuD 34

Pepper P, *Grundlagen Der Informatik* (2nd edn, R Oldenbourg 2018)

Petit N, 'Technology Giants, the Moligopoly Hypothezis and Holistic Competition: A Primer' [2016] SSRN Electronic Journal <https://www.ssrn.com/abstract=2856502> accessed 14 January 2022

Petit N, 'The Proposed Digital Markets Act (DMA): A Legal and Policy Review' (2021) 12 Journal of European Competition Law & Practice 529

Pertot T, Schmidt-Kessel M and Padovini F (eds), *Rechte an Daten* (Mohr Siebeck 2020)

Picht PG, 'Caught in the Acts: Framing Mandatory Data Access Transactions under the Data Act, Further EU Digital Regulation Acts, and Competition Law' (Max Planck Institute for Innovation and Competition Research Paper No 22–12 2022) <https://papers.ssrn.com/sol3/papers.cfm?abstract_id=4076842>

Piltz C and Zwerschke J, 'Cloud Switching nach dem Data Act aus der Beratungsperspektive' (2024) 40 Computer und Recht 153

Pitofsky R, Patterson D and Hooks J, 'The Essential Facilities Doctrine under United States Antitrust Law' (2002) 70 Antitrust LJ 443

Podszun R, *Handwerk in der digitalen Ökonomie: Rechtlicher Rahmen für den Zugang zu Daten, Software und Plattformen*, vol 5 (Nomos 2021)

Podszun R, 'Should Gatekeepers Be Allowed to Combine Data? – Ideas for Art. 5(a) of the Draft Digital Markets Act' [2021] SSRN Electronic Journal <https://www.ssrn.com/abstract=3860030> accessed 18 October 2023

Podszun R, *Der EU Data Act und der Zugang zu Sekundärmärkten am Beispiel des Handwerks* (Nomos 2023)

Podszun R (ed), *Digital Markets Act: Gesetz über digitale Märkte* (Nomos 2023)

Podszun R, Bongartz P and Kirk A, 'Digital Markets Act – Neue Regeln für Fairness in der Plattformökonomie' NJW 3249

Podszun R and Pfeifer C, 'Datenzugang nach dem EU Data Act: Der Entwurf der Europäischen Kommission' [2022] GRUR 953

Pohlmann T and Blind K, 'Landscaping Study on Standard Essential Patents' (European Commission 2016)

Polley R and Konrad FA, 'Der Digital Markets Act – Brüssels neues Regulierungskonzept für Digitale Märkte' [2021] Wirtschaft und Wettbewerb 198

Posner E and Weyl G, 'Property Is Only Another Name for Monopoly' (2017) 9 Journal of Legal Analysis 51

Prüfer J and Schottmüller C, 'Competing with Big Data' [2017] SSRN Electronic Journal <http://www.ssrn.com/abstract=2918726> accessed 10 October 2023

Raiffenstein M and Blaschek B (eds), *Konsumentenpolitisches Jahrbuch* (Verlag Österreich 2023)

Reich N (ed), *General Principles of EU Civil Law* (Intersentia 2013)

Richter H and Slowinski PR, 'The Data Sharing Economy: On the Emergence of New Intermediaries' (2019) 50 International Review of Intellectual Property and Competition Law 4

Riesenhuber K (ed), *European Legal Methodology* (2nd edn, Intersentia 2021)

Roßnagel A, Richter P, and Maxi Nebel, 'Besserer Internetdatenschutz für Europa: Vorschläge zur Spezifizierung der DS-GVO' [2013] ZD 103

Rousseva E, *Rethinking Exclusionary Abuses in EU Competition Law* (Hart 2010)

Rowley J, 'The Wisdom Hierarchy: Representations of the DIKW Hierarchy' (2007) 33 Journal of Information Science 163

Rubinfeld D and Gal M, 'Access Barriers to Big Data' (2017) 59 Arizona Law Review 339

Rücker D and Kugler T (eds), *New European General Data Protection Regulation: A Practitioner's Guide* (Nomos 2017)

Sachs U, 'Datenschutzrechtliche Bestimmbarkeit von IP-Adressen' (2010) 26 CR 547

Schillig M, in James Devenney and Mel B Kenny (eds), *The transformation of European private law : harmonisation, consolidation, codification or chaos?* (Cambridge University Press 2013)

Schmid CU, 'The Instrumentalist Conception of the Acquis Communautaire in Consumer Law and Its Implications on A European Contract Law Code' (2005) 1 211

Schmidt S, 'Daten als Zugangsobjekt: Braucht es ein "Daten für alle"-Gesetz?' [2018] Wirtschaft und Wettbewerb 549

Schmidt S, *Zugang zu Daten nach europäischem Kartellrecht* (Mohr Siebeck 2020)

Schmidt-Kessel M, 'Heraus- und Weitergabe von IoT-Gerätedaten' [2024] MMR 75

Schmitt S and Wissner M, 'Die Liberalisierung des Messwesens – Verhindert das Abrechnungsentgelt freien Wettbewerb?' (2015) 39 Zeitschrift für Energiewirtschaft 171

Schnurr D, 'Switching and Interoperability between Data Processing Services in the Proposed Data Act' (CERRE 2022)

Schulze R (ed), *Auslegung europäischen Privatrechts und angeglichenen Rechts* (Nomos 1999)

Schulze R and Staudenmayer D (eds), *EU Digital Law: Article-by-Article Commentary* (First edition, Beck, Hart, Nomos 2020)

Schumann E (ed), *Das erziehende Gesetz* (De Gruyter 2014)

Schur N, *Die Lizenzierung von Daten* (Mohr Siebeck 2020)

Schwamberger S, 'Die Klauselkontrolle in Art. 13 Data Act' [2024] MMR 96

Schwartmann R and Weiß S (eds), 'Whitepaper zur Pseudonymisierung' (Fokusgruppe Datenschutz des Digital-Gipfels 2017)

Schwartmann R and others (eds), *DS-GVO/BDSG: Datenschutz-Grundverordnung, Bundesdatenschutzgesetz (Heidelberger Kommentar)* (2nd edn, CF Müller 2020)

Schweitzer H, 'Datenzugang in der Datenökonomie: Eckpfeiler einer neuen Informationsordnung' [2019] GRUR 569

Schweitzer H, 'Modernisierung der Missbrauchsaufsicht für marktmächtige Unternehmen' (Bundesministeriums für Wirtschaft und Energie 2018)

Schweitzer H and Mestmäcker E-J, *Europäisches Wettbewerbsrecht* (3rd edn, Beck 2014)

Schweitzer H and Metzger A, 'Data Access under the Draft Data Act, Competition Law and the DMA: Opening the Data Treasures for Cowmpetition and Innovation?' (2023) 72 GRUR International 337

Schweitzer H and Peitz M, 'Datenmärkte in der digitalisierten Wirtschaft: Funktionsdefizite und Regelungsbedarf?' (Zentrum für Europäische Wirtschaftsforschung 2017) Discussion Paper 17–043

Shannon C and Weaver W, *The Mathematical Theory of Communication* (14. [print.], Univ of Illinois Press 1949)

Sidak G, 'Fair and Unfair Discrimination in Royalties for Standard-Essential Patents Encumbered by a FRAND or RAND Commitment' (2017) 2 Criterion Journal on Innovation 301

Sieber U, 'Informationsrecht und Recht der Informationstechnik – Die Konstituierung eines Rechtsgebietes in Gegenstand, Grundfragen und Zielen' [1989] NJW 2569

Simitis S, Hornung G and Spiecker I (eds), *Datenschutzrecht: DSGVO mit BDSG* (Nomos 2019)

Sokol D and Blair R (eds), *The Cambridge Handbook of Antitrust, Intellectual Property, and High Tech* (Cambridge University Press 2017)

Specht L, 'Ausschließlichkeitsrechte an Daten – Notwendigkeit, Schutzumfang, Alternativen' (2016) 32 Computer und Recht 288

Specht-Riemenschneider L, 'Data Act – Auf dem (Holz-)Weg zu mehr Dateninnovation?' [2022] ZRP 137

Specht-Riemenschneider L, 'Der Entwurf des Data Act: Eine Analyse der vorgesehenen Datenzugangsansprüche im Verhältnis B2B, B2C und B2G' [2022] MMR 809

Spiecker gen. Döhmann I, Papakōnstantinu E and Hornung E (eds), *General data protection regulation: article-by-article commentary* (Beck, Hart, Nomos 2023)

Staudenmayer D, 'Der Verordnungsvorschlag der Europäischen Kommission zum Datengesetz – Auf dem Weg zum Privatrecht der Datenwirtschaft' [2022] EuZW 596

Staudenmayer D, 'Der Verordnungsvorschlag der Europäischen Kommission zum Datengesetz – Privatrechtsregeln für Datenzugangsrechte' [2022] EuZW 1037

Steinrötter B (ed), *Europäische Plattformregulierung: DSA, DMA, P2B-VO, DGA, DA, AI Act, DSM-RL: Rechtshandbuch* (Nomos 2023)

Steinrötter B, 'Verhältnis von Data Act und DS-GVO' [2023] GRUR 216

Strubel M, 'Anwendungsbereich des Rechts auf Datenübertragbarkeit' [2017] ZD 355

Surblyte G, 'Data as a Digital Resource' [2016] SSRN Electronic Journal <http://www.ssrn.com/abstract=2849303> accessed 17 April 2020

Svetiev Y and Comparato G (eds), *EUI Working Papers: European Regulatory Private Law – The Paradigms Tested* (European University Institute 2014)

The Netherlands Authority for Consumers & Markets, 'Fintechs in the Payment System: The Risk of Foreclosure'

Thomas J and others, 'Response to the Public Consultation on the Data Act' (European Law Institute 2021) <https://www.europeanlawinstitute.eu/fileadmin/user_upload/p_eli/Projects/Data_Economy/ELI_Response_Public_Consultation_on_a_Data_Act.pdf> accessed 23 January 2023

Tombal T, *Imposing Data Sharing among Private Actors: A Tale of Evolving Balances* (Wolters Kluwer 2022)

Tucker D and Wellford HB, 'Big Mistakes Regarding Big Data' [2014] The Antitrust Source 1

Turner S and others, 'The Exercisability of the Right to Data Portability in the Emerging Internet of Things (IoT) Environment' (2021) 23 New Media & Society 2861

van den Boom J, '*What Does the Digital Markets Act Harmonize? – Exploring Interactions between the DMA and National Competition Laws*' (2023) 19 European Competition Journal 57

Vezzoso S, 'Fintech, Access to Data, and the Role of Competition Policy' in Vicente Bagnoli (ed), *Competition and Innovation* (2018) <https://www.ssrn.com/abstract=3106594> accessed 15 March 2023

Vezzoso S, 'The Dawn of Pro-Competition Data Regulation for Gatekeepers in the EU' (2021) 17 European Competition Journal 391

Wallerath M and Krause P (eds), *Fiat iustitia, Recht als Aufgabe der Vernunft* (2006)

Weber R and Thouvenin F, 'Dateneigentum und Datenzugangsrechte – Bausteine der Informationsgesellschaft?' [2018] ZSR 43

Weichert T, 'Der Personenbezug von Geodaten' (2007) 31 Datenschutz und Datensicherheit – DuD 113

Wendehorst C, 'The State as a Foundation of Private Law Reasoning' (2008) 56 The American Journal of Comparative Law 567

Westphal M and Wichtermann M, 'Datenportierung nach Art. 20 DS-GVO' [2019] ZD 191

Wiebe A, 'Protection of Industrial Data – a New Property Right for the Digital Economy?' [2016] GRUR International 877

Wiebe A, 'Der Data Act – Innovation oder Illusion?' [2023] GRUR 1569

Wilhelmi R, 'Lizenzverweigerung als Missbrauch einer marktbeherrschenden Stellung in der Gemeinschaftsrechtsprechung' [2009] WPR 1431

Wolff HA and Brink S (eds), *BeckOK Datenschutzrecht* (42nd edn, 2022)

Wolters P and Jacobs B, 'The Security of Access to Accounts under the PSD2' (2019) 35 Computer Law & Security Review 29

Worthington S, Robertson A, and Virgo G (eds), *Revolution and Evolution in Private Law* (Hart 2018)

Zech H, *Information als Schutzgegenstand* (Mohr Siebeck 2012)

Zech H, 'Daten als Wirtschaftsgut – Überlegungen zu einem „Recht des Datenerzeugers“' (2015) 31 CR 137

Zech H, '„Industrie 4.0“ – Rechtsrahmen für eine Datenwirtschaft im digitalen Binnenmarkt'

Zeleny M, 'Management Support Systems: Towards Integrated Knowledge Management' (1987) 7 Human Systems Management 59

Zunzunegui F, 'Digitalisation of Payment Services' [2018] Ibero-American Institute for Law and Finance Working Paper <https://www.ssrn.com/abstract=3256281> accessed 8 March 2023